THREADS
—OF—
SOLIDARITY

THREADS

— OF —

SOLIDARITY

Women in South African Industry,
1900–1980

IRIS BERGER

Indiana University Press
Bloomington and Indianapolis

James Currey
London

Published by
Indiana University Press
601 North Morton Street, Bloomington, Indiana 47404

and

James Currey Ltd.
54B Thornhill Square, Islington, London N1 1BE, England

The paper used in this publication meets the minimum
requirements of American
National Standard for Information Sciences—Permanence of Paper for
Printed Library Materials, ANSI Z39.48-1984.

Manufactured in the United States of America

Library of Congress Cataloging-in-Publication Data

Berger, Iris, date
   Threads of solidarity : women in South African industry, 1900–1980
/ Iris Berger.
      p.   cm.
   Includes bibliographical references and index.
   ISBN 0-253-31173-X (cloth). —ISBN 0-253-20700-2 (paper)
   1. Women—Employment—South Africa—History—20th century.
2. Women in trade-unions—South Africa—History—20th century.
I. Title.
HD6212.B48 1991
331.4'0968'0904—dc20   91-23112

1 2 3 4 5   95 94 93 92

British Library Cataloguing-in-Publication Data
Berger, Iris
   Threads of solidarity.
   I. Title
   331.409680904

   ISBN 0852550782
   ISBN 0852550774 pbk

To Ron, Allison, and Anna
and to the memory of
Anna Skolnik

Contents

IV. DECENTRALIZATION AND THE RISE OF
INDEPENDENT UNIONS

Illustrations precede Chapter 8.

Preface

As activists and political theorists alike consider the structure of a post-apartheid society in South Africa, the persistence of gender inequality is among the complex and controversial issues they confront. Discussing how a new constitution can best insure women's economic, political, and legal rights, Albie Sachs has declared bluntly: "It is a sad fact that one of the few profoundly non-racial institutions in South Africa is patriarchy."[1] The "patriarchy" of the 1990s operates in a very different context from that of the early 1930s, when Sachs's father began to organize white women in the garment industry; but the statement provides a useful reminder that, despite the distance between contemporary inequity and the "domesticity and dependency" of the past, many issues remain unresolved.

In tracing the journey through time of South African working-class women between 1900 and 1980, this book reflects my academic background in both African history and comparative women's history. While contributing to African studies by analyzing women's industrial labor in a single country, it seeks to expand the horizons of women's history beyond its dominant Euro-American boundaries. In South Africa, with its imperialist amalgam of Africa, Europe, and Asia, many themes of women's history converge. Following a common pattern, producers of food and clothing turned to female workers as ostensibly cheap and docile, and as elsewhere, trade unionism presented these women with both barriers and opportunities. Yet the economic, political, and cultural context of women's work was, in many ways, distinctly African.

By directly addressing issues of comparative concern such as women's experiences of work and political action, their cooperation and conflict across racial lines, the power of state policy to shape work and family life, and the influence of changing perceptions of gender on both women's exploitation and strategies for social transformation, I hope to encourage a deeper understanding of the uniqueness and the universality of women's lives in different historical and cultural settings. Women's historians speak often of cross-cultural dialogue but find its practice difficult in a discipline steeped in regional and national particularity. Discussion is especially constrained across the divide that separates industrialized Western societies from the formerly colonized "others" of Africa, Asia, Latin America, and the Middle East.

This concern with the threads of historical connection among women in different countries also reflects my own varied political and personal connections to the topic. The historical documentary "Union Maids" appeared in the 1970s before I began this project. Set in Chicago, the city of my childhood, it presented three strong, articulate women who channeled their anger at low wages and racial discrimination into the nascent unions of the 1930s and early 1940s. Their intense commitment and astute political understanding first inspired my interest in women's labor history. At the time, however, I had no idea of how I might express this interest in my own research. Only after the project was under way did I consciously recall another influence, stories of my grandmother's work in a New York garment factory as a young immigrant to the United States. Paradoxically, these years in a presumably squalid sweatshop were among the happiest of her life. Knowing this may have prodded me to look beyond the obvious theme of exploitation for a more nuanced understanding of how women themselves interpreted their experiences at work. For my grandmother, this seems to have been a brief period of respite from patriarchal family life. Finally, it is important to mention my many years of involvement with varied anti-apartheid organizations. This political orientation has impelled me to share my knowledge and understanding of South Africa with as wide an audience as possible in an effort to insure overseas support for a democratic postapartheid future that is free of the inequities of the present.

Without the generosity of numerous funding agencies, this project would have been impossible. I am grateful to the National Endowment for the Humanities, the Social Science Research Council, the Rockefeller Foundation (Gender Roles Program), and the Nuala Drescher Awards Program of the United University Professions for fellowships that provided me with the resources for travel and research and with essential time to write. Contributions from the Research Foundation of the State University of New York and the Faculty Research Awards Program of the State University of New York at Albany also are appreciated. None of these organizations, of course, shares any responsibility for the book or its conclusions.

The book also bears the stamp of many people, who contributed in diverse ways to its completion. The expert archival knowledge of Hans Panofsky of Northwestern University Library and Anna Cunningham of the William Cullen Library of the University of the Witwatersrand greatly enriched the source material available to me. I am extremely grateful to Jan Theron and the Food and Canning Workers' Union for permission to consult union records, both before and after they were deposited in the University of Cape Town Library. While respecting their request for anonymity, thanks are also due to the two factory owners in Johannesburg who allowed me to interview their workers.

A number of colleagues and friends generously shared their suggestions and their understanding of South African history, thereby easing my scholarly transition from the eastern to the southern section of the African continent. They include Shula Marks, Deborah Gaitskell, Belinda

Bozzoli, Julia Wells, Charles van Onselen, Barbara Trapido, Stanley Trapido, Philip Bonner, William Beinart, Barbara Brown, Martin Nicol, Barbie
Schreiner, Jenny Schreiner, and Elaine Unterhalter. In addition, Shula Marks
and Margaret Strobel offered critical suggestions on an earlier version of
the work. With extreme generosity, Baruch Hirson volunteered to read a
large section of the manuscript. His incisive comments saved me from
several egregious errors; any that remain are my fault alone.

A number of other people also contributed to the project in important
ways. Ilsa Mwanza and Julie Frederickse lent their assistance and hospi-
tality in Zambia and Zimbabwe respectively and Ray and Jack Simons
welcomed me warmly to their bustling household. I also owe a very special debt to Helen Joseph, whose insights, contacts, and friendship were
invaluable. Finally, to all the trade unionists and factory workers who
spared me time and energy and shared the stories of their lives, I am
immensely grateful. I hope they find the book an accurate reflection of
their struggles and aspirations.

Any project of this length demands so long a time commitment that it
almost becomes another family member. Fortunately, my daughters Allison and Anna successfully kept this third "sibling" from dominating my
life entirely. Ron Berger's presence in my life permeates the book in too
many ways to enumerate. Whether as historian and critic, single parent
during my research trips, or restorer of my sense of humor and balance,
he consistently encouraged and enriched my work. At the same time, his
combination of outrage at injustice, yet skepticism about human perfecti-
bility constantly challenged me to reexamine my conclusions and assumptions. To my own family and to the "family" of South African working
women who have struggled against racial, gender, and class injustice,
this book is dedicated.

Portions of this book have appeared elsewhere in somewhat different
form. The author gratefully acknowledges permission to reprint excerpts
from:

"Gender, Race, and Political Empowerment: South African Canning
Workers, 1940–1960," in *Gender & Society*, vol. 4, no. 3 (September 1990),
pp. 398–420. Copyright © 1990 by Sociologists for Women in Society. Reprinted by permission of Sage Publications, Inc.

"Sources of Class Consciousness: South African Women in Recent Labor Struggles," in *International Journal of African Historical Studies*, vol. 16,
no. 1 (1983), pp. 49–66. Reprinted by permission.

*The Politics of Race, Class and Nationalism in Twentieth Century South Af-
rica*, by Shula Marks and Stanley Trapido, pp. 124–55. Copyright © 1987
by Longman Publishing Group. Reprinted by permission of Longman
Publishing Group.

"Gender and Working-Class History: South Africa in Comparative Perspective," *Journal of Women's History*, vol. 1, no. 2 (Fall 1989), pp. 117–33.

Abbreviations

ACVV	Afrikaner Christian Women's Association
AEU	Amalgamated Engineering Union
AFCWU	African Food and Canning Workers' Union
AFTU	African Federation of Trade Unions
ANC	African National Congress
CNETU	Council of Non-European Trade Unions
COSATU	Congress of South African Trade Unions
FCWU	Food and Canning Workers' Union
FNETU	Federation of Non-European Trade Unions
FOFATUSA	Federation of Free African Trade Unions of South Africa
GWU	Garment Workers' Union
ICU	Industrial and Commercial Workers' Union
IICU	Independent Industrial and Commercial Workers' Union
IWW	Industrial Workers of the World
NTMA	National Textile Manufacturers' Association
NUCW	National Union of Clothing Workers
NUTW	National Union of Textile Workers
SAAEO	South African Association of Employees' Organizations
SACTU	South African Congress of Trade Unions
SAGWU	South African Garment Workers' Union
SAMEU	South African Mine Employees' Union
SATLC	South African Trades and Labour Council
SATU	South African Typographical Union
SATUC	South African Trade Union Council (1962, renamed TUCSA)
SWU	Sweet Workers' Union
TCMA	Transvaal Clothing Manufacturers' Association
TUC	South African Trade Union Congress
TUCSA	Trade Union Council of South Africa
TWIU	Textile Workers' Industrial Union
WEWU	Women Engineering Workers' Union
WTA	Witwatersrand Tailors' Association

I
Gender and Industrialization

–1–

GENDER, COMMUNITY, AND
WORKING-CLASS HISTORY

The continuing struggle against racial domination in South Africa has created an environment in which the actions and attitudes of contemporary popular movements often resonate with historical significance. In this highly politicized atmosphere, interpretations of the past have the power to provoke intense interest and, at times, passionate controversy. Nowhere has this interplay between past and present been more significant than in the trade union movement. As waves of strikes swept the country in 1973–74 and black workers again felt their potential power, labor organizers realized the critical need to understand the successes and failures of earlier working-class organizations. Acutely aware that ruthless government repression had crushed progressive unions during the 1950s and 1960s, new leaders sought to build a movement whose democratic strength would inhibit its destruction.

Yet, because so many union officials had suffered arrest, banning, and exile, important links between generations were weakened or severed; thus, many contemporary activists were unaware of the complex connections over time embodied in their work and their ideas. The silences and distortions of official versions of South African history further reinforced the rift between past and present. When Tembi Nabe shocked some members of the audience at a 1983 labor education workshop by speaking frankly of women's subordination within the household, she never suspected her kinship with Mary Fitzgerald, a flamboyant leader who raised similar issues in the early 1900s. But Nabe's graphic descriptions of women workers providing idle husbands with an endless round of domestic and sexual services closely matched Fitzgerald's critique of domestic inequality.[1] Likewise, when the shop stewards at a Dunlop chemical factory successfully laid a trap for a training officer who was requiring sexual favors as a condition of employment, they had no idea of their historical bond with garment strikers who, in 1931, complained of "rude and vulgar" treatment and pressure to go out with the foreman or the boss in order to keep their jobs.

This book seeks to reknit the continuity among generations of working women and to restore some of the hidden connections between past and present struggles against racial, gender, and class oppression. In doing so, it also places this history within the wider perspective of working women in other parts of the world and other time periods. This approach to formulating relevant questions and theoretical issues does not imply that gender alone is the single determining factor in understanding and interpreting women's lives, but rather that historiographical trends in the study of working-class women help to frame a context for revealing the complex interplay among gender, class, and race.

In South Africa, as in many other countries, factories usually have employed men in larger numbers than women. This trend has left women predominant in agricultural labor, domestic work in middle- and upper-class households, and independent "informal" economic pursuits ranging from petty trade to prostitution.[2] In many countries (although less frequently in Africa), home industries offered jobs to large numbers of women who resisted or were unwelcome in factory work.[3] These patterns of women's proletarianization often followed phases of the family cycle, with factories absorbing young, single, and often better-qualified women, while older married women working at home remained part of the "subproletariat."[4] Although their incorporation into factories has varied enormously in different national and local settings, common gender stereotypes have kept women concentrated in low-paid work that is defined as compatible with their "natural" tendencies. Thus, workers in the international electronics industry are valued for their "nimble fingers," as were the legions of female typists in the United States in the late nineteenth century.

Other more concrete similarities in the history of factory employment patterns for women are particularly striking. The three stages of development of the United States garment industry as outlined by Helen Safa are comparable to those in South Africa.[5] The first phase, which relied on a native female labor force, mainly the single daughters of farm families who were working before marriage, parallels a period (albeit a century later) in which newly developing South African factories turned to the daughters of rural Afrikaner families. The successive groups of immigrant women who became clothing workers during the second stage were similar in many respects to the black women who began to fill South African factories after World War II. Like their United States counterparts, they often continued to work after marriage and brought to the urban industrial experience a similar background of ethnic-based (though often-disrupted) cultural traditions. Finally, the more recent turn to runaway shops, as the industry branched out into developing countries, is analogous to the development of rural clothing factories in South Africa, where low wages match those of other peripheral centers worldwide.

Although relatively few women have worked in industry by comparison with other occupations, the experience of female factory operatives often has had broad social and political repercussions. Ivy Pinchbeck, for example, in her pioneering study of British women workers, implies that the independence young women developed working in mills and factories influenced the awakening consciousness of middle-class women.[6] In many countries, even if the percentage of women working in factories was relatively low at any given moment, this form of employment was a common phase, a rite of passage that many young working-class women underwent en route to marriage and family. In such instances, the experience might stamp women with a collective awareness that profoundly shaped their consciousness. As David Montgomery has observed in his study of the American working class in the late nineteenth century:

> The young women's work culture . . . confronted supervisors with a paradox. On the one hand, the conviviality and even the fantasy world into which pieceworkers often let their minds slip actually provided a lubrication that helped both workers and their employers accomplish their daily tasks. . . .
> On the other hand, the bonds that attached young women to one another also fostered a sense of identity and of self-respect that overseers offended at their peril. Clothes, the fashionable attire that invariably shocked upper-class observers as frivolous, became the outward symbol of that identity, on and off the job.[7]

Although expressed partially through fashion, this sense of self was not without a political edge, leading women to express bitterness and anger at "disrespectful" foremen and at many aspects of working conditions, particularly child labor.[8]

The experience of factory work left a particularly strong imprint on many South African women, creating bonds among working women that promoted their involvement in labor resistance. But these ties also might be turned to wider political ends. Thus, when the Federation of South African Women formed in 1954 as a national organization dedicated to fighting racial and gender oppression, trade unionists were disproportionately represented at the initial conference. Equally important, factory work (especially in the 1940s and 1950s) brought together in the same jobs a racially diverse group of women who, under other circumstances, would have had contact with each other only in unequal relationships. (For their male family members, much more closely tracked into racially distinct channels, such proximity would have been unthinkable.) Thus, working in factories had the potential to extend women's experience in a variety of ways, exposing them to new ideas and to people of other racial and ethnic backgrounds. In some instances, this wider contact reinforced attitudes toward race, class, and the division of authority within the family that women had learned in the more protected world of their households; but, in others, serious rifts and conflicts might arise between the different but interrelated realms of work and home. In examining the lives of women in industry, this study seeks to integrate the often-distinct categories of factory, family, and community.

In exploring these connections, it relies heavily on the insights of recent feminist theory, which has sought, with varying degrees of success, to conceptualize the relationship among these spheres of daily life. Whereas writers in the 1970s often recognized the connections between their opposing categories of public and private, production and reproduction, they sometimes tended to link them in a static, ahistorical fashion. Building on such theoretical dichotomies, writers on South Africa who combined Marxist and feminist perspectives repeatedly echoed the functionalist notion that women's reproductive roles subsidized and thereby sustained the capitalist sphere of the economy. But the two were depicted as otherwise quite distinct and separate, and gender too often was subsumed within class.

Others have approached the problem of duality with greater historical awareness and have sought to spell out the connections between categories more systematically. Joan Kelly described her view of women's "doubled vision," based jointly on sex oppression and the system of productive relations, asserting that the two needed to be understood simultaneously.[9] Seeking a theory to do so, Belinda Bozzoli turned to the concept of struggle between women and men within the household and between the domestic sphere and the wider economic system.[10] Through the use of these concepts, she creatively reexamines twentieth-century South African history. Some who counter this perspective would object to a view of racial/ethnic households simply as an arena of conflict. Instead, they perceive these families as a site of resistance to external oppression, emphasizing that economic scarcity may foster a high level of mutual dependence between women and men.[11]

If these approaches seek connections to bridge dualistic categories, Lourdes Benería and Martha Roldan insist more firmly on the need to understand both the material and the ideological aspects of women's subordination and to see patriarchy and relations of production as interconnected and mutually reinforcing, rather than as dual systems. Since women in real life have no choice but to integrate their lives at work and at home, they suggest that perhaps the only way to confront dualism is not through more elaborate theoretical formulations, but through specific historical analysis.[12] Implied in this approach is the need to overcome yet another division—between history and theory.

Much of the previous writing on South African labor history has been too narrowly conceived to be helpful in bridging any of these gaps between categories of analysis. Perhaps understandably, as trade unions reawakened after over a decade of repression, many historians of the late

1970s and early 1980s limited their inquiries to institutional analysis. Though this period produced some important research, only rarely did these writers venture beyond the factories and the union halls to examine workers' family and community lives. Even predominantly female unions often were discussed in a gender-blind fashion, ignoring the issue of whether and how women's double or triple burden influenced their consciousness or union participation.[13]

A different problem emerges in some studies of how South African women were "incorporated" into capitalist or industrial production.[14] Often valuable inquiries into economic structure, these interpretations nonetheless leave little room either for human agency or for "family strategies" in shaping women's economic place.[15] Rather than portraying women as individuals and family members who make their own choices about whether and where they wish to work for wages—however restricted their options—their approach depicts people as virtual puppets of economic forces that leave them little control over their lives.

This criticism is not intended to suggest that the often-combined weight of race, gender, and class left poor women with a wide range of choice, but rather that even within the confines of their limited economic prospects, women faced critical decisions about work, marriage, family, and politics. By drawing on husbands, relatives and children, and on church and community groups, they were able to develop strategies to confront these challenges. To focus exclusively on structures of domination is therefore to ignore individual and collective leverage, creativity, and struggle, however confined the space for its expression, and to neglect the tension between popular pressure and the controls embodied in both capitalist interests and the state.

In reviewing the historical literature on women in industrial production, perhaps no question crops up more frequently than why and how organizing women was different from organizing men. The issue is most often conceptualized as why (in many situations) women were slower to form trade unions than men and, even when organized, took less part in these working-class organizations. Still influenced by this central approach, others have examined successful efforts to involve women in unions or in strikes, or instances where women aggressively took the initiative, asking what made the difference in these particular cases. The problem is particularly pertinent to South Africa, where in varied contexts and periods observers have often credited women with more fearless and militant behavior than men. Rachael Zeeman, a strike leader in a Cape cannery, observed:

> In my opinion, the women in the union achieve more with the bosses than the men. It's like that here as well. The women will insist upon something which would be dropped by a man, women carry on. The woman does not give up. She carries on.[16]

In seeking to understand women's relationship to organized labor, historians, until recently, favored two explanations. The first, which attributed women's exclusion to anti-female attitudes among male trade unionists, arose naturally within the context of feminist history in the 1970s. To writers bent on demonstrating the force of patriarchal power across time and culture, sexism embodied in institutional arrangements seemed a logical and historically justifiable reason for women's relative powerlessness in many public settings. Writing on early twentieth-century Russia, for example, Rose Glickman argues that male unions mainly ignored women out of an "underlying conviction that women were a lower order of being."[17] The other answer grew from the preoccupation with the dual spheres of women's lives, the split between home and work. Proponents of this view argued that women's heavy involvement in domestic affairs left them neither the time nor the emotional energy to take part in working-class organization.[18] Placing less stress on unions themselves, this explanation implied that circumstances forced women to make a choice, and that (under the weight of prevailing cultural norms) they opted for domesticity.

Despite their differences, both formulations tacitly accept the idea that trade unions were the appropriate means of expressing class power and consciousness, and that how women related to these organizations was an index of their class awareness and of unions' gender awareness. Thus, whether through their domestic involvement or through sexism, women often were prevented from developing the attachments that would assure them full membership in "the working class." Yet Temma Kaplan, writing on women in Barcelona, argues that to accept unions alone as the agencies of the working class is to ignore other forms of association connected with the family, the church, cooperatives, and women's groups.[19]

As the focus of women's history has changed, approaches to the question of their involvement in unions have shifted as well. As many women's historians in the later 1970s became more interested in how women have constructed their own autonomous cultures, despite (and in response to) patriarchal constraints, they also began to suggest new ways of integrating gender into working-class history. From the perspective of women's culture, it was easier to dismiss the innuendo that women were remiss in not developing firmer attachments to trade unions and to argue instead that unions were too narrowly conceived around particular male-defined economic and political issues to adequately reflect women's concerns. If earlier interpretations had found fault with working women for their low level of class consciousness, recent writers have instead faulted the unions. Writing from this perspective, for example, Dolores Janiewski turns the old question around and asks, "Why are unions irrelevant to so much of women's lives?"[20] Furthermore, analysis based on language and discourse suggested a reason for this masculine emphasis: that, in many instances, the "languages of class," the very conception of class and, by extension, of class organizations, was gender-bound, conceiving of male experience as the universal representation of the working class.[21] For much of South African history, it might be added, this portrayal of "the" working class was both male and white.

Answers to the second question concerning women's organization—how to explain examples of successful organizing or of strikes with substantial female involvement—draw heavily on the cultural approach to women's history. They show women most inclined to become active union members when they are able to center their participation around work-based and/or community-based culture and networks or where unions have consciously and successfully incorporated women's particular concerns and informal ties.[22] These arguments suggest that the class experience of women includes not simply their conflictual relationship with owners and managers of capital, but their mutual relationships with each other, whether conceptualized as "work cultures" or as "bonds of community." Because these relationships differ from those of working-class men, they are too often dismissed as trivial, while the class content they embody is ignored. Once again, historians generalize from male experience and portray it as the universal norm.

Other discussions of women's involvement in working-class organization and action follow along the lines suggested by Louise Tilly, who hypothesized that different "paths of proletarianization" (including the organization of production and the household division of labor) are linked systematically with particular patterns of collective action.[23] In a similar argument, Carole Turbin proposed that trade union activities or participation in labor unrest may be strengthened when women's families support their involvement. Racial conflict falling along class lines also may prompt such participation by creating a community of interest between women and men. Writing on Latin America, Helen Safa found that female breadwinners, freer from male domination than other working-class women, were more likely to view themselves as "workers."[24] All of these arguments are variations on the idea that particular work and family relationships promote or inhibit women's class action in distinct ways, although Safa's case study emphasizes the absence of an inhibiting factor (male power in the family) rather than the presence of positive reinforcement through family or racial identification. They also underscore the idea that women's propensity to engage in collective action is increased when (for a variety of possible reasons) their behavior is not deemed a threat to male power.

In adopting the more recent approaches to female labor history, historians are implying that congruence between women's lives and culture at work, in the family, and in the community (with different combinations as the salient factors in particular cases) is central to strengthening working women's active class identification, to reshaping "class" in terms that resonate with their own experience. In taking this integrative approach, they follow the lead of social historians like Edward Thompson and Herbert Gutman, who analyze working classes in the combined context of work, family, culture, and community. Yet there is a crucial difference from some, although not all, of these historians, many of whom write as if "household" and "family" were integrated units, bastions of cultural creativity along class and ethnic lines against the inroads of the dominant classes. The idea of gender conflict at the heart of this haven of communal values is foreign to this perspective as it is often presented.[25]

Following working-class life out of the factory and into the community is clearly critical to any effort at reconceptualizing class to include women's experience. But in the South African context, and perhaps in others as well, the concept of community found in the writings of American working-class historians like Herbert Gutman, Virginia Yans-McLaughlin, and Tamara Hareven requires reassessment. These historians speak of "community" in positive terms to refer to groups of geographically proximate people, usually united along class or ethnic lines and embodying critically important pre-industrial, often Old World cultures and values.[26] The emphasis on culture, whether conceptualized as immigrant, peasant, or pre-industrial, is particularly important. In certain respects such a definition is valuable to African history, reminding us of the worldwide tendency for capitalist encroachment to alter earlier cultural traditions. Yet it also assumes that these working-class families and communities had substantial control over their own working and personal lives, a situation often impossible for black South Africans; harsh economic exploitation and political exclusion made their lives more comparable to blacks in the United States than to white immigrants.[27]

With South African realities in mind, Belinda Bozzoli has some cautionary insights concerning the complexity of the concept with reference to South Africa. She reminds us, first of all, of the brutal legacy of dispossession, forced removal, and continuing oppression necessarily at the heart of many South African definitions of "community."[28] In this context the idea of "struggle" is often critical to any notion of solidarity among working-class women: not simply of contests between laborers and capital or bosses over wages and working conditions, but of struggle against racial legislation, struggle to protect established communities, and struggle to define the meaning of class, ethnicity, and gender. These were often instances, then, in which class (or race) and community reinforced each other, situations that Bozzoli credits with leading to "the most effective and radical forms of class expression."[29]

Bozzoli's discussion also highlights the role of intellectuals in shaping perceptions of community. From them, she argues, come the relatively structured ideologies or systems of ideas that help to shape and to restructure individual and collective attitudes.[30] South African labor leaders like E. S. Sachs of the Transvaal Garment Workers' Union and Ray Alexander of the Cape Food and Canning Workers' Union, both from Eastern

European communist backgrounds, clearly played such a part within their respective organizations. This insight suggests that any sense of identification with others is not simply a given fact, inherent in people's material lives, but rather needs to be constructed conceptually, emotionally, and historically to have any meaning. Thus Benedict Anderson's concept of nations as "imagined communities"[31] among people who do not know each other could apply equally well to smaller groupings along lines of gender, race, ethnicity, or class.

Although South Africa has been fragmented in different ways from the United States, its division during most of the twentieth century into an African majority of roughly 70 percent of the population, an intermediate racially mixed and Asian group of 10 percent, and a dominant white minority of 20 percent has established a heterogeneous context in which struggles over identity occur.[32] Contests for power among whites have been heightened by persistent tension between the more numerous Afrikaans-speaking segment of the population and those of English-speaking origin. Both African and Afrikaner intellectuals have successfully shaped ideology and political movements around nationalist identification.

Conceptualizing class as one form of "community" (though with social and economic rather than spatial boundaries) immediately raises the question of its connections to other such groupings. On this issue, the work of American labor historians is more illuminating for South Africa than that of European historians, who usually write of an undifferentiated working-class experience in the nineteenth and early twentieth centuries. The racial and ethnic diversity of South Africa, like that of the United States, demands a more complex analysis. Thus Gutman's argument that nonclass elements such as ethnicity and race often generate the appeal of class-based identification[33] is equally cogent for South Africa where, it might be argued, most workers have rarely even conceptualized class as transcending racial boundaries.

Since gender so clearly cuts across all other categories, its relationship to them adds another layer of complexity to any analysis. Although women in homogeneous marriages share the inherited ethnic and racial identification of their family and "community," the way they conceptualize and construct this sense of belonging may be very different from that of men. (To my knowledge, this is a largely unexplored topic.) More thoroughly researched is how women and their husbands may differ, both in their objective class position and in their consciousness. This is particularly true in many African societies, where wives and husbands maintain independent control over their own economic resources.[34] Where gender is more comparable to race and ethnicity in its relationship to class are those contexts in which gender-based networks and culture among women help to reinforce their solidarity as workers. Countering the argument for separate female and male class positions within individual households, David Montgomery portrays the nineteenth-century American family as a "nursery of class consciousness," although also as a "school for instruction" in women's separate and subordinate sphere.[35]

The idea that a new form of working-class family emerged in Europe and North America during the nineteenth century is widely accepted among historians. Within this new domestic structure women, facing strong cultural pressure to retreat to the household if they could afford to do so, became heavily dependent on men's earning power. Black women in South Africa, by contrast, rarely have had the luxury of choosing whether or not to refrain from income-producing labor.[36] The combined pressures of men's low wages, male labor migration, live-in domestic jobs, acute poverty, and state regulation have undermined stable family relationships and intensified women's economic independence. On this issue, urban African-American women may be the most apt comparison.

Yet the contrast between Africa and the West may be less stark than it would appear. Many black South African families aspired to replicate the patterns of nuclear family life that European missionaries put forth as a model. Furthermore, like South African women, European and American women who remained at home sewed, rented rooms to lodgers, and sought other informal means of augmenting scarce family funds. Thus, the differences may be greater in the realm of ideology and expectation than in women's actual lives, although high levels of migrant labor have produced much greater family separation in South Africa than within white households elsewhere.

This discussion of labor history provides a context for understanding working-class women in broad terms that take account of race and ethnicity and insist on the gendered nature of historical experience and perception. This insistence forces historians to examine the connections among aspects of life too often compartmentalized but clearly critical to our understanding of the past and to women's understanding of their own lives.

Yet the distinct features of South African society make some aspects of comparison more relevant than others. Although the country's racial and ethnic complexity are more comparable to the United States than to Europe (before World War II), the tightly knit ethnic communities of North American immigrants were matched in only a few regions of South Africa. More like African Americans, most blacks who migrated to cities from rural sections of the Transvaal and the Orange Free State came not from integrated peasant societies, but from families of tenant farmers and sharecroppers. And even where peasant communities persisted, most rural areas were profoundly unsettled by the turbulent events of the nineteenth century. Zulu and Boer expansion uprooted and scattered innumerable communities and brought others under the sway of new conquerors; Christian missionaries created deep cultural and religious rifts between converts and Africans who resisted change; and intensive gold and diamond mining transformed all of southern Africa into a labor pool for wretchedly paid migrant men. Furthermore, as the commercialization of agriculture and racially based legislation intensified during the early twentieth century, land shortages and poverty became increasingly acute. In the wake of these upheavals, the reconstructed cultural traditions and gender relations that developed within urban proletarian communities become as critical to understanding working-class behavior and consciousness as the legacy of precapitalist culture.

South African realities also make state power a critical factor in understanding the lives of working-class women and their families. Often absent from social histories of women, the intrusive, authoritarian presence of the government in all areas of black life has made it impossible to ignore. Since the law has governed such basic facts of daily existence as who has the right to live in the cities and where urban-dwellers may seek housing, it has left an indelible imprint on the most intimate of family and individual decisions.

In exploring the lives and struggles of women industrial workers, this study also will analyze changes over time in other aspects of women's work, both formal and casual, since alternative options for economic survival strongly shaped the history of factory work. Overall, however, the book will concentrate on women who stitched garments, spun and wove cloth, and processed food, for they comprised the vast majority of female manufacturing workers. These three industries (clothing, textiles, and food) with their divergent ways of organizing work, their distinct patterns of ownership, their varied constructions of race and gender, and their differing relationships to regional economies provide a rich tapestry of contrasts and comparisons that illuminate the changing work and family lives of women of all racial groups. They also illustrate the "threads of solidarity," sometimes strong, sometimes tenuous, that drew women together, occasionally across racial lines, despite increasingly restrictive state policies.

Two South African unions were particularly successful at mobilizing women, at responding to their daily concerns, and at providing an atmosphere in which the contested meanings of class, race, and gender were central to formulating policy: the Garment Workers' Union of the Transvaal (GWU), centered in Johannesburg, and the Food and Canning Workers' Union (FCWU) and its African counterpart (AFCWU) in the Cape Province. Their rich histories provide fruitful insights into why and how some women became involved in collective action and how they viewed themselves in an often-threatening context of clashing political and economic interests.

The evidence from all three industries, and especially from these unions, sustains the conclusions of historians who emphasize women's greater responsiveness to organizing efforts that address their problems at home and in the community as well as at work.[37] During the periods of their greatest strength, the policies of both the GWU and the FCWU/AFCWU showed a deep understanding of how women perceived and negotiated the conflicts and confluence among these different aspects of their lives. Whenever possible, these unions sought to respond to their members not only as workers, but as mothers, daughters, wives, or widows and as members of racial and ethnic communities, whether black or white, African or Afrikaaner. Making a similar point with reference to the present, Emma Mashinini, a prominent women's organizer of the 1970s and 1980s, argues:

> The trade unions have got to follow the workers in all their travels—to get them home, and to school, in the education and welfare of their children, everywhere. The whole life of a worker needs trade union involvement.[38]

Although archival research forms the basis of this book, oral interviews (primarily in the form of life histories) provided a more individualized perspective, answering many questions on which written sources are silent. With the inevitable randomness and chance that accompany any such research, trade union leaders were followed up through a variety of personal contacts in Great Britain, South Africa, Zambia, and Zimbabwe. By the time I began the research, some key figures had died. But, with a few exceptions, I was able to meet many of the leading women unionists of the period.

I also interviewed women in two Johannesburg clothing factories: in one through a personal contact with a long-time employee and in another through a recommendation from the head of the Industrial Council for the Clothing Industry (a mediating body with both worker and employer representation). My objective during these interviews was to locate black women who had begun to work in factories during the 1940s and 1950s, a group about which little other information was available. In one of the factories the interviews were not very productive, since I was allowed to speak to the women only during the lunch break, trying to talk over the clatter of tea cups and competing conversations; in the other, the owner gave us a private room in which to meet and allowed women to take time from their machines to speak to me. The fact that both factory owners had lived in the United States for short periods may have contributed to their receptivity to my request. (One was anxious to demonstrate how favorably his establishment compared with the new round of sweatshops in cities like New York.) The lives of these women form the basis for chapter 12.

The fear and suspicion that permeate South African life undoubtedly influenced all of these interviews, even those with exiles; but it is difficult to assess or to generalize about the precise impact of this emotional climate. I never approached anyone without a personal reference, which must have helped to establish my trustworthiness. In the factories, the women to whom I spoke seemed candid about their personal lives and pleased to have an outsider take an interest in their experience. It is impossible to gauge their frankness on political issues; but the opinions they expressed were quite varied, and some women who were reluctant to speak openly found more veiled ways to communicate their feelings. The warmth, perceptiveness, and personal strength conveyed during all of these interviews (both in the factories and with union leaders) certainly made them a highlight of my own research experience. I am grateful to all the women involved for sharing their lives and their time with me. Their insights have enriched the book, and have deepened my under-standing of South African society and history.

Finally, a note on the complex question of racial terminology is essen-tial, since the designation of various groups in South Africa has operated both as a means of oppression and division and as a symbol of liberation. The Black Consciousness Movement of the late 1960s and early 1970s transformed the term "black" by applying it to all groups that the state then designated as "non-white": Africans, Asians (primarily from India), and coloureds (a group of heterogeneous origins, most numerous at the Cape, that dates back to the earliest years of European colonization). For some people, this linguistic shift has produced profound changes in per-sonal and political identification. Yet such alterations do not solve the historian's problem. Separate group designations remain fundamental to state policy, as they have been for the entire period of this study, and to many people's perceptions of themselves. Thus in some contexts these labels are necessary to understand the past and the present. Current pop-ular usage complicates matters futher, since black is used both in its broadest sense and as a synonym for African. At the risk of confusion, I will follow this pattern. The context of most statements should clarify any resulting ambiguities.

The policies of racial definition and separation in South Africa, which extend also to efforts to divide the African population into ten separate communities, mean that all racial and ethnic designations represent com-plex historical struggles over language, representation, and ultimately, power. But, because of the ambiguous racial and political position of the coloured population, this category in particular should be understood as historically constructed according to the changing needs of the state for dividing oppressed groups from each other.[39]

Whether examining language or social, economic, and political policy, the history of women in industrial labor provides unique insights into the political economy of twentieth-century South Africa. Uniting the public and private spheres, the household and the economy, formal and casual labor the topic lends itself to transcending the dualities of many theoreti-cal works. Because of the succession of ethnic and racial groups that were drawn into factory work, it also illuminates the diversity of working-class experience and its complex relationship to changing constructions of race, gender, and class.

– 2 –

DEPENDENCY AND DOMESTICITY

Women's Wage Labor, 1900–1925

Among the leading South African labor organizers in the early twentieth century was a recent immigrant from Ireland, Mary Fitzgerald, who became notorious for inciting dramatic confrontations between striking workers, scabs, and police. Whether leading her "Pickhandle Brigade" against opponents of the nascent Labour Party in 1911 and 1912, lying on the tracks with a group of women during a 1911 tramway workers' strike, or setting out explosives to keep the trams from operating, Fitzgerald consistently placed herself in the forefront of working-class struggle. She also rebelled against contemporary norms of proper feminine behavior and repeatedly challenged the elitist craft orientation (though not the racial composition) of the trade union movement. As a socialist and a supporter of the Industrial Workers of the World (IWW), Fitzgerald advocated a single general union of all industrial workers.[1] At a time when few women were involved in wage labor, she was virtually alone as a female union activist.

Both trade union organization and women's position in the economy before 1925 reflected the country's rapid industrial growth. The discovery of diamonds and gold in the late nineteenth century had initiated an abrupt transformation from an agrarian economy, integrated only partially into overseas commercial networks, to a social order driven by the demands of international mining capital. Drawing unskilled black men from all of southern Africa and skilled white men from Europe and its colonial outposts, the mining industry established patterns that came to dominate twentieth-century social and economic relationships. By 1900 divisions of race, ethnicity, and skill were clearly fixed between different groups of male workers, and employment possibilities for women were limited.

With little to attract them to the major cities, most women, black and white, lived in rural areas or small country towns. Most black men were housed in bleak and overcrowded single-sex barracks and paid wages sufficient only to support themselves. African women were therefore encouraged to remain in the countryside to provide the benefits to ill and aged workers that neither mining capital nor the state was willing to fund. Particularly in the mining centers of the Witwatersrand, however, drastically imbalanced sex ratios meant that there was a high demand for women's domestic services, sexual and otherwise, and that all of these services acquired commercial value.

Political relationships in the state and the labor movement clearly reflected this racial and class hierarchy. The constitution adopted in 1910 created a new political environment by granting South Africa autonomy from Great Britain and unifying the four formerly separate provinces of the Cape, the Orange Free State, Natal, and the Transvaal. By retaining the existing voting regulations in each province, the architects of the new order effectively disenfranchised Africans, except for a small number of men in the Cape.[2] From then on, white governments representing the interests of mining magnates and wealthy farmers used their legislative power to insure themselves a steady supply of cheap black labor and, increasingly, to etch deeper boundaries around racial groups. Between 1910 and 1924, under the successive leadership of Louis Botha and Jan Smuts, a balance was achieved between British imperial interests, mining capital, and a moderate white nationalism.[3]

Rural economic trends also favored the quest for workers, as the growing capitalization of agriculture threatened the rights of both black and white sharecroppers, tenants, and small landholders. Among the newly proletarianized, white workers were in an insecure intermediate position. Fearful of their ability to sustain their economic superiority over blacks, they expressed their anxiety politically in a dizzying succession of organizations with ambivalent and contradictory attitudes toward the industrial color bar. The most enduring of these groups were the Labour party, an exclusively white organization speaking primarily for the interests of skilled workers, and the Communist party. As revolutionary socialist organizations, the most radical groups believed, in theory, in a nonracial socialism. But during this period their recruitment practices and actual political campaigns rarely embodied this ideal.

Despite the acute polarization of South African society in the first quarter of the twentieth century, women shared many common attributes, regardless of race. Treated as dependents of their fathers and husbands, although in radically different socioeconomic contexts, their contributions to domestic life were paramount. Apart from the pivotal place of African women in rural agricultural production, women's formal role in the economy was limited. For neither black nor white women was a substantial number of wage-paying jobs available outside of domestic service, and most women sought formal employment only episodically: when economic depression, widowhood, war, low male wages, drought, or in the case of black women, discriminatory laws, forced them out of their customary dependency either on the land or on male incomes. This is not to argue that women's economic position was identical across racial lines. Jobs in shops and cafes went mainly to whites, and the new industrial openings from World War I onward became a white and coloured monopoly. Nonetheless, ideologies of domesticity and dependency and an economic order dominated by mining and farming combined to create a context that circumscribed women in similar ways and led most poor urban women to perceive casual jobs as their primary alternative to domestic labor.

Throughout the twentieth century, also, regional patterns of urbanization, demography, and industrial development have remained critical determinants of women's economic position. The concentration of mining and heavy industry on the Witwatersrand created white working-class communities whose daughters provided the earliest female industrial workers in the area. The Western Cape, a center of lighter industry and of the country's largest coloured community, has offered a steady stream of factory jobs for women dating back to World War I. The Eastern Cape, slower to develop economically than the West, was like the Transvaal in its predominance of jobs for white women until the early 1940s. In Natal, where an ample supply of Indian and African men monopolized most wage labor, women have only recently entered industrial work in significant numbers.

Conceptualizing the rapid transformation of South Africa's economy and society during the early twentieth century is complex because of the racial and gender variations in the experience. The white men who came to the mining towns formed a "proletarian" class in the usual sense of the word. Like their counterparts in Europe to whom the term first applied, they were uprooted from rural areas and forced to sell their labor power in order to survive. The process was somewhat different for African men, whose families usually retained control over rural land, and for women, black and white, who most often found means of survival not in the formal sale of their labor, but in the precarious, independent economy that flourished in the interstices of urban life. Unlike African men, however, many black women lost their access to rural land when they moved to the cities.

An understanding of women's work and family lives in the first quarter of the twentieth century requires not only analysis of these two different facets of proletarianization, but an understanding of how this process affected women of different ages and backgrounds and a realization of the careful distinctions women made among different forms of wage labor. Most striking, when women were able to choose, was their concerted effort to avoid domestic work. While poor, white women were more successful at this than their black counterparts, black women also found ways to voice their distaste for household labor. Indeed, if the black women who took part in the campaign against passes in 1913 were resisting pro-letarianization,[4] their specific fears focused on the threat of being pushed into jobs as maids.

Ideologies of female domesticity also contributed to shaping conceptions of appropriate jobs for women and strongly influenced their earning power. The sense that young women forced by circumstances to labor for wages should enter the most ostensibly "protected" and housebound of occupations generated official efforts to propel women, black and white, into domestic service. Although those who took these jobs had little individual or collective power, the widespread avoidance of such work on the part of white women, and many blacks as well, constituted in itself a form of resistance. Just as Rhodesian mineworkers, lacking the collective power to reshape their dismal working lives, resorted to wholesale desertion in the early decades of the twentieth century, many South African women engaged in a similar refusal to fill the slots that bourgeois families and state bureaucrats sought to allot them.

Not surprisingly, legal norms for both black and white women reflected and reinforced their dependent status. Under the multiple ethnic-based systems of law then in force black peasant women were considered minors; even the land they farmed was allocated through their husbands' kin groups. Under the Dutch-Roman law that applied to white women, unmarried women over twenty-one and widows were accorded the same legal status as men. Once women married, however, they became legal minors; unless protected by an ante-nuptial contract, a woman's husband automatically assumed control of her person and her property. Within the family and the household, black women felt this male authority primarily through the power that chiefs and elders exerted over extended families. In white households, it was expressed through the authority of fathers.[5]

If women moved to the cities partly in response to rural economic dislocation, many also sought greater personal autonomy than rural communities allowed. Speaking of black women, Deborah Gaitskell stresses the appeal of urban migration particularly to young women and widows:[6] the former seeking to escape arranged marriages and domineering mothers-in-law, the latter, remarriage to a deceased husband's brother. Yet, as industrialization and proletarianization eroded the bonds and institutions of earlier rural communities, and as more women sought to evade "traditional" male restraints, self-appointed guardians of the social order invested substantial energy in keeping women under control, conceptualizing them as the upholders of tradition, morality, and domesticity. Black women encountered particular pressure from mission churches anxious to curb premarital female sexuality, and white women from Afrikaans language organizations concerned to preserve the stability of the Afrikaner family.[7]

For women in the countryside, family-related economic strategies were paramount. The arduous work of rural African women, in planting, harvesting, drawing water from distant sources, and thatching houses, is well-documented, although the leverage they gained from their pivotal part in production probably varied. Women whose families held land on white farms often were expected to work as fieldhands and domestic servants. By the latter part of the nineteenth century, peasant women might travel long distances on foot to sell eggs, milk, and fowl to Europeans.[8] Those who controlled their earnings may have strengthened their position in the household. These demands on the labor of women and children increased with the growing commercialization of agriculture by the early twentieth century. One witness informed the Transvaal Labour Commission in 1903:

> We prefer women for some work. They are cheaper and they do just the same work. For instance when plucking tobacco, or reaping mealies (maize), it is immaterial whether the hands employed belong to a child or to a woman. It is not hard labour. We want men only to take out the stumps of trees. For other work we use machinery.[9]

Although rural Afrikaner women had traditionally confined their work to the household, among small farmers by the late nineteenth century the growing competition for black labor tenants meant that, like their black counterparts, poor white women and children often had to engage in such physically demanding tasks as ploughing, harvesting, and caring for livestock.[10]

In the early part of the twentieth century, powerful patriarchal constraints in both African and Afrikaner families confined most women to their households of birth until marriage. But precarious economic circumstances would severely test those norms in the coming years. For black families, in addition, the 1913 Natives Land Act, restricting African landholding to designated "reserves" in a scant 8 percent of the country's territory, made it imperative to seek economic opportunities elsewhere. Because the state continued to perceive black women as economically insignificant in urban or industrial occupations, the Stallard Commission of 1923 sought no limitations on their presence in the cities, and authorities never followed through on their sporadic and localized efforts to control women's movement by requiring them to carry identity documents. After women in Bloemfontein marched in protest to the district office in 1913 and destroyed their passes, those responsible for the new legislation eventually backed down.[11]

Two writers who hoped to attract British women of "high moral character . . . common sense and a sound constitution," in order to create stable families that would support the mother country, described in detail the labor situation for white women in 1902 and 1903.[12] Accepting without question the domestic orientation and subordinate character of most available occupations, Alys Lowth wrote, "The majority of the vanguard of women workers who go out to South Africa will presumably belong to the great army of dependants—domestics, governesses, companions, secretaries, and so on."[13] Under the conditions prevailing until the end of the Anglo-Boer War in 1902, many women who might not otherwise have been in paid employment, particularly refugees from the Transvaal, had filled some of these positions, taking jobs in domestic service or doing needlework. Others had assumed work in small match or cigarette factories.[14] But Alicia Cecil outlined a further need for women to work as dressmakers, milliners, and laundresses as well as in tearooms, "respectable boarding houses," and nursing homes.

These authors alternate between describing actual conditions of employment and suggesting ways in which enterprising newcomers might fill apparent economic niches. Lowth, for example, arguing the need for "competent, businesslike" English laundresses, dwells at length on the purportedly iniquitous, unreliable, and unhealthy Malay washerwomen at the Cape. Her description suggests that these Malay women were carrying on business quite independently and very much on their own terms: setting their own pace of work, charging "frightful prices," and acting "independent and impudent to an incredible degree."[15]

But, reflecting the insatiable demand for domestic services in the skewed demographic climate at the turn of the century, these writings underlined above all the need for "honest, sober and respectable" domestic workers. According to Cecil, "the servant question" was uppermost in the minds of South African mistresses. Indeed, supplying suitable white servants to emerging bourgeois families seemed to be as important an aim of the women's immigration campaign as populating South Africa with "the wives and mothers of the future." This campaign and its emphasis on women "who will bring with them a good and wholesome influence and raise the tone of their surroundings"[16] exemplifies perfectly the Victorian ideal of women as the moral housekeepers of society.

Yet the terms and conditions of domestic labor in South Africa were unlikely to attract permanent armies of recruits from England. Not only were servants hired overseas expected to sign contracts that obliged them to repay all or part of their passage money over a designated period of time, but they were also required to perform a wider range of tasks than their English counterparts. A cook to whom Cecil explained that her overseas duties would include cooking (with an African assistant), making beds, answering the door, and performing other "trivial duties" firmly refused the offer. More daunting still, prospective emigrants had to face a complex tangle of class and racial attitudes. Employers "forgot sometimes that a white servant cannot be spoken to in the same way as they have been accustomed to address their Kaffirs or Cape boys or girls, and then they are surprised that a British girl resents such treatment."[17] Worse yet, in the eyes of the women, their expected privileges as whites might be ignored. Miss A. Fourie testified indignantly to the Wages Board that one of those "nice ladies" for whom she had worked "in one case put a native over her, to give orders to her."[18] In addition, housing for servants was often inadequate and, as an understated government report put it, "largely of a character which would not be acceptable to European servants."[19] Further complicating matters, new arrivals quickly became demoralized as they confronted the scorn of local whites for domestic labor.

Despite the suggestions of possible business ventures for enterprising female immigrants, from laundries to market gardening and poultry keeping, household work continued to be the primary opening for women workers.[20] Yet by the time of the depression of 1906–08, the effort to fill these positions from overseas had virtually come to an end. In the Transvaal, middle-class households dispensed with relatively expensive "cooks-general" and sought new sources of cheap labor. Not only had English-speaking immigrants been costly, but they quickly sought more independent occupations as tea-room waitresses, boarding house operators, shop assistants, clerical workers, and to a lesser extent, workers in small factories. More commonly, in the immensely favorable demographic climate, they turned to marriage, which in South Africa usually offered an escape from domestic drudgery. One disgruntled employer complained that the bachelors of Johannesburg spoiled the domestic servant market.[21]

If the depression forced employers to search for cheaper labor, it also produced potential new internal sources of such workers: in the Transvaal urban, largely Afrikaner women from impoverished families and Zulu women pushed out of the countryside by a disastrous combination of drought, cattle disease, economic depression, and rebellion. Yet neither group proved a reliable source of labor. In the words of a government commission that sought workers to replace African domestic employees, white women "object to menial work, and also have a strong feeling of repugnance against working with natives in any household when these are employed."[22] A 1916 report on industrial education described young women in indigent homes as "shocked at the thought of taking a subordinate position in another house."[23] Those who had engaged in such work had no illusions about its "protected" nature. One former domestic worker, bothered by the "improper overtures" associated with the job, explained, "I'd rather go on the streets than be a servant again. It's so humiliating."[24]

African families, also fearing sexual exploitation, were reluctant to allow their daughters and wives to enter domestic service; and black women themselves preferred more independent occupations, whether legal or illegal. For coloured women too, the demand for domestic labor generally exceeded the supply; while they predominated among domestic workers at the Cape, "complaints are rife . . . of the difficulty of getting good servants."[25] In the trenchant words of Charles van Onselen, "To their bewilderment and considerable annoyance, . . .the middle and ruling classes uncovered that basic social fact that each of its generations has to discover for itself—namely, that during the severest of depressions and distress the poor prefer the communality of collective suffering to individual life-saving labor amongst alien classes."[26]

Employers in the Transvaal had their own reasons for hesitating to hire black women. Many white women were fearful that their husbands might initiate sexual relationships with female servants and, since African women and men received equal wages, there was little incentive to hire female workers in place of men. Although a disastrous drought in 1911 drove thousands of women and children into the cities and lowered the wages of black women, black male "houseboys" continued to predominate in most white Johannesburg and Durban families during this period.

Yet, despite the widespread distaste for domestic service on the part of black women and their families, regional variations and differences between urban and rural areas were marked. Reliable rural statistics are difficult to obtain because many squatters and labor tenants who performed intermittent domestic work were counted in other occupational categories; but distinct patterns of women's proletarianization and urbanization and differing histories of black-white relationships produced relatively large numbers of black women servants in the Cape and the Orange Free State by the early twentieth century and relatively few in the Transvaal and Natal.

Significant changes were occurring during this period, however. Whereas in the Cape, with large numbers of coloured women as domestics, African female servants were roughly three times as numerous as African men in both 1911 and 1921, in the Orange Free State African women's preponderance over African men jumped markedly (from 55.9 percent to 84 percent of all black domestic workers). The number of women continued to be much lower than that of men in the Transvaal and Natal; but it increased in both areas from roughly a quarter to over 40 percent of all African domestic workers.[27] These changes notwithstanding, domestic work employed only 10.7 percent of all black women over fifteen counted in the 1921 census.

Although some white women were able to obtain wage work outside of domestic service, many other women, black and white, found their options limited. African women in Johannesburg explained their difficulty earning a living in a petition that Mrs. Ellen Leeuw and 122 other women brought to the City Council in 1910. Describing kitchen and general servants' work, washing and ironing, and work in African "eating houses" and hospitals as either forbidden to them or monopolized by men, they protested: "All means whereby we could make our living are unsympathetically locked up."[28] This shortage of regular employment compelled most women to carve out their own independent niches in the urban economy, sometimes legally, but often in proscribed ways. Such flexible strategies for supporting themselves accorded with women's domestic responsibilities and orientation, allowing them to obtain an income, however small, from the sale of scarce domestic services and commodities.

In Johannesburg, black men monopolized laundry work until the 1920s, leaving illegal beer-brewing as the primary economic pursuit of most African women in the city. As a home-based, potentially profitable traditional skill that required little capital, brewing had many advantages.[29] One brewer, whose business attracted attention during an extortion case against a white police officer, had been earning the substantial sum of twenty pounds a month,[30] considerably more than the ten shillings to one pound that washing jobs might yield.[31] Police raids succeeded only in inciting public anger and confrontation, never in stopping the flow of a commodity in such demand. Attempted repression also led some women in the 1920s to shift from brewing traditional beer with long preparation time and a distinctive smell to more powerful and quickly prepared liquor such as *isiqedeveki* ("makes you drunk for a week") and *isikilimikwiki* ("kill me quick").[32]

Not unexpectedly, women charged with brewing were likely to face blame for an array of social problems. Dismissing assault charges against two black women in 1922, the magistrate berated them:

> There would be none of this trouble if you women would not make all this beer. You are too lazy to work. This has got to stop. You native women are the cause of most of the crime on the Rand. You do nothing but brew and sell liquor and the men get into trouble through it.[33]

If domestic workers, in van Onselen's words, were the witches of suburbia, brewers had become the witches of the slum yards.

Many white women, particularly those who were married, also favored informal ways of earning an income, some as outworkers in the garment trades, others by washing clothes and taking in boarders. The case of a young woman who sought work in a fabric shop illustrates the options of two generations of women:

> She is 14 years of age, her parents are very poor, the father is suffering from phthisis and cannot work and the mother has to do all kinds of things such as taking in washing and had to take the girl from school. The mother had to let off rooms in the house and do as well as she can in a general way to make things meet.[34]

Like their counterparts in Europe and the United States during the nineteenth and early twentieth centuries, many white working-class families followed a generational strategy: sending adolescent children out to work for wages while the mother pursued home-centered economic activities. A similar approach prevailed among black households, where daughters were more likely than mothers to be pressed into domestic service.

Illicitly selling small quantities of liquor to blacks represented another common means of augmenting family income, one that thrived in the racially mixed shanty towns called slumyards that dotted the urban landscape during this period. In 1916, 76 percent of the white women imprisoned in the Transvaal had contravened the Liquor Law.[35] Typical was the case of Sarah Duplessis, sentenced to six months hard labor for selling liquor to an Indian woman. A mother of two small children, Duplessis admitted her offense (from which she had earned only 1s.) explaining, "Times are very bad."[36] Many of the women charged with this violation used their earnings to supplement other sources of income: Minnie Anderson, sentenced along with Duplessis, also worked as a dressmaker; Annie Hamburg's coloured husband earned steady wages as an artisan and one of her adult daughters brought home four pounds a month as a tailoress. Annie Scott, pleading innocent, argued that she was too well-off to sell liquor. Family income included her husband's wages as a cab driver, those of a daughter in service, and her own earnings from a store at the May Deep mines.[37]

For impoverished proletarian women, black and white, sex was the other domestic service apt to be commercialized. In 1880, a local administrator in Pietermaritzburg charged that the bulk of African women had abandoned the kraal to adopt "prostitution and petticoats,"[38] phenomena he seemed to equate with each other. On the Witwatersrand, Cape coloured women, succeeded by women from an astonishing array of European countries, filled the brothels of the new mining centers. Growing male unemployment during the recessions of 1904–05 and 1906–08 forced many Afrikaner women into commercialized sex either directly, or equally often indirectly through the appallingly low pay of the jobs available to them. Similarly, in the black community, encouraged by the imbalanced sex ratios of the mining compounds and the lack of other options, some women became prostitutes. In 1911, police estimated the number of full-time black prostitutes in Johannesburg at between two and three hundred; by 1921, the estimate for all mining areas had risen to two thousand.[39] On the Rand, between five hundred and eight hundred of these women came from Portuguese colonial areas. Farther from home, they could escape more easily from rural patriarchal controls than local women. Nonetheless, they attracted the attention of mining authorities when their male compatriots voted that they should be returned to Mozambique. Not only their morality was at stake, but also the fact that their husbands and fathers had not granted them permission to leave home.[40] Thus, even in distant centers of labor migration, other local men might act as surrogates to exercise the paternal authority felt necessary to monitor women's behavior.

With few other job openings for women and a strong ideology of domesticity, government officials labored continuously to persuade young women to enter domestic service, clinging to a firm belief in its potential for building character and a sense of responsibility. They remained convinced that only a lack of suitable training facilities inhibited new armies of white women from eagerly embracing domestic work. This notion produced a rash of proposals for domestic training schools, touted by proponents as solutions to the problem of insufficient domestic labor.

Among African women, the insistent demands of mining and agrarian capital for black male labor strongly influenced the effort to push them into domestic work. Early in the century the Native Economic Commission reported:

> One branch of the Native labour question is the employment of women, and the Commission feels that it is highly desirable that every measure should be adopted which would encourage the employment of Native women in domestic work. The employment of Native women for domestic purposes would, particularly in Natal and the Transvaal, release large numbers of men and boys for employment in occupations more suited to them.[41]

As in the case of poor white women, domestic employment was favored for its reputed ability to introduce them to "higher standards of comfort, cleanliness and order." Although the Commission recognized that women's presence in urban areas "would undoubtedly expose them to much temptation and the danger of moral ruin," it looked to paternalistic employers "whose duty it should be to protect and care for the character of female servants." In order to facilitate the recruitment of such workers, the Commission recommended the formation of societies to locate positions and to provide women with homes while they sought work.[42] Ten years later similar suggestions again found their way again into government reports.[43]

The bleak economic situation of the African reserves, the commercialization of agriculture, and more varied alternative openings for African men eventually supplied more black women for domestic labor than any direct state policies. Although equally unsuccessful, the official efforts to insure the domestic orientation of white women seemed endless. Educational policies formed a critical aspect of these efforts. A 1916 report on industrial education outlined the ideology of these attempts under the revealing heading "The Needs of the Normal Girl." It noted:

> The case of the girl differs in one very important respect from that of the boy: the noble vocation of home-making is marked out for the great majority of women. In South Africa . . . we believe that every girl in her heart looks forward to being the mistress of a South African home and the mother of South African children. If she enters on some other occupation it is unlikely to provide her with her life-work, and even in that case she will probably have opportunities to make use of any training she has received as a homemaker.[44]

The authors ultimately hoped to create a contented servant class of women trained in new household technology, who were efficient and anxious to succeed; each of them would "take a pride in her work and a becoming uniform." Such a young woman, who "will take the position of a general servant and manage the internal work of the house without coloured aid," need never be "without a comfortable home, a happy useful employment, and a position in which her self-respect need not suffer in the slightest degree." And in case women continued in massive numbers to refuse such beguiling opportunities, the new methods of household science that they would have learned might enable them to dispense with servants altogether: to manage "without undue drudgery and in far less time and with far greater efficiency" than the African men who had usurped women's proper sphere in the house.[45] A 1917 report from Cape Town, after detailing the low wages and abominable conditions for women in other areas of employment, compared domestic labor with nursing. Arguing that the registration of nursing as a recognized profession had significantly raised the status of the occupation over the previous fifty years, it urged that "a similar change would take place in Domestic work if raised to the status of a profession."[46]

The educational bedrock of domesticity was the Housewife's Certificate, then offered at a number of schools in the country, usually as part of the secondary school curriculum; but some institutions, such as the Pretoria Huishoud School, provided instruction in practical housework, cookery, laundry work, and needlework without educational prerequisites. Other proposed ingredients of the general course included house management and household accounts, home dressmaking, hygiene, and physiology. The rural curriculum also introduced classes in dairying, poultry farming, beekeeping, horticulture, and fruit preservation, reflecting the fact that productive as well as reproductive labor routinely occupied the lives of farm women. With space for forty pupils, the Pretoria school had only nineteen.[47] The Huishoud School in Bethlehem, in the Orange Free State, the Schools of Domestic Science in Johannesburg and Cape Town, several different Dutch Reformed Church Schools in the Cape Province (at Graaf Reinet, Wellington, and Tulbagh), and four unnamed centers in Natal all offered a similar course of study.

If young women were not clamoring for the available domestic jobs,[48] few others were pursuing their labor power. In January 1917, the Women's Employment Bureau of the Labour Department showed that thirty women had registered during the month; six were placed in service, nine given daily needlework, and five sent to unspecified places. Although not reflected in bureau placements, clerical workers were in some demand as a result of the war,[49] and the 1916 report on industrial education also predicted new openings in light factory work in the near future: in the tobacco, textile and cardboard making trades as well as in dressmaking, millinery, and laundry work.[50]

According to the 1921 census, however, only 19.3 percent of the white female population over fifteen was economically active, as compared with 62.5 percent of coloured women, 69 percent of black women, and 12.6 percent of Asian women. Of these white women, professional jobs, over-whelmingly as teachers and clerical workers, predominated; for less edu-cated women, service occupations were the only significant possibility. Black women in 1921 formed the largest single group in service occupa-tions; yet domestic labor occupied only 10.2 percent of the economically active black female population as opposed to 84 percent of coloured women wage earners. The vast majority of black women remained in agricultural work, overwhelmingly classified by census takers as peasants, whereas most of the remaining coloured women held jobs as farm laborers or in-dustrial workers—spread equally between textile workers and general la-borers. The small number of Asian working women were divided be-tween service and agriculture.[51]

The low wages in these jobs created a high level of poverty among all working women, which kept them in an economically precarious, depen-dent state. But, particularly in time of depression, married women often faced the most acute hardships. Evidence presented to the Transvaal In-digency Commission of 1906–08 found more destitution among married white women than among those who were single. If brewing and laundry dominated the informal income-earning activities of black women, for white women a similar combination of washing, charring, sewing, and illicit liquor sales offered the primary means of putting together sufficient in-come for survival, although street beggars and what welfare agencies termed "begging letter writers" were not uncommon. Large numbers of white women on the Rand also turned to petty trade, inciting the concern of the commission investigating assaults on women in 1913.[52] Giving some indication of the main pockets of poverty, of the 455 cases that the Loyal Women's Guild investigated between May 1903 and October 1906, 16 per-cent of the women were widows, 15 percent had unemployed husbands, and 10 percent were single.[53] In the other cases, men's incomes were presumably insufficient to sustain a family.

Testimony to the Indigency Commission demonstrates the concern of welfare agencies to preserve male authority within the family. Most relief workers adhered firmly to a policy of maintaining the traditional family wage structure. Representatives of the Loyal Women's Guild, pointing out that many of their clients were the wives and children of men who were out of work, reported, "It is the men for whom we want the relief works."[54] Rev. A. M. Kriel of the Langlaagte Orphanage observed in the same vein, "in many cases we cannot even help the women because we do not want to take the responsibility from the men."[55]

The problem of child care points up a significant racial difference in the options of impoverished urban families. Whereas African parents often sent their children to live with rural relatives, whites, as a more fully proletarianized group, were unable to do so. Instead, many desperate mothers paid black families to do childcare: a privately organized foster care system that attracted official indignation because it transgressed racial boundaries. Such arrangements also incited intense fears about the threat to white supremacy from "the equally wretched habitations of poor whites and poor blacks in Johannesburg's slums."[56] Sister Evelyn, a deaconess of the Wesleyan Church who had worked among the poor for over twelve years, argued in favor of crèches for working mothers to replace the practice of giving babies to full-time paid caretakers. She expressed particular concern over the allegedly high mortality rate among illegitimate children handed over to other people. Children whose mothers had ceased payments to the foster mothers faced particularly acute difficulties. She explained:

> The mother starts paying all right, and for a time she does pay, and then gives the slip, and disappears altogether. The woman will wait and wait, and gradually she ceases the good feeding and care—she is human, often too human—and there you are. The poor little thing wastes away. Besides they are kept filthy dirty, covered with flies; I see all sorts of things in that direction.[57]

At this stage in South Africa's history, then, industry employed few women; indeed the country's secondary industries were relatively poorly developed. When skilled jobs became available, they went exclusively to white and coloured men who had passed through a formal training period. Rigid sex stereotyping and restrictive apprenticeship laws barred women and blacks from these relatively lucrative occupations.

Yet, not all production went on in factories. Outwork abounded, often under abominable conditions, and some training schemes for young women were geared to produce home workers. In 1913 the Transvaal Home Industries Board ran eight schools, instructing ninety-four students in spinning and weaving. The Board purchased the completed yarn from former pupils working at home, although they also were encouraged to weave it at home into "useful articles," whether for sale or for personal use is not clear. In the same year the Pretoria Women's Co-operative Home Industry Society found employment in making confectionery, cakes, and canned fruit for many women, "including those of the better class."[58] Eight years later, the National Service Fund tackled poverty, particularly among widows and women with "husbands whom they would be better without," by seeking contracts for sewing work from hospitals, schools, shops, and private individuals to be done either at home or in N.S.F. workshops.[59]

Beginning with World War I, an increase in factory work began to expand job opportunities for women. As local industries stepped up production of military supplies and replaced European imports with domestic consumer goods, women became an important source of low-paid labor.

In the Cape alone, by 1917, between 4,500 and 6,700 women were engaged in factory work, an estimated two thirds of whom were under nineteen years of age.[60] From 1917 to the mid-1920s, the number of women employed in industry nearly doubled. White women's employment climbed from 4,586 in 1915–16 to 8,848 in 1925–26; the number of coloured women in industry during the same period went from 3,288 to 6,349.[61] These figures, together with those for the Cape in 1917, demonstrate that most of the coloured women in industry were concentrated in the Cape and the white women in other areas, particularly the Transvaal.

Even as these new forms of wage labor were opening up for women, they remained integrated into a family economy, and many assumptions about domesticity and women's dependency continued to influence their wages and working conditions. Following a common pattern, most female industrial jobs involved the production and processing of food and clothing, extending into industry the services that women once provided exclusively in the home. In Cape Town in 1917, they were jam-makers, fruit- and fish-canners, tobacco workers, tailoresses, milliners, and upholsterers. They also manufactured soap, furniture, and sweets and were numerous among bookbinders, cardboard box makers, canister makers and solderers, match makers, dyers and cleaners, and printers' assistants. Thus, although women now created domestic commodities outside the home rather than inside, their work involved little redefinition of their roles or capabilities. Indeed, given the youth of most working women, some of these jobs simply provided training for domesticity in another setting.

Reflecting a high level of paternalism toward women workers, regardless of their age, both the state and employers perceived them as minors who were incapable of assuming responsibility for themselves. Though many proponents of protective legislation expressed sincere concern at appalling wages and working conditions, they also assumed that women were incapable of standing up to employers on their own. In this spirit, the House of Assembly established a Select Committee to investigate the wages of women and girls (defined as those under eighteen); this action was part of a more general effort to develop regular procedures for addressing a host of newly emerging industrial problems. Although the wage regulation machinery instituted in 1918 as a result of the Committee's recommendations achieved little, the parade of witnesses from industry, labor, and welfare organizations amply documented the dreadful pay and working conditions for female and child laborers in nascent industries and the underlying assumptions of employers toward these workers. Reporting in 1917, the Committee recommended the institution of a minimum wage rate for women and young persons employed in a select group of industries and trades. Discussing the draft of this bill, the Secretary for Mines and Industries noted its underlying premise: that women and children were not able to meet their employees on the same terms as "ordinary grown-ups."[62] He shared this view with the Labour Registration Officer of the Cape, who testified before the Committee that young women in the tailoring, printmaking, and sweet-making trades lacked the education to enable them to organize.[63] Neither official considered whether the absence of union organization reflected craft and gender bias among existing unions rather than female docility.

Advocates of protective legislation implied that only by government decree would the meager wages of these workers be raised; and the testimony to the Commission verified beyond any doubt the extremely low pay women received and the dreadful conditions in which many of them worked. A fifty hour work week was the norm, although lack of regulation meant frequent overtime. Most speakers agreed that even single workers could not possibly live on their wages alone. Manufacturers and labor officials cited wage rates of 4s. to 27s. 6d. a week. According to Harry Beynon, the Labour Officer for the Cape, only the wages of older women came near to the "bare subsistence for a European," enough for a man to live in a Salvation Army cubicle, eat in "a scrappy sort of way," and just barely keep body and soul together. One clothing manufacturer, Max Torbin, testified, "I do not think a decent girl over 18 years of age could live on 10s. a week, but the minimum is intended to apply to the other class; they can live on less, living as they do."[64]

Agnes Cooke, president of the Women's Citizen Club in Cape Town and one of the few independent witnesses to the Select Committee on Wages, presented figures even more stark than those of the manufacturers' representatives. In the course of preparing a report for the Juvenile Advisory Board, she collected wage data from twenty firms in the region (another 180 did not reply to her request for information) and found a minimum wage of 2s. 6d. and a maximum of 10s. for young women learning a trade. Cooke's testimony also highlighted another problem resulting from the lack of a formal training period; many firms relied primarily on "learners," firing new workers as soon as they became eligible for wage increases. Not all witnesses disapproved of the low wage levels for learners, however. Thomas Fidler, the general manager of a large shop, Messrs. Cleghorn and Harris, argued in favor of "proper apprenticeships in lieu of a salary" as a way of building the character of young people.[65]

Other witnesses cited lack of proper ventilation in shops and factories, pressure on saleswomen not to use seats where they were provided, and great variation in working hours. Although a forty-eight- to fifty-hour week seemed to be the norm, Cooke found some cafes in which women worked seventy-two hours.[66] Seasonal industries like crayfish factories might require twelve to thirteen hours of continuous work, followed by a day or two off.

Overall, however, the garment industry provoked the greatest level of concern among witnesses before the Commission. Factory production of clothing in South Africa had begun on a small scale in the late nineteenth

century and expanded gradually, especially in Johannesburg and Cape
Town, from 1908 to the beginning of World War I. As wartime conditions
increased the demand for military or "slop" clothing, competition for lucrative government contracts stimulated rapid growth in the industry and
produced numerous efforts at cost-cutting that included the payment of
shockingly low wages. According to one witness:

> The men who got these contracts immediately gathered the cheapest possible
> labour they could get around them and established work rooms. The whole
> thing was merely a question of getting the lowest wage possible, and it in-
> volved very long hours.[67]

Contracts given out for military clothing were commonly sub-con-
tracted to others who got the work done as cheaply as possible, either in
small shops or in the homes of the workers. Seven or eight "squad tailors" would oversee the labor of outworkers, each handling small contracts for a particular part of the work such as machining, pressing, fell-
ing, or buttonholing. Even in "the better class of trade," outworking was
not uncommon, both on the part of "finishers," who completed the final
stages of garments in their houses, or of full-time employees of large
manufacturers who regularly brought home piecework. In the effort to
pay rock-bottom wages, subcontractors relied heavily on the youngest
workers possible, who were usually classified as learners.[68]

Employers readily admitted that wages were insufficient to support even
a single woman; yet they felt no compulsion to pay more. Like South
African mine owners at the time, they viewed their workers as part of a
family economy that (in the case of women) would subsidize its unmarried members. Thus, only those women at the top end of the scale earned
even enough to support themselves in a meager way. Reinforcing the
theory of women's dependency, employers concurred that they expected
the woman's family of birth to make up the difference between what she
earned and the cost of her survival. Beynon, representing the Cape Labour
Department, accepted this assumption and argued against the accepted
belief that low wages drove women into prostitution. He suggested:

> Most of these girls, it must be remembered, live with their parents, and rep-
> utable firms in town, when they engage a girl as an apprentice, always ask
> who she is living with, and who her parents are so as to ensure that there is
> sufficient support.[69]

Indeed, Max Torbin of the Union Clothing Manufacturing Company "would
not engage a child unless she had one of her parents or a guardian with
her." With this protector, not with the young woman herself, did he settle on the first payment and on the wage after a trial period.[70] Employers
of shop workers were particularly prone to hire only those young women

who lived with their parents,[71] thereby reinforcing women's dependence on their families and denying jobs to those who were self-supporting.

Employers implied that families were carrying out their proper responsibilities to subsidize the continued training of their children after they had left school. They overlooked a number of facts, however: that many women were laid off after the training period, that even those who had attained the upper reaches of women's salary scales could barely sustain themselves on their earnings, and most crucial, that these employers were extracting profits from the women's labor during this period. Only the delegates of the Commercial Employees' Association directly addressed in broader terms the fact that "the difference between what a girl receives and what it costs to keep her will have to be made up somehow," whether by starving herself on a diet of bread, water and "two pennyworth of tail fat" or by relying on her parents or on charity. Charity, in this instance, meant an unrelated family "willing to take her in and keep her for next to nothing." Cooke discovered many people who let rooms to women at bare cost and then provided hot water for tea and baths without extra charge. In effect, "public charity makes up somewhat for the short payments of wealthy firms."[72] The only other possibilities, according to the Commercial Employees' representative, were theft and prostitution.

The other central flaw in the argument for parental subsidy came from the economic situation of many parents. Although some were comfortable enough to regard their daughters' earnings as pocket money, many others depended on these earnings to cover basic household expenses. Poverty and hardship were exacerbated when men who suffered from miners' phthisis were permanently unemployed or when young women had economic responsibilities as both mothers and daughters.[73] In supposing that female workers required pay sufficient only for an individual, employers were treating young white and coloured women as they did black men. In both cases their assumptions about family resources were often erroneous and always self-serving.

If many women sought steady wages to help support their parents, they also routinely left their jobs when they married.[74] This pattern implied a belief that their husbands would now assume responsibility for sustaining them, but also reflected a widespread prejudice against the employment of married women. In 1920, for example, R. Stuart, Secretary of the Cape Federation of Labour Unions, wrote to the Labour Department concerning the many cases of single shop workers who were replaced by married women following the initiation of the Wages Board, a government body empowered to set rates of pay for an industry after hearing the arguments of both workers and employers. By gathering information on married women working in commercial trades whose husbands were similarly employed, he hoped to enlist the assistance of the Chamber of Commerce in "getting the married woman to take up her home duties and thus affording the single girl an opportunity of earning a decent living."[75] The same attitude prevailed in professional occupations such as teaching, although in 1922 the Director of Education insisted on the need to continue hiring married women until all unmatriculated teachers had been replaced.[76]

Women's presumed links to a family economy, then, significantly shaped their wages and patterns of work. These ties made them a primary source of cheap labor that was readily available to meet the needs of wartime production, particularly in the garment trades.[77] Under wartime conditions, white women also succeeded in penetrating the previously male world of clerical work.[78] Newly employed in significant numbers, both employers and the state continued to perceive these young women as docile and dependent, paying them wages that necessitated continued reliance on their families. Reinforcing this downward pull was the absence of substantial competition for women workers outside the domestic sector.

Although gender served to classify all women as dependents, a stringent racial division of labor gave white women a privileged position over those classified as coloured. (Transvaal industrial establishments tended to rely primarily on white women.) In Cape Town factories coloured workers predominated in certain occupations (cigarette manufacture, jam and sweet making, and crayfish canning). In some of the larger clothing factories, the women were nearly all coloured.[79] Only one of the plants described in the Select Committee report, the United Tobacco Company, employed a relatively balanced mix of white and coloured women. But lavatory and meal facilities were segregated, coloured women worked in a separate department, and the higher paying jobs went disproportionately to whites. While Europeans comprised 63 percent of the workers under eighteen, they made up 80 percent of the higher paid employees over eighteen.

A distinct racial division of labor also prevailed in Cape Town cafes and shops. In the former, white women and girls worked as waitresses or behind the counter, coloured assistants in the kitchen. In stores, white women were shop assistants and, of course, supervisors, while coloured women sewed clothing in the workrooms. But, racial considerations aside, many shops experienced difficulties in finding "the class of girl" who could "speak properly to a lady."[80] At Stuttaford and Company, apprentices in the dressmaking workrooms, nearly all coloured, began at 2s. 6d. a week; in the all-white millinery workrooms they began at the slightly higher wages of 10s. to one pound per month. In the words of the general manager, "We cannot offer them a living wage if they are not trained."[81]

Perceptions of the relative status of different jobs clearly affected women's preferences, with shops and cafes ranking highest among poor working-class women, factories in the middle, and domestic work at the bottom. According to testimony before the 1917 Commission, women who had a choice favored working in shops or cafes to laboring in factories. Beynon, the Labour Registration Officer for the Cape, outlined the preferences of young white women: "Factory work is not popular with white girls here. They prefer to take up work as clerks or typists or go into business."[82] But both white and coloured women shared a disinclination for domestic labor. Despite a considerable increase in the wages of domestics during the preceding months, the demand for household workers continued to exceed the supply. "They would rather go into factories or shops despite the better pay of the domestic, because they dislike the restrictions imposed upon them in domestic service by their mistresses. . . . They want freedom: this lack of freedom is their objection, that is after working hours. At present they are at the beck and call of their mistresses from 6 a.m. to ll p.m."[83]

The economic rationale for preferring shop work or waitressing to factory work varied according to region. On a nationwide average, according to 1924 figures, there was little difference in the wages for these occupations. Tailoresses' and milliners' earnings were on a par with those of shop assistants and waitresses, and those of dressmakers were slightly higher. In both the Cape and the Witwatersrand, however, average pay for cafe assistants and saleswomen was somewhat higher (by 13 percent and 20 percent respectively) than for women in the trades for which figures were given.[84]

Although wage differences between coloured women and white women were relatively low, especially at the Cape, a marked disparity between male and female pay was accepted practice. The *Cape Argus,* for example, reported the case of a widow with two children who earned 2s. 6d. a day at a factory outside of Cape Town. After she was killed at work under unspecified "tragic circumstances," the company replaced her with a man who received 8s. a day.[85] While this case shows an extreme divergence based on gender, a smaller, but nonetheless pronounced difference was the norm. Between 1910 and 1924 the earnings of white women in manufacturing, clerical work, and domestic work averaged 43.7 percent of the earnings of men in the same occupational categories; a slight rise to 46.3 percent in 1915 may reflect the shortage of male labor during the war. This percentage remained relatively stable over the entire period to 1924–25, following the general pattern of a steep rise in wages during 1919 and 1920, and a gradual decline from 1920–1924 in the aftermath of the 1921 depression. Figures for industrial occupations in 1924 show a comparable wage gap. Although the relationship between male and female earnings varied greatly by occupation and by area, comparing all trades with weekly pay, women's wages averaged only 42.2 percent of men's.[86]

Whatever the inadequacies of their salaries, white women in manufacturing earned substantially more than "non-European" men.[87] In 1921 "non-European" men's wages were 43 percent of those of white women, in 1924, 44 percent. The most notable departure from these statistics occurred at the Cape, where the figures of 60 percent and 62 percent reflect the higher wages of coloured workers.[88] Thus, in industrial employment at this time, black men were ranked below white women in the pay they received and the kinds of jobs open to them. Comparing the figures for black men and white women with those of white men paid on a weekly basis, white male wages in industrial occupations were 4.8 times those of black men and 2.3 times those of white women, whereas white women received twice the pay of black men.[89]

Women's low wages undoubtedly provided a major incentive for hiring them; but their ostensible docility as workers also appealed to employers. At a time when skilled men dominated the white working class, women who tried to organize faced the combined barriers of skill and gender. This bias meant that, apart from the actions of a single, flamboyant leader like Mary Fitzgerald, women's labor activities were occasional and episodic, and their expressions of class awareness were as likely to occur on behalf of their husbands and fathers as on their own behalf. Among the earliest women involved in organized labor protest during this period were the shop assistants who took part in a demonstration in Johannesburg in 1905. Addressing the meeting, Olive Schreiner, author of the nineteenth-century feminist classic *The Story of an African Farm*, expressed her particular pleasure at the women's presence. She observed, "as the most poorly paid and heavily pressed section of workers. . . it is especially necessary that women workers should learn solidly to combine."[90] With remarkable prescience, Schreiner stressed the urgent need to organize, arguing that with a continual supply of new groups of workers willing to work for less than their predecessors, "there is always a hole in the bottom of the boat through which the water will ultimately creep in."[91] Whether she was warning these women to shield themselves from competition or to insure the incorporation of newcomers is unclear.

During the following decade, few working women were organized, although Mary Fitzgerald tried to form a waitresses' union in 1907 or 1908. But she made her most enduring contribution to women's labor history through her writing, unique for South Africa in forging a link between working-class issues and the women's suffrage movement. Never shrinking from controversy, her columm from 1909 to 1912 in the white Labour party newspaper, *The Voice of Labour*, covered contemporary debates over women's suffrage and boldly confronted the issue of marriage as a form of domestic servitude. She wrote in 1909 of the aspiring bride as "blissfully unconscious that she's giving her life to slavery, with the difference that the chains will become tighter every year and her only escape will be grim Death."[92] Advocating that husbands pay wages to wives not working outside the home, she also admonished organized working men who "bitterly resent" women's encroachment into paid labor, continuing to believe that a woman belonged "in the kitchen looking after her husband's wants."[93]

For a brief period in 1909 and 1910, Fitzgerald also managed and co-edited the first feminist journal in South Africa, published under the auspices of the Women's Enfranchisement League. Unlike Olive Schreiner, who resigned from the League because its acceptance of the vote for women on the same basis as men was racially exclusive, Fitzgerald's feminism did not include a challenge to the racial attitudes of the period. In 1915, after the municipal franchise was extended to women, Fitzgerald stood as a candidate, basing her campaign on issues affecting the poorer white women of Johannesburg. Once in office, she was particularly active in publicizing the wholesale sweating of garment workers who received charity from the city's relief funds.[94]

The era of widespread industrial unrest that swept across South Africa toward the end of World War I included some women, although their numbers were necessarily small. Early in 1917, printers' assistants in Johannesburg organized a union to represent those barred from the skilled, all-male South African Typographical Union (SATU). Cited as the first strike in South Africa in which women were the main participants, one hundred workers took action when a major printing firm refused to reach an agreement with them. The craft union supported the stoppage by instructing its members not to do any of the strikers' work and by helping to organize the Printers' Assistants Union; its leaders included two SATU members and two women, Ruth Dando and Jessie Turnbull.[95] In a similar case in December 1920, women banking clerks joined members of the exclusively male union in walking off their jobs; only after the strike was under way did the South African Society of Bank Officials decide "to admit ladies to the society at the earliest possible minute."[96] The uneasy relationship between skilled unionized workers and their newly hired co-workers forms a major aspect of the relationship between working-class men and women during this period. Women seeking to form unions faced not only organizational barriers, but conceptual ones; for their efforts challenged the widespread perception of "the working class" as both white and male.

Not surprisingly, Mary Fitzgerald founded the first South African group specifically devoted to organizing women. Beginning in 1918 under the auspices of the South African Industrial Federation, the Women's Industrial League targeted waitresses, laundry workers at the Johannesburg hospital, and women at the Pretoria mint. Influenced by the industrial unionism of the IWW, Fitzgerald sought to involve women who lacked access to traditional craft associations. She also tried to pressure the organized labor movement, putting forward a motion in favor of equal pay for women at a 1919 trade union conference. Though breaking new ground in organizing women, the members of the Women's Industrial League were all white and reflected the prevailing mood of the time in their fears of displacement by blacks.[97]

The social and conceptual climate of the period reinforced the constraints of a segmented labor market to impede both racial and gender equality. The fact that even the poorest of white families might employ an African servant established an incontrovertible racial hierarchy, lessening the likelihood of solidarity in other contexts. A low-paid government printing worker with five children, for example, testified in 1919 that she paid one pound per month "for a native."[98] Thus, the gender equity Fitzgerald advocated remained racially bounded. And even among white women, divisive sentiments were not absent. Testifying at a meeting, Fitzgerald deplored the snobbishness of some female shop assistants, and hoped that they would "quickly recognize that waitresses were their equal."[99] Furthermore, the ease with which notions of women's domestic expertise could be transferred to the public sphere acted to keep women in subordinate positions, even as members of political organizations. During the May Day celebrations in 1919, working women expressed their class awareness as the festival's tea stewards.

Skilled white workers communicated their attitudes toward women during the tailoring strike on the Rand in 1919 and 1920. From an early period, the Witwatersrand Tailors' Association included in its activities, if not in its leadership, the women who worked in tailoring shops. Among the workers involved in a strike against Messrs. Henochsberg and Co. in 1919 were eighty-eight women and twenty-four men. Acknowledging the dire circumstances of many of the women, the strike organizers exempted from the weekly strike levy all women "whose families are on strike or in distress."[100] By January 1920, eight hundred tailoring workers, half of them women, struck again demanding a 20 percent pay increase to keep up with the rising cost of living. A flyer urging other workers to contribute to the strike fund took a decidedly protective attitude toward these women. It argued:

> We ask you to IMAGINE YOUR SISTERS in this struggle. We ask you to declare that the conditions of labour on the Rand for young girls shall be such as to safeguard them from the TERRORS OF PROSTITUTION.[101]

Elsewhere in this letter, the craft-oriented perspective of the union emerges clearly in an appeal to other workers to join "in the fight against the Masters." Only later do "the bosses" enter the discourse of clothing workers as the primary antagonists in their struggles.

Black women, far less numerous in the wage labor force, were not altogether absent from incidents of workers' unrest. In 1919 washerwomen in Bloemfontein went on strike as part of a campaign for general wage increases launched by the recently organized South African Native National Congress (later the African National Congress).[102] As the Industrial and Commercial Workers' Union developed from 1919 onward into a mass movement of rural and urban workers, the organization included small numbers of women as branch leaders, officials, and representatives at conferences. At the group's initial meeting, held in Bloemfontein in 1920, Charlotte Maxeke, American-educated and articulate, brought up the problems of women workers. As the only female delegate, her "vigorous promotion" of women's rights led those assembled to adopt as a primary goal the organization of all females in industry and domestic service.[103] In many respects, then, she paralleled Mary Fitzgerald as a lone voice of female consciousness within a group of men whose primary interests lay elsewhere.

While the small number of women wage workers at this time precluded massive organizing efforts, women joined in male labor activities on many occasions, perhaps most dramatically in the tramway workers' strikes mentioned earlier that immortalized "Pickhandle Mary" in South African labor history. Like working-class wives and daughters in other historical settings, these women shared the class awareness and the anger of the men with whom they lived, a common situation in mining areas where women depended on male incomes for family survival. In such settings, Louise Tilly suggests, the community of work includes women, even if they are not themselves wage laborers.[104] In 1908, several years prior to the tramway workers' strikes, three hundred white women had acted in a similar spirit. Marching with their children to the Assembly of the Orange Free State, they sought to register their protest against the high rate of unemployment. When the Speaker refused to accept their petition, they occupied the floor of the House.[105] In this instance, women were acting politically, but as wives concerned about a shortage of male jobs. Women's motivation was similar during the 1913 mine strike on the East Rand. In support of their men, Fitzgerald and other women led many of the groups that marched from pit to pit calling out the workers.[106]

During the lengthy and violent revolt of white miners in 1922, women's actions were somewhat more complicated. The protracted gold and coal strikes that began early in 1922 placed particular hardship not only on the families of miners, but also on those women laid off, sometimes as an indirect result of the mining stoppages. In late January, a representative of the Rand Aid Association noted the "state of pressing poverty" prevailing in Johannesburg as a result of the strikes. In the worst position, he noted, were a considerable number of widows and families who could support themselves only if young, unmarried women worked. "In clothing, hat and cap factories and other establishments or as general seamstresses, they kept the wolf from the door." Now that they had lost their work as a result of lack of business or lack of power to work shop machinery, their situation was precarious.[107] By February 25, authorities estimated that relief committees were feeding some thirty thousand people.[108] It was undoubtedly these women, perhaps disenchanted with the strike because of the hardship it caused their families, to whom Mrs. Wordingham appealed during a meeting of strikers at the Johannesburg Town Hall. She did not blame them for their lack of sympathy, but rather the husbands who had done nothing to interest their wives in trade union work. Expressing a keen awareness of the burden of household chores, probably exacerbated during the strike, she warned, "Let them wait till their wives strike against sixteen hours a day and then the men would get a sorry time of it."[109] Speaking to a demonstration several days later, a member of the Women's Active League urged women to stand firm and not to induce their husbands to return to work.[110]

Disregarding the hardships, many women lent their support during the prolonged and heated "Rand Revolt," an uprising of white miners against the threat of undercutting and replacement by black workers. On February 8, 1922, a "long procession" of women, members of the Women's Active League of the Krugersdorp area, marched to the Town Hall to present the Resident Magistrate with a resolution; it urged the government to pressure the Chamber of Mines to accede to the strikers' wishes and also to open new industries that could absorb the unemployed. After shouting three cheers for the sympathetic magistrate, the women sang the "Red Flag" and dispersed.[111] During most of the major demonstrations leading up to the army attacks on strikers, women's commandos or women's sections of neighborhood commandos joined in the frequent processions, as did nurses marching together in uniform. Not surprisingly, Mary Fitzgerald appeared among the leaders of a march of six thousand demonstrators in Johannesburg on February 6. In a March 3 funeral procession of fifteen thousand people, one women's commando dedicated its banner to "Our comrades, murdered in cold blood by the police." As tensions mounted over the use of scab labor and over the issue of men who had returned to work, women joined in attacks on the men and their police escorts, despite the feeling of some in authority that they were acting inappropriately. When Minnie Sweeny was tried for obstructing the police, the prosecuting attorney asked, "Don't you think that the best place for a woman is at home looking after her babies?"[112] Following the suppression of the strike sixty-two women were among those arrested, although in the end only six were charged with specific offenses.[113] Thus, as dependent women were drawn into supporting the class struggles of the men on whose incomes they relied, some were incited to take actions that challenged their categorization in purely domestic terms. Acting to protect their positions as mothers and wives led them to contest sometimes the narrow norms that defined those roles.

Despite repeated references to young women unable to fend for themselves and to the notorious difficulty of organizing shop assistants, some women, though unorganized, devised alternative means of shaping their working lives and of struggling against the veil of docility and dependency. Although the individual nature of this protest hides much of it from historical scrutiny, the concealment is not total. Unfortunately, however, most instances came to public attention only when they involved legal action. Among domestic workers, the precarious, yet intimate, personal relationship with their employers offered considerable scope for discord. Most resistance probably involved petty theft and other forms of passive resistance; but cases of more direct conflict were not unknown. In 1915, for example, a black woman in Yeoville, Johannesburg received a sentence of four pounds or one month's hard labor; her employer complained that she had given an order three times and received no response. The accused then spat in her face, shouting, "Yes, take that."[114] In a similar case of personal defiance, a domestic worker at Seapoint, outside of Cape Town, swore at her mistress, smashed a palm pot and threatened to destroy furniture when she was asked to leave after beating her employers' two-year-old daughter.[115]

More collective signs of discontent also surfaced on occasion. Newspaper reports in 1917 noted a growing insubordination among female servants at the Cape, reflected in the number of cases at the local police courts in which women had contravened the strictly defined Masters and Servants Act and in the number of assaults on employers. The scores of boarding house employees at the Cape who left without notice during the busy Christmas and New Year's holidays were also finding a way of shaping their working lives to their own convenience,[116] as were the numerous tearoom waitresses who risked prosecution and fines by failing to sign an attendance register.[117]

Many court cases between workers and employers involved disputes over wages. In 1921, a shopkeeper had to pay a twenty-pound fine and back wages to an assistant whose salary he had illegally refused to raise from £4 10s. to eight pounds a month when she turned eighteen.[118] In a similar case in 1915, Henry Oliver was fined two pounds and forced to pay £7 10s. in back wages to a black woman named Lena whom he had employed in the kitchen for five months without payment. Oliver argued in defense that she had agreed to work for only food, lodging, and clothing; she testified that she had expected £1 10s. a month.[119]

Seeking to control their working lives in still other ways were the white servants who refused the indignity of doing "rough" work such as scrubbing floors, cleaning windows, and washing dishes, forcing employers to hire black men to perform these onerous chores.[120] Most direct and aggressive in resisting their demeaning conditions of labor, however, were the black female domestic workers on the Rand who joined the Amalaita gangs that roamed the white suburbs during 1906–08, attacking employers who were remiss in their wage payments or who were accused of treating their servants badly. Although unequal to male gang members in number or in status, the female members, clad in their own distinctive pleated skirts, black stockings, and high-heeled shoes, formed a significant element in these gangs.[121]

Overall, this period of early industrialization showed the beginnings of several distinct tendencies, some of which would remain relatively stable, while others would change as industrialization and proletarianization proceeded. The pattern for poor white families was similar to that of nineteenth and early twentieth-century Europe; by the age of fourteen or fifteen, young people were expected to work until marriage to assist their parents and younger siblings. During this period in which young women received extremely low wages, employers relied upon their families to supply room and board as a supplement to their scant earnings. The contradiction is, of course, obvious. But employers justified the wage levels on the basis of the women's low productivity as they learned the necessary skills for the job. (Most married women with children supplemented meager family budgets by taking in boarders, doing laundry, and selling liquor illegally, although some did find formal jobs.) Rural labor patterns that confined women to domestic labor and childcare when economically feasible, as well as the paucity of alternatives, probably influenced these choices. Despite the pressure from many sources, and despite the number of women with no other options, domestic labor remained too entangled in racial attitudes to attract more than the newest immigrants or the most desperate of these women.

Black women, too, sought to retain as much control as possible over their own labor by preferring informal work. Although wage-paying jobs continued to be scarce, married women in particular clearly favored brewing, laundry work, and charring, tasks that offered a degree of flexibility and allowed them to combine income-producing activities with childcare. The potential profits from brewing beer and liquor provided a distinct advantage over ill-paid domestic work, the only wage-earning alternative for women. Both women and their families resisted this option, although in the Eastern Cape and the Orange Free State, where a tradition of women's domestic labor had been established in the nineteenth century, many women were drawn into household work. Following the dictates of economic necessity as well as patterns of continuous rural labor, most African women expected no break in their working lives as a result of marriage or childbearing.

If some women wage earners of this period found varied means of shaping their working conditions and of resisting unsuitable or exploitative employment, far more sought to retain some control over their lives and perhaps to challenge the expectation of dependency and docility by refusing domestic labor and by insisting on their own strategies for economic survival. Although labor authorities were less concerned with black women's preference for other forms of work, many Africans nonetheless shared with white and, to a lesser extent, coloured women a "regrettable aversion" for domestic service. Such attitudes caused officials considerable consternation, engendering endless schemes to upgrade and professionalize the occupation by training women in childcare, cooking, hygiene, needlework, and first aid. Yet in 1922, despite these efforts, J. D. Rheinallt Jones termed domestic work an "almost unoccupied field" in which the demand for trained help in institutions and homes far exceeded the supply of workers.[122] Although some young women were forced into service because of the scarcity of alternatives, their stubborn reluctance to enter household work was perhaps the most distinct characteristic of women's protest during the early industrial period.

II
Women in the New Industrial Unions

-3-

PATTERNS OF WOMEN'S LABOR, 1925–1940

From the middle of the 1920s a new surge of industrial development shifted women's position in the labor force, greatly accentuating differences in the working lives of black and white women. With a steady increase in local manufacturing, new jobs opened up for white and coloured women, offering them an alternative to domestic labor. More indirectly, by expanding the employment options of black men, the new factories increased the demand for African women as urban household workers. While industrial growth gave poor women in the larger cities of South Africa greater scope for earning a livelihood, their options remained limited, shaped as they were by racial and gender stereotypes and by state policies over which they had no control. Patterns of rural labor and marriage, individual family situations, and the temporary scourges of drought and depression also influenced whether a woman remained in a rural community or sought to expand her choices by moving to a city.

However constrained their options, these women cannot simply be depicted as a "reserve army of labor" at the mercy of abstract economic forces. When white and coloured women chose the mechanized routine of factory jobs over domestic service, and when black women struggled to maintain the viability of casual home-based economic activities, they were striving to assume responsibility for their own lives and for the well-being of their families in an increasingly hostile environment.

As part of that effort, many young women in industrial occupations turned to trade union organizing, sometimes in partnership with women of more varied backgrounds who were affiliated with the South African Communist party. If they no longer resorted to pickhandles as implements of struggle, many women still displayed courage and defiance in the face of police violence, arrest, and imprisonment. With a few notable exceptions, black women were more likely to express their economic distress through small-scale, often spontaneous, community-based protests since they lacked access to institutionalized grievance procedures.

If these economic changes opened up new forms of collective action to some women, they also led to sharper racial divergence in employment possibilities. Gender expectations still dictated that most married women would avoid working outside the home if possible; but new options for white and coloured women, especially if young and single, created a context in which some were able to challenge restrictive gender boundaries. At the same time, black families, now proletarianized in ever-growing numbers, were increasingly unable to keep their daughters out of domestic service. Furthermore, although large numbers of women of all races still relied heavily on casual labor, the major activity of black women, brewing, came under increasing official attack, which effectively labeled overwhelming numbers as actual or potential criminals. Relying on income from brewing and prostitution, many Sotho women in particular developed a subculture in which they aggressively flaunted their independence from male control.[1]

All of these women, black and white, were products of a new economic and political climate from 1925 onward, as the emergence of new consumer goods industries, "secondary" production, became increasingly central to the South African economy. Clothing manufacture increased, greater quantities of textiles, boots, and shoes were produced locally; and the processing and packing of foodstuffs accelerated, all encouraged by new tariff policies that granted protection to this emerging local manufacturing capability. In the course of rapid expansion, many of these industries reorganized the labor process by means of increased mechanization, job fragmentation, and deskilling, undermining the position of many established employees but opening up work for newly proletarianized workers who had been denied access to skilled crafts.

During these years (the second half of the 1920s) the new "Pact" government, a coalition of the Labour and Nationalist parties, came to power. They represented respectively the interests of working-class whites and of the varied groups increasingly drawn to Afrikaner nationalism. Allied against the South African party of Jan Smuts, which was closely identified with mining capital and British imperial concerns, the Pact government under J. B. M. Hertzog introduced legislation designed to reshape the labor force and to revise the guidelines under which workers could press for increased wages and improved working conditions. Its most immediate concern was to guarantee continued white superiority by enacting public policies to insure "the political security of the white race as a whole and the economic security of its feeblest members."[2] In 1933, however, with the Depression still ravaging living standards, Hertzog and Smuts joined forces in the United party.

Their newly forged unity provided a basis for further entrenching white domination. As the state enacted racial policies first proposed during the

1920s, urban segregation increased and became more formalized, pass laws were enforced more strictly, black and white schools and churches were more rigidly separated, interracial relationships outside of marriage were outlawed, and educated and prosperous African men in the Cape Province were deprived of the right to vote. Furthermore, in the effort to eradicate white poverty after the Depression, the state devoted its own resources to creating new jobs for poor white (mainly Afrikaner) men to protect them from black competition. This repressive and racist climate combined with economic growth to deepen the rift between poor urban women of different races. Even in the past, the neighborhoods and housing of the poorest whites were usually far superior to the squalid, teeming slum yards that housed most urban blacks. But by the late 1930s the material improvements for most white families, combined with increasing segregation and differential treatment of blacks, were heightening still further the economic gulf between black and white women.

At the heart of government labor policies were several new laws, most notably the Industrial Conciliation Act of 1924 and the Wages Act of 1925, which introduced Wage Boards as a means of addressing workers' grievances. By creating new means of managing class conflicts through formalized negotiation procedures and limitations on strikes, these measures shared common features with labor legislation in other industrialized countries. But the Industrial Conciliation Act had its own uniquely South African twist: prohibiting all those required to carry passes (essentially African men) from taking part in trade unions that could be registered, and therefore legally recognized, under the new law and instituting a "civilised labour policy," which encouraged employers to give preference to white workers. Though some of these laws refrained from direct reference to race, they were clearly intended to have an impact on the racial division of labor. By contrast, the effects of these policies on gender relations were unforeseen and probably unintended. Yet, by exempting domestic service and agriculture from the operation of the Wages Act, legislators deliberately excluded a substantial number of workers (many of them women) from the potential benefits of the new legislation.

This period of accelerated industrialization had its greatest direct impact on white and coloured women, particularly in the Transvaal and the Western and Eastern Cape. Yet women's accelerated entry into industrial wage labor was not simply a function of government policy, deliberate or otherwise, but also a result of economic conditions: a succession of severe rural droughts in the late 1920s, exacerbated by the worldwide Depression of the early 1930s. Coming after a sharp decline in real wages between 1914 and 1925, many women were forced to contribute in new ways to family survival.[3]

Gender divisions in rural production, as well as the relative availability of wage work for women and men, influenced family decisions on how best to maximize their meager resources. Although poor white women took an active part in rural economic life, the cash contributions of daughters working in the cities were more essential to family survival than their labor potential on the farms. In the words of the Carnegie Commission investigating the plight of impoverished whites, "even the daughters of more comfortably situated farmers find little scope for profitable occupation, but in the poor households they can contribute practically nothing towards their own support and that of the family."[4] Accordingly, white women outnumbered white men in the larger cities and the imbalance was substantially higher among Afrikaners than among the English-speaking population.[5] Interestingly, however, the relative stability of the urban sex ratio among whites between 1926 and 1931 suggests that the exodus of Afrikaner women from the rural areas predated both the dislocations and the expanded economic opportunities of the late 1920s.

Statistical data demonstrate the dramatic rise in the number of women involved in factory production in the late 1920s, particularly in four categories: food, drink and tobacco; clothing and textiles; books and printing; and leather and leatherware, which together accounted for 86 percent of the white female employees in industry in 1929 (11,364 out of 13,128). The following table shows the specific increases.[6]

Class of Industry	1923/24	1928/29	% Increase
Food, drink, tobacco	1,532	2,980	95%
Clothing, textiles	2,362	4,999	112%
Books, printing	1,268	1,922	52%
Leather & leatherware	977	1,463	50%
Total	6,139	11,364	85%
Total no. female industrial employees	7,104	13,128	85%

Despite women's entry into factory work, few employers changed their negative attitudes toward female employment. In 1925, for example, Cape clothing manufacturers depicted such labor as unattractive to white women. Noting a decreasing ratio of white employees in the industry, they observed that "the type of white girls" who sought factory work came in "as a last resort," having failed at an alternative occupation.[7] A welfare worker, reporting in 1931 on a woman charged with soliciting, reiterated this attitude: "She is the usual factory type of girl, and not of bright intelligence."[8]

While dismissing the abilities of female factory workers, labor officials continued to perceive few alternatives to domestic service for poor young women. Their attitude provides ample documentation of how stereotyped notions of female domesticity shaped public discourse on women. Speaking in 1926 on "Careers for Girls," the head of the Durban Juvenile

Affairs Board vehemently denied that women might benefit from a scholarly education. Decrying the nervous strain and the energy-draining effects of academic learning, which also fostered a "distaste" for the bucolic life of the homemaker, he advocated the introduction of a newly designed Homemakers' Training course. Unlike the ill-suited classical curriculum, this course would remedy the distorting influence of instruction that neglected the essential core of women's lives: "the care of others than themselves."[9]

Efforts to provide training programs that would encourage female juveniles to enter domestic work continued unabated during the late 1920s, even as industrial jobs began to increase. By working with Juvenile Affairs Boards to establish and run such programs, branches of the National Council of Women were able to solve two problems simultaneously: assisting young women less fortunate than they, while creating new supplies of suitably trained servants. Yet young white women remained as resistant as ever to these "opportunities." Indeed, their resistance may have hardened at a time when official policy sought to associate unskilled manual jobs with black workers. Training centers in Pretoria, Johannesburg, Cape Town, Durban, Pietermaritzburg, and Bloemfontein met with varying degrees of success in attracting applicants, despite vigorous efforts to counter the continuing distaste for domestic service by making it more attractive: training specialists in child-care as nursery nurses, offering distinctive uniforms and badges to graduates of their courses, and occasionally trying to establish uniform wages and terms of employment. Bloemfontein officials were realistic enough to recognize that, despite these incentives, a hostel might be necessary "to accommodate girls earning very small salaries."[10] And attempts to attract a wide range of recruits notwithstanding, directors of one of the more successful centers found that recruits came overwhelmingly from "very poor" families.[11]

Only a report by the female members of the Coloured Juvenile Affairs Board in Cape Town punctured the official rhetoric on the benefits of domestic work and located the problem of labor supply not in lack of education, but in the conditions of employment: low wages, "deplorable" accommodations, insufficient time off, and the exclusion of domestic work from the Wages Act. It also noted that most (probably 75 percent) of the domestic workers at the Cape came from the country districts, both because young town and suburban women favored factory employment and because employers preferred more docile workers:

It is worthy of note that mistresses, as a rule, prefer to employ country girls . . . chiefly because they do not claim with such insistence proper consideration where food, accommodation, and "time off" are concerned. Sooner or later, though, country girls begin to seek new positions where the conditions may be presumed to be less irksome.[12]

Even after factory work became commonplace, the futile efforts to lure white young women into service continued. In the early 1930s, the Carnegie Commission report found that, although domestic service was often the only opening for the country girl seeking employment, even those "from the less intelligent classes" felt an antipathy for this kind of work. However often philanthropic outsiders repeated their refrain that the work suited "the nature of most girls," their chorus of refusals could not be muted.[13] By the middle and late 1930s, the continued expressions of optimism that the distaste for domestic labor was "only temporary" and that each new training scheme would be the one to succeed are truly amazing.[14] But, once again in 1939, the Department of Labour was forced to admit that those who had been through the Girls' Training Centre in Pretoria preferred to be placed as hospital assistants, laundresses, or seamstresses—anything but domestic service in private households.[15]

In Cape Town, coloured female workers joined their white counterparts in avoiding domestic labor, leading, by the late 1930s, to a crisis among white families over the supply of servants.[16] By that time, alleged one reporter, only "the derelicts and the slackers" were willing to become servants; "girls of real energy and intelligence" preferred clothing and sweet (candy) factories, or even the lower paying laundries.[17] Whereas ten years earlier it was "a simple matter" to find a good maid for two to three pounds a month, the "poison" of factory work had spread, creating an "appalling" servant shortage that reversed the position of maid and mistress.[18] Even in the winter months when the end of the fruit-picking and jam-manufacturing seasons had in the past left a plentiful labor supply, a serious shortage continued to prevail.[19]

By the end of the World War II economic boom, the Labour Department turned its efforts in new directions. But the thirty to forty years spent by various officials and allied white women's organizations in trying to coax white women into these jobs suggests that the gender association of domestic labor as "women's work" was stronger in their minds than the racial connection of menial labor with black or brown skin. The presence of a poor white class regarded well into the 1930s with some of the same disdain attached to racial difference helped to make this association viable. Only in the 1940s, as black women became proletarianized in increasing numbers, would the "problem" of domestic labor in the cities be "solved" temporarily.

As new jobs for women opened up in the late 1920s, some labor officials began to expand their conceptions of women's work; but gendered expectations still shaped their vision in many respects. They continued to disparage the morality of young working women, expressing the Victorian idea comfortably relocated in South Africa that domesticity was not simply a convenient or even a "natural" preoccupation for women, but a moral duty to society. Most South Africans at the time probably shared the prevailing view of women expressed at a National Party congress in

1929. One delegate reported his wife's opinion that a woman's job was to keep her pots and pans looking bright. "These franchise people know nothing of cooking and that's the job for a sensible woman."[20] The image of the feckless "modern girl" decried at the conference was at odds with such good sense: "a girl with short hair, short skirts, still shorter bloomers, with red-stained lips, who spends her days perched up behind a man on a motor bike."[21]

While continuing to tout the advantages of domestic work, Labour Department officials and the Chief Inspector of Factories also began in the mid-1920s to report on a more varied range of occupations for girls and women, always in jobs that involved the preparation of food and clothing: a rapidly growing invisible mending firm in Johannesburg; knitting and boot and shoe factories in Port Elizabeth; new food processing plants in the Eastern Cape [making sweets and biscuits (cookies) and drying and packing fruit]; and textile mills in Johannesburg. Reports consistently noted the increased number of openings for white and sometimes for coloured women, although regional variations were considerable. By April 1927, for example, the Inspector of Labour from Port Elizabeth was anticipating "a serious shortage" of European female labor.[22] The 1926 Annual Report of the Chief Inspector of Factories had observed in Natal and the Transvaal "a steady increase in the employment of female labour leading to a distinct improvement in the type of person seeking employment."[23]

Overall, 1926 showed not only a rise in women's employment, particularly in the clothing and printing industries, but a decrease in the aversion to factory work by European women, leading "women of a more intelligent type" to take these jobs.[24] During 1927, women's employment continued to expand in the Western and Eastern Cape and the Transvaal, particularly in clothing and sweets and in the Western Cape in fruit drying and packing.

Yet, the trend toward more steady employment for women in industry did not change the attitudes of job applicants overnight. At the Cape, during 1927, girls' difficulties in finding employment reportedly increased, since the majority who applied to the Juvenile Affairs Board aspired to be "clerks or shop assistants, milliners or dressmakers" rather than factory or domestic workers. The Annual Report of the Cape Juvenile Affairs Board still found that factory work lacked appeal to school leavers and was accepted only when girls had failed to find other jobs. "Deplorable" factory conditions were blamed in part for these attitudes. Young coloured women, by contrast, were very attracted to factory work, although they shared the aversion of white women for domestic labor. Indeed, prejudice against domestic work was reportedly "on the increase" among all juveniles, and those who found themselves in such jobs responded by the most efficacious means possible—getting out. Few remained in domestic employment for more than twelve to eighteen months.

Providers of girls' education responded to these new developments with considerable success. Indeed, the contrast with earlier schools providing domestic training is striking. The Trades School for Girls, which opened in Johannesburg in March 1926, had nearly 180 students by 1927. Its record spurred the opening of technical schools at Brakpan and Germiston over the next two years. At all these institutions, instructors sought to "give a sound apprenticeship training" in dressmaking, dresscutting, and millinery work to girls of any age with a Standard 6 (eighth grade) education or to less educated students over fifteen. By the late 1920s, even domestic science training emphasized a broader range of employment possibilities than were previously available. Though most candidates viewed the "Housewife's Course" as training for private domesticity, others were urged to apply these skills to nurses' training, or to working in hospital kitchens or laundries, factories, or tearooms. More specialized certificate courses now prepared girls as Certified Children's Nurses, tearoom workers, hotel matrons, or for jobs in needlework, dressmaking, or millinery. Barring available openings, however, all continued to be touted as "splendid preparation" for women's "primary careers" as wives and mothers.[25]

Officials were quick to note and to seek to influence the impact of women's industrial employment on the racial division of labor. Reporting for 1926, the Chief Inspector of Factories observed that "many factories, which had hitherto employed non-Europeans, were endeavoring to staff their factories with Europeans only."[26] The report for the following year showed similar trends, again with typical regional variations: in the Transvaal sweet industry, for example, black men were replaced by white women at a reduced wage. In general, the requirements of the Factories Act for segregation of cloakrooms and lavatories was creating a tendency "towards the employment of individual races in order to effect economy in building."[27]

With African workers excluded from the provisions of the Industrial Conciliation Act, the newly created Wage Board became one of the main instruments to shape policies concerning race and gender. But the effects of its decisions, often couched in terms of skill, were frequently contradictory and, overall, its actions had little structural impact on the division of labor in the country.[28] This ambiguity was an inevitable product of the fine line that Board members attempted to tread between high wages that would exclude black workers and increase production costs and pay so low that the demand for whites would diminish sharply. In deciding on wage issues raised by Cape clothing manufacturers who employed large numbers of coloured women, for example, the Board strongly advocated calculating wages according to the task performed, regardless of race. It observed:

> We have tried . . . to make it clear that we are not operating as a colour bar body. We want to fix wages for particular jobs, and if a native or a coloured

person is trained so as to be able to perform those jobs, then that coloured person or native must be paid the same rate as would be paid to a white man in that particular job.[29]

Yet, other decisions applied this philosophy only to skilled work in which at least some Europeans were likely to be engaged. For unskilled work, often performed by Africans "whose standard of living is much lower than that of the Europeans, of most coloured, and of many Asiatics,"[30] race might be taken into account in wage determinations.

Women, whose work was usually deemed "semiskilled," were apt to fare less well than the other members of their group according to such guidelines. But boys under eighteen and women, if white, were theoretically most likely to gain employment under the new policies, because they qualified as "civilised labour," but they might be paid little more than black men. Defining the principles on which the Wage Board operated, its chair, F. A. W. Lucas, observed that the wage paid for a particular job might be the same for a European woman and for an African man; where their skill was equal, however, the greater physical strength of the African man might make him a preferable choice.[31]

Finding the discussion of skill a smokescreen, the Communist party newspaper charged that, while theoretically ignoring questions of color, the board was actually perpetuating the existing color bar by maintaining the large gap between "skilled" and "unskilled" wages.[32] In this case, the writers also grasped an essential element of efforts to determine the ostensible "skill" level of particular jobs: that such categories bore a strong imprint of ideology, reflecting an automatic tendency to rank the jobs of women and racially subordinate groups lower than those of white men.[33]

From the start, the Board also accepted a male-female wage differential without question, outlining different gender-based principles for making decisions about wage levels. According to Lucas, a "civilised wage" for a female employee was "taken as one upon which she can maintain herself without having to look to her parents or anyone else for support," whereas for a man it must be taken to mean not a wage on which he can "merely exist," but one on which he can "maintain not only himself, but also a wife and family with a reasonable degree of comfort according to European standards."[34]

According to the underlying ideas affecting wage-setting practices, then, both black men and white women were presumed to require sufficient resources only to sustain themselves. For white women, this formulation differed slightly from notions prevalent at the time of the 1917 hearings on the wages and working conditions of women and juveniles. From assuming that women could live on wages below the standard for their reproduction because of their "natural" reliance on fathers or husbands, authorities were accepting, at least theoretically, that many women were self-supporting. The requirements of women with families to maintain or to assist were ignored. For black men, the fiction that their wives and families were able to sustain themselves in the reserves remained a convenient myth for much of the twentieth century. The reason for the shift in attitudes toward women's wages is uncertain. But, writing during the early 1930s at the height of the Depression, Lucas must have realized that many families with working daughters could scarcely afford to support themselves, let alone to subsidize the meager wages of parsimonious employers.

By 1925 wages and working conditions were scarcely better than they had been eight years earlier at the time of the Select Commission Report on women, girls, and juveniles. Pay remained far too low to cover expenses of lodging, food, and transportation, let alone other basic requirements.[35] And attitudes toward working women remained ambivalent. Even some advocates of improved pay and benefits expressed dismay at the results of women's presence in the labor force: wage cuts, the displacement of men in certain occupations, and "deplorable" (a favorite word of reformers during the period) results for family life. Fanny Klenerman, the leading organizer of white working women in the mid-1920s, favored equal pay for women, but also pressed for a suitable family wage so that women would not be forced into situations injurious to their physical and mental health. Speaking before the 1925 Economic and Wage Commission, she argued for wages that would enable men alone to support their families: "Married women and a good number of single women would leave the industrial world gladly if their husband's [sic] or fathers . . . were in a position to support them."[36] Klenerman's solution did not suit the times, however, and the coming years were to see an increase rather than a decrease in the number of wage-earning women in South Africa.

This ambivalence toward women's labor outside the home, combined with a shortage of jobs deemed suitable for them, led to restrictive policies regarding the employment of married women. In 1927, the Juvenile Affairs Board passed a resolution urging both public and private employers to eliminate married women from paid employment. Such a policy already was in effect in programs to support the dependents of miners' phthisis victims. They were hired at sixteen and could work until marriage; afterward, officials assumed that their husbands would support them.

Attitudes toward outwork also became caught up in the controversy over whether married women should take jobs outside the home. During the late 1920s, advocates of higher pay for women expressed concern at the amount of garment manufacturing going on in homes and small workshops. While attractive to married women with families, the low wages threatened prevailing pay rates in factories, making the issue a particular concern of the Wage Board.[37] Ignoring such criticisms, promoters of home industry argued that outwork would "arrest the influx of poorly educated girls" into the towns.[38]

As the 1930s progressed, the concerted efforts of trade unions and gov-

ernment agencies to eliminate outwork led to a decline in nonfactory production, but not to its total disappearance. In 1936, for example, when a
clothing factory in Pietermaritzburg closed, outworkers drawn from "the
poorer class of women" took over the jobs. One of the employers, a woman
who ran four sewing machines in her house, sometimes forced the three
women who worked for her to accept payment in kind rather than in
cash. Those who complained to Industrial Council representatives were
dismissed.[39]

Although the Wage Board condemned outwork as an impediment to
employers who wished to comply with mandated wage increases, Klenerman's report to the Economic and Wage Commission understood the
circumstances that pushed women to accept such sweated labor. She noted
in particular lengthy travel time to and from work and the difficulty of
finding adequate childcare. She explained, "If the work unfits her from
further effort in the home the married woman hesitates to accept it. This
encourages women to take work in the home, such as making shirts and
trousers; the rates for work of this kind are appalling and beyond description."[40]

The high level of outwork underlines the overwhelming number of
women not formally working, despite significant shifts in employment
patterns between 1925 and 1940. By 1936, 92 percent of Asian women, 77
percent of white women and 65 percent of coloured women were described as "dependents." Although intended only as an economic category by census-takers, this classification continued to reflect a patriarchal
construction of women's social and legal position. The small proportion
of black women depicted as "dependents" (18 percent) reflected neither
their greater freedom from family controls nor a higher degree of proletarianization, but rather the vagaries of census categories. All rural African women were designated as economically active "peasants."[41]

Apart from their lower level of involvement in wage labor than men,
most trends affecting women were as dependent on race as on gender.
For white women, with access to a growing variety of paid jobs, the changes
were more complex than for other groups. Certainly the most striking
development between 1921 and 1936 was a threefold increase in the number of white women in industrial jobs. At the same time, the number of
women working as shop assistants more than doubled, a clear result of
the deskilling process by which women were beginning to replace highly
paid men in this occupation.[42] In clerical work, however, as the percentage of men continued to increase, the proportion of women dropped. But
women alone benefited from the newly defined profession of "stenog-
rapher," which first appeared in the 1936 census. The number of both
women and men in service occupations (including hotel workers) and in
the professions also continued to increase. In the latter, a steep rise in the
"medical" category reflected the gains in the development of nursing,
while a slight fall in the number of women teachers (compared to a steep

rise for men) may indicate deliberate government restrictions on the employment of married women.[43] Finally, white women's urbanization was reflected in a decrease in the number of women classified as "farmers and farm workers."

From 1925 to 1940, coloured women continued to be more heavily represented than other women in the paid labor force. In both 1921 and 1936, an overwhelming majority of those employed were "service workers," primarily domestic. Yet industrial occupations accounted for 10 percent of wage-earning coloured women, representing a rise of 70 percent in the number working in industry. In Cape Town, where most of the industrial jobs were located, the changes were particularly striking. The percentage of women in domestic service declined from 85 to 66 percent, while the proportion in semiskilled work rose from less than 4 percent to over 19 percent.[44] The number of professional women, primarily teachers, increased during this period, but remained extremely low.

During these years black women's labor patterns contrasted sharply with those of other groups of South African women because of their overwhelming involvement in peasant agriculture. But, while the percentage of women classified as "peasants" remained relatively stable between 1921 and 1936, the number described as "other farm workers" fell sharply, probably a result of increasingly restrictive policies toward African families who lived as squatters and labor tenants on white farms. At the same time, growing numbers of black women were entering domestic service, although in 1936 this occupation still accounted for only 13 percent of black women and continued to provide employment for numerous men. Very few African women held industrial or professional jobs during the 1930s, and those in manufacturing were relegated to such tasks as wool-scouring, dried fruit packing, and rag and flock picking, all considered "unpalatable and unsuited" for other racial groups.[45]

The number of employed Asian women was extremely small between 1921 and 1936, a product both of highly protective cultural attitudes toward women's work and of the relative prosperity of some Indian families. As with white and coloured women, the percentage in agriculture decreased during this period, while the percentage in service rose slightly to become the most significant avenue for women's wage labor. The largest increase, in the professional category, represented only 4 percent of employed Asian women in 1936, and the number of industrial workers, employed primarily in sugar mills and clothing factories, remained insignificant. Because of the shortage of female labor, Asian businesses were forced to employ white women as stenographers. At Sastri College, the Asian technical school, only two women signed up for classes in office skills between 1930 and 1938; neither one completed the course.[46]

Most women who entered industry in the late 1920s and the 1930s found jobs in the newly developing production of domestic goods, whose growth was stimulated by tariff barriers erected in 1924; significant numbers of white women also continued to do less-skilled work in the printing industry. Whereas the involvement of white women in food, tobacco, clothing, textiles, leather, printing, and chemicals grew at a faster rate than that of white men during this period, white men's employment in all of these industries continued to increase.

As larger numbers of white women moved into manufacturing jobs, their work diversified and shifts occurred in the division of labor by race and gender. As the percentage of white female workers in clothing manufacture fell slightly, the number producing tobacco and footwear increased. By contrast, although clothing and food factories continued to employ the largest number of coloured women in industry, new tobacco and footwear factories primarily hired white workers of both sexes and, to a lesser extent, coloured men.[47]

Assessing the effects of changing female employment patterns, a contemporary economist concluded in 1937 "that the alleged displacement of men by women employees has been greatly exaggerated."[48] The validity of that observation varied from one occupation to another. But overall, changing patterns of labor force participation indicate that during the initial period of industrial expansion (1924–25 to 1929–30), white men gained more new jobs than any other group, with white women ranking second.[49] Although this trend indicates that the "civilised labor policy," designed to increase white employment, was having the desired effect, black men during this time gained almost as many new jobs as white women.[50] During the Depression years, however (1929–30 to 1932–33), only the number of employed white women increased. While white men and coloured and Asian women experienced some job-loss, black and coloured men were the hardest hit. As the economy recovered during the rest of the 1930s, men of all races gained significantly more jobs than women. During this period the employment of white women in industry began to decline.[51] Thus, because of political conditions and the gender segmentation of the workforce, women were not treated as a "reserve army of labor" during the economic crisis of the early 1930s.

Although white women gained more new jobs than other female employees as a result of secondary industrialization, the trend benefited unmarried women far more than others. Some married women did take jobs in industry, but others filled the ranks of outworkers in the clothing industry or continued their earlier informal ways of earning money. Indeed, these sources of income were essential to women with small children or with husbands who were either unemployed or earning wages insufficient to sustain a family. Yet the lines between formal and informal work cannot be firmly drawn, since many women survived only by combining the two.

In the late 1920s and early 1930s, poor white women continued to see illicit liquor sales as a source of extra income, a temptation because profits were potentially large and the likelihood of detection small.[52] The extent of this trade is difficult to gauge; but contemporary newspaper accounts suggest that prosecuters had shifted their attention from individual sellers to organized criminal groups. Indeed, in one case reported from the late 1920s, the alleged seller was released and her domestic servant punished for perjury.[53]

Prostitution, as another source of informal income, was probably less prevalent on the Rand than in Johannesburg's earlier days as a frontier mining town. Nonetheless, the sale of sexual services continued to provide some women, both married and single, with a sole source of income, with funds to supplement inadequate wages, or with emergency resources in case of illness or unemployment. Indeed, as the number of formal jobs for women increased, many came to perceive prostitution more as a supplement to other sources of income than as their sole means of earning a livelihood. An estimate for Johannesburg, based on statistics from 1936 to 1940, argued that at least 90 percent of prostitutes (who could earn incomes of over four pounds a month) were originally employed in semiskilled (unskilled according to the report) occupations.[54] For coloured women in Johannesburg, the difficulty in finding employment in the city in the late 1930s and the fact that they were "more or less forced to live in the poorest of quarters" also encouraged prostitution.

Some arrests for soliciting document the relationship with unemployment: Thelma Collins, 27, who had worked in the Tiger Factory and found she could only afford to live in a building in Gold St., a part of town rife with prostitutes and men who pestered her constantly; or Catherine Higgins, 29, married with three children, who lost her factory job when her wages became too high. The report suspects that her persistently unemployed husband encouraged her in this endeavor. In other cases, the women concerned reportedly found the sale of sexual services a less onerous occupation than the low-paid drudgery of factory work. One probation officer described a woman "not prepared to accept factory work as the latter is poorly paid and will only provide for her rent."[55] Freed's study, based on statistical data from the 1930s, examines the low wages for women in industry, and concludes that, because many women turned to prostitution within a few months of beginning work, the curve of the number of women in industry would provide an index to the incidence of prostitution.[56] These surveys suggest that, even as the economy recovered in the late 1930s, for some white women in the remaining pockets of poverty, prostitution was, as in late nineteenth-century Britain, very much an accepted part of working-class life.

For those poor white women less inclined toward the risk of illegal activities, some form of remunerative labor at home remained a necessity. Not surprisingly, just as sewing in factories provided the single most important source of income in the formal labor market, sewing at home was crucial as well. Some women took in outwork provided by contractors, others managed to save enough to buy a sewing machine to do dress-making at home, both for their own families and for neighbors, often with a machine acquired on a hire-purchase basis. Heading the Women's Legal Disabilities Commission in the late 1940s, Bertha Solomon heard so many cases of drunk husbands who sold the sewing machine when the wife refused them more money that she eventually dubbed the group the Sewing Machine Commission.[57] A survey of the Rand in 1930–32 found 350 home workers, nearly all in bespoke (custom-made) clothing, apart from a few who worked at stringing bags and webbing belts.[58] Yet such surveys invariably underestimated the level of women's casual labor.

Although white and coloured women were becoming proletarianized in increasing numbers, the pattern of black proletarianization, which em-phasized male labor migration, was reinforced legally from 1930 onward as state policy toward African women began to shift. In 1930 an amend-ment to the the the Natives (Urban Areas) Act of 1923 granted local authori-ties in proclaimed areas the power to exclude women from towns unless they had guaranteed accommodation.[59] At the same time that some state agencies were attempting to restrict women's movement to towns, how-ever, labor officials were beginning to look to new groups of African women as potential domestic employees. Reporting in 1930, the Labour Re-sources Committee lamented the "uneconomical" use of black men as domestic workers at a time when farming and mining faced a serious labor shortage. Recommending the substitution of African and European women, the committee bemoaned the fact that those black women most likely to leave the rural areas had not provided the "most docile" type of servant and that their exemption from the pass laws made them more difficult to control than men.[60]

Thus, new state regulation of their movement was another factor in the growing racial gap between the lives of black and white women. If pater-nalistic family relationships continued to govern the relative freedom of white women, the state came increasingly to control the geographical mo-bility of black women. As in other parts of southern Africa, such actions often reflected the wishes of rural chiefs and elders, who were anxious to keep women under "traditional" controls.

Whatever their alleged defects as ideal servants, African women were not absent from the ranks of domestic workers at this time; but the re-gional patterns of the early twentieth century still prevailed. The report of the Native Economic Commission explained these patterns partly by the proximity of black communities to the towns. Their closeness in the Cape Province apparently made parents more willing to allow their daughters to work for white families; indeed, a mother often would "be-speak" her daughter at an early age to the home where she had worked in her youth. In Natal and the Transvaal, by contrast, where the villages were rarely near the towns, parental suspicions of the "dangers of town life" made them more protective of their daughters. Although this explanation underscores the effort at family control over daughters' working patterns, it ignores the significance of changing patterns of proletarianization. Thus, while African male servants continued to be more numerous than women in Johannesburg, changes were occurring as a result of women's increased urbanization; the 5,000 female domestic workers formed one quarter of the black servant population in the early 1930s and one third by 1937.[61] A drop in wages for domestic service during the Depression reinforced this trend, since black women were more willing than men to accept the lower pay scales.[62] Just as fewer and fewer white women were being compelled to work as servants for lack of alternatives, the number of black women in this situation was rising.

As Johannesburg employers turned more often to black female domestic workers, middle-class women's organizations joined the state in seeking to address "the servant issue." In September 1929, the Women's Welfare Society in Western Native Township formed to assist African women in finding employment with European housewives. By January 1930, the group had received over 100 applications from nurses, cooks, maids, and washerwomen.[63] This gradual shift also penetrated white attitudes, leading M.K.J., in a letter to *The Star*, to urge employers to consider hiring the "thousands of decent self-respecting native women," undoubtedly more suitable than "these drinking [male] villains," but not hired because it was considered "smarter to employ a 'boy'."[64] By the end of the 1930s, still larger numbers of black women were entering this occupation; in 1938, of some 228,000 Africans in domestic service in urban areas, nearly 138,000 were women and 90,000 were men.[65]

In the turn to larger numbers of female domestic workers, one group of women attracted unfavorable attention: those trained for the position in educational institutions. Employers complained that such young women were "uppity," refusing rough work and unable to work continuously for long hours, faddish about food, and always demanding time off.[66] More to the point, in the opinion of one writer, "The majority of mistresses want a cheap servant and are willing to train an uneducated girl rather than pay for a girl properly trained in domestic science and housewifery."[67] Thus, if the ambiguity over whether young, black women were being taught to care for their own families or to labor in white households provided one contradiction of girls' education, another was the reluctance of employers to hire those who were educated.[68] Once schooled in the occupation, they no longer conformed to the docile, dependent norms that the position demanded. Indeed, although their possibilities for formal organization were limited, the actions of these women bespoke a concerted individual effort to shape the conditions under which they worked.

Advertisements for domestic workers, requiring them to be hard working, respectable, Christian, and non-smoking,[69] suggest the cultural conformity that the position demanded. And, an ostensibly free-market economy notwithstanding, domestic labor in rural areas came perilously close at times to slavery. Advertising for "farm and domestic servants," a notice in the *Cape Argus* in 1937 promised, "For immediate delivery, 100 female domestic servants, cooks, house girls and nurses, Xosas, Fingos and Basutos. Speak English or Dutch. All carry a medical examination and certificate of health." The advertisement assured prospective employers that deserters would be replaced.[70]

By the end of the 1930s, small numbers of African women in Johannesburg also were engaged in more varied economic activities, some of which might later lead to factory employment. They were substanially less numerous in these jobs than white women, but the influence of gender-determination was almost identical. Among the wide range of trades practiced in the Johannesburg, dressmaking, nursing, and midwifery were the only ones that included women. The numbers involved remained small, in nursing and midwifery limited by restricted openings in training courses.[71] Also during the 1930s, waitressing became a "new profession for girls, who are often advertised as a special attraction."[72]

Despite the growing number of available jobs, black women sometimes encountered uniquely oppressive situations. In one Pretoria laundry, they complained of being forced to work not only at their regular tasks, but also in the employers' kitchens. The Native Affairs Office customarily ignored such complaints.[73]

Though teachers were highly regarded and relatively numerous in the African community, Eileen Krige suggests that girls were discouraged from entering the profession because they would be unable to continue earning money after marriage.[74] But another contemporary study, showing that women outnumbered men as primary school teachers, surmises that fathers had economic incentives to encourage their daughters to teach. Since a woman's earnings before marriage went to her male guardian, her educational achievements would increase the level of *lobola* (bridewealth) given for her at the time of marriage.[75]

As among whites, the number of black women engaged in sewing is difficult to determine, because many who worked in their homes were not counted in this capacity. According to the 1938 census, most of the successful dressmakers and tailors' assistants had been trained in industrial schools, although the established businesses were run by older men and women who probably began work before industrial training was available. Girls learned needlework in primary schools, and the curriculum of both secondary schools and industrial schools included sewing and dressmaking as well as other domestic skills.[76] Owners of sewing machines sometimes made clothes for others in the yard.[77] Studying black life on the Rand in the 1930s, Ray Phillips found one woman, Mrs. I. E. Mshage, who carried on a successful dressmaking business, catering to customers of all races and in the process training others who began their own shops.[78]

While some black urban women were entering full-time paid employment, most others continued to contribute to family and individual survival in the informal ways of the past: beer-brewing, laundry work, and
prostitution. In this continued reliance on casual labor, the lives of poor
black and white women (those who were married in particular) remained
most parallel. Yet the context in which women performed this work was
shifting, as state policy toward white male workers mended the ravages
of deprivation, while most black families remained as impoverished as
ever. Furthermore, during the 1920s and 30s, police grew more forceful
and vigilant in their efforts to control the illicit liquor trade, making criminals of those for whom brewing was not only an economic pursuit, but
also a "wifely duty."[79] Ellen Hellmann's study of Rooiyard, a typical Johannesburg slum yard in New Doornfontein, remains the classic investigation of urban women's occupations during the 1930s. Significantly, considering the trend toward urbanization and proletarianization in 1934, she
predicted the eventual formation of a "permanent and stable urban population entirely dissociated from a rural background."[80]

Many of the patterns of women's economic activity and family life that
Hellmann documented remained fixed for some time to come: the tendency for many families to send children to rural areas to be raised (both
for economic reasons and for moral training)[81] and the economic reliance
on beer-brewing and domestic service or washing "jobs." Other studies
of Johannesburg women also add hawking fresh and prepared foods (from
coffee, tea, and donuts to green vegetables, sugar cane, and mealies), to
the list of women's remunerative activities.[82] At least in Johannesburg,
washerwomen were most likely to be part of the settled proletarian family
population, while a high proportion of the women in domestic service
(though often mothers) were not married.[83] Phillips's survey of educated
families on the Rand found that one third sublet rooms to lodgers, helping to further foster the overcrowded living conditions of the locations.[84]
Although Hellmann and Krige (see below) suggest that married women
commonly brewed beer, by the late 1930s, Bonner identifies single women
migrants from Lesotho, the eastern Free State, and southern Mozambique
as the most conspicuous producers of alcoholic beverages.[85]

In an important contrast with later years, all the Rooiyard women engaged in domestic work came home every evening, and some even returned at lunchtime. Of the one hundred women Hellmann interviewed,
only twenty-two were engaged in "legitimate" occupations, all domestic
service. But often this was not a full-time job; six women worked four
days a week, while the other sixteen did only part-time work for Europeans.[86] Full-time domestic service, which often required living on the
employer's premises, understandably attracted a high proportion of single women.[87] Not only were they less likely to have family responsibilities, but if new arrivals to the city, they were ineligible for official housing

in the new townships. Washing, by contrast, was particularly popular among older, married women and among the settled, family-oriented populations of Western Native Township, Sophiatown, Pimville, and Orlando.[88]

Eileen Krige's study of Marabastad Location, on the northwest outskirts of Pretoria (a comparatively stable, long-settled urban African community) found similar patterns, with rent and the earnings of women and children as central to household survival. But, in addition to beer-brewing, a source of income for an estimated 70 percent of women, numerous women augmented their incomes by playing Fah Fee, a Chinese game of chance played through "runners" who took bets on a particular number. The latter enhanced the game's interest by translating people's dreams into the numbers they symbolized. Women who won immediately converted their earnings into food.[89]

As in other African cities with an uneven sex ratio,[90] "prostitution" might take a variety of forms: completely casual relationships, relatively stable alliances between women and single men or those with country wives, "back door husbands" whose cash gifts helped to supplement the wife's "beer money," and women who made their living from selling sexual services to numerous men.[91] Krige's study of the longer-settled Marabastad location found little that she felt resembled "prostitution in the European sense of the word," though such relationships reputedly were common in the nearby Cape location with a more heterogeneous population. What she describes as "concubinage," however, appears similar to the longer term relationships in Rooiyard.[92]

Although illegal, brewing left mothers at home to look after their children; those working outside the home either took their children with them or left them with relatives or neighbors. Arduous and hazardous, brewing forced respectable married women to take risks that their poor white counterparts rarely experienced. Beer tins had to be buried several feet below ground level and dug out when needed to conceal them from police scrutiny. Though usually done twice weekly, a police raid could necessitate a third preparation. Proceeds at the time of Hellmann's study averaged one pound a month; but prior to the unemployment of the early 1930s, two to three pounds was not uncommon.[93] Krige was clear that, despite its illegality, "Many of the most respectable and respected women brew beer, and on the whole only a small minority of teachers and ministers of religions regard it as wrong. But even their religious scruples will never prevent them from doing their utmost to warn beer-brewers if a policeman is near."[94] Nonetheless, the violence, crime, and prostitution often associated with brewing opened all women to charges of vice and immorality.

However meager were the earnings of most women, commonly accepted practices within families granted them considerable economic le-

verage. In most relationships, Hellmann found, women controlled household income, allotting men the funds for their personal needs. She
observed:

> Her earning power secures the Native woman greater equality; it invests her
> with some measure of family authority and control. The effects of this gradual
> emancipation of women are not strikingly noticeable in the case of a harmon-
> ius marriage relationship. It is generally the woman deserted by her husband
> who gives proof of her newly acquired independence by fending for herself
> instead of returning to her people as an unwanted wife.[95]

The slum clearance movement of the 1930s was having an impact on
women's work at the time of Hellmann's study, as were changes in the
expectations of white families. Part-time domestic service was becoming
increasingly difficult to obtain,[96] possibly a result of the economic up-
swing following the Depression; and Orlando, the location to which blacks
from Rooiyard were being transferred, was ten miles from the center of
Johannesburg, leading women to fear a disruption of brewing, making
part-time domestic work more difficult, and making washing "jobs" im-
practical as a result of the time and expense of fetching clothing from
Johannesburg and transporting it to the location.[97] This trend would become more pronounced in the following decades.

Many black women not formally employed formed viable organizations
to protect their economic interests and acted militantly and forcefully when
their livelihoods were at risk. This tradition of collectivity and solidarity
would provide a heritage on which trade unions might draw, as black
women entered industrial work in later years. During the 1930s, the only
women's organization in Rooiyard was the "stokfel," a mutual benefit
society with two functions: disposing of surplus beer after the weekend
and facilitating savings. Each Monday at noon the members (commonly
three to eight per group) met at an alternate woman's house, each bringing a stipulated amount of money to the week's "owner" of the gathering. The hostess supplied beer, lemonade, and cake to the other women
and to any other visitors. In every group a bookkeeper kept track of subscriptions and entrance fees. In theory, the stokfel offered the possibility
of periodically accumulating a larger sum of money than usual, though
fluctuating membership and the lack of enforcement mechanisms meant
that the potential was not always realized.[98] Nonetheless, the cooperative
spirit connected with beer-brewing and associated dances and concerts
was noteworthy in Hellmann's study of Rooiyard, partly because of its
"conspicuous absence" in other spheres of life. Women regularly assisted
each other in watching for the police, organizing special evenings, and
brewing for sick friends.[99] Krige, writing on the very similar *mohodisana*
in Marabastad, also found a strong sense of solidarity developing among
members.[100]

Perhaps most critical to black family survival, as for white families during periods of poverty or economic crisis, was the reliance on the earnings of all members: grown children living elsewhere who contributed money to their parents or those still living at home who assisted with daily expenses. Gifts of money and in kind from friends and relatives also could be important.[101] Thus, the "family wage economy" continued to be an essential element of sustenance. Yet, despite woman's intensive contributions to family expenses, the conclusions of the Marabastad study are instructive: that the earnings of male adults (fathers and grown-up sons) provided most families with their main source of income.[102] Women's efforts notwithstanding, they received lower returns for their labor than men.

Thus, under conditions prevailing in the 1930s, larger numbers of unmarried women were entering domestic service, while many married urban women augmented family income by combining part-time work (often as washerwomen) with brewing. But brewing was also the province of many single migrants, often "refugees from marriages that had cracked under the strains of rural pauperisation and the migrant labour system."[103] Although women's days were far from idle, Hellmann found that they did have time for some leisure: talking with each other, drinking beer, and more occasionally, visiting relatives in other yards or locations.

During the period between 1925 and 1940, periodic protests, sometimes violent, erupted when the actions of white authorities threatened the essential income women derived from beer-brewing. Thus, the uprising of African women in Natal in 1929, which led to a "regular battle between African women and police," and women's opposition to establishing municipal beer halls in Bloemfontein in 1934 represent efforts to maintain control over a major source of family and personal income. The writer of an *Umsebenzi* article understood this fact well. Discussing a protest meeting in Bloemfontein that, by his estimate, drew 3,000 people, he observed: "The women saw in the new move by the authorities an attempt to secure a monopoly of the '*Utywala*' business which formerly had been in their hands."[104] Three years later, several brewers in Vereeniging, an industrial center fifty miles south of Johannesburg, unleashed a chain of events that led to two days of rioting and over 450 arrests. Sotho brewers numbered prominently among the crowds of "ululating women [who] urged the men on."[105]

The militant Natal campaign against municipal beerhalls in 1929, fueled by a regional splinter group of the Industrial and Commercial Workers' Union, the ICU *yase* (of) Natal, came at a time when many women were beginning to feel the effects of the Depression and when many were increasingly marginalized in family conflicts over resources. Helen Bradford sees their exuberant resistance, chanting war songs, raiding beer halls, and assaulting male drinkers, as part of a struggle over the distribution of male wages within the household. Pinpointing a significant trend in working women's protests, she found that women "accustomed to fighting their own battles in a patriarchal world" were disproportionately represented in the leadership. They included two groups in particular: unmarried women and wives who, because of male absence, assumed control over their households for most of the year.[106] This trend was similar to that on the Rand, where single Sotho women were at the center of numerous clashes with the police.[107]

Although large-scale resistance attracted more notice, regular police searches for home-brewed beer in the African locations turned most poor black women into continual rebels against state authority, as is beautifully illustrated in novels and first-hand accounts of the 1930s. Es'kia (Ezekiel) Mphahlele wrote of his childhood in Marabastad location:

> It was a Saturday night. Usually Saturday nights are far from dull in slum locations. Everybody is on the alert, particularly the womenfolk. . . .
>   Marabastad continued to brew beer. Police continued to raid as relentlessly and to destroy. There were Saturday and Sunday mornings when the streets literally flowed with beer. . . . Each yard had several holes in which tins of beer were hidden.[108]

With no employers in a mediating position between themselves and the state, these urban women trying to gain some control over their income faced a level of continual harassment and direct state brutality unknown in even the most exploitative of factories or in the most impoverished of white communities. In Rooiyard alone, sixty-five women were arrested for brewing during 1932.[109] While their responses to state oppression usually were unorganized, they displayed a collective force and spontaneity that could be very effective in individual situations. But the lack of power to change the laws that made their remunerative activity so hazardous left large numbers of women perpetually vulnerable to attack.

Despite the prominence of women in the Natal protests of 1929, the ICU, the main organization representing black workers during the late 1920s, gave only occasional scope for women's grievances. Women's sections notwithstanding, most male leaders operated from a sense of gender superiority, conceptualizing women more frequently as wives and providers of food and entertainment for male activists than as equal partners in political work. Only a tiny minority of officials were women and some of them apparently attained their positions through relationships with male organizers. Only occasionally, as in Natal and in the lengthy strike in East London early in 1930 (led by another regional group, the Independent ICU), did women become full participants in political action. In East London the successful mobilization of women, who worked mainly as domestic servants, turned a stoppage among rail and dock workers into a general strike. With their involvement came changes in policy: inclusion of women's wage demands into the IICU platform and a shift to support for domestic beer-brewing.[110]

Thus, during the earliest years of large-scale secondary industrialization, the options of poor women began to diverge more sharply on the basis of race. As an onslaught of discriminatory legislation during the 1920s and 1930s insured that shared poverty did not become a source for nonracial class alliances, the common dependency of poor women based on gender and class yielded to a deepening racial rift. Whereas new jobs in factories opened up for white and coloured female workers, black women seeking regular wages remained confined to domestic labor. For all three groups, however, regular employment attracted larger numbers of young, single women, while women with family responsibilities preferred more flexible home-based alternatives. Yet for black women the most common forms of casual labor involved daily risk to themselves and their families. For white women such dangers were absent. Capital and the state still had the power to manipulate the available labor supply to suit their own not always congruous needs. But by basing their work preferences on life-cycle changes, poor women were able to reduce the conflict between earning an income and family responsibilities, thereby gaining some control, however limited, over their own lives.

– 4 –

DAUGHTERS OF THE DEPRESSION

Predominantly from Afrikaner backgrounds, the girls and women who took factory jobs during the late 1920s and early 1930s lived and worked in closely knit white working-class communities. As relatively recent arrivals from the countryside, many of them came from families in which ethnicity and religion provided the basis for developing a new urban-centered identity. This Afrikaner heritage became increasingly politicized as the 1930s progressed. Seeking to wean white workers from what they perceived as a dangerous class identity, nationalist organizations encouraged instead a narrow and defensive ethnic consciousness.

These nationalist groups were responding to the strong class awareness that was emerging among Afrikaner working women. This class consciousness was a product of their shared experience in the factories, of a common culture that linked work and leisure activities, and of concerted efforts on the part of communist-oriented union officials (most notably Solly Sachs) to interpret their experience from a class-based theoretical perspective. This chapter will show how the daily lives of young working women created close bonds among them; succeeding chapters will trace their engagement in some of the central ideological and political struggles of the 1930s.

As large numbers of women were drawn into new industrial settings, some of the paternalistic attitudes of an earlier era were gradually transformed. But efforts to "protect" young women from influences perceived as deleterious also took new forms. Middle-class women's groups and nationalist organizations campaigned to prevent white women from working under the supervision of black men. They also sought to shelter them from the real and imagined dangers of urban life by encouraging women to reside in closely regulated hostels that provided a range of wholesome activities to occupy their leisure hours.

The factory environment also produced a sense of belonging and a context for interpreting the social and political realities of South Africa. Young women in industrial jobs worked together in conditions that were unfavorable at best. They earned meager wages on which they could scarcely support themselves, let alone the families who relied on a share of their income. With little opportunity for individual advancement, they worked at jobs deemed semiskilled and faced employers and policy makers who believed that women who worked, particularly in factories, might be trading their respectability for an income. Many who were unmarried shared living space with coworkers, usually in private homes; but occasionally they found lodging in hostels for working women. Though very conscious of their Afrikaner identity, some of these women, away from home for the first time, began to form a new vision of the world based around their work experience.

Conditions in most factories were wretched, often little better than those condemned in the 1917 report. Although Wage Board representatives occasionally found settings they judged "excellent," more often women complained bitterly about having to stand all day at their work, or about the available "chairs": hard boxes lacking backs or arm rests. Rest rooms merited the description of "very primitive," and inadequate wages forced some employers to inquire whether job applicants had parents or relatives with whom they might live.[1] The manager of a large biscuit factory admitted that an applicant dependent solely on her own wages "is usually told the salary of a packer will be totally inadequate to keep her on." Women survived only by finding cheap lodging where they slept three in a bed and lived on dry bread and black coffee. Illness from insufficient food was not uncommon.[2]

As in many new industrial settings, geared to wean workers from a more individually and seasonally paced rural existence, discipline could be quite stringent. One sweet factory searched employees twice daily, a biscuit factory fined workers a shilling (out of a total weekly wage of 12s.6d.) for eating a single biscuit or for dropping a package and breaking some of the contents. Arriving a minute late to work resulted in the loss of a half day's pay.[3]

The right to define such discipline could be controversial. Anna Sophia Swanepoel, who worked at the African Clothing Factory in Germiston during the late 1920s, recalled an argument about whether women could sing in order to break the monotony of the work routine. When one of the owners filed a complaint against her for leading this subversive activity, the chair of the Industrial Council rejected the grievance; he argued that he encouraged his employees to sing, in the belief that it increased production. In the Germiston case, the owner's action appeared to contradict a sign posted prominently in the factory exhorting workers to "Work Like Hell and Still Be Merry."[4]

Women in small clothing workshops owned by merchant tailors or middleman tailors endured the most shocking conditions. Some of these tailors, despite their self-identification as workers, "mercilessly exploited those who worked for them, especially the younger women." In one case reported in 1929, the owner of a small workshop kept a mother and two daughters on the premises from Wednesday until Sunday, working them long hours and giving them no place to sleep; another young woman slaved on occasion from 7 a.m. to 5 a.m. the following day with no added compensation for overtime work.[5] Sexual harassment was also a problem: one discreet observer noted that the difficulties women encountered were "not only of an economic order."[6] On the Rand, many of these small establishments were owned by Indian tailors, who relied heavily on the unpaid labor of their wives and children.[7]

The lack of concern for welfare services from either the state or employers enhanced the hazards of working-class life. When men grew too ill to continue working, mining capital put their wives and daughters to work in factories rather than offering benefits. Women who became sick sometimes sought assistance from trade unions. In 1929, Jean Ghent requested a loan from the Witwatersrand Tailors' Association (WTA) after she had been hospitalized for several months; her letter cautioned, "don't tell Mr. Ghent any thing [*sic*]—he seems to think that I have been getting money from the Union."[8] Annie Stodes, deep in debt because of illness, with a daughter out of work, similarly sought a loan to cover her expenses.[9] Even Mrs. Le Grange, a highly paid machinist earning 52s. 6p. a week, was unable to afford doctor's fees and medicine after a three-week absence from work.[10] Replying to Mrs. Le Grange and two other women with similar requests, the general secretary regretted the union's inability to assist them owing to the lack of "provisions for relief to members."[11]

Such conditions had changed little by the early 1930s, when the worldwide Depression hit South Africa. Although statistically white women in industrial employment were less severely affected than other groups of manufacturing workers, they did not entirely escape the repercussions of the economic crisis. Despite H. A. F. Barker's insistence that the clothing industry, the largest employer of women, suffered no lasting damage or diminution,[12] unemployment was a serious problem. In April, 1930 the general secretary of the Garment Workers' Union wrote to the Minister of Labour expressing his disappointment that the government was unwilling to initiate any kind of unemployment insurance. Describing the desperate plight of the six hundred female and 120 male members out of work, he urged immediate relief for the laid-off women and a state-supported unemployment scheme.[13] By mid-August 1931, widespread factory closings and short-time were exacerbating the problem.[14] Wage cuts as a result of the Depression also became a major source of open conflict between workers and factory owners during 1931 and 1932, a formative experience for a number of the young women who were to become union leaders during the coming decade.

The most thorough and detailed contemporary study of white women workers was conducted during the Depression years. Examining the lives and working conditions of 540 white women on the Witwatersrand between 1930 and 1932, Hansi Pollak discovered a wide range of factory conditions. Not uncommon, however, were factories in "wholly unsuited, congested, poorly constructed buildings" that were ill-lit, badly ventilated, and unheated. In a few clothing and boot factories, she concluded, "the accumulated dirt and debris defies description." Fewer than 10 percent of the 1,323 clothing workers she visited were provided with adjustable chairs; others sat all day on backless stools. The same dirty, untidy space usually doubled as restroom and lunchroom, so that most women preferred to eat at their machines or standing in the street. Protective clothing was rarely available. Furthermore, Pollak found that, especially in clothing and sweets, seasonal variation in employment caused frequent dismissals and short time. With very few exceptions, workers received no paid holidays and there was an "absolute lack of concern" about workers health; insurance and benefit schemes were "conspicuously absent."[15] Nonetheless, when a report by the National Council of Women exposed the shortcomings of factory conditions in Pretoria, the Chief Inspector of Factories treated the document with extreme condescension, charging that the idealism of the group must have clouded its conclusions.[16]

As in the period after World War I, wages in virtually all of the industries that employed women were extremely low, still predicated on the fallacious notion that these young women were partly supported by husbands and/or families. In fact, slightly over one third belonged to a family group with no male wage earner, while nearly one fifth were the sole breadwinners in families that averaged 4.5 members. Pollak's conclusions substantiated the findings of the Carnegie Commission: that most families had come to town because of the children's wage-earning possibilities, and that the family remained the earning unit.[17] Clothing industry representatives observed that fathers and "even mothers" often came to the factories seeking work for their daughters.[18] Indeed, during the strike of 1932, many mothers appeared at the factory gates offering their daughters' labor.[19] All of the single women living away from home assumed total responsibility for their own support; 15 percent in addition sustained dependents in their former homes.

Not only were the legally determined wages extremely low to begin with, but employers found countless ways to evade full payment, rarely granted raises when they were due, and frequently laid off workers as a result of seasonal fluctuations. Women also complained of the task work system, of routine dismissals of workers who had become qualified and entitled to higher wages,[20] of sexual harassment, of rudeness on the part of supervisors, and of mandatory overtime.[21] Considering the living standards of these young women, Pollak wrote:

It is impossible to go into any detail on whether £2 a week is a truly "civilised wage," but on the Witwatersrand it is well nigh impossible for any respectable girl to live on less. . . . The managing on £2 a week implies a careful distribution of resources and a familiarity with prices far in excess of that usually found among women industrial workers.[22]

Interviews with women who lived through this period verify the sense of struggle and difficulty.[23] Indeed, by the time of the Depression, most earned less than the two pounds a week average that Pollak describes.

If questionable working conditions and low wages helped to create an awareness of shared experience among these women, hiring practices probably also contributed to a sense of community. Although there was no shortage of potential female labor during the early 1930s, most employers preferred to engage the friends or sisters of their workers or to select from among the school girls brought to the factories in groups for recruitment toward the year's end.[24] They were less inclined to choose at random from the women who beseiged the factory doors on Monday mornings. Employers with other strategies, whether relying on the industrial schools at Standerton and Potchefstroom or on phthisis dependents or widows, seemed to follow these policies consistently.[25] Thus, in most factories women were likely to cluster in groups of kin, friends, or schoolmates who might guide one another in adapting to, and perhaps also in resisting, the demands of a new environment.

The stereotypical female industrial worker during the late 1920s and 1930s was a young, unmarried woman recently arrived from the "platteland" (countryside); but the reality was somewhat more complex and seemed to vary from one industry to another. Whereas printing and food establishments in Johannesburg employed mainly single workers, many factories had higher rates of married women than commonly supposed. In the leather industry, a considerable number of women, many over forty, had trained in Port Elizabeth and then moved to the Rand after marriage. In canvas and rope, nearly all workers were elderly married women or widows because younger women dismissed the work as too hard and dirty. Textile mills employed a "considerable sprinkling" of widows and elderly married women and clothing factories a very small number of the latter, but "quite a number" of elderly widows. The clothing industry alone, however, also had a substantial number of young married female employees, although the strong sentiment against their working led many to pretend they were single. A letter to the editor of *The Star* in 1935 expressed the widespread sentiment that, with jobs scarce, a married woman whose husband earned "enough to keep her" should abstain from formal employment.[26] Only bespoke tailoring, which rarely required more than two to three days of work each week, operated on a schedule conducive to combining work and family.[27]

Despite these notable exceptions to the stereotype, the number of married women in Pollak's sample was extremely small: 5.7 percent married, 3.7 percent widowed, 2 percent deserted wives, 1.7 percent divorcees, and 86 percent single. The antipathy toward married women working came less from employers, who often found older workers more serious and reliable and less prone to absenteeism, than from other workers. Those few who had no economic need to work were particularly resented: "We make things pretty hard for them so that they usually get sick of it and leave."[28] Women with young children who did work for wages usually relied on grandparents or an unemployed father for childcare.[29]

Outside the Rand, however, less rigid attitudes toward married women in the labor force apparently prevailed. In Kingwilliamstown, up to 20 percent of the garment workers were married,[30] while one sample of Cape garment workers showed a married total of 37 percent.[31] This difference, probably reflecting a greater tendency for coloured women to remain in the factories after marriage as a result of their husbands' lower wages, might have created a different climate for white women as well. Suggesting the same pattern, the coloured laundry workers in Pollak's sample nearly all were married women or deserted wives.[32]

Although jobs in the industrial sector created new wage-earning opportunities for women, strong sentiment against married women's employment meant that most young women remained at their jobs somewhere between three and six years. Testimony to the Customs Tariff Commission of 1934 confirmed that, with few exceptions, girls quit as soon as they married; married women who continued to work usually did so because of a husband's illness, unemployment, death, or low wages. The attitude of the Miners' Phthisis Board was not uncommon: once a woman married she became her husband's dependent and ought to leave work to make room for single applicants.[33] An incident in Johannesburg bears out the close relationship between working wives and family income: one employer lost a substantial number of married women in the mid-1930s, when improved conditions in the building trades allowed their husbands to earn eight pounds a week.[34] On the Rand, therefore, the observation that women's employment is largely "a stepping stone to marriage or better times"[35] seems valid. In other areas, and particularly among the coloured population, many married women continued to work.

The increase in the number of married women employed in industry represents a change from the period documented in the 1917 study. This shift was a result not only of industrial expansion, but also of the economic hardships of the late 1920s and early 1930s, which left numerous white men out of work and many families destitute. Of the fifty-four Transvaal garment workers who were refused confinement allowances during 1932 and 1933, nearly half had husbands or male partners who had been unemployed during the preceding year.[36]

Although certain industries did employ older women, then, the majority of workers were young. The median age of all women in Pollak's study was 20 years, and 82.4 percent were under 25. Workers were youngest in sweets and food and slightly older in the clothing industry.[37] Over time, however, the workforce in the garment industry aged, both on the Rand and in Cape Town (where women workers were consistently younger than elsewhere). Whereas in 1931 those under 21 formed 57 percent of employees in Cape Town and 44 percent in Johannesburg, by 1936 the figures had dropped to 34 percent and 23 percent respectively.[38]

The overwhelming majority of women who entered industrial labor in the 1930s, white and coloured, came from needy families; but they were not primarily the newest rural immigrants. Less educated than their urban counterparts, these were the women least likely to escape domestic labor. Indeed, the stereotype of recently arrived rural women finding their way into factories masks some of the more subtle variations among women employed in different occupations. The Carnegie Commission wrote of girls from less prosperous rural families, large numbers of whom had taken factory jobs during the preceding five or six years. Yet the commission's own data on six individual establishments confirms a contradictory assertion: "that even among the Dutch-speaking female employees in factories a large percentage were either born or grew up in the urban areas where they were working."[39]

In Pollak's sample, only one fifth of the total labor force were young single women who had migrated alone to work (over half from the Transvaal). Just over one third of the women were born in Johannesburg or on the Reef and roughly another third had lived on the Rand for over ten years.[40] Likewise, according to both Pollak and the Carnegie Commission, young factory workers were comparatively well educated. Of the women discussed in the Carnegie Report, 57 percent had passed Standard 6 (eighth grade).[41] By 1934, even the Transvaal Clothing Manufacturers' Association admitted to a distinct improvement in "the type of applicant" for jobs. Among them were women "who years ago would not dream of entering a factory."[42] Thus, the majority of industrial workers were urbanized and relatively literate, not the poorest, most recent arrivals from the countryside. To the latter women went the least desirable jobs in domestic service and small sweatshops.

Considering their strong urban backgrounds, the labor activism that developed among many of these women was an accepted part of their family traditions. With many trade unionists among their fathers, brothers, and other male relatives, the young women who were swept into strikes during the Depression often followed accepted patterns of protest in their households and neighborhoods. Only with rising Afrikaner nationalism in the late 1930s did women face contradictory demands on their political and ideological sympathies.

Wage Board reports for the clothing and textile industries convey a clear impression of the sexual and racial division of labor in these factories and of differential pay scales.[43] Classified mainly as "semi-skilled" operatives, women formed 80 to 90 percent of clothing workers everywhere but Durban. The vast majority were white and Afrikaans-speaking. But in Cape Town, Durban and Pietermaritzburg, and Pretoria, women were predominantly coloured. Women operatives earned relatively low wages, averaging £1 14s. 3d. weekly. Those working as cleaners, primarily juvenile women, took home only £1 0s. 1d. per week. By contrast, the job of presser, meriting pay almost equal to that of machinists (£1 13s. 1d. average), showed a remarkable division by race and gender. Clearly considered heavy, adult work, it was the only job in the clothing industry held by African men and by coloureds and whites, both female and male.

Skilled male clothing workers, often Jewish, were distanced from women by gender, ethnicity, and by their place in the labor process. For wages of four to five pounds a week, they marked, laid out, and sometimes cut patterns. As supervisors, they also were responsible for enforcing industrial discipline. In reporting on employment conditions in East London, the Divisional Inspector of Labour took care to emphasize the strong supervisory role of white men over a work force clearly regarded as inferior. He wrote: "the necessity to keep the European female workers as far apart from the non-European males and for watchfulness and constant supervision over both has been impressed on the proprietors and/or European supervisors."[44]

The organization of production differed in the Transvaal and Cape Town. On the Witwatersrand, in order to absorb this new female labor force, sufficient deskilling had occurred so that only those working on the cheapest clothing made the entire item. Sets or teams of two to ten people assumed responsibility for other garments, with each worker doing a specified task.[45] In the condescending words of a Custom Tariffs Commission member, the girl was unconcerned about how the whole garment would look after she had "stitched up her little job."[46] In Cape Town, however, many employees were still accustomed to making an entire garment until the mid-1930s, when some of the larger factories introduced a more efficient conveyor belt system.[47] Everywhere, the Wage Board found considerable speeding up, concluding that the strain of working for long periods without a break was "telling seriously" on workers' health.[48]

The division of labor in the textile industry was similar in some respects; but race and gender distinctions in semiskilled jobs were less rigid. Foremen, at an average weekly wage of £7 12s. 6d., were overwhelmingly white males, whereas most laborers, who earned £1 2s. 3d., were black and coloured men. White adult women and Asian and coloured men were paid £1 15s. 11d. as weavers, while black men and white women, mainly juveniles, earned £1 7s. 9d. per week as spinners. Surprisingly, though, half of the white male spinners were adults.[49] As subsequent chapters will show, this less rigidly stratified division of labor would create distinct difficulties in organizing. Most obviously, the threat of undercutting could be used to divide white women from black men. But in addition, the possibility of the two groups working together so threatened established ideas of racial and gender boundaries that it immediately galvanized conservative Afrikaners to oppose efforts at unionization.

The balance of textile employees by race and gender varied in individual factories. One of the largest textile establishments, Consolidated Textile Mills at Huguenot (Cape), had about 230 employees: 130 white women, thirty white men, and seventy "non-European" men. The women spun yarn, while the black men were laborers who moved boxes between departments.[50] Although Transvaal Textiles may have been atypical because of its heavy reliance on miners' phthisis victims, with 201 employees, there were only seven Africans, doing manual work "that is not a white occupation." Of the remaining workers, 20 percent were skilled male mechanics and the rest white women. Only twenty of these women earned the maximum rate of three to four pounds a week. At the other end of the spectrum, a few widows worked at the least energetic seated work: hand sewing, inspecting, and mending. All those defined as "experts" came from overseas.[51]

In some factories, particularly in the Transvaal, standard weekly wages had become commonplace in most industries during the years since World War I, as unions and sometimes the Wage Board attacked the widespread practice of placing experienced workers on piece rates. Pollak's study of the Rand found the payment of flat weekly earnings "almost universal" by the early 1930s, a result of industrial agreements in clothing and printing and apparently also of a general change in industrial practice.[52] In Durban, however, piece rates for women remained common as late as 1935, creating particular difficulties for beginners in completing the required work. Despite assurances from manufacturers that experienced employees on piece work could earn a reasonable income, the Wage Board concluded that it was impossible to draw up a practicable scale of rates that could be adequately administered and enforced.[53] Piece rates also prevailed in the textile industry for most of the 1930s.

Despite the beginnings of assembly line techniques, in most industries the labor process had not undergone sufficient subdivision to introduce any degree of stratification among "semiskilled" women, apart from that separating learners from qualified workers. In the sweet industry, for example, in 1938, 90 percent of employees were described as "general workers,"[54] who usually moved from job to job rather than working on one operation. In at least one factory, where most foremen came from overseas, the gap between workers and supervisors was intensified.[55]

A 1938 report on Transvaal Textiles highlights many of the common tendencies of the 1930s, though with some unique features, particularly a heavy reliance on employees from the families of phthisis victims, a policy thought to promote industrial discipline. Workers were rarely changed from one operation to another, preferring, according to the report, to remain in the section where they had started. Although theoretically women could be promoted to the supervisory position of charge-hand, at the time only two women in the mill held such posts. To deal with the high absenteeism in the factory, the inspectors recommended the appointment of a welfare supervisor, "an educated woman of a higher social standing than the factory workers" to investigate problems, keep absentee records, plan social activities, and discreetly spy on the women: "By mingling with the girls during tea-time their opinion of supervisors and fellow-workers can be gauged and differences adjusted after investigation."[56]

During this period most industrial establishments remained small, with substantial seasonal variation in the rhythm of production. Many sweet factories maintained high levels of employment only around Christmas and Easter. During the rest of the year, large numbers of workers were laid off or put on short time.[57] Fluctuations were equally substantial in the clothing industry.[58] The small size of industrial establishments was partially a result of a low level of international investment. Of 298 registered factories on the Rand in around 1930, only sixteen employed over fifty women, although a few atypical establishments had several hundred workers.[59] Textile manufacturing was the main exception to this tendency. Highly concentrated, Consolidated Textile Mills owned factories at Industria, Durban, East London, and Huguenot, while a single owner controlled South African Woollen Mills in Cape Town and Harrismith Mill in the Orange Free State.

In most of South Africa's industrial centers, the relatively uniform background of most semiskilled female employees, as well as their common place in the labor process contributed to a sense of shared experience. In Cape Town, however, the large number of both white and coloured women in the factories produced a more complex situation. This division may partially explain the inability of working women there to break the hold of unresponsive, management-oriented, bureaucratic unions. The Factories Act, which mandated separate toilet and eating facilities for each racial group, meant that many employers tried to maintain a racially exclusive workforce. Others, while paying equal wages, sometimes separated employees by race. One tobacco factory, for example, with three hundred female workers from each group, received the praise of the Carnegie Commission for having separate floors for white women (who made boxes and packed cigarettes) and coloured women (responsible for treating the tobacco leaves).[60]

If separation in Cape Town factories impeded interracial solidarity, a tendency to replace coloured women with white women in the post-Depression years must have generated overt tension between them. The timing of this movement makes it a clear reaction not to the labor legislation of the 1920s per se, but to the renewed pressure exerted on manufacturers by the Custom Tariffs Commission in 1934. After a parade of industrialists from all manufacturing centers earnestly assured the commissioners that they intended to purge their factories of "non-whites,"

Cape garment manufacturers followed their words with actions. During a crisis in the Cape clothing industry between 1934 and 1936, when total employment declined for the first time since the mid-1920s, 87 percent of those who lost their jobs were coloured, 67 percent of them women.[61]

This massive shift formed the basis of varied reports and allegations over the next few years. Visiting a huge Bally Shoe Co. factory at Woodstock in 1934, a *Cape Times* reporter was impressed at finding blonds wherever he looked. Though apparently distressed that these "strong silent women" were too absorbed in their work to notice him, he observed approvingly the switch from "irresponsible and careless" coloured workers to "efficient" white workers in the plant.[62] A similar shift came to light the following year when the Divisional Inspector of Labour for the Cape, commenting on the displacement of coloured women by white women in the clothing industry, denied allegations of government subsidies for factories employing 100 percent white labor.[63]

During the late 1930s, however, Cape employers used threats of labor replacement to keep their coloured workers quiescent. At Messrs. Shames and Company in Woodstock, almost the entire staff of 140 coloured women went on strike in 1936, protesting the victimization of the leaders of an earlier stoppage. Addressing the women, Mr. Shames threatened to close the factory and engage a new staff if the strike continued; he made a particular point of noting "his intention to employ a number of European girls." By the following day, the workers had returned to their jobs.[64]

Despite the efforts of some Cape manufacturers to "whiten" their labor force, few achieved this goal. Although most clothing and shirt factories were originally operated with coloured workers, officials assumed that a new system of customs rebates would encourage a switch to European labor. A number of employers "entered into the spirit of the suggestion," creating the impression "that all the Coloured female labour could be replaced by European labour by a gradual process." By 1939, however, the difficulties in finding the necessary white labor had resulted in a mixed work force in some establishments. Furthermore, clothing manufacture did not lend itself to total separation, nor did the difficulty of drawing strict racial divisions among the varied Cape population of Europeans, Malays, coloureds, and "a type of person who may be either European or Coloured."

Although the Divisional Inspector of Labour felt that white women at the Cape had retained a "prejudice" against working in factories,[65] he also might have mentioned the drop in average wages in the clothing industry between 1936 and 1937–38 to pre-1929 levels.[66] Under Cape conditions, then, organizing across racial lines in the clothing industry was not necessarily impossible, but it would have required leadership with a level of dedication to principle never evidenced in the established Cape union.

If the objective conditions of white female factory workers were conducive to cohesion among them, women also faced blatantly discriminatory official attitudes. Although it is unlikely that working women read government reports, they suffered the consequences of official attitudes in the form of rigid, gender-based wage differentials. When the Customs Tariff Commission lamented the loss of skill from women who left work to marry and concluded that South Africa could ill afford to "deprive herself voluntarily" of advantages that her competitors cultivated,[67] it was mourning the wastage of labor that was experienced, but also cheap. The Industrial Legislation Commission agreed, arguing that women's pay must be kept low to prevent "unbearable hardships" on industries competing in the world market. Its recommendation for female wages set at roughly two thirds of those of men rested on a mixture of projected labor supply, stereotyped visions of women, and fear. Expressing doubt that pay equity "is in the interests of women themselves," it suggested that, with higher wages, women would not choose to marry, "since the higher the wage a woman receives, the less the economic urge to enter the married state."[68] From this perspective, low wages became in part a deliberate means of social control, intended to preserve traditional notions of family life that might be threatened if women achieved greater economic autonomy.

The use of European women in factories provided South African employers with workers who were cheap, white, and generally believed to possess a "natural" aptitude for making clothing and food. Their absorption into industry resulted from a combination of factors, some of which were structural (the "civilised" labour policy and the development of new industries at a time when economic conditions for poor white families were deteriorating) and some of which resulted from individual choice, particularly women's preference for factory work over the drudgery and control of domestic employment. An analysis of wages during this period indicates where these women fit into the complex division of labor by race and gender in South Africa.

Statistics from the garment industry demonstrate that, in 1929, the most numerous workers in the Transvaal were white women, followed by African men and white men, all adults. Of the 212 workers earning less than one pound per week, all but two were black males (adult and juvenile), whereas nearly all of those who earned four pounds or more were white male adults. By far the most common wage was between £1 and £1 19s. 11d. per week, the range for most white and coloured women and black adult men. But, whereas one third of adult African men earned less than £1, the same percentage of adult white women earned between £2 and £3. The pay scales of coloured adult men, small in number in the Transvaal, ranked third, after European males, adult and juvenile.[69] By 1935, wages had increased little; the average female garment worker in Johannesburg and Germiston earned £1 7s. 7d. per week, an annual average of

£72. 15s., compared with average white wages in private manufacturing in the southern Transvaal of £256 per year and an average black wage of £49.[70]

Considering these inequities, future employers would have reason to turn to black labor, male or female, whenever possible. In the late 1920s and the first half of the 1930s, however, the combination of government pressure to solve the politically charged "poor white problem" and the availability of young white females for factory work made this a temporarily untenable way to decrease labor costs.[71]

The entry of large numbers of young white women into factory work not only increased the complexity of the racial and gender division of labor, it also created new political issues, as large numbers of white women came into new forms of contact with black men, often as coworkers and therefore in relationships of potential equality. Individual incidents of tension on the factory floor, usually a result of the racism of white women, sometimes found their way into the records of the period.[72]

But the high degree of factory segregation probably kept such incidents to a minimum. Thus, when the issue of white women and black men working together did arise, it usually came from outside; either as a politically motivated attack on the personal integrity of particular individuals or as part of a campaign to "protect" white women from ostensible dangers about which most remained blithely unconcerned. Such efforts betrayed not only a continued paternalism toward young working women, but also the terror provoked among many whites by the thought of interracial contact between white females and black men.

The most prolonged protectionist effort, the campaign from 1934 onward to enact legislation to prohibit white women from working under the supervision of black men, originated in the concern of a middle-class women's organization to shield working-class women from potential "danger." With racial motivation in the forefront, Afrikaner groups quickly took up the issue as part of their legislative campaign to win the loyalty of poor whites.

What became a full-fledged national attack on Asian-owned business began with an incident in a Pretoria factory in which an African male supervisor was sentenced to three months hard labor for an alleged "indecent insult": touching a woman on one occasion and putting his arm around her on another. Although the magistrate found "a certain amount of conflict" in the evidence of witnesses, he felt the harsh sentence was necessary because the defendant's actions showed a lack of respect for the plaintiff.[73]

Concerned about the implications of this incident, as well as with the government's lack of active concern with women's unemployment, the white, middle-class South African League of Women Voters launched a campaign for legislation to prevent the possibility of "native foremen" controlling "European girls." To combat such "wholly objectionable practices," informal inspections were simply insufficient.[74] Stating quite openly her fears about the potential implications of such contact among working-class men and women, Mrs. E. G. Jansen, addressing a public meeting on the position of European women in South Africa, argued: "This mingling led to equality, and it was this equality which was responsible for the disrespect that was being shown to European women in all parts of the country."[75]

Following an investigation by the Labour Department, which revealed that only seventy-nine white women worked under "non-white" supervision and that "in no case was the supervisor a native,"[76] the focus of the campaign, now taken up by Afrikaner nationalists, began to shift its target to the more numerous cases of black authority, which occurred in Asian-owned businesses and factories.

The blatant paternalism and political motivation of the campaign was apparent in its total disregard for the feelings of the women ostensibly being protected. When interviewed about the issue, these women expressed anger and indignation, often underlining that their current Asian employers treated them far better than had former white employers. Indeed, in terms of sexual harassment, the usually unspoken fear of campaigners, social taboos on interracial intimacy probably offered white women more protection under black employers. In the Spinning Department of Consolidated Textile Mills at Huguenot (Cape), for example, "at one stage all the work . . . was confined to European labour, but owing to the familiar behaviour of the European male employees towards the women, the management was compelled to replace a portion of them by Non-European labour."[77]

Ironically, also, this episode ended in an uneasy compromise between the government and the South African Indian Congress, the former promising to withdraw proposed legislation in return for self-policing on the part of Asian business owners. The main losers were the white women whom the Asians in question reluctantly agreed to fire: a bizarre conclusion to a campaign that had grown partly out of an effort to create new jobs for white women.[78]

Although this anti-Asian campaign eventually became caught up in the nationalist political fury of the late 1930s, its early stages evidenced a paternalistic, protective urge toward young women workers that was also evident in the movement to regulate their living spaces and leisure activities. Like the small town women whose social welfare activities Jeffrey Butler has described, many middle-class Afrikaners saw the poor members of their community in distinctly South African terms: as a group "on the way down to racial perdition, to miscegenation and therefore to exclusion from the *volk*."[79]

The continuing acceptance by both the state and employers of low female wage scales and a concern for safeguarding and supervising the morality of workers still in their teens (perceived as "girls" until marriage) led to a variety of schemes for providing low-cost housing and recreational facilities. Models for similar projects were available locally in the efforts of mission churches, dating back to 1908, to establish hostels for African women in Johannesburg. With hostels seen primarily as a means of providing safe accommodation (both morally and physically) for female domestic servants, movements advocating their construction reached a peak after World War I. The Helping Hand Club, established in 1919 by the American Board Mission, provided a successful blueprint for future projects. Like similar endeavors for white women, the issue elicited voluminous discussion and relatively limited results. "Hostels persist," concludes historian Deborah Gaitskell, "as a theme in white women's Christian endeavor into the late 1930s, although chiefly, it would appear, as a pious hope."[80] The city of Johannesburg did, however, establish a Native Women's hostel at Wolhuter, near George Goch station, in July 1930, although six years of operation and a substantial drop in rents were required to fill all 130 beds.

The white hostels, catering to a population of "factory girls," concentrated on housing workers and providing them with wholesome leisure activities. Because the labor supply at this time was sufficient, factory owners were not in the position of their nineteenth-century European counterparts, who often had to supply dormitory accommodation for their workers in order to convince families that their daughters were protected.[81] The hostels for black women had a more ambiguous purpose, however: catering to the demands of those who established them for reliable domestic servants as much as to African women's need for housing.

As increasing numbers of black women entered domestic service in the 1930s, the creation of labour bureaus to help them find work became an increasingly significant aspect of the hostels' mission. Even before that, however, the Helping Hand Club placed over seven hundred young women in domestic jobs by 1928 and added 240 in 1929 (a response to 460 applications from white employers) and another 460 in 1930–31 (with 650 requests). In preparation for these jobs, a training school began in 1930 to provide instruction in "practical housework under earnest Christian influence."[82] In addition to acting as employment services, the hostels also, like those for white women, held daily prayers and weekly church services, ran cookery and Red Cross classes open to both residents and nonresidents, and provided meeting places for community women's organizations.

Middle-class women's groups usually initiated and ran these projects on a voluntary basis. They also sought financial assistance from manufacturers, who were more willing to contribute small sums to such charitable endeavors than to pay their workers a living wage. The most outstanding success among the projects aimed at white women was the North End Girls' Club of Port Elizabeth, later renamed the Athlone Club (for Women and Girls). Begun on a small scale following a survey of industrial and living conditions among women factory workers in Port Elizabeth conducted in 1921 and 1922, the club sought to address in particular the miserable housing conditions that the study had identified. Accommodations were cramped and filthy; and in over one quarter of the houses unmarried women and men shared sleeping rooms with adolescents of the opposite sex. These conditions were perceived as threatening to both the physical and moral well-being of the women concerned.

Following the report, the Port Elizabeth branch of the National Council of Women formed a committee to organize the club. Opening in September 1923, the North End Girls' Club provided low-cost meals and recreational and educational facilities to the hundreds of poor young white women who had flocked to the city from the countryside to seek work in the newly opened factories, making boots, shoes, and clothing. After initially confronting some of the workers' fears "of either patronage or charity,"[83] the project succeeded in filling critical social needs. With joint support from local manufacturers and state and local authorities (who respectively provided the building loan and the site), the club had expanded gradually by 1926 into a hostel for one hundred workers with shared and individual cubicles, meals, recreational facilities, and a sick fund that provided free medical assistance. Recreational facilities included sewing instruction, physical culture, ballroom and country dancing, and a drama group.

Dorothie Tonkin, the Inspector of Factories in Port Elizabeth who was influential in working with the project from its inception, vehemently denied charges that the scheme was designed to enable manufacturers to secure cheaper labor; but she did find it "unreasonable and against all economic law" to expect that employees in training need be paid a living wage.[84] Such a stance prompted critics of such projects, such as Mrs. Jacobs, a member of the Germiston Town Council, to argue that rather than industries that continued a policy of "stitch, stitch in huger [sic] poverty and dirt," the city should have no industry at all.[85]

Unlike the organizers of similar projects for black women and girls, the founders of the North End Girls' Club came from a secular rather than a religious background; but a certain missionary zeal informed their efforts, alongside a large dose of social Darwinism. Tonkin conceived of the "salvation" of these young women as "the missing link in our present plans of social regeneration."[86] Expressing class attitudes tinged with biological determinism, she concluded that, based on her experience with the North End Girls' Club and on the soundness of their British, Dutch, and French heritage, these poor white girls were not of an "irreclaimable" type as some had alleged, but could "very quickly be brought to a higher standard of citizenship and of restored self-respect and efficiency."[87] Her continuing reports all expressed this mixture of condescension and optimism. One praised the girl guide troop at the club, the first company in South Africa composed exclusively of "factory girls," for being recognized as the smartest troop in a review held by Lady Baden-Powell.[88] Other projects seeking to alleviate the conditions of factory workers turned to Port Elizabeth for advice.

A similar effort on behalf of coloured young women in Cape Town was the Marion Institute, located in District Six and begun, probably in the early 1920s, as a result of conditions exposed by the "lady patrols" working at the time. In 1926 the Hostel Scheme for Coloured Girls, working in cooperation with the Institute, was beginning its fund-raising efforts. Up until then the institute had supplied reasonably priced, nourishing midday meals; classes in cookery and fancy work during the week; and entertainment and Bible classes on Sunday. One of the attractions to employers, also noted by Tonkin, was the increase in productivity that they attributed to the Institute's work.[89]

Like hostels for black women, the North End Girls' Club was not as easy to replicate as some had anticipated. The Marion Institute continued to expand its services in the coming years, but never succeeded in adding a residential hostel. In 1935, the entire Witwatersrand boasted only five hostels, providing space for no more than 160 women. Even the model North End Girls' Club appeared to be having difficulties by the late 1930s. A visiting reporter in 1938 found the beds half empty, a problem she also had observed elsewhere. Seeing these institutions partly as an effort to "divert the craving for undue independence," she attributed their problems to the fact that "forsooth a few regulations must be adhered to."[90] Demography may provide a less judgmental explanation; a gradually aging labor force, including more married women, had reduced the need for such accommodation.

Despite these signs of difficulty, efforts to build hostels and social clubs for women workers continued through the 1930s. In Germiston where, by 1938, three thousand women were employed in clothing factories, the Germiston Health and Social Club was founded by a committee of health and social workers. Limited by space constraints to 120 members, the club's activities included physical education, social activity, and programs on health and education; its organizers also intervened with labor and public health officials to publicize the malnutrition and fatiguing working conditions among their clients, urging the government (without results) to supply free milk or cheese to factory workers.[91] A hostel for clothing workers scheduled for construction in Germiston two years earlier remained unstarted in 1939, however.[92]

Greater success was achieved elsewhere. In Johannesburg residential clubs housing some 350 women were either open or near completion in Pioneer Township, Brixton, Langlaate, Bertrams, and Glenesk by early 1940.[93] Some of the later projects included representatives of the Trades and Labour Council on their governing committees.[94] In the Cape Town area, hostels existed at Paarl and at Salt River, the latter supported jointly by the Department of Labour and the Afrikaanse Christelike Vrouens Vereniging (Afrikaner Christian Women's Association or ACVV), which also controlled the institution.[95] Closely tied to the Dutch Reformed Church, the ACVV saw such projects as a means to blunt internal class divisions within the Afrikaner community. By maintaining racial and ethnic boundaries, they were helping to rescue poor whites from what they perceived as potential "contamination."[96] These expanded efforts came rather late, however, particularly in Johannesburg. By the time hostels became numerous enough to begin to meet the demand for housing, workers were earning enough so that they preferred to live elsewhere.[97]

Carrying on activities similar to those of the hostels were organizations (like the Marion Institute) that catered solely to the leisure hours of workers. On the Rand, the Girls' Lunch Hour Club held dances, gave lessons in dancing and eurythmics, and arranged excursions. With a membership of seventy in 1930, the group had received donations from twenty-three local businesses and from individual members of the Juvenile Affairs Board, the Apprenticeship Committee, and the Town Council and was hoping to encourage the Women's Federation to assume responsibility for running the organization.[98] Although operating without a central location, the Afrikaner Christian Women's Association in Paarl "took a keen interest" in the welfare of the young women employed in the blanket and spinning factories there.[99]

For both black and white young women, these hostels provided not only adequate housing, food, and leisure activities, but also a ready-made urban community, intensified in the case of some factory workers by sharing a common workplace as well. Such community ties undoubtedly were important in helping new arrivals adapt to an urban environment and to new jobs, to make friends, and to gain the information that facilitated locating and changing employment. Even for those housed privately, however, isolation was apparently uncommon among factory workers. First-hand accounts invariably speak of three or four friends sharing a room, food, and in one case, of a single good dress that they took turns wearing to church.

Trade unions (most active among them the Transvaal Garment Workers' Union) also helped to create a similar sense of community for their members by sponsoring educational programs and various forms of recreation: physical culture classes, hiking clubs, theatre groups, sports, and dancing.

On the Rand, and probably in other cities as well, the young Afrikaner women in the factories formed part of a growing and increasingly cohesive and self-conscious urban ethnic community centered around the Dutch Reformed Church. Filling an important role in working-class life, the church sponsored youth groups whose activities and outings also provided young women workers with a source of friends and community.[100] Populating a belt of white working-class suburbs extending to the east, west, south, and northwest from Johannesburg, the largest number lived in Jeppes, Jeppes Extension, and West Malvern in the east; in Fordsburg and Vrededorp in the west; and in Ophirton and Booysens in the south.[101] Campaigning for political office in Jeppes in 1938, Bertha Solomon described the area as one of small, semidetached houses and former mansions converted into boarding houses or flats, "full of people struggling to make a living." The men, she found, were generally miners, railway workers, or artisans, while many of the women were garment workers.[102] In a more stark depiction, white working-class areas of Germiston had been described two years earlier as fast becoming "a glorified slum in which live poor factory workers, poor railwaymen in conditions approaching that of a Native location."[103]

A small survey of the families of garment workers taken from the 1931 voting registration rolls in Germiston and several areas of Johannesburg found that their fathers, husbands, and brothers tended to be concentrated in three job categories: skilled laborers (carpenters, plumbers, mechanics, painters, blacksmiths); unskilled laborers; or clerks, bookkeepers, or civil servants. Germiston and the Fordsburg area of Johannesburg had greater numbers of railway workers.[104] The smaller number of garment workers in the families of miners probably reflects their higher economic standing. Since miners earned better wages than other white working-class men, their daughters and wives probably found less need to work.

Although dependence on the earnings of unmarried daughters must have challenged patriarchal prerogatives in some families, neither fathers nor husbands yielded authority readily. Anna Scheepers, who in 1938 became president of the Transvaal Garment Workers' union, was born on a farm near Krugersdorp. As one of nine children, she finished school and then spent two years struggling against her father. Despite his great financial loss during the Depression, he refused to allow her to leave home for Johannesburg, "the place of sin." Discussing women's participation in trade unions from a perspective informed by her own experience, Scheepers explained: "The Afrikaner women were very good trade unionists except in those areas where they were sort of under their husbands." In such families, "the woman had very little rights; the man was the boss, the head of the family and everybody did as he said."[105]

In the late 1920s and early 1930s, although economic hardship undoubtedly caused stress within impoverished white families as scarcely grown daughters were forced to assume (or insisted on assuming) new economic responsibilities, these young women remained in harmony with their cultural backgrounds. By the late 1930s, however, as conflict erupted between militant left-wing trade unions and Afrikaner nationalist organizations, new sources of discord developed for some women between their lives at work and their lives at home and in the community. In both periods, these relationships had a significant bearing on the course of working-class struggles.

Thus, a shared context of poverty, exploitation, relatively uniform wages and working conditions, and gender discrimination created a basis for cohesion among white women workers, particularly on the Rand. (The more varied workforce in Cape Town fostered more difficult conditions.) With a preponderance of young single workers in most factories, who were often hired along lines of family or friendship, many working women built their cultural and social lives around work-based ties and around their shared experiences in lodgings or hostels. Those who resided with their own families were likely to inhabit the same neighborhoods as their coworkers. Whether they preferred dancing, sports, or church outings in their leisure time, the women with whom they stitched or spun during the day were likely to be among their companions. Ethnic organizations, middle-class women's groups, and often their families still feared for their fate amid the supposed dangers of factories and cities, treating them with the same paternalism their mothers had experienced a generation earlier. But the economic crises of drought and depression, which impelled growing numbers of Afrikaner women to seek out new options in order to sustain their families, often represented a push for greater independence that would be a force for both creativity and conflict during the years to come.

– 5 –

COMMANDOS OF WORKING WOMEN

During the late 1920s and early 1930s, some female factory workers who were intent on improving wages and working conditions began to join unions, organize picket lines, and fight against scabs who threatened to undermine their efforts. Observers in the mid-1920s had depicted women as victims of capitalism, unable to defend themselves in the nasty business of class struggle. But eight years later, in the aftermath of the Depression and a concerted organizing campaign in the Transvaal garment industry, a group of militant young women had emerged who were fully capable of representing their own interests.

Their new awareness had significant repercussions. In addition to forcing substantial material improvements in several industries, by the late 1930s some of these women had mounted a sustained challenge to Afrikaner nationalists. By questioning the right of nationalist organizations to define the political agenda of working-class white women, and by openly declaring their socialism, they directly and aggressively confronted conservative patriarchal control over urban Afrikaner communities.

There are many possible reasons for this apparently dramatic change. First of all, it is likely that the portrayals of helpless women were based as much on assumed female characteristics as they were on a realistic appraisal of their position. In a labor movement implicitly (and sometimes explicitly) defined as male and craft-oriented, recruiting women would have required special effort. Secondly, even in the mid-1920s, most wage-earning white women were employed not in factories or mines, the traditional realms of labor organizing, but in shops and cafes, whose female employees remained outside the usual constructs of "the working class." Nonetheless, even as larger numbers of women entered factory work, the active and lively part they came to play in working-class struggles was not inevitable. Even if their earlier passivity has, perhaps, been exaggerated—or if it resulted more from women's structural marginality than from inherent gender-based characteristics, as was usually implied—the pivotal place they came to occupy, particularly in the Garment Workers' Union, still requires explanation.

With respect to the GWU, two issues are particularly pertinent: why Solly Sachs sought so actively to bring women into the union, and why he succeeded so brilliantly in doing so. As this chapter and the following chapter will suggest, the answer to the first question probably lies both in the changing structure of the industry and in the political dynamics of the contemporary labor movement. Understanding the second issue requires a broader analysis of the way in which Sachs, and increasingly, Afrikaner women themselves, combined the "inherent" identity that formed an essential part of women's ethnic heritage with the "derived" ideology of socialism and class struggle which, to Sachs (as to many other Jewish leaders of working-class movements in South Africa) remained a prominent legacy of their Eastern European past.

Understanding this success also requires reference to the occupational and organizational structure of the Transvaal garment industry, which, for a number of reasons presented conditions particularly conducive to unionization. Unlike textile and sweet factories, the positions in the labor process allotted to white women and to black men seldom overlapped. Thus, neither group had to fear competition from the other at a time when they had together become the newest sources of cheap labor for South African secondary industry. Yet the thorny problem of a combined interracial union never presented itself; for at the same time that white women were beginning to join the newly expanded Tailoring Workers' Union in the late 1920s, black men were forming their own Native Clothing Workers' Union under the capable leadership of Communist party member Gana Makabeni. Because of this segmented organization, the Transvaal union did not have to confront the racial hysteria that followed most efforts to unite white women and black men in a single group.

But structure and ideology provide only a partial explanation for the GWU's success in organizing working women. In the final analysis, the most brilliant ideological synthesis might have failed to create an active women's union without the GWU's impeccable attention to involving its members in a wide range of activities that bridged their needs both as workers and as young, single urban dwellers who sought companionship, fun, and community both inside and outside the factories. While these activities often were carried out under union auspices, the initiative for organizing them probably came as much from the women themselves as from the leadership. Only this firmly rooted but broadly defined sense of "community" provided garment workers with the strength to delineate their own position within a political context that became increasingly hostile during the late 1930s.

Even as organizing campaigns proceeded, many women continued to rely on individual strategies, switching jobs frequently to take advantage of differences in wages and working conditions. In the course of a single week, for example, twelve young women left the garment industry to take jobs at a sweet factory where a recent Wage Board decision had made starting wages 5s. to 7s. higher than those in clothing.[1] Prior to this wage determination, the sweet industry had experienced a "very rapid turnover" of employees because wages were so low.[2] Many waitresses routinely moved from one cafe to another every two or three months, despite the onerous expense of buying new uniforms each time they switched jobs.[3] Similarly, the Pretoria Juvenile Affairs Board reported disapprovingly in 1929 that, finding the work unsuitable, the majority of the forty or fifty girls recruited for fruit packing at the Zebediela Citrus Estates had returned home.[4]

Consciously following in the tradition of Mary Fitzgerald, another young white woman, Fanny Klenerman, took the first steps to organize women wage-earners during the mid-1920s. Klenerman, born in Kimberley, was exposed to socialist ideas through her father as a child. After graduating from the University of Cape Town with a degree in history and English, she taught for a short time at a girls' school in Wynburg, outside of Cape Town. Although she enjoyed the students, mainly Jewish war orphans, she already saw herself as a rebel and was unable to tolerate the school's "stuffy and repressive atmosphere." Shortly after the Rand Revolt of 1922, Klenerman left the school and turned to more political ventures. Relying on her father's connections, she began to work with the Labour party, supporting Pact candidates during the 1924 election and raising funds for the International Seamen's strike the following year.[5] Young and restless, Klenerman's commitment was again brief. Within a year she had broken with the party, objecting to its advocacy of an industrial color bar. Reflecting on her response many years later, she recalled:

> Here we've come to a country the British stole from the Africans. . . . They haven't got money to go anywhere, and you're excluding them from society and bringing them down to the level of serfs. And I said, "I can't take it."[6]

Unwavering in her political interests, Klenerman joined the South African Communist party, by that time a nonracial organization, and turned her energies to organizing waitresses.[7] Describing a tearoom workers' union that Mary Fitzgerald had formed, she charged, "Mary Fitzgerald was a wonderful speaker and a clever woman," but also, she alleged, a thief. "She stole their money and she never managed to give any sort of account, but she was so strong that nobody dared to affront her."[8]

Expressing her concern for tearoom workers and other women employees, Klenerman launched the South African Women Workers' Union, working closely with Eva Green. Since Klenerman's opposition to racialism is well documented, the union's stated goal of inducing "European women workers . . . to become members"[9] requires explanation. With the women in these occupations virtually all white, she simply may have

been describing her constituency. Alternatively, she may have emphasized race for more instrumental reasons, in hopes of having the group
registered. As it turned out, however, purely bureaucratic considerations
proved the major obstacle to registration.

The constitution of the Women Workers' Union is not dated, but the
union first attracted attention in April 1925, when Klenerman requested
donations from other political and labor groups to cover initial expenses.[10]
She also sought backing from the newly organized labor federation, the
South African Association of Employees' Organizations (SAAEO), which
in 1926 became the South African Trade Union Congress (TUC).[11] On July
11, 1925, however, registration was refused because, as a general union
open to all working women, the group failed to comply with the more
narrowly cast legal definition of a trade union.[12]

This decision forced the short-lived Women Workers' Union to divide
into independent organizations of sweet workers and waitresses. Although by 1926 each newly registered union had some two hundred
members, the Waitresses' Union experienced greater difficulty consolidat-
ing its membership than did the Sweet Workers' Union, which already
had enrolled 75 percent of potential members in Johannesburg and was
beginning to expand to other provinces.[13] Despite this success, some of
the largest sweet manufacturers on the Rand continued their threats to
fire employees who remained union members.[14]

During the brief life of the Women's Union, Klenerman concentrated
her efforts on areas of the economy where women were clustered, seeking to attract workers in bioscopes (movie theaters), cafes, tea shops,
laundries, and sweet and food-processing plants. Rarely allowed into the
workplace, she timed her visits for lunch breaks or after work. At one
sweet factory where some workers appeared "thin and emaciated, some
still young and robust, others grey and worn out," Klenerman, after wav-
ing a few leaflets, was invited into the cloakroom where she quickly tried
to persuade the women of the potential benefits of a union, to answer
questions, and to record names and addresses. She found a range of attitudes toward the issue of organization: "the girls are never hostile, but
some treat the matter of joining a union as a joke, some are earnest and
others stolid and indifferent." Even where employers welcomed her efforts, Klenerman found overwhelming anxiety. "Those to whom factories
are unknown," she reported to the Economic and Wage Commission of
1925, "will hardly believe what fear of losing one's job prevails. On more
than one occasion I received notes asking me to call at the homes of the
girls because they are afraid the employer may see me."[15]

In addition to its organizing campaigns, the Women Workers' Union
lobbied on behalf of women within the SAAEO and the TUC and before
the Economic and Wage Commission of 1925. Klenerman's testimony to
the commission stressed the inadequate wages and unregulated working
conditions facing most white women in the labor force and highlighted

the new trend she perceived among working-class families: the need for two incomes as a condition of survival. Covering much of the same ground as the testimony to the 1917 commission, Klenerman reported that women worked long hours, often exceeding the fifty hour per week limit under the Factories Act of 1918, and performed numerous domestic duties before and after work. Furthermore, she claimed, they lacked paid holidays or rewards to more experienced workers and faced constant pressure to speed up the pace of work. Women who reached the top pay levels were routinely dismissed.

Based on the hypothetical budgets she constructed, Klenerman once again found that average wages fell far short of the eight pounds a month minimum required to survive in Johannesburg. She concluded the first section of her testimony by advocating the introduction of a minimum wage "compatible with a white standard of civilisation." Arguing that trade unions had not served the needs of women workers, she urged immediate state intervention "to check the exploiter and force a minimum wage," for women were as yet unable to "use defensive weapons." [16]

Throughout her evidence, Klenerman portrayed working women as weak and unprotected, driven to fatigue, ill health, strain, and tension by their lives and working conditions. "Women all over the world," she argued, "have become the prey of the exploiter." [17] Whether this view of women as frail creatures requiring protection from exploitation (and from the temptation to escape low-wage drudgery through a life of "immorality") reflected her own perspective or her strategy for making a stronger case to the commission is at first unclear; yet by the last section of her report, Klenerman leaves no doubt about her intense concern over the "grave economic and social consequences" resulting from the entry of married women into the labor force: wage cutting, competition with men for jobs, thereby forcing men to delay marriage, and the premature undermining of the health of women and children.

Apart from a final appeal for "economic democracy," Klenerman's solutions differed from those of 1930s communists in an emphasis only on reforming the workplace, rather than on transforming the entire economic system and providing communal services to ease the burden of individual housework. Expressing the sentiment that women and their families were better off when they remained at home, she argued that women should demand the same pay and benefits as men, thereby protecting the woman "because a man will be able to keep the home without her support." She concludes on a note curiously solicitous of the needs of capital: "where because of special adaptability a woman is a better worker and necessary in the industrial sphere whe [sic] will at least be sure of adequate remuneration." [18]

This last section, then, communicates Klenerman's ambivalence about whether women should be working outside the home. Lacking either the strong feminist perspective of Mary Fitzgerald in her early days in South

Africa, or the vision of socialized domestic chores current in the late 1930s, she took the position of more conservative reformers who perceived higher male wages as the solution to women's problems.

But, just as Klenerman was expressing her despair about women's ability to effect change, the growing number of women in industrial work was forcing older craft unions to reexamine their policies, thereby creating the conditions for new forms of industrial unionism. The trend began in the clothing industry when the male-run Witwatersrand Tailors' Association organized a factory section in 1925. Within three years, 75 percent of WTA members were women. Although lacking influence in the organization and unrepresented on union committees, these new members responded readily and enthusiastically to calls for strikes.

The form and content of these actions, which highlight the new racial and gender issues posed by women's increasing entry into industrial labor, first became apparent in the strike that broke out on May 19, 1928 at the African Clothing Manufacturers in Germiston. In protest against the dismissal of three coworkers at the largest clothing factory in South Africa, 240 of the 300 women employees left work for several days. The agreement they finally reached provided for reinstating these workers, tea breaks, a closed shop, and no victimization "of either Europeans or natives."[19]

As the first large-scale action since the clothing industry's expansion in the mid-1920s, this stoppage showed two features that would become integral to women's protests during this period: a reliance on mine workers as their strongest class allies, reflected in the decision to organize collections of strike funds at as many pit shafts as possible on pay day, and an exuberant, high-spirited mood among the women. This enthusiasm led the *Rand Daily Mail* to describe "a strike of bright colours, gay processions, of laughter and joking, of music and dancing," an occasion, according to the headlines, for "negotiations and jazz."[20]

Perhaps the most significant aspect of the strike, though, was the total support it received from the Native Clothing Workers' Union, which had organized in February 1928 to represent the black male workers in the industry (one quarter of the more than four hundred employees at African Clothing Manufacturers). On the Monday following the strike's beginning (the previous Saturday), these black men voted unanimously to support the action. In the only form of solidarity socially acceptable between black men and white women, the strikers held separate meetings, each addressed by their own officials. By the week's end, this joint action had brought a settlement and both groups returned to work.[21]

This cooperation is significant not only for the interracial unity it displayed, but for the reactions it provoked: an "ominous event," in the opinion of the *Rand Daily Mail*[22] and an event to be greeted with caution in the stance of union officials. After the men had offered their support, Mr. Colraine, Secretary of the Witwatersrand Tailors' Association, "was disposed to avoid complicating the dispute in this way," but was urged (by whom is not clear) "to let the girls decide." They ceased their dancing long enough to greet the offer of solidarity with cheers. "The result was seen at one o'clock, when all the natives employed in the Germiston clothing factories came out on strike."[23] Despite "the better judgment of the more cautious trade union leaders," then, the women themselves accepted this offer of solidarity across racial and gender lines. The apparently central role of the Communist-affiliated Federation of Non-European Trade Unions (FNETU) in organizing the strike[24] suggests the importance of a counter to the more conservative WTA.

Jon Lewis analyzes this strike, and others of the period in which black and white workers cooperated with each other, in terms of the industrial labor process in the late 1920s. He argues that the similar place of many unskilled and semiskilled workers of all races laid a temporary basis for cooperation that ended with the economic hardship of the Depression.[25] Yet, an understanding of why white women felt no threat from black men, whereas the cautious tailoring union clearly did, also requires an understanding of the place of gender in the division of work. Whereas the white women entering clothing manufacturing as semiskilled operatives had their own niche in the expanding industry as machinists, trimmers, and finishers, the black men working as cutters and pressers were doing jobs that, in the Transvaal, were male-associated, but at wages substantially lower than the earnings of most white adult men. These men were threatened not by the armies of women machinists, who were hired at newly created positions, but by the "cheap native labour" of men who were being employed as pressers and at other hitherto skilled and well-paid jobs.[26] Thus, the common ground between black men and white women came not only from their similar skill level, but from the absence of competition laid down by a gendered division of work.

Reflecting the competition between black and white male workers, when the craft-oriented WTA was in charge of responding to requests for solidarity, the result was different. An incident earlier in May of 1928 led to a strike at the Clothing and Shirt Manufacturers that began on June 7. Responding to management refusal to reinstate an African employee who had been dismissed, nine other men left work with him, and the striking workers paraded through Johannesburg seeking to persuade other blacks to join them. By contrast with the solidarity exhibited earlier, the representatives of the Witwatersrand Tailors' Association who investigated "came away satisfied that the firm's decision was justified" and decided not to call a sympathy strike of white workers.[27] Although the attitudes of the white women involved are difficult to gauge, they apparently did nothing to counter the decision of WTA officials; but, most likely, their opinions never were sought.

Another strike the following year, in October 1929, highlights the unusual twist that the employment of young women gave to union tactics, underlining the conceptualization of these workers as closely attached to and strongly influenced by their families. It also suggests that both officials and striking women saw this family environment as sympathetic to trade unionism, perhaps another indication of the essentially urban background of the majority of the women. The strikers again acted with their characteristic exuberance.

On October 5, 1929, young women working at the Enterprise Clothing Factory in Johannesburg ceased work in protest against management refusal to join other Rand manufacturers in an agreement to prevent undercutting. During the first day's lunch hour meeting that attracted hundreds of women, strikers led a "good-humoured charge" (according to the *Cape Times*) into the factory. Blocked by the police, they hurled eggs and potatoes at the factory windows. More inflammatory in its treatment of these events, the *Rand Daily Mail* proclaimed in its headline, "Police Hold Stairway Against Wild Women."[28] Two days later, after a demonstration in front of the city hall, workers "marched in columns of route" to interview the parents of those who had continued to work. Women at the meeting resolved to blacklist the non-strikers, "and if their fathers did not influence them to conform to the Association's mandate, they, too, if they belonged to organised labour, would be black-listed by their unions." Seven of the hold-outs reportedly responded to this form of pressure.[29] Noteworthy here is that the women themselves initiated contact with the families of other workers. As the Depression cut into working-class finances during the 1930s, family attitudes toward strikes grew more ambivalent.

Several aspects of these strikes during the late 1920s require further comment. The tendency of both union officials and striking women to perceive family pressure as a way of encouraging participation in stoppages indicates the degree to which these workers remained emotionally and economically attached to their parents. For young women from urban backgrounds, then, the working-class culture they shared with their families provided positive inducement to take part in strikes when they occurred. The attitudes of union officials further facilitated women's involvement by allowing them to infuse their own culture into strike-related activities. Gay processions, singing, and dancing turned stoppages into ceremonial occasions that provided a break from the daily routine of labor and allowed women to bring their leisure-time pursuits into the workplace. By the early 1930s, disputes between workers and employers grew more intense, and strikes more complicated. But the late 1920s provided a transitional period, when young women could engage in relatively mild labor protest with their parents' support, in an atmosphere more akin to a holiday procession than to serious political confrontation. Although women carried their exuberant tendencies into later, more heated contests, the exposure of some women to new forms of public action in a relatively protected context may have helped to prepare the way for the confrontational politics of the Depression years.

Despite the occasional militance of young women workers, the image of "European girl" factory workers as lacking the interest or ability to organize themselves persisted into the early 1930s. Pollak, writing in 1932, found women far less organized than men and therefore more open to economic exploitation.[30] Yet, by 1935, the Wage Board Report on the clothing industry observed: "It is interesting to note that on the Rand women workers in the clothing trade, most of whom are Afrikaans speaking and therefore with no industrial tradition, have organised into what is quite a strong union."[31]

This startling change in the garment industry had several causes, most notably an energetic policy of industrial organization, fueled by large scale strikes during the Depression years of 1931 and 1932, and the impetus provided to female leadership after the male craft-oriented tailoring workers seceded from the GWU in 1934. Following the general strike of 1931, newly involved women were elected to factory committees and assumed positions as shop stewards, the first of a generation of dedicated, Afrikaans-speaking young women to become trade union leaders.

Bitter strikes in Cape Town and Johannesburg in 1931 and 1932 arose directly from the Depression, as employers tried to save money by decreasing wages and increasing production. The Transvaal strikes of these years were among the most heated class conflicts of the decade. When the agreement with the GWU expired in 1931, employers sought a 25 percent pay cut to bring wages down to the level of Cape clothing workers; the union countered with a demand for substantial increases and shorter working hours. The management-proposed "compromise," a wage reduction of 15 percent and a change in the ratio of qualified to unqualified workers by which one hundred workers in Johannesburg would be dismissed, was unacceptable to the union. After several months of fruitless negotiations, a strike seemed unavoidable. On October 26, 1931, responding to a GWU decision, some 2,300 workers in Johannesburg and Germiston, predominantly white women (only one hundred white men) left work. A "fairly peaceful" strike because of solid worker support, the several-week stoppage also was sustained by the efforts of other white workers. When the strike committee organized teams to collect money throughout the Rand, the women found, as in 1929, that miners were among their strongest allies.[32] Recalling the spirit of the late 1920s, Johanna Cornelius, a later union leader, described "members signing on at the Union's offices in the Trades Hall daily being sent out to collect funds, otherwise dancing."[33] The African Federation of Trade Unions, a Communist party affiliate, cast a more critical eye on this infusion of popular culture into the grimly serious activity of labor conflict: "The strikers are kept in the Hall dancing all the time whilst the union officials from time to time have a talk to the bosses."[34] But GWU officials, less doctrinaire in approaching the women whose loyalty their efforts required, never sought to restrain such activities.

These apparently mild tactics notwithstanding, employers finally agreed to drop the demand for a wage cut, while the union withdrew its insistence on an increase. The new agreement expired in nine months, however, and as the Depression cut more deeply into the clothing industry and many workers were given reduced hours, the next set of negotiations was doomed to failure from its inception. But as a result of the strike effort, some of the young Afrikaner women in the union became involved for the first time. Elected to factory committees and to positions as shop stewards, they began to inject a renewed spirit of militancy into the union itself, although the "old guard," in Sachs's words, retained financial and administrative control.[35]

White men, still part of the same union, joined women in the strike of 1931; following the official pattern of the 1920s, no effort was made to gain the support of the black male union. This neglect of black workers led to heated denunciation of the GWU by the AFTU, which accused the union of ignoring requests for united action on the part of the black male Clothing Workers' Union, and of leaving the eight hundred African cutters and pressers "starving in the street" during the course of the strike.[36]

Despite its shortcomings, this action on the Rand was far more successful than the strike effort mounted in August of 1931 by the South African Garment Workers' Union, the Johannesburg-based rival to the Cape Garment Workers' Union (SAGWU) which, at the time, existed only on paper.[37] Targeted primarily at the introduction of short-time working hours at the African Clothing Factory, the abortive strike effort formed part of a lengthy rivalry between the Cape-based and the Johannesburg-based unions over the loyalties of garment workers in the Western Cape. Their differences centered on the well-grounded fear of workers on the Rand that lower pay in the Cape threatened their own wage standards.[38] By 1931, the South African Garment Workers' Union had established a presence in Cape Town and beckoned its comrades there to rise up in struggle; following a cut-back in working hours, it threatened to call a strike. The Cape union quickly dissociated itself from these strike threats, attacking its rival as Communist-influenced. A strike called several days later at the African Clothing Factory met with only limited success in the mild estimation of the *Cape Times*; Martin Nicol, a recent historian of the Cape garment industry, deemed it "suicidal." Because work in the factory already was "practically at a standstill," only some seventy of three hundred workers supported the action.[39]

Although the organizers undoubtedly misjudged conditions, their errors also may include a lack of sensitivity to gender, still prevalent among their contemporaries in Johannesburg. Describing the course of the strike, the *Cape Times* observed that nearly all of the women stood by their em-

ployers, while most of the men were on strike.[40] Men's greater vulnerability partially explains this divergence; at that point, they alone faced the
threat of retrenchment.[41] Yet by sending two men to organize an industry
that was 85 percent female, the union certainly conveyed an insensitivity
to gender. Although the intensity of the economic crisis in the African
Clothing Factory was undoubtedly central to the strike's failure, it also
seems likely that the union was not appealing in a viable fashion to women
workers. If the Johannesburg strike of 1931 represented the beginning of
a change in such policies, the much more heated, though ultimately unsuccessful, strike of 1932 solidified that tendency.

The 1932 strike on the Rand achieved fewer of its immediate aims than
in 1931, but it did succeed in the long-term goal of continuing to identify
and to build up a group of strong and effective women leaders. Left without their wage cuts in 1931, clothing manufacturers turned to various means
of increasing productivity: intensifying the task work system, victimizing
and intimidating union members, routinely firing women who had become qualified, and strictly controlling the amount of time spent at the
lavatory. The "rude and vulgar" treatment of women was a continuing
complaint.

The previous year's agreement was due to expire on August 15, 1932.
On August 1, manufacturers notified their workers of a 10 percent wage
cut to be implemented the following month. The union perceived this
move ominously, as the beginning of an effort to decrease wages to Cape
levels, potentially by as much as 30–60 percent. Workers' response was
"immediate and emphatic."[42] On Wednesday, August 17, seventy-five
employees of S. Malk went on strike when the factory introduced the
wage cuts before the announced date. Stoppages in two other factories
followed soon thereafter, one in Johannesburg, the other in Germiston.
This time, however, police were called in to disperse strikers, ushering in
a period of bitter, sometimes brutal, clashes between police and strikers
in which numerous women received severe injuries. No longer did dancing and singing pervade the atmosphere of the union hall.

Johanna Cornelius later recalled a feeling on the part of many women
that wage cuts, also widespread in other industries, were "a trend of the
times"; they therefore lacked confidence that a strike could succeed. Although the action was tightly organized under leaders of small groups
who reported to an elected commander, the smaller number of strikers
and larger number of scabs contributed to the heated and divisive battles.
As picketers outside the factories struggled to prevent strike-breakers from
entering, they invariably prompted police intervention, leading to frequent scuffles in which the police attacked the strikers with batons, clubs,
and boot spurs and, at times, charged them on horseback. Following a
public protest after one woman's back was broken, the horses were withdrawn. "This was all very frightening," Cornelius observed, "as most of
us were teen-agers and were not used to such treatment."[43] For the first

time since women had entered the industry in large numbers, supporting a strike involved risk and danger that demanded a new level of commitment.

In further efforts to control the women, police arrested numerous strikers, usually releasing them on bail immediately. The Saturday morning that Cornelius and Gertie Guytes were arrested, however, they were taken into custody. In an effort to mask their distress, they alternated singing and playing a mouth organ that a friend had dropped into Cornelius' pocket. Locked into a filthy cell, they wrapped one of their two blankets around the sanitary bucket in a vain effort to lessen the nauseating odor.

To console themselves they sang, their selections indicating the cultural and political amalgam that lay at the heart of the union's appeal. Their songs ranged from Afrikaner folk tunes such as "Sarais Marais," to music from the socialist repertoire like the "Red Flag" and original compositions ("Scabby, Scabby," among them) that vividly conveyed the concerns of the strike.

> Scabby, Scabby
> Give me your answer do,
> We'll be happy,
> If we can get a hold of you,
> It won't be a proper hiding,
> The police are always siding,
> But you'll look sweet,
> Between the sheets,
> With a bandaged limb or two.[44]

Later in the evening, as they lay shivering and fearful, unable to sleep, the cell door burst open and a group of men in civilian clothes (such as the Germiston police wore during the strike), informed them that they were free to leave. They refused, hesitant to depart at night with strangers in an unfamiliar city. Laughing, one of the men identified himself as the Secretary of the Mine Workers' Union and explained that Sachs had sent him and some other miners to free them. They were escorted to the Church of Christ Hall near the jail, which was overflowing with miners and their wives and children. Armed with axes, spades, and guns, the crowd had threatened to storm the prison if the local Magistrate did not release the two women. Lifted over the crowd to the front of the hall to shouts of "Speak, girls speak!" Cornelius made her first public presentation. She later recalled only "that I compared the whole event as a real fairy story, being saved from imprisonment by a commando of furious working men and women."[45]

Once again, and perhaps more intensely and vividly during this strike than during any others, the resounding white working-class support for these young women was expressed through the miners. Though their actions convey an edge of paternalism in seeking to "rescue" the women from imprisonment, the men also accepted them as "fellow" workers, the most recent additions to a racially centered class alliance. That mine workers played this part is not surprising. Like the artisans in other contexts who frequently articulated and transmitted working-class ideologies,[46] these men were among the most established, respected members of their communities. The legacy of the Rand Revolt of 1922, then the longest, bloodiest battle in South African labor history, was not easily forgotten. Indeed, if these young women guided their actions by any ideological prescriptions at this time, it was not yet as socialists, but as "rebels' daughters," the offspring of Afrikaner men who had led an armed uprising against British domination in 1915–16.[47] In seeking to explain her actions to an Afrikaner audience in a late-night impromptu speech, it is noteworthy that Cornelius sought her ideological backing not in the labor movement, of which she apparently knew little, but in the national struggles of the Afrikaner people. "Our fathers fought for freedom," she reminded her audience, "and we are their daughters."[48]

By August 24, the union had refused to submit the employers' proposal to arbitration, raising the probability that the strike would be extended to all factories in Johannesburg and Germiston.[49] The situation in Germiston was more complicated than in Johannesburg. Employers there were more hostile to the union and an up-coming by-election made police and authorities fearful about the impact of a lengthy strike.[50] By early September, the four largest factories delivered an ultimatum that unless those on strike returned to work they would be replaced. In three of them however, the majority of women had been working all along.[51] By Friday, September 3, over six hundred of the seven hundred employees in the four main factories had returned.[52]

At the same time in Johannesburg, the action continued in full force. According to a report the following Monday:

> The clothing strike was intensified today, when following a resolution taken at a meeting yesterday, strikers paraded the streets and pulled out workers at one factory after another.
>
> Eight more factories ceased work early this morning, when strike pickets prevented girls entering the buildings. One of the men was badly bruised and cut about the face.
>
> There was a clash of strikers and girl workers outside another factory. One girl was scratched and her clothes ripped as she made for the doorway, but, after a struggle she gained admission.[53]

Not until the following Saturday was an interim settlement reached. The five to six hundred strikers were to be reemployed and the dispute over wages and ratios turned over to a Conciliation Board and then, failing satisfactory settlement, to an arbitrator.[54] By the end of the process, the workers were forced to accept a pay cut of roughly 10 percent.[55]

Like the 1931 strike, this was an action by the white workers alone. In a curious African Federation of Trade Unions' trial of several garment workers believed to have strayed from exemplary revolutionary behavior, one of them described his view of the issue. "I advised the natives not to come on strike, as, after the strike, we would tell the native workers to go to the devil." He defended this attitude "Because the white workers said that they do not want to mix up with the natives. . . . My personal opinion is that the natives and whites should work together, but my opinion and the opinion of the workers do not coincide."[56] Sachs himself, by this time supporting the AFTU action in holding the trial despite his earlier expulsion from the Communist party, admitted that union policy had been incorrect in not organizing the black workers before the 1932 strike.[57] Correct or not, the structure of work in the industry and the political climate in the Transvaal seemed to guarantee the continued separation of the black male union and its white, increasingly female, counterpart.

The trial also suggests some possible insights into the question of why Solly Sachs worked so hard to integrate the semiskilled women into the union. Brian Touyz, in his study of the politics of the GWU, suggests that Sachs encouraged Afrikaner participation out of a combination of "genuine sympathy" and an effort to strengthen his position vis-à-vis the Communist party group represented in the AFTU.[58] Although both explanations are undoubtedly significant, Sachs also must have realized as fully as anyone that the changing structure of the labor force demanded women's participation if the union were to survive. The implications of his own position could not have escaped him. As a Jewish male leader of an increasingly female Afrikaner union, and as a communist and an outsider to the new membership, he could only create a strong organization by incorporating these women into leadership positions and by including their wishes and their concerns among union goals. Furthermore, the Eastern European model of Jewish revolutionary groups provided a basis for building a working-class organization centered on an ethnic constituency. The need for such an emphasis would become more pronounced in the years to come.

Among the most notable aspects of the 1931 strike, like that in 1929, was the way in which union officials involved the womens' families in the process of gaining support for their actions. During the second week of the 1931 stoppage, the GWU called meetings at the Railway Institute in Germiston and at Trades Hall in Johannesburg to inform the strikers' parents of the issues at stake and to enlist their support. The Johannesburg meeting attracted close to 350 people: fifty parents, one hundred female strikers, and two hundred men belonging to other trades. The union meetings apparently were convened in response to a gathering called several days earlier by one striker's father, a Mr. de Beer, and chaired by another, a Mr. Small. At the Germiston meeting, Mr. Kramer of the Germiston Clothing Factory spoke for the employers, Sachs for the workers, producing a lively occasion that caused "periodic outbursts of protest, hoots and cat calls."[59] At both meetings, the parents ended by unanimously pledging support and sympathy to the strikers and backing for the union.[60]

During the 1932 strike, a number of Germiston parents again intervened, this time, however, supporting their daughters' willingness to return to work. This shift may indicate that continuing depression made children's steady wages more essential than ever to family survival.[61] Since railway workers, a significant element of Germiston's white population, were facing severe wage cuts and retrenchment at this time, such family pressure is not unexpected.[62]

By the end of 1933, as South Africa emerged from the Depression, workers became more independent. Union bargaining success in that year, combined with an intensive organizing effort, boosted GWU membership to over three thousand in a period of six months. The following year, the predictable rift between skilled male tailors and women operatives led to a split between the tailoring section of the union and the newly formed Garment Workers' Union of South Africa, a development that finally put the union in the hands of a new generation of young women. Prominent among them were Johanna and Hester Cornelius, Anna Scheepers, and Dulcie Hartwell, all but the latter from an Afrikaner background.[63] At the same time, changes in union organization encouraged wider participation based on an active shop stewards' group and on general members' meetings. These well-attended gatherings were held at least four times a year.[64] With a more flexible and responsive structure in place, GWU activities expanded in new directions. Building on the popular May Day picnics of the early 1930s, the union established a flourishing cultural and political community by the latter part of the decade that provided the resources, network, and ideology to link women's work with other aspects of their lives.

The women active in the GWU were among the country's most influential white trade unionists during the coming decades. They tried to build on the white working-class solidarity that mine workers and, at times, their own families had exhibited during periods of crisis. Yet a changing political climate was beginning to create rifts within the Afrikaner community that would challenge the extent of that solidarity. To insure the continued loyalty of working-class women, and to try to minimize their distance from their own families and kin, union leaders sought to redefine the bonds of ethnicity in class-oriented terms. This effort formed part of a broad-based left-wing effort to expand the boundaries of unionism to include larger numbers of women (both white and coloured) and black men, who became increasingly numerous in industrial production as the Depression yielded to a period of economic expansion.

− 6 −

A LENGTHENING THREAD

During the second half of the 1930s, female labor organizers became part of a broad-based effort to involve new industrial workers, primarily white women and black men, in a struggle for improved wages and working conditions. While Transvaal garment workers reached out to women in other industries and to clothing workers in the low-wage coastal areas, Communist party activists at the Cape found a high percentage of women among the unskilled and semiskilled workers they sought to mobilize. Active among black men, the most numerous beneficiaries of new factory openings, was Max Gordon, a Trotskyist who founded a number of new unions in Johannesburg. As in other periods of heightened labor activity, even domestic workers, notoriously difficult to organize, formed short-lived organizations to protect their interests.

Integral to this movement, trade unionists sought not merely to create formal union members, but also to shape people's attitudes and consciousness. The concerns of the period extended beyond work-related issues to the larger political environment: the threat of fascism at home and overseas, the struggle for socialism, and the relationship of capitalism to women's exploitation. In formulating their ideas on gender, organizers drew primarily on contemporary socialist discourse. In addition, the Transvaal garment workers, under attack from Afrikaner organizations, formulated a position on nationalism that sought to maintain the loyalty of their Afrikaner members.

Whether unionizing efforts were successful depended on the composition of the labor force in particular geographical areas and in particular industries. The relatively homogeneous female workforce in the Transvaal garment industry certainly facilitated organizing. But even with this favorable foundation, the union's ideological approach and the scope it gave women to express both political and personal concerns were also decisive. By the end of the 1930s, few other working-class efforts of the decade had surmounted the initial challenges of a labor movement divided by skill, race, and gender. In a political environment increasingly suspicious of contacts across racial lines, textile workers encountered open hostility when their aspirations and behavior challenged community norms. And under the weight of an emerging Afrikaner solidarity, increasingly defined in terms that opposed "nation" and "class," many women persuaded of the logic of socialism had to confront families who no longer supported their union commitments. In the Cape the owners and managers of clothing factories allied themselves with long-established bureaucratic craft unions that rarely pressed for industrial reform. Yet Cape workers were wise to be wary of the racial attitudes of Johannesburg trade unionists, their militancy notwithstanding.

Gender occasionally became a political issue during the late 1930s. For most groups concerned to improve the lives of working-class women, however, it was usually a subsidiary matter, either to class solidarity or to racial protection. With women now prominent among the ranks of non-unionized laborers, activists felt compelled to recruit them into working-class organizations. Yet questions such as wage inequality and the heavy domestic burden on working women merited only occasional discussion in the pages of left-wing newspapers. Apart from efforts to achieve better terms for maternity leave and some discussion of crèches, these matters rarely penetrated union demands. To middle-class women's associations and Afrikaner nationalists, white women were part of an ostensibly superior racial group; thus, respect for them on the part of men of other races had to be insured. These racially motivated interventions harked back to the paternalistic conception of women (or, at least, of white women) as weak creatures in need of protection.

Regardless of their motivation, few of the groups representing or purporting to represent working women were demanding gender-based wage equality. The lack of emphasis on this issue indicates how far working women or their advocates were from reconceptualizing a society not based on gender differences, which were still perceived as fundamental. Even to progressive thinkers of the period, the abolition of racial barriers was perhaps a more conceivable goal than an end to gender inequity.

In the Transvaal garment industry, the period from 1934 onward marked a new era of cooperation between the GWU, employers, and the Industrial Council for the Clothing Industry; [1] but the union's militancy did not subside. Instead, these new leaders, at first very much under the tutelage of their General Secretary E. S. Sachs, turned their energy to the low-paid garment workers of the Cape and other coastal areas, whose wages represented a continual threat to the gains of the Transvaal union. They also organized or assisted fledgling unions of other women in sweet, textile, and tobacco plants. Sachs wrote in 1935:

> Having put our own house in order temporarily, we decided at the beginning of the current year on a policy of national organization with a view to raising

the level of the coastal workers and thereby incidentally protecting and improving our own standard. We placed our whole Union, with its financial and organisational resources, at the disposal of the garment workers of Cape Town and Durban.[2]

In 1935, the Transvaal GWU leaders still perceived the Cape union as ineffective and resistant to involving rank and file women, white or coloured, in policy-making positions. Johanna Cornelius depicted it as "a completely inactive Union, under the leadership of a group of reactionary old men who did everything possible to stultify the workers' urge for better conditions."[3] Under these circumstances, both manufacturers and the union naturally resisted the new Transvaal-based campaign. Cape officials characterized their Transvaal counterparts as acting on "a revolutionary policy of smash and grab,"[4] arguing that, of the four thousand garment workers in the Peninsula, nearly three thousand belonged to their union.[5] Their membership lists at that time, however, included only 496 people, 82 percent of them women.[6]

Sometimes using relatively unorthodox methods, the young activists from Johannesburg gained valuable organizing experience in the Cape campaign. Again led by Eli Weinberg, but this time with a more representative group of assistants (Johanna Cornelius, Lucy Combrink, and Lettie Swanepoel), the women took jobs in clothing factories under assumed names in order to collect first-hand information on conditions. Cornelius, who worked at the African Clothing Factory as Mrs. Malan, reported to a mass meeting in Johannesburg on the harassment that was routine in the factory. One foreman commonly expressed his displeasure by cursing and hitting the women working under him, "white and coloured alike."[7]

These women from the Transvaal were in the forefront of the strike that broke out the following year at the I. L. Back garment factory in Cape Town. Beginning over the issue of whether workers should receive pay for a mandatory half-day holiday on the day of mourning for King George, the lengthy action led to the arrest of twenty-two strikers and five union leaders, among them Rosie de Freitas, 17, an organizer of the South African Garment Workers' Union; Dora Alexander, 26, a machinist; and Minnie Walsh, 17, a garment worker.[8] On March 6, during demonstrations over their trial, Johanna and her sister Hester Cornelius were arrested along with Ray Alexander, a woman on her way to becoming a singularly impressive union organizer. Transvaal intervention again raised the ire of Cape Town reporters, who depicted one episode of the strike as a "fierce encounter" between police officers guarding the I. L. Back factory and "a mob of Communists, garment workers and skolly boys [gangsters],"[9] apparently all equally objectionable.

This strike, one of only three that ever had occurred in Cape clothing factories (in 1917, 1931, and 1936), grew extremely bitter. Cornelius was arrested several times: for painting slogans on factory walls at night, picketing, getting into scuffles with nonstrikers, addressing open air meetings, and not dispersing when instructed to do so. After one arrest, she discovered that the police had kept a file on everyone with a past record. Hers was marked, "Public Enemy No. 101."[10]

Despite strenuous efforts, the Transvaal union succeeded neither in forming a successful and lasting rival to the Cape union, nor even in improving conditions there. A Trotskyist newspaper, *The Spark,* attributed the failure to timid leaders, who refused to transform the stoppage in one factory into a general garment workers' strike that would have rallied all Cape Town clothing workers.[11] Whatever the causes of the defeat, without a strong union, conditions continued to deteriorate. By 1938, despite incredibly low wages, the Cape industry suffered from widespread slack, short-time, and unemployment, and qualified workers continued to face the choice of being dismissed or applying for exemption from the wages to which they were entitled. Under this procedure, employees whose length of service merited a pay increase could "choose" to continue working at the lower rate. Between four and five hundred Cape garment workers reportedly were unemployed, and probably 90 percent of the rest were working on short time.[12] Furthermore, under the pressure to hire white workers brought by the Customs Tariff Commission, many coloured women felt compelled to apply for exemptions from regulation wages in order to gain employment or to keep their jobs.[13]

In seeking to protect prevailing wage standards, the Transvaal union also campaigned aggressively among women workers in Durban, East London, Port Elizabeth, and Kingwilliamstown. As highlighted in the National Council of Women report on Durban in 1935, conditions there were unspeakable, outwork was common, and some women in factories earned as little as fifteen shillings a week. The post-Depression efforts of the Transvaal GWU led to a meeting in May 1935 attended not only by Sachs, who was still orchestrating these efforts at unity, but also by Johanna Cornelius and Lucy Combrink.[14] As part of the organizing drive, factories guilty of underpayment were charged with violations, fined, and made to pay workers their lost wages.[15]

In East London, Kingwilliamstown, and Port Elizabeth several women became independent local organizers: Rose de Freitas and Hester Viljoen, who brought together garment workers in Port Elizabeth; and Dulcie Hartwell, who formed garment and sweet workers' unions in East London and became secretary of the local Textile Workers' Industrial Union. Hartwell, a life-long labor official, began working in a dress factory in 1934 and in 1937 was appointed as assistant secretary of the GWU and elected to the national executive of the South African Trades and Labour Council. After a threatened strike at Mosenthal's over the firing of three trade union leaders, Port Elizabeth clothing employers consented to meet with the union and came to an agreement that raised wages and established a closed shop and a sick fund.[16]

In order to avoid the regional wage differentials that plagued the garment industry, organizers of sweet workers, among the lowest paid industrial employees in South Africa, sought to form a single national organization. Following their first general meeting on August 4, 1937, Cape sweet workers, with Eli Weinberg as honorary secretary, contacted their counterparts in Port Elizabeth, East London, and Johannesburg about making a joint application for a Wage Board investigation.[17] By late September, in an effort to attract additional members and to raise funds, the Cape union had organized its first dance, whose proceeds went toward exposing the "rotten conditions" in the industry.[18] Johannesburg sweet workers held an organizing meeting in mid-November. Supporting the demand for a new determination, they condemned the use of pay scales set in 1932 at the height of the Depression.[19]

During the following year joint organization persisted. Cape activists continued to expose conditions in the industry and to press for higher wages. They also held dances, visited the homes of nonmembers, argued for protective masks and gloves for workers in dangerous jobs, and worked out a plan for free drugs and medical care. By April 1938 the separate unions were sufficiently organized to apply for joint registration. Reflecting the union's origins in the Transvaal GWU, the first SWU constitution designated E. S. Sachs as president and Dulcie Hartwell as national secretary. Despite this intense activity, some areas such as Port Elizabeth proved resistant to union efforts, and only in mid-June 1939 was the Wage Board decision finally announced. Condemned by all branches, the Board recommended lower wages for some categories of workers, regional wage differentials, and legalization of piece work.[20] This response to union efforts provided a graphic reminder that, in many industries, official bodies would not willingly legislate improved pay and working conditions.

Fragile though some of these new unions were, they succeeded in extending the influence of the Transvaal GWU across the industrial map of South Africa and in providing arenas in which newly mobilized young female leaders could put their organizing skills to the test. The reputation they established for toughness and determination, reflected in the horrified accounts of newspapers throughout the country, created a new image of working women that began to undermine the stereotype of fragility and helplessness. It does not seem unlikely that the defiant posture of these female union activists alarmed the architects of Afrikaner nationalism as thoroughly as did their socialist ideals.

Some of the leading women from the Transvaal also supported organizing efforts in the textile industry, an arena of intense struggle during the 1930s. The most bitter of these conflicts, the 1936 strike at Consolidated Textile Mills at Industria, near Johannesburg, began in stages on May 11. Two days later, approximately three hundred employees had ceased work in an effort to collect back pay for Jubilee Day, a compulsory holiday on

May 6, and to secure recognition of the Textile Workers' International Union.[21]

As soon as employers began to meet with Department of Labour officials to discuss the strike, another issue surfaced: a proposal to substitute black men for eighty European spinners, who ostensibly would be absorbed into other sections of the factory. The union was cynical about employers' motives for this shift, condemning it as a cost-saving move camouflaged as concern for the safety of women traveling to and from the mill at 5 a.m. and 9 p.m.[22] Workers were not uninterested in security; Martha Hurn, a spinner, had recently been murdered on her way home from work in the evening. But as the strike continued, employers revealed their motives more openly. According to a manager at Consolidated Textiles: "The spinning trade is quite unprotected and has to compete with overseas countries where wages of 9s. to 10s. a week are common."[23]

During the lengthy stoppage, strikers and police clashed frequently, as did those who had returned to work and those who remained out.[24] A newspaper report on June 18 spoke of "A wild rush of police, strikers and non-strikers across the veld from Industria towards Langlaagte," ending in a mass meeting of the Transvaal Textile Workers' Industrial Union late that afternoon.[25] Commenting on the increasing number of returned workers, the manager described his strategy of sending prepaid postcards to all employees offering them the positions they had left. Those who arrived that morning by train had to be accompanied from Langlaagte station by police.[26]

Later that week, disturbances continued as police arrived to escort strikebreakers back to the station. During the conflict between strikers and nonstrikers, a "swirling mob" of about three hundred people fought for nearly a quarter of an hour; but before police reinforcements arrived the strikers had restored order. By June 26 thirty of the returnees had rejoined the strikers, and only fifty women actually were working.[27]

As the strike continued, so did arrests for involvement in the disturbances. Convicted on June 28 were Johanna Cornelius (23), President of the GWU; Lucy Combrink (20); Mary Masson (17); Bettie Honman (du Toit) (25); and Johanna Raata (24). In an act unheard of for white women at the time, the accused chose imprisonment rather than paying their fines. According to Bettie du Toit, a charge of provocative behavior against Cornelius was not altogether unjustified. Angered at two sisters who had organized scab labor and encouraged friends on the police force to escort them into the factory, "Johanna . . . had decided to use physical force. All persuasion had failed and there seemed no way to teach the blacklegs a lesson."[28] Despite weeks of explaining, the two young women continued to visit workers in their homes, trying to persuade them to break the strike. Cornelius had asked du Toit, at the time inexperienced in organizing, to take charge of the picketing outside the factory. Joined by Lucy Combrink, a garment worker, and by Mrs. v.d. Westhuizen, a striker, Cornelius physically attacked the sisters. When one witness expressed dismay at seeing "nice Afrikaans girls fighting and brawling in the street like common women," Combrink warned her: "Stand aside lady, I'll deal with you later."[29]

Cornelius described the arrest somewhat differently. While recalling that all five were taken into custody for assaulting scabs while on the picket line, she identified her offense merely as "bumping off the hat of a non-striker."[30] Two of the arrested women protested that they could not go to prison, arguing, "Our husbands will kill us. They're Greyshirts [fascists]," Cornelius replied: "And if you don't come, I'll kill you. You bring toothbrushes and you come."[31] Refusing bail, they were imprisoned at the Johannesburg fort.

The youth and naïveté of these women come through in Cornelius' recollection that, at the time, they were unaware of the meaning of "soliciting," the most common offense of the other women prisoners.[32] Du Toit remembers Cornelius bursting into tears at the sight of the ghastly food, but urging du Toit never to reveal that she had cried. "And I promised her faithfully that I never would and I haven't, but now it's unimportant."[33] After five days and payment of a fine, all were released.

Because the strike centered on the displacement of white workers, expressions of support were likely to carry racial overtones. Union hesitancy to put the issue so baldly did not deter a Labour party conference from passing a resolution urging all other workers to "support these women workers who are defending the great principle of a white South Africa."[34]

As a conciliation board began its unsuccessful meetings on June 8 to discuss the Industria strike, the state began to exercise new forms of coercion: using pick-up vans (hitherto reserved for black pass offenders) to convey scabs to and from work; charging the union with collecting for a charity without permission when it sought strike funds from other organizations; bringing charges against selected strikers; and regularly calling in the police. Once again, mine workers were among the most sympathetic allies of the women on strike, responding enthusiastically to women who visited the mines to collect money for strike pay.[35] Once again, also, their stance combined protection and militance. Those on the East Rand sent a telegram to General Smuts informing him that unless the conflict was settled quickly, they would go to Langlaagte "to protect the girl strikers against the police."[36] The rift between nationalist and progressive unions was still to come.

Countering these efforts on behalf of the strike, police were used during this period "to visit the strikers at their homes and to endeavor to persuade them to return to work."[37] But strikers also took their case into the community, painting "SCAB" in large letters on the houses of some of those who had returned to work.[38] Although parents did not intervene directly, the actions of the mine workers again suggest a strong measure of approval from a critical segment of the white working-class population.

Whatever the weight of these threats and of persuasion on both sides, the strike was settled early in July through negotiations between employers and the union. The Department of Labour acted as mediator. *Umsebenzi*, calling it "one of the most militant and powerful struggles of workers on the Rand since 1922,"[39] did not judge the settlement a complete victory. All strikers had to be rehired; but rather than recognizing the union immediately, employers agreed to meet with the Trades and Labour Council in two months on the questions of union recognition, a closed shop, and a sick benefit society.[40] Shortly thereafter, a completed Wage Board investigation made some improvements in wages and working conditions.[41]

A number of issues continued to preoccupy the Textile Workers' Industrial Union (TWIU) during the last half of the 1930s: putting continual pressure on the Wage Board to improve the terms of employment and, starting in 1938, struggling against widespread short-time and unemployment resulting from the import of cheap cotton blankets and rugs from Italy and Japan; arguing for better tariff protection for the industry[42] and against new speed-up policies by which workers had to operate two weaving machines at a time;[43] and pressing for the abolition of piecework.[44] A TWIU letter sent to every member of the House of Assembly argued that without better protection, South Africa could not compete, "unless it goes down to the level of slave labour conditions."[45] Only after World War II did large-scale changes in the industry, including the infusion of overseas capital, respond systematically to these pressures.

As in the garment industry, militant struggles and heated confrontations with police drew new young women into union affairs, and the lengthy strike at Consolidated Textile Mills gave the "girl strikers" a new taste of the use of state power against working people. Although I. Wolfson remained secretary of the textile workers' union, Miss Claessens became "chairman" and, as in the garment industry, women assumed much of the responsibility for local organizing: Joey Fourie in Durban, Ray Alexander at Paarl and other areas of the Cape, and Bettie Honman (du Toit) in Cape Town and Huguenot. But the division of labor in the industry, in which white women and black men either actually or potentially held the same jobs, made all organizing efforts during the 1930s extremely tenuous.

As white women became a major force in the expansion of textile organizing, new issues connecting race and gender arose. According to the union's official history, a branch initiated in Durban in 1932 was unsuccessful because the organizers' concern only with white workers created divisions within the heterogeneous labor force.[46] The union that began in Johannesburg in 1934 took a more open attitude, resolving to include Africans in the union.[47] Yet the racially exclusive reputation of Johannesburg unions made its expansion in the Cape problematic. The Secretary Organiser in Paarl wrote on July 2, 1935, of the delicate position there because of friction between "Europeans and non-Europeans."

I was first of all given to understand that I was to endeavor to organise ALL textile workers into one union, irrespective of race, creed or colour, but since the arrival of the Chairman from Russia yesterday, I am given to understand that the organisation only caters for European employees. . . . Whilst this would make my task easier, there is a definite danger of allowing the Cape Federation to make propaganda of an attempt to organise a Union with a colour bar, and I would like your instructions on this matter.[48]

The concern was repeated shortly thereafter when the organizer of a Cape Peninsula branch wrote to I. Wolfson, "my work is rendered more difficult through reports having reached the coloured section (which incidently is a very large section of the industry here) that your organisation has a 'colour bar.' "[49] Wolfson responded immediately, denying the existence of racist policies, and affirming the group's openness to all members, "Natives, Indians and Coloureds."[50] The issue of race was paramount in Johannesburg at the time because the lack of organization of black workers during the Consolidated Textile Strike had led to their use as scab labor.[51] In August, union representatives reaffirmed their intention "to organize the Native workers on the same basis as Europeans."[52] Indian complaints of segregation at meetings were addressed by a new organizing effort and a change in leadership of the local union.[53] Some of these issues seem to have subsided by the time of a strike at the Afritex Mill in Durban in 1937, in which whites, blacks, and Asians worked together. Yet the racial problem did not entirely disappear. In 1939, the Cape Town executive refused to allow the branch to participate in the union's proposed sick benefit scheme because of its restriction to Europeans only.[54]

Such racial suspicions pervaded many efforts at unity between Transvaal and Cape-based unions. Because of their large coloured membership, the latter voiced continuing fears about the racial policies of their potential allies to the north. Repeated assurances from progressive union officials rarely convinced coloured garment or textile workers that ordinary white union members would sustain policies of interracial equality or cooperation.

When Bettie du Toit arrived at the Cape in 1938 to organize two Cape Town mills (employing young white women and coloured men) and a mill with white women and African men at Huguenot thirty-five miles away, an explosive combination of racial and gender issues confronted her. Lacking the factory floor experience of many of her contempories, she learned her work through experience, and through her mistakes. "Because I didn't know a thing and I would go thumping into the Department of Labour and they would say, 'Yes, but under section so and so you can't do so and so.' And I would say, 'Well, what can I under what section?' "[55]

Although she succeeded in forming a nonracial branch at the Cape, her success was short-lived.[56] After du Toit had organized a committee with equal numbers of white and coloured representatives, the group decided to hold two separate dances to raise funds. At the coloured event, she danced with the coloured union chairperson, who returned to the factory and boasted, "Oh, yes, Bettie du Toit's not like any of you, she danced with me, a coloured man." "Ah," she recalled, "the resignations came in fast and furious. Oh, my heart was broken." Through great tact, she managed to rebuild the union, but never quite to its former strength; white women continued to charge: "That's not a white girl. No white girl would behave like that."[57]

At Huguenot, a more rural setting in the fruit and wine growing area of Paarl, du Toit aimed only to organize the white women at first, for the union felt that "at this stage to ask Afrikaner girls on the platteland to unite with black Africans would be very provocative."[58] "This was much too severe a problem," she later admitted, "and truthfully one didn't even really think of them [Africans] as workers."[59] Although du Toit was successful initially, she soon was forced to confront the brunt of Afrikaner nationalist organizing against the trade union movement. Thus, once again, the lack of a homogeneous body of workers and the intense suspicions and fears triggered by any hint of an alliance between white women and black men created barriers to organizing much greater than in the Transvaal garment industry. In addition, the highly concentrated patterns of ownership in the industry undoubtedly enhanced the power of employers to oppose unionization.

In addition to the work of Transvaal unions in the Cape in the late 1930s, a group of Cape-based Communist party members sought to publicize miserable conditions and to organize across racial lines in factories and shops. Ray Alexander, an immigrant from Latvia and a member of the South African Communist party in Cape Town, was involved with at least a dozen new nonracial unions, many with large numbers of women workers. Breaking from the old Cape policy, which accepted "non-Europeans" as members, but relegated them to a secondary role, these unions encouraged black members as organizers, chairpersons, and secretaries.[60] Women brought together as part of these campaigns worked primarily in meat and fish processing plants and chemical factories. Although they sometimes were delegated to distinct tasks, many of them labored alongside men. With some of the most arduous and ill-paid jobs in the area, these factories relied largely on coloured workers, and therefore did not present organizers with the racial divisions of local clothing establishments.

Conditions in food processing plants were indescribably miserable and unhealthy. Publicizing such conditions formed an important aspect of the organizing effort. Workers in the Western Cape spent their days in wet, freezing rooms. But only under union pressure did the women receive clogs and protective clothing without deductions from their wages. Although required to report to the factory daily at 6:30 a.m. in case any fish had arrived, work days varied substantially from three or four to twelve hours. In one particular week, total earnings ranged between 1s. 2d. and 5s. 3d.; but even these meager wages were regularly reduced by 2s. 6d. until the full cost of protective clothing was covered. Pay envelopes had to be picked up at the factory each Friday, ostensibly a day off. Despite the high incidence of colds and rheumatism, no sick pay was provided.[61]

Equally disagreeable conditions prevailed in the Cape meat industry. Although employing primarily men, at Imperial Cold Storage Pty., "tucked away in a corner near the abbattoirs" were thirty-three women who worked as gut scrapers for 16s. per week. Once again, clogs and aprons were supplied only after a union appeal to the Department of Labour. A visitor to the factory found the workers' canvas aprons soaked through, the floor of the factory running with water, and an icy wind blowing through the room, chilling the women, but not dampening the "unbelievable" smell of the offal that they scraped into piles on tables. That which found no use for sausage skins was sold at a stand across the road from the factory.[62] One reporter, arriving at midday, found the women sitting outside eating their "lunch": hunks of dry bread. During the cold weather, they huddled around burning braziers to try to keep warm.[63]

Organizing efforts in 1937 among the ill-paid women in fish canning and curing factories revealed workers more eager than their organizers to express their grievances forcefully. A meeting of two hundred women held at dawn on July 19, 1937, brought out a "determined looking" crowd, "clasping in their hands huge sharp fish gutting knives." A more formidable group of workers could hardly be found in the Cape Peninsula, noted one reporter who described the protestors as "200 sturdy coloured girls."[64] A recent death (on July 17) that was attributed to cold, damp working conditions exacerbated anger over the lack of free protective clothing and sick pay. Mounted police, eyeing the long gutting knives, withdrew to safety, but the presence of union officials tempered the women's actions. "A few of the more hot-headed among the girls were calling for a strike forthwith," according to the *Cape Times*, "but the speakers [Eli Weinberg of the SATLC and F. G. Richfield secretary of the Fish Curing and Allied Trades Employees' Union] advised that negotiations would be a wiser course."[65]

As the fish workers' campaign against victimization of union members proceeded, "trouble was brewing" among the thirty-three women in the gut factory adjoining the abbatoir at Maitland. Reacting to employers' refusal to pay a raise recommended by the Department of Labour, the newly organized women had decided to take action. A meeting on July 30 of the Maitland section of the union, "fully supported" by the women's section but poorly attended by men, announced wage increases that would bring most wages to 17s. 6d. or 18s. 6d., still short of the minimum of twenty shillings they were demanding.[66]

In February 1937, under the auspices of the Cape District Committee of the South African Trades and Labour Council, an organization campaign also began among Cape chemical workers, many of whom were women. While the South African Trades and Labour Council (SATLC) undoubtedly took a sincere interest in these campaigns, an article in *Umsebenzi* on women meat workers included a revealing insight into one aspect of their motivation:

> The position of women workers in South Africa requires special attention by the trade unions. Their wages are as low as Native wages and are a serious threat to European men.[67]

Although beginning with a male president and vice president, Ray Alexander, as secretary, became the prime figure in the Chemical Workers' Union. Its five committee members included three women: Miss S. Dudley, Miss M. Jacobs, and Miss J. Daniels. By July the new union had registered, applied for a Wage Board investigation, arranged for a dance, and was particularly successful in attracting the interest of the women in the industry. In September a branch formed in Port Elizabeth and, by the end of the year, after months of negotiations, an agreement was reached granting wage increases and holiday and sick pay and establishing a single pay scale for male and female minors. By March of 1938 successful branches were operating in Port Elizabeth and Johannesburg and efforts were under way to form a national union.[68] In addition to continual pressure for changes within the industry, the union also pressed for amendments to the Factories Act, including a forty-hour week, more frequent breaks, overtime pay, free protective clothing, adequate light and ventilation, and improved sanitary and safety conditions. Periodic dances provided occasions for members to gather more informally.

As an organization representing large numbers of women, the Chemical Workers' Union remained aware of the need to respond to their particular position. In July 1939 officials requested that a woman be appointed to the Wage Board prior to its investigation of the chemical industry, since the majority of employees were female. In its memorandum to the Wage Board, the union referred to the "condition of women workers, many of whom are independent breadwinners." Because of the nature of the work, they faced great physical strain, exacerbated by undernourishment and overwork. In the interests of health and efficiency, work hours had to be reduced and definite rest periods established.

This memo is instructive in outlining the concerns that Alexander would express throughout her organizing career. Written slightly more than a decade after Klenerman's representation to the Economic and Wage Commission of 1925, its attitude toward working women is totally different. Although Alexander, too, is concerned about stress and overwork, she sees the solution not in women's withdrawal from the labor force, but in improved working conditions. In her vision, working women are an accepted part of economic life, rather than mothers and daughters whom crisis conditions have drawn into an unwelcome situation. The change reflects not only the particular attitudes of the two women, but also the dramatic shift in women's employment that had occurred since the 1920s.

As part of the campaign among chemical workers, Alexander also sought to keep members abreast of international events related to local political issues. In October 1939 she informed executive committee members and shop stewards that the industry would soon benefit from the wartime removal of foreign competition, and alerted them to the potential for demanding wage increases. Continually emphasizing workers' education, the union also began classes to train shop stewards, executive members, and other interested workers; lectures stressed the importance of understanding and seeking to alter the system under which workers lived. The strong emphasis on political education and participation, characteristic of many Communist unions of the 1930s and 1940s, would be evident throughout Alexander's career. By early 1940 the chemical industry, although well organized, remained among the lowest paying industries in South Africa.[69]

Organizing these women presented Alexander with many challenges. "Some of the women, because of the low wages, were at night on the street," receiving greater remuneration from the sailors than from the factory. Undaunted, Alexander later described making the rounds of workers' houses. "I had to become a moralist, talk to them against their style of life." Not surprisingly, she found their parents receptive as she sought not only to organize them, but to involve them in leadership positions.[70]

Women in nonindustrial occupations also joined in the organizing efforts of the late 1930s. Under the leadership of Joey Fourie, a former waitress, the Western Province Restaurant Employees' Union (established in October 1937) worked to change conditions that still included widespread underpayment of wages, lack of free food or uniforms, and lengthy "spread over" days, which stretched nine hours of work over thirteen hours. As part of their effort, the union sought assistance from the Cape Town branch of the National Council of Women.[71]

Shopworkers also began new campaigns. In the Transvaal, the National Union of Distributive Workers was formed in 1936. Two years earlier at the Cape, Ray Alexander had worked as secretary and organizer, seeking improved wages and shorter hours and gaining the support of several prominent local women and the National Council of Women. As the Commercial Employees' Union, the group was committed to a nonracial membership policy. Taken over by Katie Silpert (Kagan after her marriage in 1937), an immigrant from Russia who had arrived in South Africa in 1924, a drive began in Cape Town in July 1937 to compel the city's shops to close at 6 p.m. on Friday. Quickly the issue spread to Johannesburg, Durban, and Port Elizabeth, in all centers eliciting a high degree of public support and the enthusiastic assent of shopworkers. In Cape Town alone, union membership increased from two hundred to nearly a thousand as a result of the campaign. By early 1940, Kagan, now based in Johannesburg, had become the union's national organizer.[72]

In the late 1930s, then, working-class women were no longer perceived as passive victims of economic exploitation. Their unions were successful at gaining recognition and at forcing changes, sometimes significant, in wages and working conditions. Their degree of success depended to some extent on geography, since Wage Board decisions tended to retain lower wages for coastal areas than for the Transvaal and lower wages still for rural centers (a problem for the textile industry in particular). Only where it was possible to organize a national union and a national Industrial Council could women overcome these regional disparities.

But despite the remarkable organizing surge among women, both regional distinctions and gender limited their possible success. Under the prevailing assumptions in South Africa, where divisions of both race and gender inhibited efforts to achieve unity (and therefore maximum strength) in the organization of workers, if white women's wages grew too high in the estimation of employers, their attractiveness as cheap labor would be eroded. Although the end result of this pressure was somewhat different in the Cape (where replacement meant turning to a larger coloured female labor force) than in the Transvaal (where the alternative workers were coloured women and black men), the end of the 1930s marked the closing of an era for white working-class women in South Africa.

Recognizing the extent of women's organization as well as the need for further unity among female workers, the Transvaal Garment Workers' Union convened a conference in Johannesburg on August 30, 1938. Indicating the GWU control of the meeting, Johanna Cornelius was elected chair, while Solly Sachs outlined the objectives of the meeting: "to coordinate the activities of the trade unions, which have large numbers of women members, for the purpose of championing specifically the cause of the women workers."[73] Thirty-seven delegates representing eight organizations attended the meeting, which received messages of support from the Cape unions with a large female membership: the National Union of Distributive Workers, the Sweet Workers' Union, the Chemical Workers' Union, and the Waitresses' Union. Women such as Dulcie Hartwell, Ray Adler, Anna Scheepers, and G. Haywood dominated the general discussion, although W. H. Andrews, I. Wolfson, and Sachs also took part.

Formed as the Federation of Women Workers, the organization drafted an ambitious charter that went beyond the specific goals for which most of the unions had been working. They included equal pay for equal work; prohibition of overtime, task work, and piece work; criminal penalties for workplace abuse; housing and recreational facilities; state and municipal crèches; and various proposals concerning wages, hours, breaks, vacations, and confinement leave. Although clearly articulating the most significant gender-based class issues, its Johannesburg origins were reflected in the absence of any reference to race, of greater interest in the predominantly coloured labor market of the Cape than among the primarily white female workers of the Transvaal. And, despite the theoretical need it filled, this organization probably never fulfilled its initial promise. Union records fail to mention it again, and at least one of the participants, admittedly some years later, had no recollection of the group.[74]

As yet proletarianized in small numbers, African women were not part of the formal unionization effort in the industrial or commerical sectors of the economy. But a few did take part in the organizing drive among domestic workers that began in the late 1930s. The difficulties of the domestic workers' unions in both Cape Town and Johannesburg reflect as much the privatized conditions of household labor as the sentiments of the workers. For this reason, the Cape union tried to assuage fears of victimization by assuring prospective members of the group's gradualist approach to improving conditions.[75]

In 1937, as trade union campaigns intensified at the Cape, domestic workers were able to take advantage of the growing shortage of household labor to increase their bargaining power. The coloured women who formed the Domestic Employees' Union under the aegis of the National Liberation League[76] voiced a number of complaints: a 50 percent drop in pay over the previous decade, jobs that required double duty in two different households, long and irregular hours, and dishonest employers. Particularly objectionable was the common practice of employers planting an object with a servant's belongings at the end of the month and then charging her with theft, threatening to call the police if the woman objected to being discharged without wages.[77] Such individual harassment highlights sharply the vulnerability of household workers.

The Domestic Employees' Union managed to survive for several years, holding regular meetings on Wednesday evenings in District Six, the coloured section of Cape Town, and investigating individual complaints about wages, filthy and inadequate living quarters, and lack of holidays. Complaints were handled by personal contact with the employer in question rather than through legal action. Despite the large number of such cases brought to the secretary, Mr. L. Mosley Turner, the small membership by January 1940 was leading to plans for a recruiting campaign.[78] The difficulty in attracting members was typical of such organizations. With workers isolated from each other and directly subject to the whims of individual employers, joining a union involved considerable risk. The constant demand for domestic labor provided their only leverage.

Some of the group's goals were typical of other trade unions: enrolling members, beginning a sick fund and medical service, and working for better wages and shorter hours. Others indicated the more bourgeois concerns that also permeated the campaigns for hostels for African women: opening a Labour Supply Bureau to assure members of good positions and "mistresses of reliable employees," and raising the general standard of domestic service. "Well-run homes," the union argued, "are the basis of a prosperous nation."[79] Yet, despite this suggestion that workers shared in the prevailing ideology of domesticity, reports of meetings do suggest a class-conscious edge to the deliberations. "So independent has this particular class of worker become," wrote a *Cape Times* reporter apparently nostalgic for the days of cheap, reliable maids, "that they resent the term 'servant' and have called their union the 'Domestic Employees Union'."[80]

A strong social service ideology and paternalistic aims also permeated the Johannesburg-based efforts at organizing domestic workers. In 1937, Lucy Twala, who had trained at Inanda Seminary, formed the Bantu Domestic Service Association, aimed at protecting the interests of the elite group of ex-boarding school servants to which she belonged. She also tried to open an employment bureau to safeguard the women's interests at work and to encourage good relations between employer and employee. Discouraged by her lack of success, she later commented that her appeal "fell on the stiff necks and dumb ears of the girl who does not understand the value of unity and the power of union."[81] Twala herself, under her married name of Lucy Mvubelo, would later put that understanding to work in the garment industry.

A successor to Twala's union, the African Domestic Servants League, was formed in 1938 by Mr. Mvula, a former assistant editor of *The Bantu World*.[82] One-time Communist party member G. J. Coka revived the group after Mvula's death and became its leader. In an appeal for assistance to the South African Institute of Race Relations (SAIRR), he spoke in all seriousness of "the large influx of ignorant and untrained African Servants" and of the racial friction that arises "wherever houseladies have to deal with impertinent and cheeky servants." By September 1938, the group had been reorganized under a committee that included: Mr. D. R. Twala, chairman; Miss Sellina Rampa, vice chairlady; Mrs. M. Nongauza, treasurer; and Miss E. T. Daba, secretary. Three other women and J. G. Coka, author of the report, also were elected to the governing body. The group worked throughout 1938 and 1939, holding a cookery demonstration and placing small numbers in employment. At the end of 1939, Coka estimated a membership of sixty, with about forty servants a month being sent out to employers. Despite severe financial difficulties, plans were under way to set up a training center for domestic workers.[83] A newspaper article of September 1939 sounded less optimistic, however, describing the membership as "apathetic" and noting that the two paid assistants had given up their positions.[84] The League continued into the 1940s, but available records give little indication of its activities, membership, or finances.[85]

While some household workers were forming legal organizations designed to improve their working situation or to help them locate employment, others, taking more direct action, engaged in their own form of social banditry. Heirs to the tradition of the Amalaita, "squadrons of Native girls" in Bloemfontein were applying for jobs, then remaining in the house only long enough to round up all the handbags and money they could find. During a single week in 1937, one detective alone had handled five cases. Other similar incidents apparently were numerous.[86]

During this period, trade unions also expressed concern about the quality of working women's lives outside the factory, developing sick funds and medical insurance schemes and seeking to increase solidarity among the workers, many of whom were newly urbanized, by sponsoring dances, picnics, and other social activities that encouraged informal contacts. The Transvaal GWU, for example, held classes in first aid, physical culture, and personal hygiene. The GWU also gained support by campaigning actively on issues of concern to women such as confinement allowances and crèches; in 1930, as the Depression set in, the union began a system for distributing food among its neediest members.

As part of their efforts, the most active unions also sought to shape the attitudes and consciousness of their members. For all except the Transvaal GWU, the extent to which these ideas were widely internalized is uncertain. Under the leadership of Ray Alexander, the Chemical Workers' Union in Cape Town collected funds to assist the Republican forces in Spain and to aid people starving in Namaqualand on the southwest coast. Members also elected delegates to the Peace Council and took part in the struggle against segregation and the extension of the color bar in the Cape, urging the Non-European United Front to organize a boycott of the Dutch Reformed Church.[87] Like much progressive labor organizing in South Africa in the 1930s, these efforts were informed by attitudes of the South African Communist party. Except for explicitly Trotskyist organizations, this was true even in unions like the GWU, whose leader, Solly Sachs, was no longer a party member.

Left-wing discourse of the period depicted communism in the Soviet Union as the ideal model on issues concerning labor and women. International Women's Day became a standard occasion for celebration, and the struggle for women's equality was depicted as part of the overall fight against capitalism. A 1937 article entitled "Can Women Obtain Emancipation in a Capitalist State?" clearly articulated this position, although it was more perceptive than most in condemning drudgery and slavery in the home as well as in the workplace.

Home life without drudgery and the subjection of the woman and mother should be the slogan of the call for woman's emancipation, and such can only be obtained by the complete economic equality of women with men.[88]

The focus on unions with large numbers of women in the late 1930s was not always a major concern of the South African Communist party, however. In an article discussing International Women's Day in 1935, *Umsebenzi* chastized:

Unfortunately in South Africa the Communist Party has neglected to work among women and no demonstration or meetings of any sort were held here. The Party must learn from this failure and must endeavor to set up special organisations for drawing the women into the struggle.[89]

The demands put forth by the Political Bureau the following year rectified this omission, under a program paternalistically dubbed "Protection of Mothers and Children." They included crèches for working mothers and leave with full pay one month before and two months after confinement. Equal pay for equal work was listed as a theoretical goal; but as an "immediate practical measure" a three-pound-per-week minimum wage for all female workers in commerce and industry was suggested—comparable to the ten-shilling-per-day minimum for unskilled Europeans and double the five shillings proposed for black workers.[90] Rather strangely, by October the Draft Program of Demands for a planned United Front conference had reduced the amount for women to a minimum wage of thirty shillings a week, rising after three years to three pounds.

But during the 1930s it was the Transvaal Garment Workers' Union that sought most deliberately to reshape the consciousness of white working-class women to encourage a sense of class loyalty. When South African fascist organizations began a campaign to win over workers to their nationalist agenda, the union waged a counter-attack. Seeking to reformulate Afrikaner identity in a new, class-oriented fashion also meant an effort to transform the racial superiority that most young Afrikaner women had learned from an early age.

The effort to create a class-conscious union membership took many forms, all of which expressed the conviction that trade unionism and politics were inseparable. Sachs summed up these strategies in a report on his organizing trip to Durban and Cape Town in 1935. Describing the work there as only beginning, he elaborated:

We have the recruits, and we must now turn them into class-conscious, loyal and disciplined soldiers, by propaganda and agitation; by building up a cadre of leaders, shop stewards, voluntary helpers, a properly functioning Central Committee, and, above all, by protecting the interests of the workers.[91]

The union worked toward this goal partly by its practical and successful advocacy of workers' interests, both inside the factories and in the larger political community. By the late 1930s the Transvaal garment workers were the highest paid female workers in industry. But leaders also helped to mold a sense of both national and international working-class unity by encouraging participation in annual May Day demonstrations, sending prominent women on trips to Russia sponsored by the Friends of the Soviet Union, and by publishing articles in the union newspaper, the *Garment Worker*, expressing a pro-Soviet, antifascist stance.[92] Women from the GWU also organized mass rallies against fascism and Nazism and sought to create and transmit a specifically working-class Afrikaner identity. During the Voortrekker Centenary Celebration of 1938, a dramatic mass reenactment of the Great Trek, garment workers donned bonnets and long skirts and took part explicitly as union members.[93] In response to nationalist attacks, they formed a cadre of union guards to protect their meetings. Parading at demonstrations in a military fashion in blue and white uniforms,[94] their presence contributed to a sense of strength and solidarity.

The union's political efforts also extended into educational and cultural activities that effectively encouraged these young women to build their lives around union-related pursuits. Even sports teams, ostensibly apolitical, contributed to creating a working-class culture that integrated work and leisure. Through lectures on working-class history and contemporary issues, pamphlets on trade unionism, and well-used libraries in several different centers, the GWU leaders effectively conveyed their political vision to large numbers of women. The newspaper, political meetings, and other events gave members the opportunity to express these insights. They wrote plays and poems, often didactic, that spoke of their struggles in the workplace and at home and portrayed the fight against misery and poverty and the tension in families when men were forced to depend on women's wages. "Die Offerhande" (The Sacrifice), a play published and produced in the early 1940s, indicts capitalism as a rotten, exploitative system and lauds the new nonoppressive government of workers and farmers in the Soviet Union. At strikes and rallies, women not only sang familiar left-wing songs like the "International" and the "Red Flag" translated into Afrikaans, but they composed their own lyrics as well, condemning scabs who "smell of rotten fish," seeking unity against "slavery and fascist law," and urging women to fight for national progress.[95]

As part of the same antifascist effort, Johanna Cornelius and other leaders addressed numerous meetings in Johannesburg, Pretoria, Vereeniging, and other towns in the Western Transvaal, Natal, and the Orange Free State. Cornelius castigated the Nazis in South Africa as "a vicious crowd" who broke up antifascist meetings with bicycle chains, knives, and guns. These "Hitler agents" gathered support by labeling their adversaries "communists," "kaffir boeties" and "agents for the Jews." Reflecting on some of the successes in these campaigns, she recalled:

> Farmers used to arrive at these meetings on horse carts, bringing their whips and threatening to chase out the "communists." Invariably we found the farmers very honest, straight-forward people and once given an opportunity of hearing our version they, more often than not, announced that they would not use the whip on us, but in defense of us.
>
> At one meeting a farmer tore the black shirt off his back and said that he was given the shirt by the black shirt leaders and he sincerely believed that Hitler was the saviour of the people, but since listening to us, he would not wear it on his back although he had no other shirt in his possession.[96]

Johanna Cornelius later admitted the importance of the union in challenging the racial and ethnic exclusivism of her background: "It took me years," she observed, "to get used to the notion that even the English—let alone the natives—were human beings."[97] Only through a deliberate effort, inaugurated by Sachs but soon taken up by many Afrikaner women, were Cornelius and others like her able to transcend the racial attitudes of their past.

Nationalist attacks on the union from the late 1930s onward formed part of a carefully orchestrated campaign to keep the Afrikaner working class within the nationalist fold, fighting the danger of "contamination" with ideas of class consciousness that might threaten the entire racial (and class) order in South Africa. The GWU and associated unions were natural targets, as militantly progressive groups often with visible Jewish involvement and leadership. The prospect of Afrikaner women departing from the authority of church and family seemed particularly threatening. Indeed, one of the cultural groups formed to intervene in the struggle with the GWU was composed of clergymen anxious to prevent the "spiritual enslavement" of women workers.[98] When Bettie du Toit tried to organize women working in textile factories in the "sleepy little village" of Huguenot in 1938, an alliance of nationalist groups and the Dutch Reformed Church forced her out of her job and out of the women's hostel at Paarl. During her absence one weekend, placards in the streets and predikants in their pulpits condemned the "terrible Communist viper" that had intruded on the community; a search of her room revealing a letter from a black friend discussing African nationalism had led to accusations that she believed in free love and intermarriage, both anathema to these self-designated upstanding citizens. Although many "ordinary Afrikaner working women" objected to this politicization of the church, "the pressure from church and parents was too strong for the girls to resist."[99]

In struggling against such attacks the GWU tried to use the symbols of Afrikaner nationalism for its own purposes, developing a counter notion of what one speaker called "healthy Nationalist aspirations": nationalist loyalties associated with the working class rather than with exploitative capitalist interests. This idea was articulated in varied public formats. Addressing a mass meeting in the 1930s, Johanna Cornelius urged:

> As workers we must fight against all capitalists whatever their nationality may be, and we must not allow our ranks to be broken by the filthy racial propaganda of Greyshirts.[100]

A flyer some years later expressed a similar sentiment:

> We have no quarrel with the decent, honest Nationalists. Our quarrel is only with the rich land-owners, financiers, estate agents, etc. who are exploiting the noble Afrikaner traditions for their own selfish ends.[101]

Placing greater emphasis on the positive attachment to her culture, an unidentified woman worker recorded: "I too love our culture, our traditions, our language, but above all my fellow Afrikaner workers, and I refuse to hate people, merely because they belong to another race or speak another language." She added, "I consider myself a much better Afrikaner than all those learned people who deplore so much, but do not lift a finger to improve our life."[102]

When union leaders were attacked internally, they received the overwhelming support of the membership. Such loyalty was probably as much a product of the GWU's practical achievements as of its success in shifting the content of nationalist consciousness. In the late 1930s, it was also related to the low level of interest that the "convoluted formulations" of nationalist groups had managed to generate.[103] Nonetheless, the struggle between the progressive unions and nationalist groups to formulate a nationalist discourse with which working-class Afrikaner women could identify was a central issue of the late 1930s. In the 1940s and 1950s this competition intensified.

Feminism formed another potential body of discourse around which women might have been organized in the 1930s. The South African feminist tradition was remarkably weak, however. Whatever the debates in European and American history over the extent of working-class participation in the struggle for the vote, in South Africa the women's suffrage movement, which won the vote in 1930, was manifestly white and middle class.[104] Furthermore, the virtual universality of domestic labor has given middle-class and many working-class white women in South Africa respite from the household chores that remain a critical feminist issue. Instead, the discourse on women, and the form of the GWU appeal to women workers, came from the socialist-feminist position developed in Europe in the late nineteenth century, most notably in the writings of Engels, and further elaborated in the course of the Russian Revolution. Through

the relatively close contacts between South African and Soviet communists, and through trade unionists like Ray Alexander and Katie Silpert,
who grew up in proximity to the ideas about gender prominent after 1917,
this socialist heritage became an integral part of labor movement perspectives on gender in South Africa.

In this spirit, trade union appeals to workers as women were intended
to solidify their class consciousness rather than to foster any independent
feminist solidarity. Articulating the GWU position on women's issues, a
1936 article by Sachs espoused strong theoretical support for women's
rights, but went on to attack bourgeois women's organizations for con-
centrating on the rights of wealthy and middle-class women and for ignoring such concerns as low wages, substandard housing, government
callousness toward expectant mothers, and the absence of unemployment
and health insurance for working women.[105] In organizing millinery, sweet,
and tobacco workers and in founding the Federation of Women Workers,
the GWU sought to attack the problems that other women's groups had
ignored.

Another element of the effort to mobilize women focused on changing
their self-image as factory workers and encouraging greater public respect
for them. Pollak related a conversation with "an experienced trade unionist" who had justified lower pay for women than for men because women
did not expect equality. Comments she reported from women workers
connected their low economic expectations with low self-esteem:

Ach, I'm only a woman, my work isn't worth more to the boss.

I'm getting as much as a woman can expect to get.

He's a man and ought to get more than me. [106]

In an effort to alter such attitudes, the *Garment Worker* printed letters that
encouraged women to respect themselves and to demand respect from
others.[107]

Women's entry into industrial labor drew them into social relationships
new to them and, in some respects, novel in South Africa. Previously,
even relatively poor white women had little regular contact with black
men not in subordinate positions. In some factories, however, they worked
in close contact with each other, if not always side by side. Providing
much of the semiskilled and unskilled labor in secondary industry, the
two groups were not set far apart in either status or pay. The structural
gap between both of them and skilled white men was far greater than
that between them. The division between white men and other workers
intensified during the latter half of the 1930s, as state-sponsored jobs for
Afrikaner men proliferated, part of an effort to guarantee their place among
skilled, relatively well-paid workers. Between white and coloured women
the division was either nonexistent or very slight indeed. Although some

factories separated white and coloured operatives or tried to maintain a racially exclusive labor force, where the two did work together, it was usually at similar or identical jobs and pay scales.

While Afrikaner nationalist groups occasionally lashed out at straw men (such as the tiny number of Asian factory and shop owners who employed white women), they were correct in sensing the danger to their notions that absolute racial separation was necessary to preserve white identity and "civilization." For, exposed to other groups in a potentially cooperative setting, and on a basis of greater equality than ever before, there was a distinct possibility that a class analysis of South African society might come to make more sense to some of these women than a racial analysis. While their close ties to church and family as well as strong social prohibitions discouraged close personal friendships across lines of color, an active group of Afrikaner women (whose numbers are difficult to determine) came to take a political stance unique for their community. Particularly shocking because these ideas and actions came from women, the response of female trade unionists to the conditions of the 1930s represented a serious threat to conservative patriarchical control over Afrikaner womanhood. Changing social and economic conditions in the 1940s and 1950s would challenge the strength of class-based attitudes among these women; but these transformations also produced a new generation of black activists with their own ideas on gender, class, and nationhood. As these women entered factory work, they brought to the experience their earlier traditions of solidarity, resistance, and mutual cooperation.

III
A New Working Class and the Challenge of Diversity

−7−

NIMBLE FINGERS AND KEEN EYESIGHT

Women in Wartime Production

Wartime conditions between 1939 and 1945 created new demands on an already expanding economy. Local industries turned to manufacturing artillery, munitions, uniforms, and military equipment in order to support the general Allied effort and to sustain South African troops in North Africa, Madagascar, and Italy. Since only white men could join combat units, they were more numerous than blacks among the 300,000 South Africans who joined the armed forces. Not surprisingly, the absence of so many skilled workers created enormous gaps in the labor force, which led to some changes in women's work. But by contrast with Europe and the United States, black men filled most of the occupational vacuum created by departing white soldiers.

The opportunities of wartime did lead a small number of white and coloured women into nontraditional jobs, however. Under conditions that epitomized their use as a "reserve army of labor," some found work in munitions factories. Women's entry into these jobs, like that of black men into semiskilled and skilled positions, created intense fear among white male trade unionists. Only through detailed negotiations that precisely defined women's wages and working conditions were these anxieties assuaged. The smaller number of women who entered other traditionally male jobs helped to fuel a general shortage of trained female labor that shifted the balance of class power to workers' advantage, particularly in the garment industry.[1]

In munitions factories the demands of military production led to new tensions between unions on the one hand and the state and manufacturers on the other. Although white craft unions sought to shape the use of female labor so as not to threaten existing gender or racial boundaries, the pressures of war gave the state a temporary stake in challenging these established relationships in order to fill military quotas. Companies short of workers were likewise eager to hire women in formerly male jobs. And, to the continuing distress of the unions, they had reason to dilute this work whenever possible in order to keep it classified as unskilled or semi-skilled. Once deskilling was accepted, employers were able to reap additional benefits by further restructuring the labor process, often using women as a pretext for mechanization.[2] Ironically, perhaps, in order to protect their own interests during the war, unions that were bastions of white male working-class power ended by creating the first officially recognized female trade union in the country.

The wartime experience highlights significant aspects of the relationship between race, class, and gender under emergency conditions. Both the state and industry were willing, when it suited their interests, to press for a reshaping of gender restrictions in the labor force. Indeed, gender, during the war, was perhaps incidental to the critical task of eroding craft privilege in order to accommodate new groups of workers. But, as engineering workers defended their position, gender became virtually a surrogate for race. Lurking behind the small number of women whom the industry absorbed under explicitly temporary conditions, established workers and their unions saw a larger threat to wage standards from black men. Thus, while the women (primarily white) who were hired as "emergency workers" struggled to be recognized as equals, powerful forces conspired to keep them in a marginal position from which they could easily be ousted when the conflict ended. These forces included traditional attitudes toward appropriate female roles, the desire of industry and the state to discount the cost of women's labor, and fears of setting a precedent for equality between established craft workers and newcomers from hitherto disadvantaged groups.

Economists who sought the most rational means to fulfill South Africa's wartime requirements were acutely aware of the impediments of gender and race. Writing on full employment in 1942, R. J. Randall observed: "Any extensive transfers of women workers to industrial occupations will be opposed by the male workers on the grounds, not unjustified, that many of the women so transferred will not be willing to resume their old tasks at the end of the war, while the relatively low wages generally paid to women will make employers very willing to retain them."[3] Also concerned about a shortage of workers, he described the war effort as "only a shadow" of what it might be "if full advantage were taken of Native labour."[4]

The economic growth following the Depression continued during the war; between 1939 and 1945 the value of manufacturing output rose by 116 percent. With over 300,000 men conscripted into the army, nearly two thirds of them white, an acute shortage of skilled labor developed, necessitating the entry of new groups into the industrial labor force. Thus, from 1938–39 to 1944–45, while the industrial workforce grew by 53 percent, only 19,000 of the 125,000 new workers were white, and a significant number of the whites were women. As in World War I, the cut-off of competing overseas imports led to an increase in the local manufacture of consumer goods.[5] Wartime production also stimulated a move toward increased mass production techniques and job dilution in critical industries like metals and engineering, shifts facilitated by state intervention and resisted whenever possible by existing craft unions.[6]

Given the South African political climate, however, the wartime boom produced difficulties as well as benefits. Inflationary pressures increased the retail price index by 32 percent, exacerbating the problems of depressed black wages and of official lack of concern for the housing needs of the black families flooding the cities. Clustering in make-shift shantytowns for lack of more substantial shelter, African squatters formed a volatile political force during the early years of the 1940s. A ban on strikes by black workers under War Measure 145 of 1942 and the low level of dependents' allowances for the families of African soldiers also contributed to economic hardship. Furthermore, the continued hostility of the white craft unions to training black men helped to keep their wages abysmally low, to keep most blacks in menial jobs, and to create other economic difficulties: a reduction in the supply of civilian goods, a scarcity of material required for the military, and a continuing shortage of skilled workers.[7] Nonetheless, despite these impediments (or perhaps because of them), a powerful and militant black trade union movement developed during the war, leading to a brief period (from 1942 to 1945) in which the black-white wage differential actually closed slightly.[8]

While for Africans, both women and men, the war initiated long-term shifts in patterns of employment and political activity, for white women workers the second World War was but a temporary episode. From the beginning of the conflict, one area of the economy pulled in white women almost immediately: munitions manufacturing. Acknowledging the need for their labor, the Director of Technical Production under the Director-General of War Supplies noted in 1941, "The only immediate source of white labour remaining for munitions production is women, and it will be the women of the country on whom a large portion of the burden of munitions manufacture must inevitably fall. . . ."[9]

Yet the employment of female labor in munitions work raised complex political issues. The *Guardian* interpreted the shortage of skilled workers and the consequent need to dilute and intensify labor to meet emergency needs as a direct result of the past failures of government and trade unions. Had they allowed "non-European" workers to acquire industrial training and to perform skilled jobs, an ample number of workers would be available.[10] But even the employment of white women, a transgression of gender boundaries if not of racial barriers, was allowed by the trade unions only under strictly defined conditions.

In March 1941, representatives of the Mechanic Unions' Joint Committee and the Gold Producers' Committee met to arrange mutually suitable terms for the utilization of emergency female labor. Committee members agreed to allow such labor "for the duration of the war only," provided that the women not perform any "normal mine work or skilled work," and that they be excluded from the closed shop agreement. Hourly rates of pay were carefully defined and women's freedom of movement was limited to prevent them from changing jobs in search of higher wages.[11]

Prior to this agreement, the issue of female labor had caused considerable controversy between the unions and employers. In November 1940 G. H. Beatty, representing the mining industry, wrote of his frustration in trying to reach an agreement with the Engineering Union. While the union was insisting on equal wages for female and male "dilutees," (starting at 2s. 1d. per hour and rising to 2s. 4d. by the third three month period), he deemed this demand "absurd."[12] Correspondence in late 1940 and early 1941 conveyed an air of tension, as representatives of the Chamber of Mines accused the unions of bad faith for retreating from an earlier decision of the Joint Committee on the principle of employing female labor; the Amalgamated Engineering Union challenged their right to employ women in the absence of an agreement on their wages and working conditions.[13]

The March meeting did not settle all the issues between the engineering union and the employers of female munitions workers. Specific types of operations sometimes came under the scrutiny of union committees based on requests from employers. While union officials decided to allow women to use specific machines not necessarily envisaged in the original agreement (cylindrical and surface grinders, shapers, and precision measuring instruments), they insisted that those using these machines or tools at the Central Ordnance Factory be paid the same rates as male emergency workers on journeymen's work and, once again, that certain strict conditions be met: that they be employed "on machines being used for repetition work only" and not on assembling work, or on "jobbing work of a non-repetitive character" and "that no woman will be employed when a skilled man is available."[14] Thus, not only were men to be protected from possible undercutting by female labor, but the women involved were to acquire the minimum possible exposure to skilled operations.

As the war continued, however, and the need to increase munitions production intensified, the union was forced to become more flexible in its attitude toward skilled work and was compelled to argue for the principle of equal pay for equal work in order to protect its own rates of remuneration. By 1942, recognizing that the country lacked a sufficient number of artisans to fuel the war effort, the union was willing to broaden the work that women would be allowed to do, but expected them to be paid at wages "commensurate with the work upon which they are engaged." These conditions were defined quite stringently: "In any cases in which women carry out the entire job of a mechanic without special assistance, guidance or supervision, the standard basic rate applicable to skilled mechanics who would normally perform the work should apply." Confident that these conditions would be met, the union secretary was even willing to admit to an argument based on principle rather than on expediency, observing that the wartime emergency had proved "in some cases" the equal efficiency of female labor. "Therefore differential treatment on the grounds of sex is not countenanced by the Amalgamated Engineering Union."[15]

Despite theoretical accord between manufacturers and the union, the latter was vigilant in policing conditions in individual establishments to insure that its prerogatives were not being violated. In October 1942 the Amalgamated Engineering Union complained to the Transvaal Chamber of Mines about the situation at Modderfontein East Gold Mine, where a woman had been transferred from the munitions shop to the main machine shop, displacing a male apprentice. The letter of complaint noted in particular the presence of some eighteen apprentices who might have filled any skilled labor shortage in the main shop.[16]

As the need for labor power intensified, government officials, in conjunction with manufacturers, took the offensive, making every effort to stretch the categories of work that women were allowed to perform. In November 1942 A. C. Payne, representing the Controller of Industrial Man Power in Pretoria, met with East Rand Engineering and with the head of the Moulders' Association to discuss allowing women to perform the journeyman's job of light core-making. Using women in this largely automatic work, in which he felt they could be as productive as men, would free trained moulders for more difficult work.[17] Indeed, although the details of this redefinition continued to be subject to negotiation, the principle already had been conceded in Government Notice No. 979 of May 29, 1942, which allowed companies to apply for permission to engage female emergency workers in journeymen's occupations.[18]

Despite stringent regulations concerning the employment of women, some firms openly violated them by training women in a wider range of operations than the agreements specified. Inspectors at the New State Areas Mine in Springs, for example, found two women who received an hour of daily instruction in arc welding without permission from either the union or the Controller of Industrial Man Power.[19] Other firms hired women without authorization, forcing the office of the Controller of Industrial Man Power to insist on written confirmation of its decisions to be sure that firms did not exceed their quotas and that they paid women in accordance with the operations to be performed.[20] Women's pay remained a controversial issue, however, and many companies and mines persisted in classifying their labor as unskilled and paying them accordingly, even when the jobs they were doing should have merited higher wages.[21]

The shortage of skilled labor also led to the intensification of work. Arguing that the absence of suitable safe accommodation for women workers left them short-handed, a Johannesburg firm manufacturing air-craft bombs applied in June 1942 for permission to increase the work day of eight female emergency workers from forty-eight hours to fifty-six hours a week. The move was ostensibly temporary, pending the completion of a new workshop that would add another twenty-eight women to the labor force. The Controller of Industrial Man Power immediately approved the request and a similar one from West Rand Engineering Works Limited.[22]

Not all authorities accepted the temporary nature of women's new positions, however. To some engineering experts, wartime conditions offered the opportunity to train women in permanent occupations "more appropriate to them than to men." For cleaning and reassembling telephones and for repairing smaller machine tools, women's "nimble fingers and keen eyesight" made them ideal candidates.[23]

Wartime needs fostered close cooperation between the state and capital, with officials paying close attention to how they might aid private employers in meeting their labor requirements. Surplus trainees from the Central Ordnance Factory (Cofac) were made available to private employers through the Controller of Industrial Man Power.[24] Labor officials also tried to facilitate the use of women wherever they might be substituted for men. Writing of a box factory in Pretoria in 1942, an employee in the Office of the Director General of War Supplies suggested that women might be hired on a number of "light and simple operations." He sought advice from the Secretary of Labour because of the firm's impression that it was prohibited from using women in woodworking.[25]

Not every area of the country was found equally amenable to the blurring of gender boundaries in employment. In addition to considerations of "skill," racial issues might create new sets of concerns. Writing from Durban, for example, the Personal Representative of the Controller of Industrial Man Power judged the engineering industry there unsuitable for expanding the number of female workers in wartime production. Much of the work was not of a repetitive nature and, furthermore, employing women raised problems in providing rest rooms and lavatories as well as in the presumed need for racial segregation.[26]

Available figures on the number of women who entered the engineering industry vary according to the number of centers included. Returns for April 1943 counted a total of 3,113 workers, excluding Pretoria, Bloemfontein, and Durban. By far the largest number according to these statistics was the 2,630 women working in Johannesburg.[27] By December 1943 a more complete count showed 6,457 such employees; 4,909 white and 1,548 coloured. Their geographical concentration was substantial: the coloured women all in Kimberley, over half of the white women on the Witwatersrand, one-third in Pretoria, and seven percent in Cape Town. Durban, Bloemfontein, Port Elizabeth, and East London shared the remaining workers. The most substantial increase during this six-month period came in Kimberley, where the number of colored females expanded from twenty-one to 1,548.[28] By the middle and end of 1944, the total figures seem to have stabilized at a monthly average of 3,412 from June through September.[29]

Labor officials at this time held firm, if sometimes opposing ideas on the appropriateness of particular jobs for women of different ages. For the sedentary job of overhauling, cleaning, and reassembling old telephones, the Controller of Industrial Man Power judged that elderly women would be more suitable than their younger counterparts. He foresaw telephone repair jobs as a possible means to absorb the three hundred women then registered for factory work who were judged too old for munitions production. He cautioned, however, that their need to employ domestic labor at home would make it impossible for them to accept the wages of 6s. 6d. per day that the Braamfontein Workshop was proposing.[30] The Chief Engineer at the workshop disagreed, arguing that because these jobs provided training for permanent careers, older women would be unsuitable.[31]

The ban on strikes among African workers represented one of the most stringent controls on labor under wartime conditions. Yet, in war-related industries such as engineering, the state also had other wide-ranging powers: to prohibit any individual or class of individuals from leaving a controlled industry, to transfer and dismiss workers, to decide any dispute with an employer, and to regulate wages and working conditions.[32] This strict regulation notwithstanding, full employment and inflation provided an environment conducive to the development of new trade unions.[33] Beneficiaries of the heightened organizing campaigns included not only the substantial numbers of new black industrial workers, but also the women involved in emergency work.

The common wartime policy of extending working hours, speeding up production, and intensifying labor to compensate for the shortage of skilled workers was a common source of grievance. During June 1942, for example, Barratt and Pillans fired all twelve of the female emergency workers in the Munitions Machine Shop for repeated absence from work (ranging from eight to forty-nine days) and for refusing to follow instructions. The Managing Director explained to the Industrial Council for the Iron and Steel Manufacturing and Engineering Industry:

> The Superintendent, Munitions Department, had instructions from me to particularly speed-up production during the week 10th to 16th instant and, instead of the women workers coming to his assistance, they neglected their duties by absenting themselves from work for reasons best known to themselves, thereby disorganising the arrangement of shifts resulting in serious loss of production.[34]

The speed-up, according to his figures, was dramatic, raising the number of bombs produced monthly from 14,225 to 35,600.

Though the formation of a union for women engineering workers might help to alleviate such pressures, women's entry into formerly male jobs presented the skilled trade union movement with a dilemma: either support the concept of equal pay for equal work, or face the possibility of displacement. Those who mulled over this question were ultimately less concerned about the small number of white women likely to remain permanently in steadfastly male industries than about what they perceived as a potential onslaught of black men into their racially exclusive sanctuary.

Unions' general political orientation and the skill level of the workers they represented dictated their responses to this predicament. At the Annual Conference of the South African Trades and Labour Council (SATLC) in April 1942, Katie Kagan, secretary of the progressive National Union of Distributive Workers (an increasingly deskilled, female occupation), proposed a motion calling on the government to grant democratic rights and liberties to the whole working class. She warned that without adopting the principle of equal pay for equal work, women would cut men out of their jobs when they returned from the front. Countering her motion, Mr. Payne of the Amalgamated Engineering Union argued that to extend such logic to "the Bantus" was "the expectation of madmen."[35] Narrowing his comments to the issue of gender, Mr. J. J. Venter, president of the South African Council of Transport Workers, warned of the "menace" that female labor in transport presented because of the danger of wage dilution. He did not oppose women's employment, but favored paying them equal wages.[36]

The concern of these unions with the issue of displacement is not surprising. For, in addition to their work in engineering plants manufacturing war equipment, women also assumed some male positions in shops and transport. As early as 1939, women were being trained as bus drivers and conductors in anticipation of the exodus of large numbers of men to active military service.[37] Women also became railway employees during the war.[38] In Pretoria, female bus conductors earned £3 10s. a week, compared with male salaries of seven pounds.[39] Shop workers faced similar differentials. One woman complained that she was replacing two men who each earned twenty-five pounds a month, while her labor merited only eleven pounds.[40] For unions and for the workers in them, these inequities represented both an injustice to the women and a threat to the wage standards of the men they replaced—yet another reminder of the way in which the segmented South African workforce continually threatened high-wage workers with displacement, while graphically reminding their low-wage counterparts that their labor was being exploited.

Responding to these challenging conditions, the Women Engineering Workers' Union mounted a sustained and successful effort to organize the female wartime workers. The initiative came not from the women themselves, however, but from the SATLC, which, in 1941, recommended that they be organized. Meeting together, the executive body of each member of the Joint Mechanics' Union (including engineers, electricians, moulders, and boilermakers) first agreed that each union should work with the women in its own particular trade. Following this decision, the Amalgamated Engineering Union, which would have been responsible for about 80 percent of the women, realized that its constitution would not permit female membership. As an alternative, the joint body charged the SATLC with forming a union specifically for emergency workers.[41] Thus, from its inception, the new union represented a protective effort on the part of craft workers.

Communication about the decision to create a women's union must have been slow, for two weeks later the secretary of the Pretoria District Trades and Labour Committee complained of his committee's "repeated unsuccessful attempts" to get the Joint Mechanics' Union to agree to organize women munition workers. He added that members were "greatly perturbed" that such a large body of workers remained unrepresented.[42]

By early February 1942, however, the confusion apparently was resolved. The Secretary of the SATLC wrote to the Amalgamated Engineering Union seeking financial support and stating the intention of organizing first at the Pretoria Mint, where a large number of women were employed on a permanent basis, and then expanding to other parts of the country.[43] Acknowledging the "paramount importance" of the effort, the engineering union contributed one hundred pounds, but with the proviso that the Mechanics Unions' Joint Executives be consulted on the organization's constitution.[44]

As the campaign proceded, the SATLC kept firm control over its initial efforts, instructing the newly hired organizer, Frances Engela, very precisely in what was expected of her. Hired for a period not exceeding three months at a salary of twenty pounds per month, she was to call a meeting of women working at the Pretoria Mint as soon as possible. Those who attended were instructed to pass a motion resolving to form a union called the Women Engineering Union.[45]

Engela, then living in Pretoria where she had been the local secretary-organizer of the National Union of Distributive Workers, had also, by 1944, become the only female member of the SATLC National Executive Committee. Although a colleague interviewed for the Labour party newspaper took care to describe her lucidity and cogent thinking, he was not adverse to emphasizing her "rare qualities" of brains and beauty. The reporter, clearly annoyed at Engela's refusal to be interviewed, could not restrain his jabs at women; her reluctance "cuts right across the prevailing idea that women are not adverse to publicity, and that they love to talk, especially about themselves."[46]

Despite the union's care to approach management tactfully, the Director of the Mint expressed reservations about the organization of his employees. He wrote to the SATLC in April to explain that since mint employees were public servants, arrangements were being made to have the Public Servants' Association represent the white women. He therefore advised Engela to confine her efforts to the coloured women at the Kimberley branch of the mint.[47]

An angry response from W. J. de Vries of the SATLC not only indicated that the Public Servants' Association had "no great desire" to accept these female employees, but accused the mint's administration of openly obstructing organizing efforts. He related Engela's complaint that a welfare officer at the mint, acting on instructions from the deputy director, had warned workers to keep away from her and had cautioned her to stay away from them. "The effect of this action has been to frighten some of the girls, and is being looked upon by us as nothing less than intimidation." Citing violations of the Industrial Conciliation Act of 1937, the letter ended with a threat to bring these incidents to the attention of the Minister of Labour and the Prime Minister if these acts could not be explained.[48]

These threats, coupled with intervention from the Labour Department and from "other [unnamed] influential people," accomplished their intended purpose. Within three weeks Engela had received regular access to employees and the assistance of several welfare officers, and more than seven hundred women had applied to become members of the union. Apparent interference from the Public Servants' Association also ceased when the group agreed to end its efforts to sign up mint employees as members.[49] Although the role of this association in the effort to block women's organizing is unclear, it seems that the management of the mint continued to prefer this presumably more compliant union.

By June 1942, the Women Engineering Workers' Union was planning to extend its organization to Kimberley, this time at the urging of the mint director who described the coloured women there as "anxious for an organisation." He expressed the fear that "if something is not done soon, I consider it likely that attempts by unauthorised bodies may be made to represent them."[50] Although he refrained from specifying these "unauthorised" groups, the comment suggests that, within a very short time, the women's union affiliated with the SATLC had come to occupy a safe position by comparison with the more politicized forces, perhaps connected with the Communist party, that might seek access to these workers.

Writing to a colleague in July, seeking help in the effort to organize in Kimberley, the Secretary of the SATLC summarized the success of the women's union up to that point: a membership of "well over 1,000," including most women in the engineering industry in Pretoria and in the large ordnance factories in Johannesburg.[51] Kimberley was then the only substantial center that remained unorganized.

Arriving in Kimberley shortly thereafter, on July 13, 1942, Engela faced a mixed response to her efforts. The management at the mint welcomed her this time, as did the members of the coloured Juvenile Affairs Board who "expressed their gratitude to the European element for this gesture of friendship, which would assist them in climbing the ladder of economic and industrial progress." Still deferential, these officials also emphasized their unwillingness to "go where they were unwanted."[52] Leaders of the Amalgamated Engineering Union, the Boilermakers, and the Engine Drivers were less enthusiastic, declining to speak at a public meeting of Engela's union because their head offices had not notified them of her arrival. Under these conditions they judged it imprudent to openly support the women's union. This rebuff may point to differences between the national unions and their local branches, or it may imply that, having created the women's union, the parent bodies expected behavior that they defined as properly submissive.

Engela, allowed open access to potential members, not only addressed the women at work, particularly during lunch breaks, but also approached the many families, usually newcomers from the country, whose members worked together at the mint. Visiting them in their homes, she tried to dispel any mistrust they might feel toward her efforts. Although she found that some urban women understood the value of trade unionism, her main difficulty lay in the "suspicion and antagonism" of coloured people toward Europeans, "who have in every way repressed and belittled their activities."[53] Under these conditions, Engela felt pleased at signing up 560 new members during her visit.

Her attempts to involve coloured women in the union were reflected in the composition of the union committee, elected at a mass meeting on July 21. Out of eleven members, nine were coloured and two white. Engela saw this heavy participation as a sign of her success, expressing confidence "that it is only a matter of time before the Europeans will realise the uselessness of their ill-founded prejudice."[54]

The optimism of Engela's final report did not fully reflect her feelings in the midst of the organizing campaign, however. On July 23 she wrote disparagingly to Mr. de Vries, criticizing the AEU for doing "everything in their power" to retard her work and lamenting the fact that the European women were "holding aloof" from the union out of active opposition to the idea of a union for coloured workers. Although many coloured women were suspicious, she felt that enrolling five hundred out of a potential eight hundred women (with another 150 anticipated before her departure), represented a significant achievement.[55]

Confirming Engela's perceptions about the hostility of some of the white craft unions, a supportive representative of the Typographical Union wrote to de Vries describing the AEU Joint Mechanics' Union officials as "hostile." Those who attended the first of her two mass meetings adopted a "strict say-nothing attitude." They declined to attend the second meeting altogether. The letter also noted the importance of speakers from the coloured community in convincing women to join the union.[56]

Because of the high proportion of coloured women among them, Kimberley workers were unrepresentative of the women hired during the war. Nonetheless, it is instructive to compare them with samples taken a decade earlier. With 40 percent of a survey of fifty-six emergency workers in Kimberley married, they represented a much higher proportion than was common among white women during the 1930s. This figure suggests a definite shift in attitudes toward the employment of married women under wartime conditions. But the high incidence among the married women of widows (43 percent) and of those without children (32 percent) identifies them as the categories of female workers most likely to enter munitions work during the war. Differing significantly from Pollak's sample of white women in Witwatersrand industries in the 1930s, the median age of widowed or divorced women in Kimberley was forty-six as opposed to thirty-three in the earlier study. The single women, by contrast, were not markedly different from those in Pollak's sample, with a median age of twenty.[57]

Engela's report conveyed the urgency of her organizing campaign because plans were then underway to expand the labor force to one thousand white women and two thousand coloured women within the next six months. To meet the housing needs of women from the countryside, the municipality was planning to build a hostel for eight hundred coloured women based, appropriately for the period, in military bungalows.[58] Partitioned off into six rooms sixteen feet by ten feet, each bungalow was expected to house two or three women who would share a wardrobe, a chest of drawers, and a dressing table; each was provided with a chair. The complex of twenty-three bungalows also included a separate bath house and lavatory, a dining room, hospital accommodation, and a recreation hall. While trees and lawns were to provide an atmosphere "conducive to restfulness and contentment," the military imagery of the period nonetheless crept into the report when the author speculated on how soon the first occupants would "assume duty."[59] Engela, although grateful to the authorities at the mint for facilitating her organizing efforts, did record the workers' concern about the cement roofs and concrete floors of the planned bungalows, which she, too, judged to be "unhealthy and unpleasant." Otherwise, with her usual conciliatory tone, she evaluated the scheme as "beyond reproach."[60]

Once organized, the union argued cogently for the interests of the women it represented, alleging that those with dependents in particular were being forced to make great sacrifices to assist the war effort because their wages were so low. A long "training" period also debased pay scales. While women did not reach the maximum wage until they had worked for six months, most jobs took only two to three months to learn. Furthermore, despite the high rate of inflation, only the women who were unmarried or widowed received a cost-of-living allowance. Other complaints echoed those of the women who had entered industry a decade earlier: wage differentials among women doing the same work, lack of payment for overtime work, filthy cloakroom facilities, outside water taps as the only washing facilities, backless stools at machines, lack of protective clothing (particularly rubber-top boots and boiler suits), lack of information on medical and burial funds, and inaccessible first-aid equipment administered by "abrupt and incivil" employees.[61]

Other complaints, framed in ways specific to these particular women, provide insight into their lives and work. The resentment against a weekly deduction of sixpence for a recreation fund "when in fact, most employees have neither the intention nor the inclination to participate in sport," suggests their high level of domestic responsibility, whether as mothers or as daughters of families with absent men. Remarks on holidays and complaints about inadequate and "chaotic" restaurant arrangements, both using the agreement for the engineering industry as their standard of comparison, suggested the union's determination to have its members viewed not as another group of ill-paid women, but as engineering workers who should be treated accordingly. When employers opened discussions of wages in 1943 by comparing scales at the mint with those in the garment, tobacco, and leather industries, the union protested that other engineering workers should be the appropriate standard of comparison.[62]

A complaint of "unfair discrimination" against old and proven workers based on the number of supervisory personnel (foremen, overseers, charge hands, and protection and welfare officers) appointed from outside, suggests a higher level of aspiration among these women than among their counterparts a decade earlier. The union charged that newcomers placed in these positions were not only unfamiliar with the work they were supervising, but, equally important, were "entirely ignorant" of the psychology of the South African women workers in the engineering trade. The union alleged: "A good deal of friction and ill-feeling have resulted between the workers and these officials who are definitely impudent and arrogant to a point of exasperation."[63]

Over a year later, many grievances remained unresolved. Wage calculations for those involved in piecework were both arbitrary and ridiculously low and a number of categories of work required upgrading in the opinion of the union: gaugers, telephonists, cloakroom attendants, and patrol gaugers and weighers. The latter employees, despite their responsibility for the efficiency and reliability of production, were ranked on the same level as kitchen assistants.[64]

Despite difficulties in achieving its objectives, the existence of the Women Engineering Workers' Union posed a challenge to the Amalgamated Engineering Union, whose exclusive policies had necessitated the formation of the first gender-based union in South African history to receive official recognition. During 1942, the same year that the WEWU began its intensive campaign, AEU members voted in favor of admitting women to the union. Commenting on the decision, the union's journal observed: "We shall base our policy on the principle of equality—not only in respect of equal pay for equal work, but in respect of the union organisation too."[65]

By the time of this decision, arrived at only "slowly and reluctantly," the women's union already had expanded to all the major centers in which female munitions workers were employed, apart from Cape Town. Only here, where the number of women in the industry was comparatively low, was there any opportunity to implement the new policy. On June 14, 1943, a number of women were initiated into the Cape Town branch. They apparently did not feel altogether comfortable among their new colleagues, however. The union reported that, despite the wishes of local members to elect one of the women onto the district committee, they were "too bashful to come forward."[66]

As the controversies over women's employment in munitions factories and over the formation of a specifically female union subsided, the documentation on women wartime workers grows sparse. If the WEWU kept independent records apart from those retained by the SATLC, they remain to be located. These women only became an issue again during the period of demobilization, when munitions plants closed down and other factories ceased to produce armaments. Because of the temporary nature of their work, agreed upon with the craft unions at the beginning of the war, numerous women found themselves unemployed. Those residing in hostels faced not only loss of work, but loss of housing, as the wartime facilities were vacated and their occupants sent home. The Department of Labour did not view these jobless women as a problem, however. Officials noted only that the large number who preferred to return home rather than seeking employment in other factories had left a scarcity of "the right type of worker," particularly in the clothing industry.[67]

Thus, in accord with their designation as "emergency workers," the story of women employed in munitions factories occupies only a brief chapter in the history of women's work in South Africa. These women were very much a "reserve army of labor," drawn into new forms of production to meet the country's wartime requirements and then shunted back home when overt hostilities ceased. Despite their successful adaptation to new kinds of labor and their continuing struggle for recognition as engineering workers, few shifts occurred in prevailing stereotypes about women's capabilities. Indeed, the reports of labor officials abound with traditional assumptions about the kind of work suitable for them, and trade unions remained extremely protective of skilled jobs.

Labor officials would have channeled some of these women into other factory jobs. But for the white women most numerous in emergency war work, postwar employment patterns led in other directions. If some women did penetrate the long-standing gender-based barriers of the craft unions, they also understood at the outset that their elevation to new forms of labor would be brief. Furthermore, as the female workforce began to shift during and after the war, only a reduction of barriers based on race as well as on gender would have admitted the women destined to assume most new industrial jobs in the coming decades. For, if some aspects of women's labor during the early 1940s proved impermanent, others heralded significant changes in women's position both as industrial workers and as trade unionists.

Demonstration in Johannesburg to protest the banning of Solly Sachs in 1952. Johanna Cornelius and Sachs in the lead. Archives, Garment Workers Union.

Scene from 1952 demonstration in Johannesburg. Archives, Garment Workers Union.

Hetty du Preez, organizer, Garment Workers Union, No. 2 Branch.
International Defence and Aid Fund for Southern Africa.

Card issued by the Food and Canning Workers Union in the early 1940s. Archives, Food and Canning Workers Union.

Officials of the Food and Canning Workers Union (1952), left to right, Bettie du Toit, Oscar Mpetha, Ray Alexander, Maria Williams, and David Jantjies. International Defence and Aid Fund for Southern Africa.

Frances Baard, Secretary, African Food and Canning Workers Union, Port Elizabeth. International Defence and Aid Fund for Southern Africa/Eli Weinberg.

COSATU

Women and the Living Wage Campaign

Cover of pamphlet issued by COSATU, the Congress of South African Trade Unions in the late 1980s. Popular History Trust, Harare, Zimbabwe.

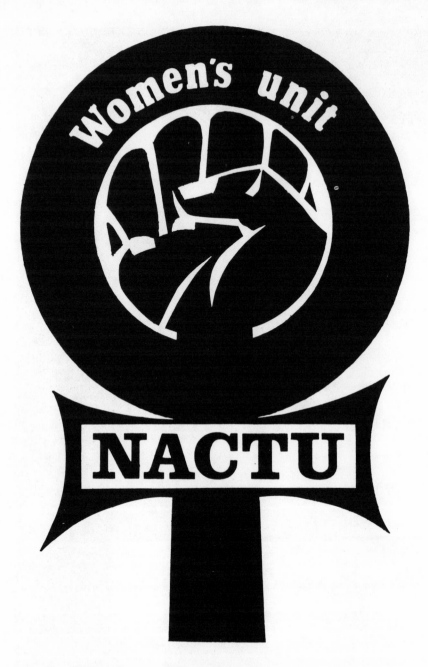

Cover of pamphlet issued by NACTU, the National Council of Trade Unions, in the late 1980s. Popular History Trust, Harare, Zimbabwe.

–8–

A NEW WORKING CLASS, 1940–1960

Many aspects of the political economy of South Africa changed sharply between 1940 and 1960. Wartime economic growth continued in the post-war years, partly as a result of expanded overseas investment in industrial production. With new sources of capital came new pressures on manufacturers to modernize equipment and to rationalize the labor process following the latest techniques of overseas management. As this philosophy impinged upon South African manufacturers through such bodies as the Board of Trade and Industry, increased mechanization and more efficient use of labor became significant criteria for evaluating local production. The new industrial climate had varying influence on the sectors of the economy that employed women.

In the wartime and postwar searches for cheap labor, black men came to supply the vast majority of new workers in secondary industry, following a trend that began in the late 1930s. The "poor white problem" was now substantially solved as a result of policies enacted by a unified white political bloc during the 1930s. The Fusion government (merging the South African party and the National party), which came into being during 1933 and 1934, created new work for Afrikaner men in the post-Depression years; they now occupied skilled jobs in industry and were moving into positions in trade, commerce, and the professions. Under these improved circumstances, young Afrikaner women could be more selective and began to seek economic opportunities in higher-status areas of the economy. As the earlier white ambivalence toward women's factory work reasserted itself, black women, first drawn into industry in small numbers during the war, moved into the openings they left. In the Transvaal, these black women joined increasing numbers of coloured women, previously employed there only in small numbers. At the Cape, coloured women continued to predominate in the clothing industry and also occupied an important position in the rapidly expanding food processing plants that flourished during the war. In textile production, however, postwar expansion led to a shift in the gender composition of the workforce, as black men rather than black women filled most of the demand for cheap labor.

Although most industrial employers still showed little interest in African women, these changing labor market patterns influenced them indirectly nonetheless. As black men were swept into manufacturing jobs, they vacated domestic occupations in droves, leaving these ill-paid positions primarily to women. The drawbacks of this work were manifest; but household labor provided access to housing in overcrowded cities where legal accommodation was scarce and offered young women from the countryside a temporary "bridging occupation" between school and marriage. Furthermore, the burgeoning urban population created new demands for food and clothing that women could fill on a casual basis. Among those who took on the challenges of survival in the cities were an increasing number of single women and widows, whom choice or circumstances had freed from rural patriarchal norms and constraints.

Closely entwined with these economic developments were the political issues raised by the increased number of black women and children who had moved to the cities.[1] The postwar period presented South African policy makers with two possible options: either to accept the trend toward higher levels of black urbanization and to create conditions in which families could live comfortably and freely, or to advocate stricter controls over black residential and family life, interpreting any liberalization as a threat to white domination.

The Nationalist victory in 1948 indicated white majority support for the second alternative. Based on a broad Afrikaner alliance of farming and petty bourgeois interests, labor, and emerging capitalists, the National party was determined to design new policies to curb the growing black working-class presence in the cities. These measures had innumerable consequences for women. Most immediate and direct was the move to extend controls over African labor and mobility to women as well as to men, by forcing women to carry passes. But other policies were equally disastrous: the Group Areas Act, which pushed urban Africans into new ghettos more distant from white areas; increasingly restrictive laws regarding the movement of blacks, particularly women and children, into urban centers; new curbs on African membership in trade unions; and policies of industrial decentralization which, particularly in the garment industry, threatened the economic gains of all urban factory workers. Furthermore, the crackdown on political opposition that intensified after 1948 (particularly through the Suppression of Communism Act) deprived many predominantly female unions of experienced leadership and left numerous women labor activists either banned, banished, or imprisoned.

This political environment made efforts to organize across racial lines more hazardous. While some unions continued to make the effort, as they had during the war, others were daunted by the overwhelming obstacles to racial justice. During the 1950s such opposing attitudes and policies produced a deep and enduring split within the trade union movement.

Among women, then, the postwar era was the beginning of changes that accelerated more slowly than for men. Black women moved into industrial production only in small numbers in the period before 1960, and white women in industry, increasingly ill-paid and considered low-skilled, could not fall back on craft privileges to protect themselves from competition. For a brief period the position of the white women who remained in industrial jobs was more similar to that of their black female coworkers than to that of their white male kin. But the political and structural impediments to an alliance between the two groups of women were overwhelming: the black-white economic divide increased as Afrikaner families moved out of poverty and, from 1948 onward, as apartheid intensified the pressures on blacks of all class backgrounds. As racial oppression became the overwhelming political issue for black workers, the white trade union movement was increasingly split between those willing to oppose apartheid policies and those who chose the safer avenue of avoiding risky political confrontation in order to preserve the economic gains of the past. In a political and economic context dramatically different from that of the 1930s, working-class women of all races faced new sets of pressures and new choices; the politics of class, gender, and race assumed new meanings and new forms.

Although the large-scale movement of white women out of industrial production became most pronounced after World War II, it was apparent as early as the mid-1930s when Labour Department analysts observed that some young white women were refusing to accept factory employment, preferring jobs in shops, offices, and restaurants. These choices were producing a shortage of labor in Transvaal clothing factories.[2] By World War II, when thousands of factory workers took jobs in munitions plants or volunteered for the armed forces, few young Afrikaans-speaking women were entering the clothing industry. Many other women left factory work because, with their husbands' relatively high military wages, they no longer needed the supplementary income.[3] As the war progressed, women's actions continued to indicate that they valued marriage more than their jobs. Some quit with little notice when their husbands returned from active duty; others left to get married.[4]

Overall, however, wartime conditions imposed many hardships on white working-class women. Those who signed up for military service fared less well than white men. In the clothing industry, employers refused even to discuss paying enlisted female employees the allowances granted automatically to enlisted men.[5] Married women who continued in the labor force found their domestic work more onerous. High inflation levels and scarce consumer goods made shopping more difficult and time-consuming, domestic labor had grown scarcer and more expensive, and the system of distributing military allowances only at designated centers forced many women to skip work in order to collect their money. Under normal conditions women bore the primary responsibility for domestic labor and childcare; but the widespread absence of husbands must have intensified these obligations.[6]

As young white women turned to new occupations or left the paid workforce altogether, the ensuing labor shortage became a major preoccupation of manufacturers. As early as 1940, the Transvaal Clothing Manufacturers' Association (TCMA) urged its members to inform all employees who signed up for active service that they would be assured of their jobs when they returned.[7] As the scarcity of workers intensified during the following year, the organization sought the assistance of the Juvenile Affairs Board in locating available workers and began to consider such innovative strategies as advertising vacancies at bioscopes.[8]

The paucity of workers shifted the balance of class power in the industry, forcing many manufacturers to pay wages higher than those specified in the agreement with the union and offering trained women in particular the possibility of seeking work wherever the pay was best. Though the TCMA officially condemned the practice of "enticing" qualified women by offering them wage increases, members who engaged in such practices defended their actions and the Garment Workers' Union argued strongly in favor of workers' right to seek jobs with the highest possible wages. Nonetheless, in several cases, the TCMA executive committee decided that the woman concerned should be sent back to her former employer.[9] Despite dissension over the issue of enticement, and despite threats to dismiss offending employers from the association, the practice continued throughout the war, offering many women the possibility of gaining substantial pay increases.

The considerable energy that the TCMA exerted to hold down wages suggests that the women who remained as clothing workers benefited substantially from wartime conditions. In Germiston, for example, "wholesale increases" in some factories caused a wave of discontent to spread to neighboring establishments. Led by a shop steward, fifty women in a nearby factory requested equivalent wage hikes. Fearing this trend, and concerned to insure that increases would be rescinded after the war, the association approached the Controller of Man Power about making clothing a controlled industry.[10]

Workers in other factories were quick to take advantage of the favorable conditions. In April 1943, all the women employed at the Ideal Clothing Manufacturers in Johannesburg walked out during the afternoon tea break, returning the following day with a letter signed by a union official that listed the names of manufacturers prepared to increase wages. The owner's testimony to the TCMA executive committee demonstrated the balance of power quite clearly: unless the association could advise him of an alternative, he would be forced either to close down the factory or to grant the workers their request.[11] When a strike was imminent in late

April and early May of 1943, manufacturers chose the former option. Afterward, however, in a self-designated gesture of goodwill, they decided to pay employees for the three days that factories had been shut "as the employers did not really want the workers to suffer."[12]

The availability of so many jobs also gave women increased leverage in dealing with unpleasant working conditions. When Mr. Salamson, a factory owner, complained that four or five of his "expert girls" had quit after he had discovered them spoiling work, the chair of the TCMA was not particularly sympathetic. Reminding Mr. Salamson of the repeated complaints the Industrial Council had received about Mrs. Salamson, he urged that she be instructed to fire inadequate employees at once. But those who were good "should be treated decently, otherwise he must expect to lose them."[13]

The labor shortage also led to occasional support for welfare measures outside the factories, although such cooperation seemed contingent on relationships with the union. In 1940, for example, the TCMA agreed to donate £120 per year to the Factory Girls' Club in Germiston.[14] Yet a suggestion several months later for a project directly related to women's ability to work in the industry elicited a negative response. The association decided against donating money to build a crèche jointly with the union until such time as the GWU "showed cooperation on trivial matters."[15]

Manufacturers who judged the wartime scarcity of workers to be temporary were in error. Even after munitions work ceased, many unemployed women preferred returning to their homes rather than to industrial employment.[16] Immediately after the end of the war, footwear manufacturers in Port Elizabeth reported difficulties in attracting a sufficient number of European women workers. As elsewhere, women appeared unenthusiastic about working outside the home "now that their menfolk are returning from active service."[17] Footwear makers expressed the emerging postwar consensus about white women's employment: that factory jobs no longer appealed to them by comparison with work in commerce or in government offices. Lamenting this shift, shoe manufacturers saw two possible sources of new female employees: whites from country areas and "non-European girls," who preferred factory work to domestic service.[18] Intensely concerned with the issue of labor supply, the shoe industry hired researchers to study the causes of absenteeism as a means of utilizing existing workers more fully. Anxious employers now responded to women's problems for the first time, recommending increased crèche facilities to assist the child-care arrangements of married women.[19] Reflecting the rationalizing spirit of the times, the Council of Scientific and Industrial Research carried out "Cape Town's first major experiment in mass industrial aptitude testing" among five hundred coloured clothing workers in order to seek ways to employ them more efficiently.[20]

The labor shortage during the war provided numerous openings for successful class action on the part of white working women and created a climate favorable to cooperation among white and black workers, particularly in the sweet industry. GWU leaders still spearheaded organizing drives in efforts to establish new unions in tobacco plants and sweet factories with high levels of female employment. Working successively with Pauline Podbrey and Joey Fourie, they also sought to organize millinery workers at the Cape, once again confronting the company unionism of R. Stuart and the Garment Workers' Union of the Cape Peninsula.[21] Transvaal activists also formed an apparently short-lived Working Women's Federation, which sponsored a widely supported protest against increased tram fares in the city.[22] Workers' demands in the notoriously ill-paid tobacco plants included the basic staples of early union organizing: wage increases and union recognition, as well as a specifically war-related claim to the 5s.-per-week bonus that other workers were receiving. Representing a varied constituency, the Tobacco Workers' Union also took a strong stance on racial issues; seeking to include Africans in negotiated benefits and organizing demonstrations to demand equal war bonuses for all workers.[23]

One of the most heated struggles occurred in September 1940 in rural Rustenburg, where the United Tobacco Company paid wages substantially lower than those prevailing in Johannesburg. Led in a two-week strike by Johanna Cornelius, the Afrikaner women there faced police attacks and tear gas bombs.[24] A tribute to Cornelius two months later conveys the atmosphere of union functions of the time. As in the 1930s, they combined political speeches, didactic entertainment, and dancing, seamlessly intertwining Afrikaner symbols and traditions with those of an international working-class culture. The cultural segment of this particular meeting included a dance entitled "Revolution," which portrayed the "bitter struggles of the workers until they discover that their strength lies in their own hands" and use this strength to "attain Freedom." The program also featured recitations in Afrikaans and English, a tap dance, and singing, including a song composed for the occasion by several of the men present:

> When workers fight with all their might
> The rich will shake with fear,
> For the sun is setting on the bosses' night
> And workers' day is here.

Singing of the Transvaal anthem and the "Internationale" symbolically concluded the formal meeting. Afterward the workers danced to the music of a "Boer" orchestra.[25]

The Sweet Workers' Union, by 1941, remained "weak and ineffective," despite several years of organizing effort.[26] But the rising cost of living during the war supplied the impetus for a new surge of activity, leading in February 1943 to a strike in which Anna Scheepers was assaulted by a police sargeant in the course of struggles between picketers and police.[27] An interview with E. J. Burford, the secretary of the Sweet Workers' Union at the time of the strike, reveals the union's successful strategy for uniting the industry's racially diverse employees, but also the problems inherent in such an effort.[28] Sweet workers were divided equally between Afrikaner women and African men. Within a few months of organizing under Burford, about 80 percent of the women had joined the union, despite intense resistance from a predominantly "rotten bunch" of employers.

As a newcomer from England lacking prior experience of South Africa's intense racial divisions, Burford had first intended to organize the black and white workers into a single union. Once he became aware of the difficulties inherent in this strategy, he formed instead an African Sweet Workers' Union with its own organizer and worked diligently to keep the two groups on an equal footing. He later recalled, "I made it a point to organise them simultaneously and ensure constant regular co-ordination between the white and the black committees, meeting in the office at the same time."[29]

This joint activity continued during the 1943 strike, with no friction and no complaints from whites. Black and white committee members met daily to coordinate activity and to make decisions on such issues as strike pay and emergency allowances, and the women agreed that the Africans should receive their full wages as strike pay, although a shortage of funds meant that the white female workers received only half of their normal wages. Nightly marches to the City Hall steps reflected the separate collective identities of the groups: Burford at the head, the women in the front ranks, and the Africans at the rear. When conflict did occur between pickets and scabs at one factory, Ornstein's, the ensuing clashes with the police were intensified because many of the pickets were the wives or daughters of the policemen. Burford, returning to the factory after making fruitless efforts to deter the police, described the scene:

> The fight was still going on; it was bitter, and the girls were like furies tearing the policemen's clothes off of them and scratching them, and the cops were at a disadvantage because some were their wives and sisters and daughters; they [the police] were doing more injury to the men than they were to the women. Some even had their trousers torn off and their shirts ripped to pieces.[30]

As in some of the strikes in the late 1920s involving black men and white women, the Africans supported the action solidly, many of them, according to Burford, eating better during the strike (from donations of oranges, eggs, bread, meat, and other food) than they did in ordinary times. This high degree of solidarity undoubtedly contributed to the strike's success, which enabled the Johannesburg branch to revive other branches of the union in East London, Port Elizabeth, Cape Town, and Volksrust and, eventually, to form a national union. Burford concluded from this experience that "with proper leadership the black-white barrier could be broken down and a great measure of mutual understanding reached although the gulf was enormous." While he conceded that "things went back to their old ways," after the strike, remnants of cooperation remained. As of 1948, African workers were refusing to cross the picket lines of the registered union, and the latter was demanding equal wages for blacks and whites.[31] Burford probably was correct in stressing the importance of leadership; but the labor scarcity of wartime also may have contributed to the union's success in encouraging temporary cooperation across racial lines.

In the textile industry in the early 1940s, the climate for organizing was less favorable. Earlier animosities persisted and many white women continued to oppose unionization. Adversaries of the TWIU showered Anna Scheepers, Violet Friedland, and Jacoba Augustyn with eggs, tomatoes, and other missiles and then physically attacked them when they tried to hold a lunchtime meeting at Consolidated Textile Mills in 1941.[32] By contrast, Johannesburg flock workers, mostly African women, who earned as little as five shillings a week, readily came out on strike a year later when one hundred workers were fired for union organizing. Led by Louise Roussouw, they won a significant wage increase.[33]

If attitudes toward unions changed substantially in the postwar period, the shortage of white female workers did not. Garment manufacturers felt the shrinking labor pool particularly acutely. According to the Wage Board Report on the clothing industry in 1947:

> Owing to the shortage of European labour during the war and postwar years, girls have been finding work in spheres of employment more congenial to them than industry, and especially in the service trades. The result has been an almost complete absence of new European entrants into the trade, and the consequent aging of the European labour force.[34]

The 1957 report of the Industrial Tribunal added:

> Factors such as the raising of the school-leaving age, the more agreeable nature of the work, the higher status and better rates of remuneration, especially in regard to the commencing wages, the freer atmosphere and the less exacting discipline, attracts girls to the service trades generally rather than to secondary industry.[35]

The shift in white women's employment patterns, partially a result of the changing nature of the family economy as the class position of urban Afrikaner men was transformed,[36] led some industries to make gradual changes in the racial composition of the labor force, but to remain predominantly female industries. In the case of textiles, however, postwar conditions led to a predominance of black men for several decades. Only in the late 1960s and 1970s would the gender composition of the industry shift once again.

Spurred by a new partnership between the state-sponsored Industrial Development Corporation and overseas capital, textile manufacturing developed rapidly during the postwar period. Although judged to be a light industry requiring manual dexterity rather than physical strength, and therefore supremely suited to the labor of women, juveniles, and families, textile mills during this period became employers primarily of African men. Between 1938–39 and 1947–48, the percentage of female labor declined from nearly 30 percent to about 15 percent at a time when the total labor force increased nearly two-and-a-half times. Whereas the number of white women in all sectors of the industry (excluding knitting and woolwashery) decreased only slightly, from 863 to 765, the number of African men rose from 776 to 4,034.

Contemporaries attributed this dramatic shift to the declining numbers of white women willing to work as operatives at existing wage rates and to protective legislation that prohibited women from working after 6 p.m., thus preventing manufacturers from using them in the double and triple shifts that had become typical in the industry. Only in the woollen and worsted factories of the Western Province, Port Elizabeth, and Uitenhage were any significant numbers of women employed (predominantly coloured) because the textile workers' union had agreed to allow double shift work for women in these areas.[37] Another small cluster of women remained in the lowest-paying, most tedious job in the industry. Classified as flock workers, these African women and men picked, washed, and sorted rags, often sitting outside the factories in the sun without access to cloakrooms, washing facilities, or canteens. After struggling to be allowed to represent them, the Textile Workers' International Union was only able to win a weekly wage of one pound for the "female labourers" engaged in this work.[38] Despite the overwhelming shift to male operatives, manufacturers still perceived women as the most "normal" textile operatives, and the prospect of workers who in some areas could legally receive two thirds of ordinary wages remained tantalizing to both employers and the state.[39]

Those sectors of industry that continued to employ female labor could choose from a large and increasing pool of African women, many of whom migrated to the cities during and after the war as new jobs in secondary industry opened up for black men and as rural reserves grew increasingly impoverished. For those who sought full-time employment, factory work was among the most attractive of possibilities: less demeaning and considerably more lucrative than domestic service, more palatable to married women and higher paying than the professional opportunities open to them. In an article discussing the need for an African Housewives' League in 1938, *Umsebenzi* had criticized the fact that African women were "debarred from the right of working in factories" and were therefore forced into doing washing at the unspeakably low wages of 7s. 6d. a month.[40] Within a very short period of time, industrial labor came to be recognized as a principal economic activity for black women, despite the small numbers involved. By 1941, "working in factories at 15s. a week" had entered the depictions of the hopeless and ill-paying possibilities open to them, alongside domestic drudgery and beer-brewing.[41] Two years later, during protests over increased bus fares, a statement entitled "Specially Presenting the Women's Case" gave high priority to the needs of factory workers.[42]

This awareness of the growing importance of black women in industry represented a realistic appraisal of future trends. By contrast, some manufacturers viewed their employment as a temporary product of the wartime labor shortage, destined to end when "normal conditions" resumed.[43] But, as more work in garment factories opened up to African women, the figures on labor turnover indicate clearly the value of these jobs and their relative appeal to black and white women. In 1946, 37 percent of white women left before working for three months; only 11.4 percent of black women did so.[44]

Despite this new source of employment for African women, the dominant trend of the postwar period was not their movement into factory work, but their entry into urban domestic labor in ever increasing numbers as African men moved out of household work and into secondary industry. The demand for female domestic workers, coinciding with the stream of families entering the cities, created an insoluble dilemma for black urban women: not only did they have the usual strains of working a full day outside the home and then returning to another round of domestic chores and childcare, but they faced the virtual impossibility of combining live-in domestic service with any reasonable family life. Under these conditions it is hardly surprising that married women in particular clung tenaciously to their informal means of producing income.

In Johannesburg, by 1945, women had assumed the dubious honor of definitively outnumbering men in domestic employment. Of 60,000 employed full time, 32,000 were women and 28,000 men. Enhancing the significance of these figures is the fact that women in household service were more numerous than all other adult women in the city, whereas the men in domestic jobs accounted for less than a quarter of the total.[45] Furthermore, 14 percent of the men (but only 5 percent of the women) were 45 and over, indicating younger men's aversion to this kind of work. As other male occupations opened up, the view of domestic service as a humiliating and unmanly occupation could now assert itself.

A study of 204 servants in sixty-eight households conducted by the Bantu Welfare Trust revealed how profoundly domestic labor disrupted African family life, particularly for women. Although many of the women were mothers, none of them lived with their children. Women spent less time than men visiting children in the countryside, probably because of their more limited rural resources and obligations. Most men maintained permanent homes in their birthplaces, preserving family-based rights to land and cattle. By contrast, nearly half the women came from families lacking any right to land. (And, as women in patrilineal societies, who could gain access to land only through fathers or husbands, their rights would have been tenuous or nonexistent in any case once they had left the countryside.) Although all of the women allotted part of their earnings for relatives who maintained their children, women's higher level of proletarianization made their contacts both with rural kin and with their own children more limited than those of men.[47]

The profoundly disrupted family life of female domestic workers explains why independent means of producing income remained fundamental to African urban women; indeed, urban-born women (like poor Afrikaner women a generation earlier) were more loathe to enter full-time domestic service than newer rural arrivals. But employers also preferred country women for their willingness to live in and for their allegedly greater reliability and honesty.[48] As Afrikaner men rose in the economic hierarchy, the earnings of women and older children grew less critical for survival; but among black families, the wages of most men remained far too low to support children and a wife who produced no income. Furthermore, according to an African social worker writing of the postwar period, "the *majority* of fathers [emphasis in text] do not give a reasonable proportion of their earnings for the use of their families. This is the case even where the wages are adequate."[49]

The patterns of informal labor in the period up to 1960 remained similar to those during the earlier years of the century, although in some cities black resettlement was undermining established sources of income. Women with families still sought work charring or washing for white families on a daily basis; but a study of Durban in 1959 concluded that the increasing spatial barriers between black and white communities as the Group Areas Act was put into effect made such jobs increasingly less possible and less remunerative.[50] In Johannesburg, the imposition of a 10d. charge for each bundle of wash on the railway appeared to be shifting the site of laundry work from the townships to the white suburbs.[51]

In an account that celebrates the independent entrepreneurial spirit of black women, Ellen Kuzwayo describes them trading in liquor, selling dagga, receiving stolen goods, playing Fah Fee, sewing and hawking homemade clothing, vending foodstuffs, and operating coffee stalls. She also refers to "extremely capable" business women who not only "own and run shops and taxis, but as hawkers of a great variety of goods . . . go as far afield as Ermelo, Witbank, Welkom and Bloemfontein."[52] Many of these women were accumulating sufficient resources to invest in property, either stands or houses in the open freehold areas left in the towns, or in the country. Speaking of the most successful among them and of the increasing number of black teachers, nurses, and social workers, Kuzwayo saw a new type of African female emerging among two groups: the independent widow and the unmarried woman so self-sufficient she found marriage unappealing.[53]

Clearly, the range of success in the pursuit of independent economic activities could be considerable. In dressmaking, for example, an occupation that expanded in the 1940s and 1950s as the urban gender balance grew more equal, differentiation developed between cheap and expensive dressmakers. Women in each group catered to a different African clientele and priced their goods accordingly. Possessing a skill that could serve equally well in the home or in the factory, they often switched from one setting to another according to individual circumstances.[54] Many women employed in factories augmented their formal incomes by sewing at home, either for their own families and neighbors or as outwork for their employers.

Although the need for independent income among most African women was indisputable, not all observers shared Kuzwayo's optimism about the fruits of their labor. Ethel Wix's pamphlet, *The Cost of Living*, added several additional forms of income to those Kuzwayo mentions: rent from tenants, children's earnings, and gifts and loans from relatives. Acknowledging the difficulty of obtaining precise figures, she estimated that in 1944 the average net income from laundry (after deducting for fares, washing materials, and fuel), was £1 10s. 6d. per month and, by 1951, £2 19s. 6d. Domestic jobs contributed from £3 10s. to £5 10s. a month to the family budget.[55] Although many women undoubtedly pieced together income from several different sources, their combined earnings rarely exceeded the average male income of over eight pounds a month. Indeed, their intensive labor notwithstanding, Wix shows women contributing on average only 13.5 percent of family income.[56] Outside of the large cities, earnings might be even more meager. Studying Kimberley in 1955, a researcher estimated wages in domestic service at 7s. 6d. to 30s. a month, with an average of 15s. Those who worked for coloured families received only 5s.; but the better paid jobs as servants went to coloured women rather than to Africans.[57]

Kuzwayo's praises of female entrepreneurship also neglect the continuing hazards of economic activities that authorities deemed illegal. Police routinely harassed coffee cart owners and other petty traders for not having hawkers' licenses. One group of women was arrested in 1955; because their carts lacked wheels they were charged with illegally running refreshment stands.[58] Brewing continued to be a source of conflict, although protests now indicated tensions among women themselves. During some of the volatile conflicts over municipal beer halls during the 1940s and 1950s, differences emerged between highly successful "skokiaan queens" and ordinary women who brewed in their homes primarily for family and friends.[59] Once again, also, official policies added inescapably to women's burden, creating new forms of antagonism between black women and the state as municipal governments in the 1950s sought new sources of revenue and new means of controlling the African population.[60]

Yet these pressures also generated collective action by women in order to preserve the conditions that supported their remunerative activities.[61] If black women's struggles against the extension of passes to women reflected one form of resistance to wage labor, their periodic battles against municipal beer halls and participation in bus boycotts marked desperate efforts to maintain their sources of independent income in the townships.

Compared with the past, these protests were more often connected with organized, broadly based community expressions of dissent. Among the most militant and exuberant were the eruptions in Natal in 1959. In Cato Manor, the major home of Durban's African population, municipal destruction of stills as part of an effort to improve sanitation created a new source of resentment. Already angered by municipal beer halls, which claimed income that women saw as rightfully theirs, some two thousand took to the streets on June 18, invading and burning beerhalls and clashing with the police. As violence in the townships spread, crowds destroyed city buildings and vehicles. Observers recall vividly the way women used traditional forms of sexual insult: arriving at beer halls with breasts exposed, pulling up their skirts when confronted with lines of police, and on one occasion removing their panties and filling them with beer. Because of the close ties between Durban and the Natal countryside, rebellion soon spread to rural women, whose livelihood was equally threatened by cattle limitation and dipping schemes, new systems of land allocation, and a new tax on wives — all in the context of passes, influx control, and forced removals. With some twenty thousand women involved across the province, cane fields were burned, police stations and magistrate's courts attacked, and nearly three quarters of the dipping tanks destroyed.[62]

Similar signs of revolt crystallized during the periodic bus boycotts that erupted in townships across the Rand. In Evaton, thirty miles from Johannesburg, women conducted much of the picketing during a 1955 protest, while in Pretoria in 1958, women, prepared to use force if necessary, insisted on prolonging a boycott of local buses after men were willing to settle the dispute.[63] The economic needs that underpinned their militance were best articulated during the bus boycotts of the early 1940s in Alexandra, a freehold township nine miles from the center of Johannesburg. With the "powerful agitator" Lilian Tshabalala among their leaders, women found the boycott strategy a way to address critical grievances: crowding, long delays, and a flat-fee fare system. Washerwomen had to pay a double rate to allow room for their bundles and weekend surcharges penalized live-in domestics, who relied on the buses to sustain a viable family life. Although these protests involved township women in a wide and complex community of interests, they allowed those engaged in casual and domestic labor a powerful, if occasional, means of voicing critical collective grievances.[64]

Different patterns of informal economic activity prevailed among coloured women at the Cape. As in Johannesburg, casual labor remained most attractive to older, married women. Those who were Muslim seemed to prefer the relative privacy of laundry work, which women could do in their own homes. Flower sellers, who usually came into the trade through parents or spouses, were predominantly women (about four fifths) and mainly Christian. The majority were married (though some were divorced or widowed) and between thirty-five and sixty years old. A researcher in the early 1960s judged their earning prospects as greater than in most other work open to unskilled women from their community.

Laundry was done both in women's homes and at municipal washhouses. Many washerwomen began working as children, under the supervision of their mothers. Of those surveyed, twenty-one of twenty-two were Muslim, seventeen of whom were over forty-six years of age (nine over sixty); only one woman was single, the others married, widowed, or divorced. Roughly three quarters of the women had been washing for more than fifteen years and never had held any other paying job. Although a small number were training their daughters to continue their work, most felt their daughters would do better in factories.[65]

Statistical data reflect some of these changes in women's occupations; but they are also deceptive, particularly in the categorization of rural women. Figures showing a sharp decline in the number of African women in agriculture between 1936 and 1960 (from 86.5 to 23 percent) in fact reflect the misleading reclassification of peasant women in the reserves as "housewives." The census does, however, confirm a shift into service occupations, which employed twice as many African women in 1960 as in 1936. As late as 1960, few women were engaged in primary production or in professional work (mainly as nurses and teachers), although the number in both groups was growing.[66]

Among white women, the most striking trend was the steady rise in the percentage of clerical employees (from one quarter of paid women workers in 1936 to half in 1960),[67] accompanied by a dwindling number in service occupations. Likewise, the proportion of women in production declined from a high of 18.5 percent in 1936 to 6.3 percent in 1960. In the sales and professional/technical areas, the percentages declined slightly between 1946 and 1960.[68] The number of white women in agriculture became insignificant during this period.

Like African women, over half of employed coloured women worked as domestic servants in 1960 (56.7 percent). But this represented a drop from 84.5 percent in 1936, whereas the proportion of African women in this occupation was growing steadily. Nonetheless, during this time, the absolute number of coloured females in domestic employment continued to increase. Although African women were beginning to move into industrial production during the wartime and post-war periods, the trend was most significant for coloured women, one fifth of whom worked in industry by 1960. In professional, clerical, and sales occupations, however, the percentage of coloured women remained extremely low.[69]

Most Indian women continued to be relatively marginal in paid employment, although some shifts occurred among those who worked. Most notable were a gradual rise in the importance of industrial production (employing slightly over one quarter of working women by 1960), a sharp drop in the importance of agriculture, and a steep decline in service between 1936 and 1946, followed by a leveling off in 1960 at one quarter of the female workforce.

Statistics on industrial workers by race and gender dramatize the overwhelming importance that African men were assuming in the production of goods in South Africa. From 58.7 percent of production workers in 1933–34, they had risen to 76.7 percent twenty years later. By then (in 1953–54), white men held less than one fifth of industrial jobs and white women a mere 3.5 percent, a drop from 11.1 percent during the 1930s. Although the proportions of African women remained small, their numbers rose from 1,254 to 10,878; the number of coloured women increased from 11,263 to 38,031. The overall drop in the percentage of whites in factories was especially acute in industries that had begun with high levels of women workers.[70]

As the industrial labor force grew more varied, wage differentials by race and gender became more complex; but they continued to reflect the standard racial hierarchy, headed by whites and followed (in order) by coloureds, Indians, and Africans. Men always earned higher pay than women in their group, causing a particularly sharp gender differential among white workers. Women's ranking did not always follow these divisions exactly, however. During the 1940s and 1950s, Indian men earned substantially more on average than coloured women and in a single year, 1951, African women received slightly higher pay than African men.

The figures in the table below demonstrate with striking clarity the increasing racial divide as apartheid policies took effect.

| | Percent of White Men's Wages | |
Category	1944–45	1956–57
WF	45.6%	45%
CM	43.1%	30.4%
IM	37.7%	29.2%
CF	30.6%	21.9%
IF	25.6%	19%
AM	23.5%	16.4%
AF	20.6%	14%

Although white women continued to earn slightly less than half the average wage of white men, the pay of coloured and Indian men followed closely in 1944–45. A decade later, however, these two groups of men had lost their relative advantage as the wage gap between white men and women and all black people widened. White women had made no gains by comparison with men of their own group; but their standing had risen sharply by comparison with even the highest-paid black men since the early period of industrialization.[71]

Women's labor activity formed an integral part of the intensive organizing drive that began in the late 1930s and continued during the war, although this effort was most significant for drawing unprecedented numbers of black men into trade unions. By the postwar period, however, these unions had fallen into disarray and suffered widespread defeat.[72] New segregationist laws and new restrictions on African working-class organizations in the 1950s created serious splits among white trade unionists on the most appropriate response to these racist measures. Out of the divisions a new nonracial, politically committed federation developed, the South African Congress of Trade Unions (SACTU). Closely allied with the African National Congress, SACTU attracted many of the organizers of progressive unions during the late 1950s: Rita Ndzanga, Mabel Balfour, Mary Moodley, Viola Hashe, Elizabeth Mafeking, Frances Baard, and Liz Abrahams.[73] African nurses, facing the threat of passes and of segregated professional organizations, also engaged in new forms of collective action.

As state pressure on nonracial organizations intensified, their task grew more difficult. The SACTU union in the textile industry struggled nonetheless to create alliances that crossed racial and gender boundaries. At a woolwashery outside of Durban in the late 1950s, for example, twelve elderly Indian women were dismissed when they refused to buy chickens from their employer, who routinely deducted the cost from their wages. The African men with whom they worked supported their protests and even persuaded potential workers in the Zulu reserves not to enter the mill as scabs. Only a threat to evict the men from the municipal barracks and send them back to the countryside forced the union to settle the conflict, although the women were not reinstated and the union had to find other employment for them. This incident illustrates the ultimate weakness of trade unions within a coercive migrant labor system; but it also suggests the potential for interracial cooperation on class lines, despite numerous legal, social, and economic obstacles.[74] The Textile Workers' Industrial Union in Worcester in the Western Cape, with a workforce of African men and coloured women, created a similarly strong alliance that produced strikes and a successful local bus boycott in the mid-1950s.[75]

For predominantly white unions with earlier traditions of militancy and working-class solidarity, pressures from the state and from independent Afrikaner organizations posed a challenge. Most continued to belong to the SATUC (later TUCSA, the Trade Union Council of South Africa), which first decided to bar black unions in an effort to appease its white constituency and, in the following years, vacillated hopelessly on the issue of whether to include African workers in defiance of the government. The National Union of Distributive Workers, among the most progressive of these groups, supported the organization of African workers for many years, and many of its leaders favored the nonracialism of SACTU. But fearful of SACTU's political orientation, unable to sway white members, and under the pressure of red-baiting and efforts to establish rival white unions, the group finally affiliated to the SATUC in 1961.[76]

These examples from the wartime period and the early apartheid years suggest that no predetermined scripts governed the individual or collective actions of working- class women during this era. Although ideological discourse shifted to some degree in the years after 1945, the factors governing consciousness on the basis of class, race, and gender were complex and the results of particular struggles were not always predictable. A detailed examination of women in the Transvaal garment industry and the food and canning industry at the Cape clarifies the possible economic, political, and ideological choices of these workers and the ways in which the state, manufacturers, trade unions, and family influence all contributed to shaping different forms of consciousness and action among the women in each group. Neither the progressive, nonracial stance of the Cape women nor the retreat from class consciousness and socialism of those in the Transvaal is explicable without a full understanding of the multiple pressures and possibilities inherent in each historical situation.

-9-

SOLIDARITY FRAGMENTED

Garment Workers in the Transvaal

As the largest and most active female working-class organization during the 1930s, the Transvaal Garment Workers' Union succeeded in shaping the political and social consciousness of a significant number of white women in industry. Although not all GWU members accepted the political orientation of Solly Sachs and the union leadership, their support was sufficient to sustain a highly cohesive and militant industrial union. Based on the common ethnic background of most of the women, their shared poverty, and their relatively uniform place in the labor process, the union fostered unity by taking up issues of specific concern to female workers and by fashioning and sustaining a class-centered Afrikaner identity. Confronted with the problem of undercutting, the GWU waged aggressive, though often unsuccessful, campaigns to organize branches in the low-wage coastal areas. But geographical specialization among clothing producers minimized the threat of coastal standards to workers in Johannesburg and Germiston.

By the late 1930s and early 1940s conditions were changing in ways that tested whether the commitment to class solidarity transcended racial boundaries. From the mid-1930s, small numbers of coloured women began to work in garment factories, entering in much larger numbers by 1940. Higher paying opportunities for white women during World War II and the expansion of clothing production to meet wartime needs also drew African women into the industry. In the Transvaal, while the number of white female employees rose slowly—from 5,923 in 1937 to 6,322 in 1943 and to 6,979 in 1947—the number of coloured women in the same years multiplied rapidly, from 250 to 1,850 to 3,078. The number of Africans grew from 8 to 454 to 873. In effect, the proportion of whites among the female labor force decreased from 96 percent to 64 percent between 1937 and 1947, while the percentage of coloured women rose from 4 to

28. By 1947 African women comprised only 8 percent of women garment workers in the Transvaal.[1]

The growing number of black women in garment factories, partly a result of postwar employment trends, also reflected the industry's continuous efforts to seek new and cheaper sources of workers. By the late 1940s the industry had made little effort to rationalize production or to implement the techniques of scientific management favored by their overseas counterparts and by the Board of Trade and Industry. Rather than using conveyor belts, most South African factories still relied on a cumbersome system by which bundles of clothing were carried from one stage of production to another. Efforts to scientifically test and train workers for the industry had yielded few useful results.[2] Lowering labor costs thus remained a primary means of saving money.

In theory, the relative lack of sophistication in rationalizing the labor process should have favored a continued class-conscious cohesion among the workers as new groups of employees were hired. This was true to a degree. When factories first began to engage African women, their numbers jumped very rapidly in a brief period because they received lower pay than other workers under the terms of an out-of-date wage determination. Manufacturers justified their action by claiming that the Industrial Council agreement did not apply to Africans. The union and the employers' association promptly contested the issue and finally resolved that the Industrial Council should take the matter to the Supreme Court. The GWU maintained that African women were "employees" in terms of the Industrial Conciliation Act, while employers flatly refused to accept the union's interpretation. Ruling on November 9, 1944, the court agreed with the union, arguing that since women were not required to carry passes, they were exempt from the provisions of the Industrial Conciliation Act that prevented "pass bearing" Africans from belonging to registered trade unions and sharing in the benefits of Industrial Council agreements. Immediately after the judgment, the union, now able to control undercutting, demanded that the Industrial Council claim back wages for all the African women who had been underpaid. It also began to recruit African women as members, appointing a black shop steward, Lucy Mvubelo, as organizer.[3]

Through this challenge to racial exclusiveness, combined with the union's strong record of militant confrontation with employers, the GWU earned a reputation throughout South Africa as somehow "different" from other initially white trade unions. Explanations of this distinctiveness have varied. Although "openness" often has been a successful strategy among industrial unions,[4] other unions in the same position took more popular exclusive stances, so that this explanation alone is insufficient. Sachs attributed this political and ideological difference to the subordinate position of Afrikaans-speaking women that, he argued, made them less prone to feel a sense of racial superiority.[5] However attractive this notion might be from a feminist perspective, the life histories of many of the women who became active fighters for a multiracial union indicate that they once shared the racist attitudes of their families. Johanna Cornelius offered a more materialist explanation, grounded in the low pay and hard work endured by garment workers and the industry's long international tradition of working-class organization and struggle.[6] Whichever explanation is most accurate, the coming years offered challenges that severely tested the racial attitudes of white garment workers. By the mid-1950s, belief in the union's nonracialism was severely strained.

Despite the very real and important benefits the 1944 court decision granted to African women in the industry, it left intact many divisive aspects of the labor process. In its general report on manufacturing, the Board of Trade and Industry strongly pushed not only greater rationalization of production, but also the idea of stimulating industrial development through deskilling. Stressing that the optimum use of labor resources involved not simply the formal classification of work categories, but, more crucially, the wage rate granted to each category, the Board strongly favored breaking down categories "so as to derive the full benefit of the large resources of comparatively low-paid, non-European labour."[7]

During the 1940s such fragmentation had not yet occurred in the Transvaal clothing industry, and new workers were incorporated into established job categories at existing pay scales. Women were classified either as "learners," with weekly wages rising every three months, or as "qualified," after a period of thirty months. One of the few major changes from the 1930s lay in the industry's attitude toward skilled workers. Formerly under union pressure to retain a ratio of one qualified employee to every three learners, management now sought desperately to retain the shrinking pool of qualified machinists.

Despite the absence of change in the labor process, the GWU was alert to the threat of deskilling. Officials argued cogently that, although wages had improved over the years, they remained far too low. In 1946 learners' pay began at £1 11s. per week, rising to £3 12s. 6d. by the end of the qualifying period. The union estimated, however, that a "self-supporting female employee without dependents" in Johannesburg required seven pounds a week to live "in frugal decency (not in comfort)."[8] In order to prevent any further debasement of workers' living standards, the GWU strongly condemned the extreme subdivision of work in the coastal areas as leading to "disgracefully low wages" and hampering efficiency. A memorandum to the Wage Board noted:

In the Transvaal where all female workers excluding cutters (who need special application and education) receive the same wage irrespective of the operation they are engaged on, it is found that they are given more opportunity to become first-class tradesmen. Not only do some workers get a chance to learn how to make every part of a garment but through experience it is proved that workers change their employment so as to enable them to make all types of garments in the industry, and it is common for an experienced woman machinist to be able to complete all classes of men's and women's garments in the Transvaal.[9]

Although leaders of the Garment Workers' Union continued their efforts to forge a self-conscious body of working-class women during the 1940s, the tone of union discourse shifted in a number of important respects, particularly after 1945. Such changes in emphasis reflected the greater conservatism of the postwar period. With growing white prosperity and the vigorous campaigns of Afrikaner nationalist organizations, heightened anti-communist sentiment made class analysis increasingly suspect.[10] By 1948, in Dan O'Meara's estimate, Christian nationalism had become "a powerful mobilising ideology with a clear resonance in the daily consciousness of Afrikaans-speakers of all classes."[11] The *Garment Worker* continued to attack racial prejudice and to support the struggle for trade union rights in South Africa and abroad; but the highlighting of selected modern factories and the brief introduction of "women's pages" discussing dress, appearance, recipes, and knitting suggest an effort to acknowledge both the altered political climate and the changing age, marital status, and economic aspirations of many of the workers.

Despite the union's continued theoretical commitment to nonracialism, the attitudes of some members forced GWU leaders to make policy decisions that, by their own admission, violated this principle. And, union proclamations notwithstanding, there is substantial evidence that Sachs, always a pragmatist, was more concerned with the white working class than he was with organizing across racial lines.[12] In 1940, as increasing numbers of coloured women entered the industry, they were incorporated into the union as a separate number two branch. Thus, while the union worked vigorously to organize all garment workers, the relationship of black women to the parent body posed difficulties. In light of much later arguments advocating black separatism, some justifications of the decision to create a segregated coloured branch may appear plausible. But considering the ideological context of the 1940s and the fact that the organizational initiative came from the registered union rather than from the coloured workers, these arguments cannot help but seem a rationalization for steps the union felt compelled to take. Moreover, once introduced, segregation gradually spread until it included separate entrances, lifts, and offices for black and white garment workers.[13]

On September 26, 1940, the *Guardian* reported that the coloured garment workers in Johannesburg had decided to form a special section to cater to their particular needs. The workers had elected a committee to look after their interests and to advise the Central Executive Committee on matters concerning them. Although a number of workers objected to the section's formation as a form of segregation, a union official called this a misunderstanding, explaining that the new members would retain all the rights of main branch affiliation, but would also be able to attend to their own interests and train their own leaders. In an argument that became common later, the spokesperson continued:

> It had been felt that the Coloured workers always remained in the background at general members' meetings, that they hardly ever express their views on questions affecting them, etc. therefore, the formation of the section serves a need which must be satisfied.[14]

According to Sachs, the union started to organize coloured workers in the mid-1930s and soon thereafter began to solicit the opinions of members and shop stewards on how to structure their participation. About 10 percent favored complete equality without racial discrimination, while over 80 percent preferred a parallel organization with separate black and white branches. The overwhelming majority was against mixed meetings, but only an "insignificant number" completely opposed coloured entry into the union. The prevailing sentiment favored a parallel branch whose members had the unqualified right to manage their own affairs and finances, to elect their own officials, and to have an equal say in determining union policy and in making industrial agreements. Sachs therefore explained to the coloured workers that, while the union leadership favored complete equality, the majority of members did not. The number two branch was then established along the parallel lines suggested above; "by unanimous decision," however, its members decided to allow the Central Executive Committee to administer all finances. While judging such a racially defined structure as "against all trade union principles," Sachs also felt that "in practice it worked well."[15]

Clearly, then, many white workers resisted a policy of complete non-racialism. Aware of the benefits to capital of such divisive sentiments, officials explained them by reference to racially biased Afrikaner traditions maintained by workers' husbands and families. In the words of Johanna Cornelius:

> We have been brought up on the platteland where we are taught to hate the Africans and coloured people, as also Jews. The majority of the people on the platteland still have these views. We very often go to the factories, but the trouble is that the workers are married to men who work on the mines, or who come from families who live on farms, where they treat the Africans like dirt.[16]

Although the union had succeeded in reshaping some of these attitudes, its work was far from complete.

Cornelius was undoubtedly correct to emphasize the strong influence of family racial attitudes. Ideas of racial separation were not simply an atavistic heritage from the farms and mines, however. As O'Meara has shown, the political and economic climate of the postwar period produced favorable conditions for the growth of new forms of Afrikaner nationalism based on an antipathy to class-based or nonracial organization and to trade unions with "foreign" (mainly Jewish) leadership.[17] As nationalists assumed control of other Afrikaner unions, the basis for the 1930s alliance between progressive garment workers and white working-class men (particularly mine workers) was destroyed. Indeed, this change in the political climate left many white Transvaal garment workers distinctly split between their politics at work and their politics at home.

During the 1940s the union was called upon not only to devise an organizational strategy for incorporating new workers that was both workable and principled, and to continue the struggle against threats of undercutting, both in the Transvaal and by coastal manufacturers, but also to confront racial conflicts in the factories.[18] In an effort to minimize such friction, officials tacitly accepted legally mandated measures to insure shop-floor segregation. They worked actively to see that employers put up "proper partitions" between white and coloured workers and suggested staggered starting hours to facilitate racial separation. Thus, officials made no effort to challenge the views put forth by Anna Scheepers as typical of the white membership: "We do not object to their working in the factories but we do not want to mix with the coloured workers." Dulcie Hartwell, then secretary of the Clothing Industry's Unemployment Benefit Fund and Medical Aid Society, echoed this position. "It is absolutely untrue to state that the Garment Workers' Union stands for social equality of European and non-European. Whatever the individual opinions of officials may be, they have . . . never tried to get members to accept the non-European workers as their personal friends."[19]

In the most celebrated case of the decade involving shop floor relationships among workers, two Germiston women, Mrs. Nell and Mrs. Moll, were expelled from the union (which, under the closed-shop agreement, meant loss of employment), for having incited a strike to protest the hiring of two coloured women as machinists. While union officials proclaimed their commitment to insure everyone's right to work, the local secretary sought to defuse the incident by accepting the dismissal of the coloured women. Furthermore, the union lacked the local power to avert the outcome of the protest: an informal agreement by Germiston employers not to hire black machinists that lasted into the following decade. After this incident an Action Committee representing the three Afrikaner churches, which was formed on behalf of Moll and Nell, began to investigate and attack the GWU. As part of this campaign, Dutch Reformed ministers sought access to the factories and preached strongly partisan sermons on the evils of interracial contact.[20] Thus, for many garment workers during this period, the conflict between work and community was far from abstract. Particularly through the churches, women faced heavy pressure to conform to the norms of an emerging nationalist consensus.

This transformation of the Afrikaner working class had a profound impact on white union members. The strength of the GWU in the 1930s and early 1940s had derived jointly from its successful efforts to improve wages and working conditions and from its ability to respond to the social and political needs of its members. The success of this strategy created a community of working-class women that extended outside of the factory and into women's leisure activities, thereby helping to strengthen their bonds with one another. As the ideological consensus of urban Afrikaner life shifted, these women faced formidable conflicts. While workplace friendships and networks undoubtedly remained personally significant, the class-oriented culture conveyed by the union no longer reflected the values of women's families and neighbors. For all but a small and militant minority of women, the meaning of the GWU in their lives inevitably changed.

The division of the union into racially based branches also led to tensions. Although over a period of two decades such conflicts were relatively infrequent and usually were solved through discussion, the outcome of these talks nearly always reflected the inequalities of power between the two groups. Not surprisingly, the single most difficult issue was how black workers were to gain a voice in the affairs and decisions of the mother union. From the beginning, the new workers pressed for representation on the Central Executive Committee, the union's policy-making body. Sachs argued that, since forcing the question would split the union, "this matter must be discussed from a view of tactics and not principle."[21] Furthermore, black workers should temper their complaints because they were well represented by the number one branch. Suggesting that the lack of a voice on the C.E.C. could be solved by giving the number two branch a copy of the minutes, Sachs asked if the C.E.C. "had ever decided on anything which was detrimental to interests of the No.2 Branch."[22] In the end, Sachs's viewpoint prevailed (with only one white official, Ray Adler, dissenting). But the feeling behind the issue did not disappear. When the union constitution was amended in 1953 to give the number two branch representation on the C.E.C., the political climate of the country was already in transition. Three years later the Industrial Conciliation Act of 1956 mandated that only whites could serve on the governing body of a mixed union. Recalling their earlier struggle for representation, many members of the number two Executive Committee felt autonomy would be preferable to such subordination.[23]

Other matters also prompted periodic disagreements between the two branches. Usually initiated by the black organization, these conflicts reflected its continuing sense of grievance against the dominant white union. Early in 1942, for example, the number two Executive Committee members expressed concern that they never had been formally presented with a union balance sheet.[24] Later complaints voiced irritation at not being invited to testify to the government's Commission of Enquiry on the union, discontent over the division of space in the union's new office building, annoyance that "non-Europeans" never were invited to address public meetings, even of their own membership, and anger at their limited access to the single union car.[25] Dramatic evidence of the unequal power relationship came in 1951, when Sachs judged the administration of the number two branch to be unsatisfactory. He immediately placed R. de Freitas in the office to work with its secretary, Hetty du Preez, who would be sacked if she failed to "reform completely and unreservedly."[26]

During the 1940s, then, as new groups of workers entered the industry, the GWU was successful at preventing undercutting and at resisting changes in the labor process that might have subverted the intention of incorporating black women at equal pay by multiplying and diluting the work classifications. But the political climate within the union led to the creation of two separate and inherently unequal branches. And this segregation had numerous consequences. In combination with the spatial segregation of workplace facilities mandated by the Factories Act, it made it more difficult for women in the industry to develop the friendships and informal networks that might have helped to extend the sense of working-class consciousness on a nonracial basis and it created tension over the inequalities between the two groups. The Nationalist victory in 1948, leading to the elaboration of new forms of racial domination, further reinforced the existing tendencies toward separation. A pattern emerged during the 1940s that solidified further during the 1950s. The union engaged in strong and militant action to prevent newcomers from receiving lower wages than those already established, but it compromised when necessary on questions involving union organization. The GWU never succeeded, however, in preventing geographically based undercutting from lower paid workers in other areas, white or black. This failure later assumed major significance.

The 1950s saw the ever-increasing incorporation of black women into the labor force and the greater power of employers, supported by the state, to enforce work fragmentation that allowed their inclusion at lower wages. By this time, capital was determined to lower wage costs, and did so partially by investing in unregulated "border industry" factories in which pay was so low that it threatened the standards of even the low-wage coastal areas. Further exacerbating the fears and divisions that these developments fostered came new state policies. Determined to prevent the formation of a transracial unity that included the massive numbers of proletarianized blacks who were joining the industrial labor force in the 1940s and 1950s, the government finally prohibited all Africans, women included, from belonging to registered trade unions.

Following the rapid development of the war and postwar years, the clothing industry had become the fourth most important secondary industry in South Africa, surpassed only by iron and steel, metal products, and construction. By 1951–52, nearly half of all black women (47 percent) and over one quarter of all white women in secondary industry manufactured clothing. Just as women had begun to replace men in the late 1920s and 1930s during the transition from craft production by skilled tailors to mass production by lower paid, semiskilled machinists, there were similar shifts in the 1950s that eventually allowed the industry to incorporate large numbers of new workers. Between 1947 and 1952, the number of women workers in the Transvaal clothing industry rose from 10,930 to 15,061, an increase of 38 percent. During this five-year period, black women predominated in meeting the demand for new sources of labor; 2,029 coloured women joined the industry, an increase of 66 percent, while the number of African women increased by 1,243, a rise of 142 percent. By 1960 the number of white women garment workers had decreased dramatically from 52 percent (in 1952) to 25 percent of female employees. The proportion of coloureds rose from 34 percent to 44 percent, although with a very small increase in absolute numbers (from 5,107 to 5,612), and the percentage of Africans rose from 14 percent to 31 percent.[27]

This striking shift in the composition of the labor force in the postwar years reflected the increased proletarianization of black women. Driven into cities by rural impoverishment and a desire to keep their families together, some were perhaps drawn by the increased possibility of factory employment. These women, like their counterparts in the 1930s whom a generation of Labour Department bureaucrats had sought to turn into household workers, found factory work more attractive than domestic labor. Furthermore, the class struggle of earlier trade unionists had improved conditions in the majority of urban factories.

Yet white workers were not simply pushed out of the industry as National party propaganda maintained. As noted earlier, once the most devastating effects of the Depression had begun to subside, young white women opted for white collar jobs. As the economy expanded after World War II, new sources of wage employment in the clerical and distributive sectors began to open up to them. This change in employment patterns caused a drastic shift in the age composition of white garment workers compared with the 1930s. Whereas then the majority of women were under twenty-five and single, by 1957 only 9 percent of white women in the clothing industry were in the 16–24 age group; 65 percent were 35 and over. Their median age was now 39.2.[28]

Although it would be imprudent to assume any simple correlation between advancing age and conservatism, this drastic change in age structure meant the vast majority of white women probably were married and possibly less independent politically than they had been as young single women, particularly if they had lived apart from their families. Furthermore, while married women's earnings remained extremely low, the greater prosperity and social mobility of large numbers of Afrikaans-speaking male workers during the years since the Depression made them far more comfortable than they had been a generation earlier. Indeed, union officials in the postwar years referred frequently to the workers' rising social aspirations.[29] Yet, despite these aspirations, which were reflected in the occupations of their children, the low level of mobility within the industry may have shaped a consciousness among white women that was distinct from that of their husbands. As noted earlier, the changing political climate in Afrikaner communities made the implications of this split particularly acute.

The Transvaal Garment Workers' Union was concerned at the changing composition of the working population. In the context of a highly segmented labor force, it severely threatened the union's previous gains. Thus, in March 1957, the GWU distributed a questionnaire to its members entitled, "Why Is Your Daughter Not a Garment Worker?" The responses were virtually unanimous on two points: the work was too hard and the pay too low. Some of the respondents also referred to their uncertain future in the industry and to the difficulty of achieving better wages and working conditions. Of those whose daughters already were working, most were engaged in office work, often in banks or post offices. The intended jobs of those whose daughters were not yet employed were similar, although slightly more varied: primarily typing, general office work, and nursing.[30]

But the sources of working-class disunity lay not in the transformation of the labor force alone, but also in the way in which capital and the state chose to manipulate these changes. By 1950 manufacturers clearly expressed their unwillingness to continue to absorb new groups of workers without pressing for tangible benefits in return. In a letter to the general secretary of the GWU in that year, E. Reyneke of the Transvaal Clothing Manufacturers' Association proposed a new wage category to cover certain classes of female workers: cleaners, folders, stampers, markers, and sorters. Arguing that special provisions in the agreement for less-skilled workers would merely stabilize the current practice, he wrote:

> Today, learners are engaged on these types of work and when they reach a scale where it is no longer economic to employ them, they are dismissed and replaced by new workers.[31]

A "realistic" wage scale, he observed, would make such dismissals unnecessary.

A new state policy put into effect shortly thereafter came to the rescue of manufacturers concerned about "excessive" wages in the industry. The Native Labour (Settlement of Disputes) Act of 1953 forbade any Africans from belonging to a registered trade union. From the standpoint of the government and capital, the legal anomaly that had kept the wages of African women "unnaturally" elevated was laid to rest. As soon as the new law was passed the GWU established a separate branch for African women. At the request of the Minister of Labour, the union then asked the Industrial Council to consider extending the agreement to all African workers. The employers' representatives reportedly were amenable with respect to African women, but they were unwilling to include African men, although Johanna Cornelius reported in a letter to Solly Sachs that "it appears as if they (employers) were prepared to consider the matter favourably provided we can find a solution maybe through different grading and classification."[32]

This apparent honeymoon with capital was shortlived, however. By March 1954, the union was reporting cases of drastic wage reductions for African women already employed and of efforts to replace higher paid white women with Africans. Cuts at the Star Shirt and Clothing Company, for example, affected thirty African women as beginners' wages were reduced from £2 15s. 6d. to £1 10s. 9d. and the pay of experienced workers from £6. 14s. 2d. to just over four pounds. Within a week, over one thousand African women held a protest meeting in Johannesburg pledging "to be in readiness for any action which our Union or the GWU of South Africa may call on us to take." They also demanded the reinstatement of wages at the level of the Industrial Council agreement and the payment of back wages to all women whose pay had been reduced. By early April, four more factories had lowered black female wages. A union telegram informed the Minister of Labour of the high degree of unrest among the workers and urged his prompt intervention. Yet, by the end of April, not only were increasing numbers of employers reducing black women's pay, but some also had begun to replace white and coloured workers with Africans.[33]

Throughout this period, workers remained united in their attitudes toward these cuts. In a letter to E. S. Sachs, Johanna Cornelius reported:

> The workers in our industry, European as well as non-European were up in arms immediately and they are prepared to take part in a struggle even if it would mean strike-action to protect their present wages and working conditions. This fortunately is not only the opinion of the European and Coloured workers who have a great deal to lose, but the African women are 100% united with us on this issue.[34]

By April she reported: "The position at the present moment looks explosive. I doubt whether we will be able to avoid strikes from breaking out in the various firms."[35] Finally, in early June, just after the old contract had expired, employers agreed to extend coverage to all workers in the industry if the union accepted several conditions: the further subdivision of certain categories of work, extension of the learnership period for some categories, and reduced wages for designated groups of qualified workers. The resulting fragmentation was dramatic: an increase in the number of work classifications from six to seventeen. Predictably, African employees were concentrated in many of the new areas.[36]

The issue of competition from cheaper labor did not end with this wage agreement, however. During 1955 and 1956 one employer began switching from all white to all black labor, thereby replacing a largely experienced workforce with one primarily composed of learners, while another, employing African men, applied for an exemption from the wage agreement.[37] By 1956, the GWU finally was forced to accept the introduction of two sets of wages for each category of work, effectively lowering wages for the new groups of black workers in the industry still further, since the reorganized work categories already had reduced the pay of many black workers. The new category B pay scale applied to all new employees and to workers of certain classifications who had less than a specific minimum of experience or who were receiving less than specified minimum wages by November 30, 1956. H. A. F. Barker, author of the most comprehensive economic history of the South African clothing industry, sees this new set of wage categories as "not based on any racial discrimination," but rather as part of an ongoing struggle between labor and capital: the outcome of a "determined stand" by the Transvaal employers to arrest the steep rise in wages of the preceding twenty years that was undermining their competitive position by comparison with lower-wage coastal areas and as the employers' first successful attempt to rationalize the wage structure.[38] The new wage agreement represented a triumph for the employers, a sign that under changing economic and political conditions the union would have difficulty maintaining a strong bargaining position.[39]

As a result of these structural changes, the division of labor in the industry assumed a new and more complex shape. A skilled labor shortage broke down some of the gender barriers among white workers, while black women replaced white women in the lower levels of the hierarchy. By contrast with the 1930s, 86 percent of supervisory employees (foremen/women, supervisors) were now women, overwhelmingly white, although most women remained machinists and tablehands. Nonetheless, the work of white women was defined more rigidly than that of black women. For, in addition to doing the stereotypically female work of the industry, black women also worked as pressers and general workers alongside African men who formed over half the workers in each of these categories.[40]

Ultimately more threatening to the living standards of Transvaal garment workers than any local structural and labor force changes was the widespread development of unregulated garment factories in the areas bordering on the African reserves. The GWU, since its inception, had expressed continual concern over the challenge to workers' wages resulting from lower paying clothing factories at the coast. This concern was reflected in endless unsuccessful efforts to form a single national union that would raise all wages to Transvaal levels. But now capital began turning to sources of labor that were more difficult to organize and whose unions, if organized, could not receive official recognition. Indeed, the government-sponsored Tomlinson Commission specifically encouraged the development of a rural clothing industry with lower wages and longer working hours than those in the urban centers. The Wage Board contributed to further reductions in labor costs in the uncontrolled areas. Its members decided not to establish a ratio of qualified workers to learners, effectively sanctioning the dismissal of workers who had passed through the learnership period, and to allow longer working hours and less annual and sick leave.[41] Before the Wage Board investigation, the GWU had estimated the wages in the rural factories at approximately one-third of those prescribed in the Transvaal agreement. The new ruling gave clothing establishments additional incentives to withdraw from the urban areas.[42]

This continual pressure on wages created a great deal of anxiety, particularly among the white women in the industry. In a letter to the Minister of Labour the GWU protested:

> Needless to say our members are in a state of unrest. The majority of them are older workers who are not in a position today to successfully adapt themselves to new posts. Their contention, therefore, that in no other industry will they secure employment for the same wage they have been receiving is quite logic [*sic*] and justifiable. The six thousand garment workers will, in the event of them not being prepared to offer their services for a wage that will suit the pockets of the hard-minded employer of cheap labour, have no alternative but to face unemployment.[43]

Yet, while some official policies threatened the livelihood of female garment workers, others sought to undermine class-based, nonracial organization and to create a situation in which their fears of displacement by cheaper labor would be translated into racial terms. These policies sometimes backfired, however. In 1952, Sachs's banning provoked a multiracial demonstration of some fifteen thousand women that could only have served the interests of working-class solidarity. Similarly, the development of rural garment factories affected all workers in the urban centers and, in theory, provided an issue around which they might unite.

Two state measures of the later 1950s—the Industrial Conciliation Act and job reservation—served to keep the racial division of the working class in the forefront of people's consciousness and attempted to split workers on political as well as on racial lines. The Industrial Conciliation Act of 1956 forced the number one and number two branches to divide even further into two completely separate unions. Progressive members were persuaded to accept this move only because nationalist supporters were threatening to form breakaway all-white unions. Under the new provisions, the government would recognize mixed unions only if a majority of members supported them. An article in the *Garment Worker* pronounced the decision to divide the two branches "absolutely contrary to the principles of trade unionism."[44] Yet, during the ensuing months, the issue of maintaining the union's strength came to be seen in racial terms as three competing white unions sought ways to unite. In its invitation to the executive members of all the number one branches to hold a joint meeting, the GWU Central Executive Committee argued that unity among white garment workers was the only way for them to maintain employment in the clothing industry:

> With the danger which is on our doorstep of the clothing industry going into the hands of cheap native Labour—which has already made its entrance at places such as Charlestown Location, Standerton, Ladysmith, the Transkei and Vryburg in the Cape, . . . we in the Transvaal cannot afford to fight among ourselves.[45]

By the middle of 1956, two racially based unions were in process of forming and seeking registration: a new GWU of European workers and the GWU of South Africa (Coloured, Malay and Asiatic), with members in the Transvaal, the Eastern and Northern Cape, and the Orange Free State. During the following year, however, the clamor for an all-white union subsided, and a mixed organization with separate white and coloured branches was maintained.

In addition to encouraging racially separate trade unions, the Industrial Conciliation Act also granted the Minister of Labour the power to reserve certain categories of work in any industry on a racial basis. Thus, while the white union was still attempting, less and less successfully, to protect its members through inclusive strategies, the government made an effort to erect artificial, and ultimately unworkable, barriers to limit competition from subordinate urban workers. On October 27, 1957, the Government Gazette announced that as of November 4, the work of machinists, supervisors, choppers-out, and table hands in the clothing industry would be reserved for whites, who then accounted for only 4,500 of the forty thousand employees in these categories. When most of the 22,000 black workers doing "reserved" jobs in Johannesburg, Kimberley, Port Elizabeth, and Germiston stayed away from work in protest at the urging of the union, three hundred factories were forced to shut down.

The measure was so totally unworkable—as the government tacitly admitted by immediately granting exemptions—that by the end of the decade it was modified yet again. This time a complicated plan was devised to prevent the percentage of whites from falling below a certain level (different for each region) and to check the employment of Africans in urban factories. The high level of disruption and uncertainty that these policies caused to both capital and labor prompts the suspicion that their ultimate intent was to promote the growth of the rural clothing industry, under a smokescreen of "protecting" white workers.

The intense pressures that the Transvaal garment industry faced in the 1950s, the relentless efforts of the state to blame the difficulties on competition from black workers, and the generally heightened racism promoted by Afrikaner groups led to a number of ideological changes during the decade. But, within the industry, these changes had a clear material foundation. For the increased workplace stratification had, in itself, created new divisions among workers through the multiplication of job categories, the creation of A and B wage scales, and the relatively high wages paid to some women, partly because of their lengthy employment in the industry. Figures relating hourly wages to the retail price index make this point starkly. Whereas in 1946 the index of hourly wages ranged from 163 to 189, in 1958 it ranged between 81 and 331.[46] Although these divisions did not invariably fall along racial lines, whites tended to earn considerably more than the minimum for their job category, while blacks always earned close to the minimum.[47]

Other developments of the decade, like the enforced separation of trade unions, also helped to focus these status distinctions on race, as did the pattern of extensive workplace segregation. Not only did factory facilities have to be segregated, but this mandatory separation meant that the vast majority of garment workers during the 1950s labored in factories that employed only a single racial group. By requiring separate facilities, the Factories Act gave employees a financial incentive to seek out a homogeneous work force.

The GWU received intensive criticism from the left during the 1950s for its ostensible ideological changes. Discussing the Industrial Conciliation Act of 1956, Oscar Mpetha of the African Food and Canning Workers' Union charged, "Even the GWU, left inclined formerly, had turned practically right and decided to persuade all non-Europeans to accept the present Act."[48] Ray Adler, a dissident member of the union, chided the GWU leaders for acting with "indecent haste" as the first union to accept the principle of separate black and white unions and for remaining obsessed with complying with legal formalities in order to maintain their registration, rather than embracing all sections of the population "in united and democratic trade union organizations."[49]

Some of these criticisms are valid. In the context of a more highly stratified working class, now divided much more starkly on economic as well as racial grounds and in a new national environment concerned with institutionalizing more rigid forms of racial separation and domination, GWU ideology reduced its emphasis on class struggle and working-class internationalism and stressed instead a pragmatically based unity that might, if necessary, operate in a multiracial (and hierarchical) rather than in a nonracial, democratic fashion. The main purpose of this unity remained, now as before, to prevent undercutting and the destruction of the gains that the workers had built up through struggle. Reluctantly accepting this reality, Johanna Cornelius expressed a typical sentiment of the period when she depicted the time as a "tragic stage" in the South African trade union movement, but added:

. . . we must never forget that the main object of a Trade Union is to get the
highest wages and best working conditions for their members. The Trade
Unions are being forced, by the introduction of the Bill, to reorganize themselves differently to what has always been believed was proper, but we libe
[sic] in a different time and may have to change our methods to suit the
circumstances.[50]

Despite the GWU's pragmatism on questions of union organization, it
did not drop its theoretical commitment to social justice. In a speech to
the 1958 conference of the Trade Union Council, for example, Johanna
Cornelius condemned job reservation for the suffering it would cause
workers of all races.[51] In its memorandum to the Industrial Tribunal on
the reservation of work, the union insisted on the tribunal's responsibility
to consider the interests of all groups of employees rather than recommending measures that would favor one group over another.[52]

The membership seemed to approve of this moderate position, which
may have accurately reflected its ambivalence. In 1951, Johanna Cornelius
had told the English journalist Basil Davidson that the union had about
six hundred shop stewards who took a progressive attitude on the color
question within the union, although many of the same women also voted
for the National party.[53] Shortly thereafter, however, Cornelius wrote to
Sachs that "the Nationalists did make quite a bit of progress amongst our
European Garment Workers with their outrageous attack on the Trade
Union Movement under the cloak of communism."[54] A few months later,
discussing union efforts to politicize the workers, she lamented, "Unfortunately they do not wish to take our advice and somehow the Nationalist Party with their vile propaganda seem to have a better hold on them
than we can muster."[55] Yet on the next page she expressed greater optimism. After describing the union as advocating the closest cooperation
with Africans but, if necessary, organizing on parallel lines, she added
that this policy was working perfectly. "I do not think that our members
were ever as united as they are at the present moment." This sense that
most members outside of the Nationalist stronghold of Germiston agreed
with the leadership was borne out in the election following the creation
of the European union. Anna Scheepers and Johanna Cornelius, running
respectively for president and general secretary, each received 78 percent
of the vote against the two male opponents put up by the Nationalists.
After extracting the Germiston vote from these totals, the support for these
women was substantial.[56]

Despite the violation of trade union principles implied in the division
of the unions along racial lines, this separation did afford black women
some opportunity to develop their own leaders and their own political
positions. Their support of non-union organizations involved in fighting
primarily against racial exploitation and oppression points to the impact
of state policy as well as industrial policy on workers' consciousness. As

the Nationalist government continued to intensify the control and exploitation of black labor and to introduce controls over African women that had been absent previously (through an extension of the pass laws), garment workers readily supported resistance on racial as well as on class grounds. As labor force segmentation increased during the 1950s, so did the ideological gap between different groups of workers, although their dependence on the white GWU undoubtedly shaped the choices of the black leadership.[57] In the late 1940s, however, the number two branch initiated donations to the Passive Resistance Movement, to the leftist newspaper, the *Guardian*, to the South African Institute of Race Relations, and to the First People's Assembly.[58] It also joined the Council of Non-European Trade Unions and the African National Congress.[59]

As individuals, many black garment workers also took an active part in progressive groups of the period that organized around both women's and working-class issues. Although some white workers may have joined them, the union leaders were not among them. Hetty du Preez, organizer of the number two branch, was involved in 1947 in an effort to form a left-wing, nonracial women's organization, and she, along with Lucy Mvubelo, Sybil Hedley, and Betty Flusk were among the convenors of the first national conference of the Federation of South African Women, the multiracial women's organization that spearheaded the decade's massive anti-pass demonstrations. Hetty du Preez also became a member of the first National Executive Committee of the Federation.[60] The organization's vice president, Lilian Ngoyi, at one time on the Executive Committee of the GWU of African Women, also served on the National Executive Committee of the African National Congress and as Transvaal president of the Women's League. Having worked in clothing factories from 1945 to 1966, she recalled the demonstration of thousands of garment workers after Solly Sachs's banning as one of her formative political experiences.[61] There is no indication, however, that the GWU of African Women ever formally affiliated with the Women's Federation, as did the Food and Canning Worker's Union, a progressive, nonracial union with a large female membership.

The left-wing, nonracial South African Congress of Trade Unions (SACTU) also attracted some of the same leading militant young black women who were active in the GWU of African Women. The main branch of the GWU, by contrast, continued its involvement in the South African Trade Union Council, which excluded Africans, although GWU leaders repeatedly pressed the SATUC to liberalize its racial policies. Lucy Mvubelo, the most prominent SACTU activist among garment workers, was elected as a vice president of the organization in 1955 and then unanimously reelected in 1956. In that year twenty members of the GWU of African Women attended the SACTU conference in Cape Town. Mvubelo also was selected as the SACTU representative to the Women's Federation conference in Johannesburg in May 1955.

On November 26, 1956, under circumstances that remain unclear, the Executive Committee of her union unanimously decided to disaffiliate from the Congress. According to the SACTU minutes, the decision resulted from the formation of a Liaison Committee with the South African Trade Union Council that would serve "the interests of all garment workers, irrespective of their colour or creed." In a later interview, however, Mvubelo attributed the action to SACTU's decision to affiliate with the ANC; her union voted against the motion because "politics was a death-knell to us." The alternative trade union federation, FOFATUSA, the Federation of Free African Trade Unions, which garment workers were instrumental in forming in 1959, was ostensibly aimed at keeping "trade union activities within the bounds of worker grievances."[62] Whatever the politics involved, Mvubelo did not remain totally silent on the political struggles of the decade after her break with SACTU. In 1958, on the occasion of a large-scale protest, she took a strong public stand "on behalf of all the African women in my organization who are opposed to the passes."[63]

This wavering on the part of black garment workers is not unexpected, for the pressures they confronted were enormous. In a subordinate position to the white union, the GWU of African Women would have risked a rupture of this alliance, however unequal, had it pressed to remain politically independent. Furthermore, for many structural reasons, there were greater barriers to building a united community of black garment workers than there had been for white women in the 1930s. With the initial energy and excitement of the union's early organizing years long past, much of its business had grown bureaucratic and routinized by the 1950s, a trend interrupted only by the periodic attacks of nationalist organizations and the state. Equally, or perhaps more important, under the onslaught of apartheid legislation, cohesive black urban communities (most notable among them Sophiatown) were being destroyed in the 1950s and their inhabitants scattered far from the center of Johannesburg over the bleak expanses of the newly constructed township of Soweto. As the decade progressed, it became less and less likely that the women who worked alongside each other, and who shared their lunch breaks on the sidewalks outside the factories, also would share the kinship and neighborhood connections of their white counterparts a generation earlier. Although some black women vividly recall the comradeship of May Day picnics and of the demonstration after Sachs's banning, the extent of black involvement in a work-based political and cultural community that encompassed women's leisure hours was severely restricted. As predominantly married women with families, they found their time too limited for the sports, plays, and lectures that had filled the lives of many young, single white women and had reinforced their sense of belonging to an active, class-based community. Finally, for those women inclined toward politics, the inequity of race was more pressing than that of class. Even the wage-lowering thrust of the 1950s did not erase the advantages of garment factories, whose pay and working conditions remained considerably more attractive than other occupations open to African women. By contrast, the threat of passes for women, the new insult of an inferior "Bantu education," and the forced removal of long-established communities provided relentless reminders that racial oppression was an inescapable fact of daily life.

During the 1930s, then, when the GWU developed its strength and support among a relatively homogeneous working-class population composed of large numbers of newly proletarianized Afrikaans-speaking young women, its success lay not only in the organizing skill of the leadership and in its ability to gain substantial improvements in wages, benefits, and working conditions, but also in the fact that the vast majority of women were semiskilled operatives who stood in roughly the same position in the labor process. During the period the phrase "poor white women," combining a joint appeal to class, ethnicity, and gender, applied to the overwhelming majority of workers.

By the 1950s, a more stratified workforce had developed. Despite the continued gender uniformity, rapid job fragmentation was producing substantial inequalities among different groups of workers. These status divisions, combined with increased racial diversity and pressure from new state policies and from Afrikaner nationalist organizations, made class-based unity more tenuous. At a time when both capital and the state were deliberately manipulating fears of racial competition, the GWU was forced into great defensiveness. Without wholly abandoning its earlier inclusive industrial trade unionism or its theoretical commitment to workers' equality, the drastically altered material situation of the industry and the growing strength of the apartheid state mitigated against a primary emphasis on a nonracial, class-centered ideology. In place of the working-class consciousness of the 1930s, the GWU emphasized a more narrowly based trade union consciousness. And, in the face of government pressure, it abandoned its earlier belief in the inseparability of politics and trade unionism, fashioning instead an ideology of apolitical "bread and butter" unionism that it passed on to its African counterpart. The areas of compromise remained selective, however. While the GWU continued to fight vigorously and militantly to prevent undercutting, it was willing, as it had been in the 1940s, to make concessions in areas relating to union organization. Thus, opponents of the GWU were correct in noting a shift in ideological emphasis during the 1950s. But the change was not as total as they portrayed it and resulted as much from changes within the industry as from a deliberate policy of "appeasement to racialism."

Whatever the reasons, however, the Transvaal Garment Workers' Union was no longer in the forefront of progressive politics during the postwar period. The community of women active in forging a new political and cultural synthesis had gradually eroded, replaced by a narrowly focused union bureaucracy. In addressing the critical issues from 1948 onward, and in making the pertinent political connections between race, class, and gender, a heterogeneous Cape-based union in the food processing industry emerged at the center of the struggles of working-class women, now increasingly black. Unlike Afrikaner women of the 1940s and 1950s, who experienced a growing divergence between their political lives at home and at work, these new groups of factory workers confronted similar issues in both settings. The newly formulated policy of apartheid had begun to permeate all aspects of daily life.

-10-

FOOD AND CANNING WORKERS AT THE CAPE

The Structure of Gender and Race

Events of the 1940s and 1950s challenged Transvaal garment workers in ways that ultimately changed the character of their union. At the same time another group of working women replaced them on the cutting edge of progessive political change: the food and canning employees of the Cape Peninsula. Living and laboring in small rural communities in the heart of the fruit growing areas, their experience differed from that of most clothing workers at the time, whether in the north or in nearby Cape Town. Tiny houses clustered in townships and camps near the factories contributed to a deep involvement in local issues. Before the Group Areas Act enforced strict residential segregation, their racially mixed communities and factories provided a basis for nonracial solidarity. Though women made up a high percentage of the labor force, gender was conceptualized not as an independent political issue, but as an integral part of struggles defined on class or racial grounds. In these struggles, however, and particularly in the campaign against passes for African women in the Cape, female food and canning workers played a significant role.

Women's labor history is replete with examples of mixed (or even female) unions in which women had only a muted voice; but men dominated neither the Food and Canning Workers' Union (FCWU) nor its African counterpart (the AFCWU).[1] Not only did women hold a disproportionate number of leadership positions, but in strikes and political actions, they often were far more involved than men. Suggesting explanations for this apparent anomaly requires an understanding of the structure and history of both the industry and the union, the focus of this chapter, and of the approaches the union formulated to the issues of race, gender, and class, the subject of chapter 11.

This analysis suggests that two primary structural factors shaped women's activism: their predominance in seasonal labor, which gave them few individual options for improving their situation, and the support of working-class communities in which women, men, and children often labored in the same factories. But union policies made the most of this situation. A strong commitment to local issues kept women workers politically involved during the off-season, and a tendency to interpret gender concerns as family issues helped women minimize the conflicts between their working lives and their household responsibilities. Thus, women became active supporters of an organization whose leaders understood the broad-ranging conflicts and tensions in their lives and worked actively to address them, both inside and outside the workplace.

Yet neither the union nor the community existed in a vacuum. Without the highly charged political climate resulting from discriminatory and repressive state policies and from the efforts of a multiracial nationalist movement to respond with extensive political mobilization, women's place in the union might have been different. Although repression rather than liberation followed this period of nationalist ferment, as in many revolutionary situations, the high level of social unrest was conducive, at times, to drawing everyone into the struggle.

The food industry in South Africa dated back to the late nineteenth century, when the first jam factories opened in Stellenbosch and Paarl; fruit canning began early in the twentieth century. By 1925 there were twelve fruit processing factories in the country, among the most prominent H. Jones and Company at Paarl, built with Australian capital. Development of the industry remained limited until World War II, when heightened demand for locally produced food led to investment in new factories and machinery and to new technological input from overseas.[2] Reflecting the rapidity of the expansion, total output more than tripled between the beginning of the war and July 1941 and the number of employees rose sharply: from 1,867 in 1938–39 to 4,647 in 1940–41.[3] During the five years of the war, the number of factories nearly doubled and the gross value of output increased by 517 percent.[4]

Following the wartime boom, the industry continued to change. A shift in emphasis from jams to canned fruits, more in demand as exports, led to greater dependence on overseas markets, especially in Britain, and made international competitiveness of prime importance. The shift also meant that 75–80 percent of the industry's total production came from the deciduous fruit-growing regions of the Western and South Western Cape, while other regional specialties assumed less importance: vegetables from the Transvaal, pineapple and tropical fruit from Natal, citrus fruits from the Eastern Cape, and pineapple from East London. Although the level of mechanization increased in the postwar period (particularly in cutting, skinning, and depipping) the industry remained highly labor intensive.

The predominance of South African capital in the industry, and particularly of financial interests based in Cape agriculture, gave growers significant control over the disposition of their crops and over wages. In an effort to retain labor, they used their influence to keep factory pay from competing with farm wages. Furthermore, as participants in the movement to accumulate capital in Afrikaner hands, most owners of fruit and canning factories fully supported National party political initiatives. Although financial control was relatively diffuse in the immediate postwar years, the mid-1950s, following a period of expansion in the industry, saw an increasing concentration of capital. After 1955 two companies were dominant; the Langeberg Kooperasie Beperk (L.K.B.) and the South African Dried Fruit Company of Wellington.[5]

The development of both the industry and the union were informed by the distinct characteristics of the Cape, both east and west. In the latter area, where large-scale, mechanized farms relied almost totally on wage labor, both coloured workers and the settled black populations of small rural towns were totally proletarianized. Driven from farms in large numbers as increased mechanization and the fencing of grazing camps reduced the need for agricultural labor in the years before World War II, these men and women provided a ready source of workers for the canning factories. Their communities were desperately poor, with high levels of unemployment and irregular employment. Many workers lived in towns, but were drawn back to the farms in the peak months to harvest or pack fruit, accustoming women in particular to the seasonal rhythm of labor in the canning factories.[6] Under these impoverished conditions, families formed earning units that relied heavily on the contributions of women and children.[7] Houses, overcrowded, unsanitary, and unhygienic "to a degree that can hardly be described," were constructed mainly of sack, reed, tin, or rusted galvanized iron.[8]

A recent appraisal of the Food and Canning Workers' Union suggests that the class homogeneity of the rural Western Cape may have contributed to successful union organizing. Discussing the reputed apathy of coloured workers, the writer suggests "that the working class is dominated and made to feel inadequate in almost every way—whether it be at school, church or at home. This difficulty does not exist in the rural areas of the Western Cape, where a larger proportion of these communities are ordinary workers."[9]

The level of poverty in the Western Cape was hardly atypical in South Africa. But contrary to the situation in many of the country's largest cities (although not unlike Port Elizabeth and East London), the black population of these smaller urban centers was long-established, sometimes over a period of generations, which fostered fairly even gender ratios and stable family life.[10] This stability, combined with a lower degree of residential segregation than elsewhere, created a distinct racial climate, noted with alarm by the 1937 Commission on the Cape Coloured Population:

Among many of the lower classes of Cape Coloured living among the Natives in locations and otherwise under the same social and economic conditions, there is a weakening or absence of that feeling of difference and of superiority which tends in other cases to keep the two groups apart. Some of these Cape Coloured mingle racially with the Native, so that . . . there is a growing class of "Coloured" with an infusion of Bantu blood.[11]

To the east, Port Elizabeth and East London also differed from most urban centers in South Africa. As cities that had encouraged the migration of black families in order to establish a settled, semiskilled workforce, both had relatively balanced sex ratios that contributed to women's employment in industry and to their participation in politics; indeed, in both cities, women outnumbered men and families lived together. By the early 1940s the black population of Port Elizabeth was concentrated mainly in the newly developed and relatively unregulated location of New Brighton.[12] In these predominantly Xhosa-speaking areas, ethnic homogeneity contributed to political unity. In East London, however, as Tom Lodge documents, many factors produced a level of political mobilization considerably lower than in Port Elizabeth: closer ties to rural relatives in the Ciskei, a greater cultural rift between educated Christians and more rural-oriented people, higher levels of poverty and unemployment, and a more repressive local administration.[13] This difference was reflected during the women's anti-pass campaigns.

As the food industry developed in the late 1930s and early 1940s, working conditions were appalling and wages extremely low. In 1939, a *Guardian* article exposed the complaints of young women in Paarl jam factories who earned 12s. 6d. for a forty-eight hour week. (Worcester wage levels of 7s. 6d. and 8s. 6d. a week would have shocked investigators several decades earlier.) The women lacked boots or protective clothing, although many stood all day in water. Those who ran the tin cutting and lining machines for eighteen shillings a week were involved in labor that was better paid, but dangerous; women who lost fingers while working these machines received no compensation. Workers were granted no paid leave for vacation or public holidays and pregnant women were routinely sent home in order to avoid paying them a confinement allowance.[14] The first agreement negotiated by the Food and Canning Workers' Union established wages of £1 10s. and £2 5s. per week at a time when the poverty datum line for single women and men in Cape Town was £2 13s. 3d. and £2 17s. 10d. respectively.[15]

Rapid wartime expansion produced shocking housing conditions around the factories. Living in a location that belonged to the Langeberg Kooperasie, for example, the 650 canning workers in Ashton had access to three types of dwellings: pyramid "pondokkies" (huts) made of reed and clay with floors of cow manure and doors of sacking that could only be entered on all fours; huts with bare earth floors made of sacking stretched over a wooden frame; and better houses of clay brick constructed with iron roofs and clay floors. Not atypical, one hut 12 feet by 15 feet housed two families—four adults and ten children. The entire camp had only a few communal lavatories and a single water tap; the nearest doctor lived six miles away.[16]

During the season, the pace of labor was intense. When Elizabeth Mafeking worked for H. Jones at Paarl in the 1930s, hours were unregulated, so that workers were on duty from 6:30 a.m. until 1 a.m. the following morning, with only a half hour break for lunch. After work they walked the several miles between Paarl and their homes in Huguenot. Even out of season, the working day did not end until 7 p.m. Reflecting on such conditions in 1939, a journalist issued a challenge that was soon to be taken up: "It looks like a case for organisation. What about it, trades unionists?"[17]

A number of other characteristics of the food and canning industry shaped both the process of unionization and the consciousness of the workers involved, women and men alike. No matter how large and successful the industry became, labor continued to be seasonal; in the absence of salaries that could sustain workers throughout the year, many were forced to seek other employment during the off-season. The number laid off could be substantial; at Associated Canners at Daljosaphat, for example, the eight hundred to a thousand workers during the height of the canning season dwindled to three to four hundred during the off-season.[18] In Port Elizabeth, roughly half of the workers in the industry were employed on a seasonal basis.[19] Even during the season, delays in fruit shipment might cause frequent breaks in work, often followed by excessive overtime.

The association of women with seasonal work was the most striking aspect of the sexual division of labor in the industry. Another was their responsibility for most aspects of fruit preparation, while men tended and operated the machines. Complaining of speed-ups in a Durban factory in the early 1940s, one of the workers, Annie Miller, described the women's work.

> As soon as all the girls arrive in the morning, they have to see that the conveyer belts and the scales have been properly cleaned. Then, as the tin containers are carried along on the belt, we have to fill them with vegetables and meat. This belt system compels us to work very fast, and recently, although a number of girls have been put off, the numbers of tins that we are producing per day still remains the same. . . . We have to work like machines. But while a smaller number of us are giving more of our labour, our wages still remain the same.[20]

In fish canning factories, which a former union official compared with California's cannery row as depicted by John Steinbeck, a complex division of labor separated not only women and men, but the small number of permanent workers (10 percent) from more numerous contract laborers. Women worked only at two jobs: gutting, earning in one factory only 5d. an hour, and packing, considered a more responsible job and paid according to the item. Two other factories paid women a pittance of 3s. 1/2d. ordinary rate and 6d. overtime.[21] The labor here was particularly arduous. Magrieta Wynand, who worked in Lambert's Bay, disclosed the process of skinning the fish in graphic detail.

> The skin had a hard part that would tear your hands. The fish scales would stick underneath your fingernails. Your fingers would swell and become sore. We would work so hard the blood ran from our hands. We would have to go to the doctors with our own money to have the nails pulled out.[22]

As the primary group of seasonal workers, women occupied the least stable positions, whereas men predominated among permanent employees and qualified workers, those who had gained a degree of recognized skill. Assuming that women could be dismissed with impunity during the off-season, employers treated them as they did African male contract laborers who, in Luderitz Bay, for example, were kept on only between February and May.[23] They also might dismiss the entire labor force during a strike, mistakenly believing that nonpermanent workers were difficult to organize and would not respond to such provocation.

Women's temporary positions led to continuing conflict between the union and the state over whether they should be eligible for unemployment insurance. Officials and employers consistently argued that since alternative work was available, primarily in domestic service, such payments would foster idleness. The union countered that seasonal workers required time to recuperate from months of intense labor.[24] However great the need for rest, few women had this luxury, and most were forced to seek other jobs during the off-season, mainly as domestic workers. Yet some women also found more varied, if not necessarily more appealing work: farming, planting trees, or working in the factory store. The youngest and most fit, like Mary Mafeking, might be hired to break stones, arduous labor for which the factory paid 7s. 6d. a load, and farmers 2s. 6d. a day.[25]

Many aspects of work and of the labor process remained relatively stable until the early 1960s, when the level of mechanization increased rapidly; and, although shifts occurred over time in the composition of the labor force, the overwhelming majority of workers during the 1940s and 1950s were coloured and African and included both women and men.[26] While overall figures available for the 1940s exclude Africans, 1948 employment statistics from L.K.B. indicate a typical pattern. The two largest groups of employees were coloured women (32.7 percent of the work force) and African men (25.9 percent); coloured men and African women formed almost equal proportions, 13.7 percent and 13.5 percent respectively. The much smaller number of Europeans (men, 11.1 percent and women, 2.7 percent) were primarily administrative and clerical employees with distinct interests and concerns.[27]

Despite the continuing predominance of coloured women and African men throughout the 1950s, some shifts did occur. In the early period of the industry's expansion, the numbers of coloured men and women were roughly equal, although (apart from the years 1939–40 and 1946–47), men always outnumbered women. In 1950–51, however, the number of coloured men dropped substantially and remained significantly lower than the number of coloured women throughout the decade. The figures for that year are typical of the 1950s: 15 percent of the total labor force was coloured men, 31 percent coloured women. Thus, as union pressure for raises took effect, women's lower wages and their perceived flexibility (a seasonal reserve army of labor) made them increasingly attractive employees.

Similar efforts to reduce costs by seeking the cheapest possible workers are evident in the employment trends for African women, whose numbers rose steadily throughout the 1950s. While in 1950–51 they represented 9.4 percent of the total labor force in the industry, by 1958–59 they comprised 20.1 percent of the total. Curiously, however, in the crisis that hit the food and canning industry in the late 1950s, leading to a reduction of over 7,000 employees between 1958–59 and 1959–60, women were the hardest hit: while 29 percent of employees were coloured women in 1958–59, their numbers had fallen to 20.8 percent in 1959–60. African women dropped from 20.1 percent to 16.3 percent of the total.[28] Although in the case of coloured women, the reason for this drop is unclear, for black women, it probably represents the increasing success of the apartheid state in including them in influx control. As a result of these tightened controls on the number of African women in urban areas and particularly in the Western Cape, which was designated a "coloured preference area," large numbers were expelled to rural reserves.

A similar tendency to favor the cheapest and ostensibly most easily controllable labor is evident in the changing proportion of black and coloured workers in the course of the 1950s. Whereas in 1950–51, 46 percent of workers were coloured, their proportion of the total dropped gradually over the course of the decade to 40.5 percent in 1958–59, and then rather precipitously to 33.4 percent the following year. By contrast, the percentage of Africans grew steadily during this time, rising from 37.3 percent of the workforce in 1950–51 to 48.1 percent in 1959–60.[29]

Although not substantial for most workers, a gender-based wage gap helps to explain women's attractiveness to employers. In 1947 women laborers under eighteen earned 93.5 percent of male wages, reflecting the meager remuneration for all youth. When workers turned eighteen, however, the gender gap widened, and women received only 80 percent of men's pay. A similar differential of 83 percent held among Grade 4 workers (the lowest in the graded hierarchy).[30] Gender inequality increased substantially among higher paid workers: women supervisors earning 67 percent of the pay of their male counterparts, while forewomen earned only 56 percent of the pay of foremen.[31] Considering women's greater prevalence in seasonal work and probably among casual employees paid on a daily basis, their yearly earnings would have been substantially less than those of most men. Yet the lower differential in the most menial jobs gave employers less incentive to replace men with women in these positions. Indeed, in 1955 the Wage Board proposed a significant decrease in the wages of women laborers, which the union saw as introducing a new form of discrimination against women, thereby asserting the "superiority of the male" and providing employers with cheap labor. The Board expressed the belief that it was "normal" in other countries to employ women in such work.[32]

The distribution of gender-specific wage scales documents the clustering of women in the lower grades of work. By contrast with the separate male and female wage designations for Grade 4 employees, the lack of distinct scales for the higher grades (1–3) suggests the absence of women from these jobs. Although equally prevalent as "laborers," many black men occupied these graded positions, as well as jobs as food boilers, beginning at £2 1s. a week, but with steadily rising wages. After three years, a qualified boiler earned £5 17s. 6d. a week. Most women who had escaped the classification of "laborer" became fruit molders or packers, earning £2 2s. 6s., but lacking any possibility of increasing their wages according to the length of their experience. (No parallel grouping existed for men.)[33]

Although the absence of racial segregation in factories and in many communities formed a strong base for building solidarity among all food workers, the structure of the industry, with its great demand for unskilled or semiskilled laborers, contributed as well. The figures on this are striking: in 1945 in the dried fruit industry, 70 percent of total employees were classified as laborers and nearly 95 percent as either general workers or laborers.[34] Although general workers earned slightly more than laborers, the difference was not great; in Cape Town, for example, all wages in these two categories fell between £1 3s. and £2 4s. 1d. per week. The other two sources of distinction, apart from gender, were region and age.[35] Thus, although social relationships in the factories did not necessarily transcend racial boundaries, black and coloured food workers did not face the degree of wage or skill distinction that was built into the structure of the garment industry. This relative equality was reflected in most instances of conflict, where workers usually supported each other without hesitation, often forcing employers to seek scabs from outside the factory to keep production going.

If the forms of labor necessary for food and canning production encouraged interracial unity, even at a time when state policies pointedly sought to intensify divisions among working-class people, the structure of the industry made this group of workers more difficult to organize than in most other comparable sectors of the economy in the 1940s. Industrial decentralization created similar problems for clothing and textile organizers from the 1950s onward. Not only did the seasonal nature of work make it difficult to keep branches active during the off-season, but of the twenty-seven union branches listed in the 1957 Annual Report, twenty-four were scattered across the rural areas of the Eastern and Western Cape and up the coast of Namibia (then South West Africa), a center of the fishing industry. The remaining three included Cape Town, Durban, and Johannesburg. Holding together such a dispersed organization required continual effort. But it also necessitated responsible and independent local leadership, thereby fostering attempts to encourage a high level of democracy within the union. Frances Baard, an African union leader in Port Elizabeth, recalled the intense concern of the first general secretary, Ray Alexander, with training local branch leaders. "She taught us how to run the union, and we learnt administration and taking minutes, how to chair a meeting, and about shop stewards and so on, so that the union should be properly run."[36]

If racial barriers were more easily bridged than in other parts of South Africa, a gap between permanent dwellers and workers brought in from outside remained a significant source of division, especially in smaller centers like Ashton, Wolseley, and Worcester. In Wolseley, for example, where migrant workers were either transported back and forth daily or lived in various forms of factory accommodation, the resulting residential dispersal was the major impediment to unity among employees. Richard Goode judged that between the two groups "there was little mutual assistance or contact, nor was there much cooperation and community solidarity."[37] Furthermore, those who lived in factory housing faced the prospect of eviction if they took part in work stoppages.

Although these structural conditions created particular constraints and opportunities that influenced the organizing of food and canning workers, both women and men, the strongly articulated political orientation of union leaders was equally vital in shaping the direction of the FCWU. Bettie du Toit, who had sharpened her skills in the textile struggles of the 1930s, initiated the organizing process in Johannesburg and became the local branch secretary there. But the center of the union lay in the Cape, where its energetic founder, Ray Alexander, took up the challenge of the Guardian article, bringing to the task her energy, her dedication to a non-racial South Africa, and an ideological perspective strongly shaped by the contemporary concerns of the South African Communist party.

Born in Latvia into a religious Jewish family, Alexander became involved early in illegal communist activity. By the age of fifteen, when she went to Riga to study for a teaching certificate at the technical college, she belonged to an organization whose members faced the continual threat of arrest. Learning that the police were searching for her daughter, Alexander's mother arranged to send her to South Africa. She arrived in 1929, not quite sixteen, but already an ardent advocate of the Eastern European and Soviet revolutionary tradition. It did not take her long to find political companionship in Cape Town.

Shortly after her arrival, Alexander began assisting the organizers of a number of different unions, doing office work, visiting workers in factories and homes, and taking part in picket lines during strikes. She improved her English by working through Olive Schreiner's classic *Woman and Labour*. From 1933 onward Alexander played a key role in forming numerous new local unions: the Commercial Employees' Union (forerunner of the National Union of Distributive Workers), the Oatmeal Workers, and the Non-European Railway Workers' Union. Later in the decade, as a moving force behind the new surge of unionization in Cape Town, she worked directly with chemical, sweet, laundry, and tin workers, and with shoe repairers. In 1940, Alexander turned her organizing abilities to the food and canning workers whose numbers were mushrooming under wartime conditions.[38] At the time of her banning in 1953, a union flyer detailed her philosophy and the range of her concerns.

> She not only organised workers in trade unions but fought against injustice to the workers, and has always been in the forefront of the struggle for freedom and justice. She also took part in the recent campaigns against apartheid on buses, fought for the reduction in the price of bread, against the introduction of the Separate Representation of Voters Bill and has always been in the forefront of the struggle for democratic rights for all working men and women, and for an independent and democratic Trade Union movement.[39]

A special meeting held at the time of her banning expressed a sense of reverence for Alexander and her accomplishments. As the main speaker, Oscar Mpetha of the African Food and Canning Workers' Union drew out emotional audience responses that have the ring of a church service: "Until Ray came we were slaves," and "If Ray dies we must die. Hand in hand and with all our hearts we must try to get Ray back." Mpetha concluded, "Watch out that your children don't curse you when you grow up because you did nothing. If you feel she must come back, then say so." To which members responded resoundingly: "Yes!!!!"[40]

Alexander initiated the FCWU at a meeting in Cape Town on February 6, 1941; the Paarl branch, formed the following month, held its first gathering on the banks of the Berg River because a hall was unobtainable. Less than a year later, in January 1942, a national union was created, and by the end of that year the Wage Board was conducting its first investigation of the industry (a process that failed to yield the promising results the union had anticipated). Under inflationary wartime conditions, how-

ever, and appealing to workers lacking any access to alternative rural resources, the union spread quickly. Within three years branches had developed in Paarl, Wellington, Worcester, Groot Drakenstein, Stellenbosch,
Wolseley, Ashton, Lamberts Bay, Robertson, Port Elizabeth, Port Nolloth,
Grabouw, Saldanha Bay, Ceres, Prince-Alfred Hamlet, and Doornbaai.[41]
Successful strikes in a number of areas, leading to increases in pay, helped
to galvanize support, forcefully convincing workers of the material benefits that membership could offer them. By the time Alexander was banned
in 1953, she had successfully won over workers of all communities. In a
tribute to her success, the women of the African townships of Langa and
Nyanga gave her respectively the names of Nozizwe and Nothemba,
meaning "trustworthy."[42] Frances Baard, a leading union activist, remembers the great affection workers felt for Alexander: "We used to call
her our mother."[43]

Highlights of the early years included a strike in September 1941 at H.
Jones and Company in Paarl. Angry over the firing of an employee for
trade union organizing, workers soon expressed grievances over wages
and working conditions. These events established a pattern of equal female and male involvement in local union activity. Although the dismissed employee was a man who had worked at the factory for thirteen
years, the other two workers penalized during the strike, for arranging to
have the Inspector of Labour visit the factory to investigate complaints,
were Mrs. D. Adriaanse and Miss Eva Arendse. Arendse soon became
the organizer for Paarl and the union vice president.[44]

With the success of the Paarl strike, other branches quickly followed
suit, over the protests of canners, one of whom complained that the workers
always had been "happy and content" until Ray Alexander came along
and "upset" them.[45] Many of the early stoppages, at the Cape and elsewhere, showed patterns of solidarity that were to mark the history of the
union during this period. On November 29, 1941, 150 women at the factory of Associated Canners at Daljosaphat ceased work demanding pay
increases; the "lorry loads of girls" brought from Wellington as scabs refused to work when they realized why they were there.[46] In Durban that
December, four hundred employees of Morton's jam factory left work,
also over wages. For the coloured, Indian, and African workers, both
women and men, the precipitating incident came when forty African
women were put on short time. The pitifully paid women piece workers
who, lacking a guaranteed wage, had to appear at the factory each morning in case there was any work, reportedly reacted with joy to the increase they received when the strike was settled two months later.[47] Similar instances of cooperation occurred repeatedly. During a 1957 strike at
the Spekenham meat factory, for example, legal for the coloured workers,
but not for the Africans, the coloured union raised money to pay the fines
imposed on African participants.[48]

This solidarity extended to efforts to divide workers on the basis of gender. In 1959, when workers at L.K.B. were notified that pay cuts decreed in Wage Determination 179 of the previous year were to begin with men in the carpentry shop, these men filed out and submitted their reference books for discharge. As the strike spread to the entire factory, the managers tried to call separate meetings for men and women. The women refused to be separated and chastised management for its divide and rule policies, in particular, for telling the men that the women already had accepted the cuts.[49]

The Wage Board recommendations for the food industry announced in July 1943 provoked another round of strike action. Instead of raising salaries, the proposals degraded certain categories of work from higher paid "general workers" to "laborers."[50] When managers of the Rhodes Fruit Farms Canning Factory attempted to implement these recommendations, a lightning strike forced them to restore all cuts.[51] Local strikes at Wellington and Stellenbosch shortly thereafter reflected the general discontent that the determination had created.[52]

The union's success, partly a product of the wartime demand for food, also generated new grounds for protest among the workers as numerous union activists were victimized; being female sometimes seem to provoke particular management disfavor. A labor official investigating the degrading and firing of a number of women involved in the union called in Annie McKenzie, one of four who had been dismissed, and demanded to know why she had called on people to strike. When asked why he had singled her out, the official replied "it was because she appeared to have brains."[53] Frances Baard was penalized somewhat differently: by being demoted from a supervisor to an ordinary worker. In fact, the union argued, she ought to have been classified as a forewoman because her work entailed instructing others.[54]

Women's dominance during the late 1953–early 1954 strike in Wolseley further illuminates their significance in union affairs. Although mainly a dispute about pay, early in the negotiations another grievance surfaced: the company's decision to hand out wages on Saturday instead of Friday. Primarily affecting women, this new policy left them no time to buy food for the week because of early shop-closing on Saturday. Whether this decision angered women particularly is uncertain; but their heavy involvement, apparent from the start, is not. The *Cape Times* described the action as a strike of "several hundred Coloured and Native women," a depiction verified by arrest figures: of the 131 people tried for striking illegally, only eighteen were men. Nor did these women lack domestic responsibility. The 380 strikers arrested on January 21, 1954, included ninety-six women with small children for whom relatives and friends pooled their funds to raise bail money. Equally significant, the leaders of the action were exclusively female. Dismissed from their jobs as the union's "leading members" were Annie McKenzie, Rachel Williams, and Margarita Bastiaan. Three other women, Rachel Sass, Janetta Crotz, and Sophie

Kriger, were credited with insuring regular strike committee meetings and keeping up worker morale.[55]

The union's successes in the early years did not imply an absence of problems, either internal or external. Some branches were better organized than others, and the strength of branches varied over time. All had to address common critical issues: the attitudes of some male organizers, who assumed that union women were at their disposal; high rates of illiteracy that made communications difficult; and suspicions about the financial probity of officials, which lingered as a legacy of the Industrial and Commercial Workers' Union.[56] In addition, falling behind in collecting subscriptions was not uncommon; but it became a serious problem at times when conciliation boards were appointed and the Labour Department checked union registers to ascertain whether the union was sufficiently representative of workers in the industry. In 1953, for example, in a memo headed "S.O.S.," Alexander reminded officials in Paarl, one of the stronger branches, to see that all workers were paid up. Emphasizing the need for ongoing organization and communication, she noted, "The trouble is that our members have forgotten what the Union has done for them, and they do not realise what their lives would have been without the union. They also do not realise what the Union is still capable of doing for them if they stand together!"[57]

The seasonal nature of the work force also presented continual organizing problems, as Frances Baard recalls. Not only did many work for no more than six months a year, but the same people were not necessarily hired year after year. "The first people to come there get a job. And so each year we must start educating the workers again." Furthermore, branches sometimes lay dormant during the off-season, possibly finding it difficult to maintain their momentum at a time when only the most skilled, best-paid workers were employed. "Every year," Baard explained, "we used to get some new people on the committee too, because those others were perhaps gone, or they won't be taken back into the factory when work starts again because the managers know them now as union people."[58]

Despite the union's unquestioned success in many areas, the structural difficulties imposed by geographical dispersion and the problems of organizing a seasonal and partly migrant labor force were impossible to overcome completely. And, by the late 1950s, severe new external pressures compounded these difficulties. For one thing, the expansive conditions of the early 1940s had ended. In 1958, a government study concluded that the food and canning industry had entered a period of stagnation.[59] A wave of dismissals reflected this economic crisis; but political pressures created equal concern. Ray Alexander, Becky Lan, and other officials had been banned under the Suppression of Communism Act, and the Industrial Conciliation Act of 1956 threatened to expel the few black workers in higher level positions in order to replace them with whites.[60] Two years later, the Minister of Labour, disregarding union objections, introduced Wage Determinations Nos. 179 and 180, which actually reduced the wages then in effect.[61] Further blows came in 1959. Amendments to the Industrial Conciliation Act increased pressure for racial segregation in the union and the government classified food canning as an "essential service," making strikes in the industry illegal.[62]

While branches always varied in their effectiveness, these pressures weakened the organizing efforts and the morale of even the strongest centers. The Annual Report of 1958 noted that the union newspaper *Morning Star* had not appeared for six months, while Oscar Mpetha of the AFCWU lamented the following year that Paarl lacked "the same spirit as they had before." He wondered whether this was due to the banning of Comrades Ray Alexander and Frank Marquard.[63] At the same time, the response to new organizing efforts in East London was described as "poor," a result of employer intimidation and police interference. A letter to the Port Elizabeth branch expressed shock that its officials had not notified the central office that the employers intended to cut pay in accordance with Wage Determination 179.[64]

In April 1959, in the midst of these pressures, a disturbing event occurred. Intruders who designated themselves as the Klu [sic] Klux Klan vandalized the head office, destroying typewriters and adding machines, setting fire to a duplicating machine, tearing up and pouring ink over files, and writing obscene slogans on the walls in Afrikaans and English. In a deliberately symbolic act, they destroyed the English dictionary, but not its Afrikaans counterpart. This violent assault, coming at an uneasy moment, must have made members and leaders alike feel that, under contemporary South African conditions, their principles were growing increasingly dangerous to maintain.[65] Yet the union's commitment to equality was not easily shaken. For both its ideological base and its daily work rested on firmly held ideas not only about race, but also about gender, class, and community.

-11-

STANDING UNITED

The labor process in the food and canning factories provided organizers with both problems and possibilities. In their efforts to transcend the structural constraints of a seasonal and partly migrant labor force and to address the challenges of increasing state racism, they developed policies toward gender, race, and community that helped to nurture women's full participation. While the political orientation of the FCWU and the AFCWU encouraged women to resist taking passes under union auspices, an emphasis on nonracial unity created space for solidarity and friendship between African and coloured women. Thus, by contrast with black Transvaal garment workers after the mid-1950s, women were encouraged to bring political struggles into the factories. Equally critical, the union's responsiveness to family and community issues helped to bridge the conflicts between women's working lives and their lives at home. Sustained by an organization shaped in so many ways to their particular needs, women, especially those permanently settled in the areas in which they worked, became the union's backbone in the 1940s and 1950s.

Maintaining a nonracial trade union was a continual struggle. The first threat came in 1945 when the Blanke Werkers Federasie, supported and financed by the National party and the Dutch Reformed Church, tried to form unions of European food workers in Ashton, Worcester, Robertson, and Paarl.[1] With the small number of white production workers, these efforts were far less destructive than in the garment industry. In 1947, however, Labour Department officials threatened to deregister some FCWU branches if black membership continued, forcing the union to form a separate African Food and Canning Workers' Union.[2]

Because they were exempted from the pass laws, the inclusion of African women presented a separate problem. Although a 1944 Supreme Court ruling had allowed them to join the Transvaal GWU, the Department of Labour was slow to extend this decision to the food industry. Only in 1951 was the union informed that "this office has always regarded Native females as employees in terms of the Industrial Conciliation Act."[3] The decision came late, however; within two years the Native (Labour) Settlement of Disputes Act forced African women to return to a racially exclusive organization.

Though separation caused innumerable practical problems, union officials made every effort to insure that the two groups were as equal as possible, given official recognition only of the coloured union. By contrast with the GWU, representatives from the black union took full part in meetings and discussions, although the minutes had to list them as "visitors" to avoid violating the law and risking deregistration. When Alexander learned that African women could be incorporated into the FCWU, she immediately scheduled new elections to insure their representation on the union committee.[4] Frances Baard recalls, "We worked together all the time like we were one union. We always had our meetings and discussions together, and all our strikes we did together too."[5] Even after the Group Areas Act mandated separate offices for the black and coloured unions, the Port Elizabeth branch resisted segregation, suffering continual police harassment as a result.[6] Reflecting these ideals in both a symbolic and a practical way, the secretaries of the registered union and the African union usually traveled together in their regular visits to the branches.

Within the wider trade union movement, there was controversy over how best to express the commitment to nonracialism. Until 1953 the FCWU at the Cape belonged to the nonracial South African Trades and Labour Council (SATLC), a federation dating back to 1930. Following Alexander's belief in a united union movement, she opposed membership in the Transvaal-based Council of Non-European Trade Unions (CNETU), advocating instead that this group affiliate with the SATLC.[7] But in 1953, when the SATLC caved in to pressure from the state and right-wing unions and decided to exclude Africans, the FCWU was critical, emphasizing its "persistent and constant fight against race discrimination in the trade union movement."

By 1955, FCWU leaders were among the trade unionists who split from the SATLC to form the South African Congress of Trade Unions (SACTU), affiliated with the Congress Alliance and committed to a broad nonracial struggle against racial and class oppression. Leon Levy, branch secretary of the Johannesburg FCWU, became its president and a number of women from the union became SACTU branch secretaries: Rachael Green in Benoni, Delores Telling in Port Elizabeth, and Louisa Kellerman in Cape Town.[8] The close connection between the SACTU and the union meant that many other organizers and officials, such as Mary Moodley and Mabel Balfour in the Transvaal and Frances Baard in Port Elizabeth were involved simultaneously in both organizations. Under their influence, the union campaigned actively in 1957 to support SACTU's drive for a minimum wage of one pound a day.[9] These women also may have shaped the instructions that SACTU drew up to assist speakers in publicizing the campaign. The guidelines were particularly interesting in acknowledging the importance of domestic work. They called for the recognition of housewives as workers and for a sharing of household tasks in families where women were wage earners.[10]

In all of its work, FCWU actions and policies reflected the conviction that industrial, political, community, and international events were inseparable and that educating workers politically would make them feel part of a wider community struggling against oppression and exploitation. Annual Reports in the late 1940s emphasized the union's connection to a vibrant worldwide progressive movement with a prolabor, anti-imperialist character. The reported support of these forces for the antiracist struggle in South Africa helped to sustain hopes for democratically inclined internal change. Like Solly Sachs in the Garment Workers' Union, Ray Alexander used every opportunity to provide a broad context for union actions, connecting local struggles in the workplace to the "derived" ideology of international communism. How many workers adopted this perspective is uncertain; but it is worth noting that expressions of concern for world peace and other global issues often found their way into local branch resolutions, alongside demands for paved roads, telephone booths, and better street lighting.

While expressions of optimism were understandably muted by the mid-1950s, continual and determined opposition to the laws and policies of the apartheid state pervaded union records and actions, through scathing attacks on job reservation and other racist policies and through active support for the multiracial liberation struggle. This broad-based movement centering on the "Congress Alliance" of the African National Congress (ANC) and affiliated coloured, Indian, and white organizations led campaigns of passive resistance during the 1950s against all forms of oppressive legislation. The spirit behind the union's work was expressed in a class-oriented explanation of the Congress movement. Analyzing apartheid as not simply a form of racial domination, but as a means "to supply the employers, farms and mines with cheap labour," a circular letter of the late 1950s explained more fully: "Whilst the bosses pile up more and more profits, the workers and their children have to starve. The people cannot and will not accept these conditions. They must organise and unite in the struggle against racial, national and class oppression."[11]

Among the strongest trade unions at the Cape, the FCWU and the AFCWU played a significant part in involving workers in contemporary political campaigns. These nonracial struggles drew on a complex history of cooperation and distance between black and coloured political activists in the Western Cape, first in the burgeoning Industrial and Commercial Workers' Union of the early 1920s, before coloured members were expelled from the organization, and then in the brief but intense period of militant political action among the rural proletariat in 1929–30 under the aegis of the African National Congress in the Western Cape. Distinct both for the joint participation of black and coloured people and for the inclusion of women, these movements formed part of a tradition on which the FCWU could draw.[12]

The union's left-wing political orientation and its deep involvement with SACTU and the Congress Alliance led naturally to a close connection with the Federation of South African Women, as did Ray Alexander's position as a founding member of the group. Formed in 1954 (the year after Alexander was banned and forced to give up her position in the FCWU), the Federation took up numerous issues related to women's racial and economic oppression and became especially involved in the struggle against passes for women. In addition to Alexander, those who issued the call for the initial conference included a number of union members: A. M. Coe, Frances Baard, and L. Diedrichs of Port Elizabeth and Martha Nqxesha of East London. Union branches lent money to support women who attended the organizing conference in Johannesburg and also elected delegates to a later regional meeting in Cape Town.[13] The heavy representation of trade unionists (from the food, textile, tobacco, furniture, and tin industries), suggests that unions provided the main strength of the Federation in the Cape.[14] During 1955 the Management Committee of the FCWU resolved to affiliate with the Federation and appealed to its branches to cooperate with the organization.[15]

Such close ties between the union and the most significant women's group of the 1950s encouraged politically aware women in the food and canning industry to combine labor and political work and created a climate conducive to disclosing the connections between these two arenas of struggle. Broad-based grassroots organizing was characteristic of the early years of the Federation, particularly in areas like Paarl with strong union branches. Women campaigned around such issues as rent increases and the removal of the municipal vote from coloured women and Indians. By 1957, however, under the aegis of the coalition group, the Cape Association to Abolish Passes for African Women, the issue of passes became dominant.[16]

The extension of passes to women in the Cape formed an important aspect of the effort to expel the region's black population in order to create a "coloured labor preference area." The registration of African women throughout the Western Cape began in earnest in 1954, accompanied by massive arrests, prosecutions, and deportations. Within two years, 2,500 families had been "endorsed out" of the area and over 2,800 African women illegally in the Cape were ordered to leave.[17] The distribution of passes to women followed late in 1959, and within three months some twelve thousand had been issued.[18]

If the towns of the Cape were the first to experience the full force of apartheid legislation regarding women, many of these centers in both the Eastern and Western Cape were well equipped to respond. Worcester and Paarl, with strong union branches, had staunchly supported the Defiance Campaign against racial legislation in 1952 and, in struggles infused by a mood of religious fervor, Port Elizabeth and East London had produced the largest number of arrests in the country. Resisters in Port Elizabeth also routinely combined civil disobedience with strike action.[19] Nor was the strong alliance between the ANC and the unions unexpected: in Port Elizabeth, "consistently the strongest centre of ANC mobilisation, trade unions had in the 1940s thrown up a political leadership and generated an organisational expertise that made the ANC a much more constant local political influence than in most centres." By 1952 trade unionists dominated local ANC leadership in the city.[20]

In the struggle against this new turn in the pass laws, the FCWU and the AFCWU played a leading role, in alliance with the African National Congress. In rural areas like Worcester and Paarl, where communication was difficult, most women came into the Federation through the union and their organizations virtually coincided.[21] Women from these two communities provided strong backing for a march against passes held in Cape Town in May 1957 and addressed by Louise Kellerman of the FCWU and Elizabeth Mafeking of the AFCWU and the ANC Women's League; they also led local protest demonstrations to location and town officials. In Worcester the women were determined either to return all reference books or to burn them.[22] Adopting tactics the union had used effectively in its early organizing years, women went from door to door to mobilize support.

Not surprisingly, Port Elizabeth was the scene of some of the most successful women's struggles, often factory-based actions forceful enough to postpone the introduction of passes for protesters. At L.K.B., the city's largest canning factory, the management posted notices in November 1956 informing workers that all African women should bring passes from the Labour Bureau. The strong and immediate response was appropriate to a city with an active ANC presence and uncontrolled African movement prior to 1953. Women decided to ignore the directive and to go to work as usual, but to remain at the gate as others entered the factory. When the manager ordered those who wished to work to come forward with their passes, the women replied, "We want work, not passes." As men left their jobs in a gesture of support, the manager was forced to meet with a workers' committee and agreed to take the women back without passes.[23]

Frances Baard, an activist in the campaign in Port Elizabeth, relates the way in which the government encouraged employers to demand passes from their workers even before it was legally required, frightening many women who feared they would lose their jobs if they refused the new documents. Sending trucks into the township to issue the passes was a chief tactic. Describing the efforts to persuade women to resist, Baard explained:

We would see the trucks standing in the townships giving passes to the women. Then we would go and stand next to the truck and talk to the women who have come to collect their passes. We would talk to them and tell them what it will be like if we take these things, how the government wants us to take these things so they can control us more easily, and tell us where to live, and where to work, and that we can't do this and this.[24]

In other such incidents, however, the women were not as fortunate. When factory owners in Paarl took women by lorry to the registration office, many women, whether they refused passes and went to jail or accepted them, ended up without permission to remain in the area. Others were issued permits that allowed them the temporary right to retain their work at the factory.[25]

Although the anti-pass effort encouraged many African women workers to resist this new extension of state power, the emphasis on passes may have distanced them in new ways from their coloured coworkers. Mafeking's words, urging coloured women "not to stand by idly while these things happen to their African sisters," but to "join with us to fight this evil"[26] convey an ambivalent message. While expressing the union's tradition of working-class solidarity, the need for such a plea may indicate that in this new phase of action against the state, necessitated by racial rather than class oppression, black women felt they were struggling alone. Supporting this interpretation, J. Schreiner suggests that as the ANC Women's League, closely allied with the Federation and the union, eclipsed earlier nonracial women's organizations in the Western Cape (such as the Cape Housewives' League and the Women's Food Committee), new initiatives among coloured women were blocked.[27]

Analyzing the anti-pass struggles on the Witwatersrand during the 1950s, Julia Wells suggests that the main impetus came from women struggling against proletarianization, and particularly against domestic employment that would require lengthy periods of separation from their homes and children.[28] But for factory women, apparently at the core of the Cape anti-pass movement, the motivation was different: to protect the jobs on which their families depended, and to retain the right to remain in areas where wage labor was available. Rather than resisting proletarianization, they were guarding their urban proletarian position and trying to avoid being expelled to unfamiliar, impoverished rural reserves. Both groups of women, however, sought to escape from the controls on their labor and their movement that passes had imposed on African men.

While leaders exposed members to the discourse of resistance in a way that galvanized many to take part in opposition politics and to share their critique of racism and capitalism, perhaps the union developed its greatest strength through its active concern with health, housing, childcare, and other aspects of community and personal life. In this respect, the AFCWU and the FCWU were as much vehicles for community organizing as they were an effective trade union. This emphasis, undoubtedly shaped by women's strong presence in the union, allowed them to integrate the worlds of work, family, and community and contributed to the ability to mobilize when communities were threatened with destruction under the Group Areas Act. Indeed, the union's strategy of organizing around such varied issues was, in itself, a challenge to the separate boundaries of work and community. In an industry with high levels of seasonal female labor, this organizational approach and this involvement with daily local issues had the potential to keep women active, even during the off-season.

A 1953 survey of two rural towns in the Western Cape, Ashton and Montague, conveys an impression of working-class life in the areas from which many of the stable workers were drawn. Most households had two adult members and nearly four children, two fifths of whom were in school. With an average of six people, each group occupied 3.24 rooms. Relatively stable, these families had lived in the same place for an average of twelve years; two fifths of the sample were long-time residents of fourteen to twenty-five years. Subsisting on household earnings of £2 14s. per week, rent took an average of 6s. 3d., but often less. Typical of working-class budgets, food absorbed the bulk of family income, with bread as the staple, supplemented by meat and milk. Other important items included sugar, coffee, beans, vegetables, and mealies (maize meal). Coal and wood for fuel, and paraffin and candles for lighting indicate the absence of electricity. Although cigarettes, doctors, and insurance were noted among "other expenditures," contributions to churches was the most common item in this category.[29]

If daily life lacked luxury, it was far better than in the camps for migrant workers. Drawn from both urban and rural slums, these women and men were assured upon recruitment of free housing sufficiently spacious both for babies and for the older children who cared for them while their parents worked. Instead they found cramped and filthy accommodations. Houses in Wolseley, for example, had two rooms, each measuring ten feet by twelve feet, bare apart from a coal stove for cooking. Twenty unrelated people, all sleeping on the floor with only thin sacking for blankets, might be crowded into each house. Sanitation facilities were shocking: a single water tank two hundred yards from the houses, no washing facilities, and bucket closets directly behind the houses. A union letter informed the Secretary for Public Health: "The filth under which these food workers live has to be seen to be believed."[30]

These families had little choice, however, for conditions were no better at home, whether in the urban squalor of Elsies River or in rural areas like Kraaifontein, where perilous health conditions prevailed. A handwritten letter to the union from Kraaifontein, a community northeast of Cape Town from which workers were recruited, explained: "Now that the Health Inspector in the first place condemned our animales such as donkes cows sheep goats even fowels now he is condemned our houses puting it all down to ill health. I like to give an explanination to all our friends." The explanation detailed dangerous roads of deep muddy water on which children had to travel to school; inadequate supplies of stagnant, stinking drinking water, which the health inspector refused to see as a possible cause of sickness; indiscriminate policies of destroying livestock and houses; and an inadequate road system on which an ambulance recently had been stuck for six hours. By the time it reached the hospital, the occupants had died. The letter concluded, "Kraaifontein is a very poor village and got no work. We have to go out to work. We are not dissatifide to better our selfs if the Board will be so kind to assist us."[31]

By contrast with the predominantly youthful, unattached female factory employees of the 1930s, the women who canned fruits and vegetables at the Cape in the following two decades were more diverse. Often married with families or widowed, many women worked beside their daughters in the factories. Regardless of marital status, women's earnings were a dire necessity, whether as the family's only source of income or as an essential supplement to the wages of other household members.[32]

Liz Abrahams, who became general secretary of the union in 1956 at the age of twenty, was among those who followed a family tradition of working in the canneries. Speaking of her past, she explained:

> I grew up here in Paarl and we were eight children, four brothers and four sisters . . . my father was a sickly man; I had two brothers in the army . . . I was in the middle. I decided to leave school [after the sixth year], so that I could help my mother; we just couldn't afford for me to go on. My mother worked in the factory when there was no union yet, and that's where I joined her. My younger sister stayed home and looked after the younger children.[33]

Despite laws that prohibited children under the age of fifteen from working in factories, child labor provided another means for families to sustain themselves (and for employers to gain the cheapest, most expendable workers). A report from L. K. B. Worcester observed, "When it is season time the school children run to the factories for employment."[34] Similarly, union officials visiting Ashton in February 1957 found the factory employing children between the ages of nine and thirteen.[35] Reflecting the frequency of such violations, a union letter to the Labour Department demanded action on the grounds that "Our Union has submitted complaints of this nature to your Department year after year."[36] The 1956 Annual Report, noting the large number of children found working during the fruit seasons and school holidays, appealed for educational efforts so that parents, and particularly mothers, would not to allow their children to work in the factories.[37]

All of these families were engaged in a continual struggle for survival. Wages were insufficient for daily necessities, making it impossible to save any money to cover expenses during the off-season. In the winter, workers bought food and clothing on credit, hoping to earn enough during the season to pay off their debts.[38] Some tried to supplement their wages by farming, but the possible earnings were judged "negligible." Poverty also led to severe malnutrition among children and to high child death rates from tuberculosis, rickets, and scurvy.[39]

The implementation of the Group Areas Act from the mid-1950s onward, threatening the removal of long-established coloured communities, created new forms of fear and insecurity. As the prime political organization in an area like Paarl, the union took the lead in 1956 when ten thousand coloured people were threatened with displacement at the request of the European Ratepayers' Association. In her appeal to mobilize everyone possible against this forced removal (trade unions, churches, sport and benefit societies, schools, and any other cultural organizations), Liz Abrahams argued, "This is a crisis facing the Coloured people in Paarl and many of these workers are members of our Union."[40] Abrahams described long-standing white and coloured neighborhoods of neat, well-built houses whose coloured occupants would be forced to move to barren and stony areas far from shopping centers and workplaces. As if to sharpen the indignity, those displaced would be forced to bear the costs of developing the new areas.[41]

If many of the union's campaigns reflected an effort to mobilize people in the interests of present and future justice and egalitarianism, state policies of the 1950s also prompted another equally poignant sentiment: the desire to preserve communities and traditions (such as the right to vote) threatened by state power ruthless in pursuit of its own vision of a more rigidly segregated future. Indeed, as the decade progressed, many working-class actions (such as the campaign against passes for women) drew their strength from appeals to preserve the rights of the past, whatever their shortcomings. Although the women's pass movement may be an exception, some of these efforts to resist Nationalist policies also helped to intensify the community of interest between the black and coloured populations of the Western Cape.[42]

Wide-ranging branch resolutions at annual conferences indicate the degree to which the struggle "for a better life" provided a means for members to relate varied local issues to a larger ongoing political movement. Extending from critiques of job reservation, restrictions on strikes, high rentals, and taxes, to demands for crèches, maternity homes, bus shelters, and better housing, these resolutions prompted discussion of the connections between national and community issues. Rather than a weakness, a substitute for shop floor organizing, as some critics of progressive unions in the 1950s have argued, these concerns strengthened the union's place in the daily lives of its members, carrying on a tradition that Alexander articulated at an FCWU conference in 1943. Observing that in many country districts, the FCWU was not only the first trade union, but the only working-class organization, she argued: "It is our duty to attend not only to wages and conditions in the factories, but to help people build a better life outside the factories."[43] Highlighting the continuing importance of such work a decade later, the union newspaper urged:

> Branches must take part in the economic, political and social lives of the members in their areas, which means that it is the branch's business to see that the streets in which the workers live should be clean and lit at night, that the children should have crèches, that there should be enough schools for the children, that there should be pre- and post-natal clinics, a district nurse, and above all to see that the people struggle for democratic rights to vote and be elected to all governing bodies of our country.[44]

The concern with housing and community life went far beyond rhetoric. Officials aggressively investigated and sought to address complaints on all aspects of community and personal life: pressing for the development of municipal housing in Paarl in the early 1940s;[45] gathering evidence on housing, health, and medical care to present to the National Health Commission;[46] seeking an inquiry into housing and health conditions for 350 African families living in a municipal location outside of Worcester; and demanding the construction of maternity hospitals, dental clinics, and crèches.[47] In June 1952, protesting vigorously against plans to bulldoze an interracial squatters' camp where many members had lived for the previous five years, the union insisted that no homes be demolished until decent alternative accommodation had been provided.[48] Beginning with the union's first May Day celebration, held in Paarl in 1942, the union also established the right of coloured people in the Western Cape to assemble in the city halls of the region.[49]

Such activity was particularly intense in the early 1950s, perhaps reflecting a period of relatively stable organization and leadership. Concerns at the time included rent increases for municipal housing in New Brighton,[50] transportation for school children in Wolseley,[51] telephone booths for residential areas in Wellington, Worcester, and Paarl,[52] bus service to H. Jones & Company in Paarl,[53] and the construction of new housing throughout the Western Cape.[54] Finally, the union continually advocated the building of crèches, a necessity in an industry employing so many women. Occasionally these efforts succeeded, as in 1953 when facilities were built in Zuider Paarl for the workers at H. Jones & Co.[55]

Tying in closely with the philosophy of nonracial unity and community organizing was a strong stress on democracy and education within the union. To train leaders in political economy and in practical skills, the head office provided weekend courses, issued frequent circular letters and widely distributed annual reports, and published two successive newspapers: *The Food and Canning Worker* and *Ikwezi Lomso/Morning Star*.[56] Literacy classes began very early in the union's history, when Alexander learned that some branches were paying a local teacher to write their letters to the head office and then to read the replies. In addition to politics, the newspapers sometimes addressed other, more personal topics, such as keeping children busy, prenatal and maternity care, and proper vegetable cooking.[57] In a similar vein, a union conference held in 1954 considered ways of making workers more health conscious, discussing in particular the possibility of showing films on tuberculosis and its symptoms.[58] As Ray Alexander observed when informed that some workers did not want to pay their subscriptions and join the union, "It is our duty to explain, explain and explain again to the workers, and educate them so that they can take their places in society and bring about the necessary changes."[59]

J. Schreiner has criticized the political movements of the 1950s for adopting a strategy of occasional mass mobilization from above rather than one that involved participants closely in ongoing organizations.[60] But the strongest union branches, it may be argued, developed forms of shop-floor and neighborhood organization that succeeded in training local leaders and in involving members in decision-making. This grassroots emphasis undoubtedly drew in many women who otherwise would have remained politically uninvolved, and it provided the continuous engagement absent in political groups of the period. Strong community roots probably also account for the union's ability to mobilize its members for political campaigns, since the African National Congress was relatively weak in the Western Cape.

The extent of this community involvement undoubtedly reflects the composition of the labor force in the industry as well as the union's political commitment. With the canneries as a major source of local employment, families in which husbands, wives, and children all worked in the factories were not uncommon. Such employment patterns created a broad-based working-class culture in which women experienced little objective split between work and community. If the Garment Workers' Union, by the late 1940s and 1950s, had to work to forge a common political and cultural community outside of the factories, often in opposition to women's family loyalties, the AFCWU and the FCWU could shape their political strategies and discourse around workplace, community, and political problems that were closely connected with each other and with the daily lives of the women and men in the union. Furthermore, concern with such community issues often informed women's politics in South Africa.

While assigning high priority to the problems of working women and acknowledging the significance of gender-related differences in working-class experience, officials did not conceptualize women's distinct interests as an impediment to class unity. These gender differences, based on women's domestic and childbearing responsibilities, led to intensive campaigns around issues related to women's ability to combine factory work with family life. This approach to the relationship between gender and class was similar to that of the GWU.

A memorandum to the Women's Legal Disabilities Commission of 1947 outlined the perspective that shaped union policies on women: blaming an outdated legal system for women's difficult position and seeking support from capital and the state for social services and protective legislation to alleviate their double burden. Analyzing women's disadvantaged position as a survival from an era in which they had been excluded from public life, the memo argued that the law, while not creating inequality, "expressed and maintained" their inferior status. Now anachronistic because of increasing numbers of women in the labor force, legal inequities led to "glaring discrimination" in wage rates, which harmed both sexes by undervaluing women and by threatening men with displacement from cheaper female labor.[61]

Now that women had established a permanent place in economic life, according to the memorandum, the law should give them special consideration on account of their dual roles as workers and mothers. At a time when the birthrate was declining, "society must encourage the bearing of children and make it compatible with the employment of women in industry."[62] Diminishing the conflict between work and family would require improved confinement allowances, more adequate resting and dining space for non-European workers, more numerous crèches and nurseries and, finally, communal kitchens to free women from the double burden of "working hard in the factory and at home."[63] Appropriate to testimony before a state commission, the memorandum located the problem and its solution with the state and employers; by supporting collective solutions, these bodies also might address the issue of inequalities in the household division of labor.

A recent interview with Frances Baard highlights the difference between this approach and later analyses that confront the division of household work and power more directly. When asked whether the Women's Federation ever had taken an interest in the position of women in the home, she hesitated. But, after grasping the question's meaning, she replied firmly, "No, not husband and wife, wife and husband in the house, no. I don't think that (laugh). . . ." [You think those were not important?] "No they were not important for us. Of course, as a friend I would go to a husband and say why do you do this and this and this." [But you didn't see that as a political issue?] "No, No."[64]

This depoliticization of domestic relations did not mean, however, that leaders ignored the division of power within the family. Ray Alexander was intensely concerned about the issue, particularly as it affected women's ability to spend time on union-related and political work. Accordingly, she often intervened to persuade reluctant husbands to be more flexible in their attitudes and to share responsibilities in the household.

In the effort to minimize the conflicting pressures on women members, the union continually confronted several issues: night work, overtime work, and maternity benefits. These concerns, and the way they were formulated, reflected a persistent emphasis on easing the lives of women who had no choice but to combine full-time work with motherhood and family responsibilities.

Although national legislation prohibited women from working between 6 p.m. and 6 a.m., frequent infringements of the law and the practice of granting exemptions to employers under specified circumstances made the issue a focus of persistent negotiation between workers and management, punctuated by angry reactions to particularly gross violations.[65] In one instance, women and juvenile workers remained on duty from 7 a.m. until 4 a.m. the following day, with only a brief break for a "meal" of a single piece of fried fish. Leaving work at 4 a.m., they were instructed to return three hours later. When two women were dismissed after nearly fainting on the second day of this grueling schedule, the union intervened on their behalf.[66] Responding to such violations, officials repeatedly sought to prohibit night work for women because of their domestic responsibilities, but they also deemed such work "not beneficial to anyone regardless of sex."[67]

Conditions in the industry were not conducive to maintaining this principled stance without compromise. In December 1948, all employers received permission to allow women to work until 10 p.m. for a six-month period at overtime rates of time-and-a-half.[68] When canning companies attempted to extend women's hours even further in the early and mid-1950s, women argued for strictly defined conditions, including transport to and from work and the payment of time-and-a-half for any shift that extended into the prohibited periods.[69] Despite continuing union efforts to control the conditions of night and overtime work, by the late 1950s all workers were permitted to work up to seventy-eight hours per week, whereas in 1948 women were limited to a maximum of sixty hours. These escalating concessions led the union to request a moratorium on future exemptions to take effect the following month.[70]

While principled, opposition to exemptions from laws that restricted women's working hours had potential dangers. In the early 1950s, for example, one fish-canning factory responded to prohibitions on overtime work by introducing new machinery to be handled by men and then laying off the women previously responsible for these jobs. Neptune cleaning, cutting, and packing machines introduced at Lambert's Bay could process six thousand fish in an hour.[71] In discussing possible reactions to the new technology, union members feared it might "eliminate female labour in the factories."[72]

The issue of women's working hours naturally provoked discussion not only of their double duty, but also of how domestic labor was perceived under South African conditions. When discussing policies toward working women, insensitive officials required repeated reminding that not everyone could afford servants. A manager at H. Jones, for example, failed to understand why women lacked the time to eat breakfast at 5 a.m. before coming to work.[73] When a dispute arose at Tulbagh over Saturday absences from work, Abrahams explained to the Divisional Inspector of Labour:

> The workers complain that they are required to work excessive overtime everyday including Saturdays and Sundays, therefore they have insufficient time to attend to family and personal needs such as buying food and other household necessities, washing, keeping their homes clean and generally doing those tasks that have to be performed by housewives who have no servants.[74]

The question of maternity benefits elicited similar struggles with employers and the state, first, to persuade the Secretary of Labour to allow payment to seasonal workers[75] and then to insure that women were able to collect their benefits. Even after women who worked for at least 130 days per year had won the right to a confinement allowance, individual employers sometimes refused to process the claims and the Labour Department occasionally refused to enforce its own policy.[76]

Seasonal employment also led to conflicts over unemployment benefits. In April 1949, when sixty-four women laid off at L. K. B. sought to collect unemployment compensation, their request was refused because domestic work was available fifty miles away in George at wages substantially lower than in the factory. Married women objected not only to the meager pay, but also to the potential impact on their family lives if they were unable to be home in the evenings or to afford the cost of child care. They also expressed reluctance to have single daughters take jobs that would require them to live away from home.[77]

Both daily union work and political campaigns encouraged women's leadership at all levels. In testimony to the Industrial Legislation Commission, Alexander responded to a question concerning women in trade unions:

> Women workers make as good trade unionists as men, and it is no more difficult to organise the women than the men. In fact they are often more loyal to the Union than the men as the Union has not only helped to improve wages and conditions of work but also raised their status.[78]

Later reports verify this observation about women in the union. At the annual conference in 1950 the vice president complimented women members for their "splendid work" in organizing, while criticizing a number of "men comrades" for insufficient effort. Similarly, in her comments on discussions of the annual report in 1950, Ray Alexander "particularly complimented the women comrades for their good contributions."[79] Although she might have intended to encourage hitherto reluctant participants, there is little indication that this was the case. On two separate occasions in 1955, the minutes of the Paarl branch noted that only the female workers regularly paid their weekly subscriptions.[80] Rachael Zeeman (Sass), a Wolseley leader interviewed by Richard Goode, argued that women were more persistent and less easily swayed by arguments of the bosses: "They stand more united than the men!"[81]

Analysis of the union's leadership confirms this anecdotal evidence and verifies women's full involvement at all levels of leadership. Holding the most influential position in the union, all the general secretaries or acting general secretaries were women (Ray Alexander, Becky Lan, and Liz Abrahams), as were many shop stewards and branch secretaries, among them Mary Mafeking and Frances Baard. From 1947 until her banishment and dramatic escape from Cape Town in 1959, Mafeking served as vice president of the AFCWU, as secretary of the Paarl branch, and then as the union's president. Although the same two men held the positions of president and vice president during the latter half of the 1950s, the treasurer was female (from 1958 to 1960 the president's wife) and women were prominent among officials. Alexander recalled recently how she personally prodded women who were reluctant to assume responsibility. To women who insisted, "Oh, I can't do it," she would respond, "Look, comrades, I don't know what you can do. But, I'm a woman and I do it, and there's no reason why other women can't do it."[82]

Information on union-wide committee members for the years 1957–1960 indicates a consistently favorable gender balance: in 1957, four of seven were women; in 1958, six of eight; in 1959, five of eight; and in 1960, four of nine.[83] A list of FCWU committee members in Port Elizabeth included sixteen people: twelve women (half married and half unmarried), two men, and two unidentified.[84] The African union, with considerably higher male membership, still had five women among eighteen committee members.[85] Because the union valued local self-reliance and workers' education, female activists must have learned useful organizing and administrative skills, while deepening their political understanding.

The women who assumed these positions came from impoverished backgrounds and clearly responded to the union's call to struggle "for a better life." Elizabeth Mafeking began working at H. Jones in Paarl in the early 1930s at the age of fourteen in order to support the grandmother who had raised her. Married to a worker at the Langeberg Cooperative in Paarl in 1938, Mafeking took a month off for the birth of each child and then returned to work with the baby on her back. She became a shop steward in 1941 and an organizer in 1946. As an active member of the ANC Women's League, Mafeking refused to take out a pass and was dismissed from her job in 1953 after working twenty-one years for the same firm. Her political involvement not only brought her into contact with women from all over South Africa, but took her to Eastern Europe, China, and the Soviet Union. Shortly after she was elected vice president of the Women's League in 1958, Mafeking's banishment prompted an uprising of three thousand supporters in Paarl. According to newspaper accounts, crowds marched along the dusty roads, clashing with police, chanting "Mrs. Mafeking will be avenged," and "Kill Verwoerd, kill De Wet Nel, kill the police."[86] Not willing to endure this threatened isolation in Southey (a remote town in the northern Cape), she fled across the mountains into Lesotho (then Basutoland) with her two-month-old child. He was aptly named Uhuru, the Swahili word for freedom.[87]

Frances Baard, like Mafeking, was a leader never far removed from the women and men among whom she worked. After various jobs, including domestic work and a teaching post from which she was fired because a man was preferred in the one-teacher school, Baard decided at the time of her marriage that she preferred to work in a Port Elizabeth canning factory. When the union formed at the Jones factory (in 1948), she was elected organizing secretary. Drawn to an ANC meeting after her shock at seeing people forced to sleep outside on a cold, rainy night for lack of accommodation, Baard soon was involved in the Women's League and later became a member of SACTU'S National Executive Committee. After her husband's death in 1952, she assumed sole responsibility for raising their children.[88] In 1956 Baard was among 156 people arrested in the famous Treason Trial, which drained the energy and resources of many leaders of the Congress Alliance until their eventual acquittal in 1961. Among those released before the end of the trial, Baard continued her trade union and women's organizing until her banning and arrest in 1963.

Many explanations are possible for women's high level of participation and leadership among food and canning workers. They faced many instances of discriminatory treatment. Apart from differential wages and job categories, allegations of assault and complaints about the use of abusive language by supervisors came particularly from women, housing was often provided only to male workers,[89] and employers sometimes forced women to perform gender-related tasks completely unconnected with their work. In 1959 Sheila Koopman was declared "useless" and fired from her job at Continental Food Manufacturers, Elsies River. Her misdeed: refusing to wash clothes for her foreman.[90]

But discrimination alone is only a partial explanation. Ray Alexander certainly encouraged female involvement, and it is arguable that the democratic traditions of the union created an environment in which women felt comfortable. Equally important was the stress on community issues. Undoubtedly shaped by women's participation, this emphasis meant that women could express a wide range of concerns through the union, thus partially bridging the tension between work and home. Because union involvement could create new conflicts for women whose husbands resented the amount of time they spent at meetings, the combination of concerns was particularly important.[91] Community involvement also provided a means to retain the interest of seasonal workers (mainly women) even when they were unemployed, thus helping to overcome the problem of fluctuating membership. Indeed, the union's cultural and educa-

tional activities were concentrated during this period, when either workers were laid off or the pace of labor was less intense.[92]

Women's high level of seasonal employment also provides another possible reason for their union involvement. As an industry in which trade
union activists suffered high levels of victimization, women risked less
than men. Rarely able to become permanent or qualified employees, and
rarely the beneficiaries of work created to extend employment to the off-
season,[93] the union provided their only vehicle for effecting change. Unlikely to improve their situation through individual effort as were some
of their male coworkers, they turned instead to collective solutions. Black
women, in addition, doubly threatened with forced removal from the Cape
and with the need to carry passes, had added incentive to take part in an
organization prepared to protect their position, which was rapidly becoming more precarious than that of black men.[94]

The union's conceptualization of gender concerns as essentially family
issues also reinforced the sense of connection between home and work.
By seeking to minimize the stresses on family life from women's overtime
and night work, the union tacitly accepted household labor as their responsibility. (Individual activists were sensitive to domestic conflicts but
tended to address them on an individual basis, rather than as collective
political concerns.) This emphasis on family also helped to build a sense
of women's common experience on the joint basis of class and race; for,
as black working-class wives and mothers, they faced far different circumstances than middle-class white women, who rarely held paying jobs and
who relied on domestic workers for childcare, cleaning, and cooking.

As the two largest groups of organized women engaged in industrial
labor during the 1940s and 1950s, Transvaal garment workers and food
and canning workers at the Cape faced contrasting material situations
and differed markedly in their responses. The GWU was more and more
divided between a shrinking group of older white women and growing
numbers of black women. Despite the increasing distance between the
two groups, the place of white women in the industry also was eroding
and most of those who remained did so because they were too old to
retrain themselves to join the new armies of female white-collar workers.
Torn between loyalty to a union that had served them well since the
Depression and families and churches becoming more vehement in support of Afrikaner racism, these women amended their class conscious ideology of the past, which theoretically would have meant inclusion of all
workers across racial lines. They retreated instead to a less ideological
trade unionism that allowed for cooperation with black women within the
confines of increasingly racist legal constraints.

The situation was very different for food and canning workers. In this
industry, objective differences of gender and race were considerably less
marked than in the garment factories and the distinct conditions in many
parts of the Cape until well into the 1950s meant that nonracial slums

often housed both African and coloured families. While some apartheid laws of the decade affected the two groups differently, they were not necessarily pitted against each other, and both groups were increasingly deprived of even the meager rights they once had possessed. Although the discourse of union leaders shifted between 1940 and 1960, from a primary emphasis on working-class solidarity to a more defensive concern with struggles against racially based policies and legislation, this change represented a necessary response to new state pressures rather than an ideological departure from the union's past.

Reflecting and helping to maintain the involvement of all women was a continuing and active concern with community welfare and a class- and family-oriented approach to gender issues that emphasized the reduction of women's double burden through shorter working hours and expanded support services. Although the anti-pass campaigns of the late 1950s involved African women more intensely than their coloured counterparts, there is no indication of significant divisions among women as a result. Thus, throughout the 1940s and 1950s, the theory and practice of the FCWU reflected the philosophy outlined by Ray Alexander in 1952:

> We have learned from our day to day work in factories, and from union meetings, that workers irrespective of race, colour and creed, can get together with a view to bringing about a happier state of affairs for themselves and their families, and do not want to cut one another's throats.[95]

Even as pressures on the union intensified during the following decades, this commitment did not entirely fade.

–12–

NEVER FAR FROM HOME

Family, Community, and Working Women

As the first group of white female industrial workers in South Africa, the Afrikaans-speaking women who took factory jobs in the 1920s and 1930s attracted the interest of officials and scholars alike. Whether reflecting an attempt to eradicate white poverty or a paternalistic effort to protect young women from the imagined dangers of teeming, heterogeneous cities and racially mixed factories, such inquiries conveyed some understanding of these women's lives. Their black coworkers in the 1940s and 1950s, by contrast, passed through the factory doors virtually unnoticed, apart from a few scholarly studies set in Cape Town. Only in the 1980s did the combination of sharply rising numbers of black women in industry and expanding academic interest in gender produce a comparable level of interest and concern.

Yet despite the absence of easily accessible information, to write only of women at work would ignore a fundamental insight of feminist scholarship: that women's working lives are best understood in the context of their experiences of home, family, and community. In one of the few contemporary studies of female factory workers, Anna Weiss, writing in 1950, depicted them as "never far away from home." She continued, "Their domestic problems, their emotional attachment are of major importance to them and determine and influence their working life."[1]

This assessment supposes a mutual influence between home and work but leaves the nature of the relationship unclear. Did factory labor create the opportunity for new forms of independence or simply reinforce earlier patterns of gender hierarchy? Did it expand women's political horizons or have little influence? These are unresolved issues in the literature on gender and industrialization. The varied South African material suggests the difficulty of answering these questions definitively, partly since "independence" is an ambiguous, culturally dependent category. Furthermore, in South Africa, industrialization coincided more closely than in the West with capitalism, urbanization, Christianity, and western education, all equally significant in shaping the relationships between work and family.

Wider economic and political events and the nature of the community in which women lived also shaped these connections. If many young, white garment workers during the 1930s drew away from their families socially and politically, they usually remained part of a family economic network, particularly during the Depression, and retained a clear cultural and religious identity as Afrikaners. Food and canning workers at the Cape during the 1940s and 1950s faced no such split, even implicitly. Part of a larger community in which the canneries provided work for women and men of all ages, jobs in the factories were an integral part of local cultural and political life.

For black garment workers in Johannesburg, however, the situation was different. As central urban communities were destroyed and their inhabitants scattered in distant townships, the cohesion of inner-city working-class neighborhoods was broken and the potential for connections between home and work eroded. The breakdown of families within this environment caused particular alarm among both black and white observers of township life. Thus, many Transvaal clothing workers lived in communities in flux and under constant threat. But unlike their counterparts at the Cape, they could count on union support only for a very narrow range of economic issues, not to sustain the political and community struggles against state policies that undermined the security of their families.

Mainly married, and often mothers when they began to work as machinists or finishers, most black women favored industrial work over domestic labor, the only other option for most of them. Because of its relatively high pay (by comparison with household work), they were able to survive, often as single parents raising children alone after older husbands became ill or died. Such women may have contributed to the paradigm of the "independent" urban woman, which informs the perspective of many contemporary South African writers on urban women and families, as it does some of the comparative work on women and industrialization. But, while some factory workers may have sought such autonomy in their youth, as soon as they had their own families, they were forced to forge kin-based networks of mutual support with other female family members and as they grew older, with their children. They also found solace and companionship in the activities of established churches. Though many became autonomous "breadwinners," their goals were concrete: to feed, clothe, and educate their children. If in the process they forged new norms of female independence, this had seldom been their intention.

Black women rarely interested postwar researchers as industrial workers; but their lives came under the scrutiny of those concerned about Africans in towns and, more specifically, about urban family life. Prompted by rising levels of delinquency and by a sense that constraints, controls, and socialization patterns within the black community were crumbling in the larger cities, officials, scholars, white liberals, and socially concerned educated Africans (though often disagreeing violently in their solutions) all perceived urban family structure as a central issue. Encoded in their writings, whether explicit or not, were assumptions about the proper roles of women and about the effect of cities (and "modern" life) on women's position.

Although some anthropological studies frankly refrained from tackling the "complication" of women's status,[2] others included women in their samples, finding that they sometimes migrated to cities for the same reasons as men (poverty, landlessness, illness and death, or preference for town life). In other cases, however, their motivation was distinct: accompanying or following a husband; escaping from marginal positions (as widows, divorcees, deserted wives, or unmarried pregnant girls); or fleeing, as young married women, from the difficulties and demands of being daughters-in-law in patrilineal, patrilocal societies.[3] Though as "outcasts of the rural system," women tended to perceive town life as an end in itself rather than as a means to support a rural home,[4] the cities (particularly from the mid-1950s onward) provided no refuge from vulnerability.

Women who came into towns in the 1940s and 1950s certainly gained the possibility of greater control over many aspects of their personal lives. But the kind of contrast between "traditional" patriarchy and "modern" individualism emphasized in many contemporary accounts is misleading: it omits the erosion of women's place in peasant societies under the joint encroachments of capitalism and land scarcity, and it underemphasizes the extent of male domination in the fully "modernized" societies held out as models.

Nonetheless, the possibility for women to assert themselves in new ways and to try to establish new forms of marital relationships is undisputed. Ellen Hellmann wrote of small numbers of families in which a more egalitarian family life prevailed, but observed:

> It is far more common to find families under strain because of the unresolved conflict between the husband's patriarchal conduct and the wife's new role as wage-earner, manager of the household budget and educator of the children. Men, including educated men, seem to resist the emancipation of women which modern conditions promote. The cry of many women is that husbands continue to exercise an aloof authority and to demand unquestioning obedience from wife and children, while at the same time refusing to co-operate in bringing up the children and, in many cases, making their fair contribution to household expenditure. There is little evidence of a desire by women to usurp the man's position as head of the home, but what they want is more communication and co-operation.[5]

This statement is instructive. Although assuming that African women seek greater male interest in family life and more egalitarian decision making, both the author and the women concerned apparently concurred in accepting men as the "natural" heads of household. The "egalitarianism" of which Hellmann speaks might be described more accurately as greater joint involvement in household matters.

Writers of the period attributed changing relationships between women and men within the family to varied factors, particularly to women's relatively high level of education and their possibilities for wage labor.[6] L. Longmore, who saw the option of economic independence as having a significant impact on household power relationships, wrote:

> The sale of their labour as a means of independent livelihood has disrupted the solidarity of the urban African family and, by offering an escape which formerly did not exist, has undermined the authority of the father and wrought immense changes in relative status positions, and modified behaviour patterns. The possibility, or necessity, of wage-earning for women has raised their status and given them a considerable degree of independence and authority.[7]

Unlike Hellmann, who saw continued male power as the essential issue, Longmore believed that independent access to economic resources had challenged that power.

Monica Wilson and Archie Mafeje's classic study of the Cape Town township of Langa reached similar conclusions. Emphasizing education and employment as causative factors, they described women as earning and saving money, often controlling the family budget, and taking responsibility for their children's education. Symbolizing this developing equality between husbands and wives, they now ate together rather than in the gender-segregated groups common to rural homesteads.[8]

Sensitive to both the negative and the positive aspects of these changes, Ellen Kuzwayo, among the first African women trained in social work, celebrated the new independent woman but also expressed concern over the burden of responsibility for those with families.

> With her [woman's] growing financial economic stature, she has no doubt, also increased her difficulties. Many of these advanced and independent women find it difficult to marry. All too often a jealous husband has prevented his wife from fulfilling her potentialities, and so we are witnessing today the emergence of that new thing, entirely new in the traditional society, the unmarried independent career woman . . . who is changing the traditional ideas and values of African society beyond recognition.[9]

While believing that a woman's accomplishments should guarantee her right to treatment as "an equal, a partner, a companion," she also described the substantial "setbacks and hardships" that urban women faced:

lack of cooperation and assistance from fathers in bringing up children and running the home and the failure of many men to adequately share their earnings with their families.[10]

Thus, as in many other African contexts, the other face of this ostensibly greater authority within the family was increased vulnerability, often for those women who were most autonomous.[11] Pauw's study of East London found that women's education did not necessarily translate into better jobs. A large proportion of women with a secondary-school education were either unemployed or engaged in unskilled work.[12] Since towns seemed to attract larger numbers of unattached women than unattached men, and since the divorce rate was high in urban centers,[13] the difficulty of gaining suitable employment increased the problems of survival and probably encouraged women's involvement in informal relationships with men. Such arrangements might provide not only financial support but, sometimes more critical, access to housing.

Certainly in many urban communities the percentage of female-headed families was high. In East London, Pauw's sample of 105 urban-born households indicated that two fifths of family heads were women (one quarter unmarried mothers) and that households, while often large and multigenerational, tended to lose the father at an early stage.[14] Although in the new township of Soweto only 18 percent of families had female heads, among the 660 families in the older-established Eastern Bantu Township, women headed 41 percent of families, establishing a pattern that Hellmann feared might represent the future for newer African communities.[15]

Accepting women's place in the wage economy as necessary for survival, most writers of the period nonetheless shared an ideal of domesticity, deeming the family to be women's primary responsibility and concern. In Langa, for example, although unmarried girls and older women consistently worked for wages, as did most professionally trained middle-class wives, young married women in other classes expected to remain at home.[16] At least part of the reason for this pattern lay in the primacy of domestic labor among the available jobs for nonprofessional women. But the difficulties of finding childcare also must have played a part. Family members were not necessarily available and the number of crèches in the townships hardly began to meet the demand for them.[17] Deborah Mabiletsa expressed the prevailing consensus about working mothers: "If wages for Africans could be increased, the African mother would not have to work all the time, especially when the children are very small. She would in this case be able to devote more time to her family . . . [so as] to fulfil her natural role."[18] The sentiment reflected here remains close in spirit to Fanny Klenerman's testimony to the Economic and Wage Commission over forty years earlier. Now, however, the women entering wage labor in increased numbers were black rather than white.

If urban residence had contradictory implications for African women (varying by class and with the stages of their lives), pressures from the state had no such ambivalence. With the progressive introduction of apartheid legislation throughout the 1950s, new controls on the movement and the labor of African women assumed primary importance. Implemented through the pass laws, these new strictures were intended to limit even more severely than before the number of women and children legally eligible to reside in the cities.

The first serious restriction on women's right of urban residence came in 1952 when Section 10 of the Urban Areas Act (which applied uniformly throughout the country) forbade any Africans, female or male, from remaining in town for more than seventy-two hours unless they came under one of four exempted categories defined by place of birth, length of urban residence, and length of time working for a single employer. By 1964, however, a new set of even more draconian laws was passed, this time no longer assuming that wives and unmarried daughters of qualified men could reside with them in the cities; indeed, from that time onward, it became extremely difficult for new African women to enter the proscribed areas.[19] These new controls put an end to the dramatically rising urban female population which, between 1911 and 1960 had increased by 1,377 percent (compared with a male rise of 393 percent).[20]

During the 1940s and 1950s, African women engaged in industrial labor formed a very small group within the urban female population; among coloured women at the Cape, factory work was more common. Yet the family and community lives of all black women shared many common elements. At least one observer felt that African women factory workers on the Rand constituted a quite distinct group within their own community. Noting the tendency of suitably skilled women to alternate between private dressmaking and factory work, Mia Brandel wrote somewhat condescendingly of the contradictions she perceived in the position of these women:

> These skilled garment workers furnish an interesting illustration of the confusion caused through European influences, and through different European ideas about class. Many of these women come in touch with Marxist ideas, and are habitually in an atmosphere where Marxist terminology and "class" notions fill the air. They have somehow adopted the Marxian class-consciousness, and talk proudly about themselves as "we workers". It needs all the natural placidity of the African women to cope successfully with two such contradictory attitudes as the Marxist workers' class-consciousness and the capitalistic class-consciousness of being amongst the highest paid African women and, as to social contacts and friendships, belonging to the upper class layer of the "fashionable" set.[21]

What Brandel fails to discern is the degree to which class-conscious militancy was responsible for wages that, however meager, placed garment workers among the highest paid African women in the townships. The emphasis on high social status also may mask another issue, well-described in Anna Weiss's study of coloured garment workers in Cape Town: the alternating periods of poverty and prosperity at different stages in the family cycle. Among both Muslims and Christians (the majority of the workers), women between thirty and forty, whether married or formerly married, faced the most difficult period of their lives: with husbands (if present) unable to sustain the family adequately and children too young to work. Often, however, women supported families alone.[22] Not atypical of working women, Weiss found those she visited at home always engaged in some productive activity; even when "resting," they knit, mended, sewed, or did embroidery.

Weiss's study is particularly valuable for illuminating the life-cycle changes among different groups of Cape clothing workers, although her mode of analysis may overemphasize husbands' economic standing as the primary indicator of women's class position. While she argues that the absence of a male partner almost invariably placed women among the most impoverished wage workers, her model types are too static, neglecting the variations over time in male presence or absence. Nonetheless, her overall picture remains remarkably close to those of working-class families in nineteenth-century Europe.

In the Cape Town coloured families that Weiss designates as "upper middle class," where husbands earned their living as teachers, ministers, clerks, or businessmen, daughters rather than wives were employed in the factory, leaving work either at marriage or at the birth of a first child. Relative comfort notwithstanding, children's wages went directly to their mothers as a contribution to household expenses. Although women with small children rarely held jobs, the mothers of grown children sometimes returned to the factories, particularly if widowed or concerned about maintaining a comfortable standard of living. They usually engaged a household employee to relieve them of the burden of domestic labor. Both working patterns across the female life cycle and the dependence of women with children closely approximated white ideals of the period. But white women from comfortable backgrounds entered the labor force in white collar and professional positions, not as factory workers.

"Middle-class" families (in which the men worked as artisans, drivers, or government employees) aspired to the "upper-middle-class" pattern, but under economic circumstances that fluctuated significantly during the family cycle. Although the cushion of two incomes meant relative comfort for newlyweds, circumstances quickly changed as children were born and couples felt pressure to find their own homes. Women rarely returned to work at this time unless an elderly, nonworking relative was available to do childcare. Yet prior financial commitments, such as furniture bought on a hire-purchase agreement, continued to consume resources, now scarce in the absence of the woman's wage. The "continuing struggle against poverty," of the following years ended only when at least one child turned fifteen and was able to bring wages home to the mother. As children departed from home, however, the youngest child tended to be left supporting aged parents. By contrast with the relative comfort of their more prosperous coworkers, flats and houses were small, with no bathroom and often only one water tap in the kitchen or the yard. Children's education had to be curtailed in order to contribute to family expenses; health problems (tuberculosis, cancer, blindness, or malformation) and infant death were common. Even for young single women, household responsibilities filled much of their leisure time, allowing for participation in perhaps a single sports club, attendance at Sunday school, and an occasional visit to the cinema. Despite their "middle-class" designation, no one in these families escaped the experience of poverty and hardship at some stage of life.

By contrast with their more comfortable coworkers, women in families designated as lower class lacked the choice of remaining at home to care for their children. Mothers routinely continued working, often supporting several children on their own and sharing accommodations with other family members in order to survive. One such household included a widowed mother and an unmarried daughter, both working in the factory; a married son and his wife (also a factory employee); and a married daughter who remained at home with two small children while her husband worked as a foreman. With each family segment occupying a single room, they shared a kitchen and were able to save money by pooling resources.[23]

June Stevenson's later study of coloured women in the Cape Town clothing industry confirmed some of the same patterns.[24] Most workers were relatively young, 32 percent between fifteen and twenty and 47 percent from twenty-one to thirty-five; 62 percent of the workers never had married, 34 percent were married, and only 4 percent were widowed, separated, or divorced. Based on her own sample and on a study by the Bureau of Market Research, Stevenson concluded "that the Coloured working wife would appear to be less common than is often supposed," totaling 25 percent of wives in the market research sample. The difference between the two figures on married women workers is reasonable, given class differences in the pattern; in families in which the husband earned less than R60 a month, the proportion of working wives rose to 30 percent. Stevenson also found that most wives controlled the household budget, while unmarried women under twenty-one who lived at home routinely handed over their wages to their mothers.[25]

One of the greatest strains on these garment workers came from external factors, particularly the forced removals from settled coloured communities such as District Six to the barren, outlying area of the Cape Flats.

Exposed and cold in the winter, lacking heat and hot water, houses were often far from the grandmothers and aunts whose proximity helped to ease the lives of many working mothers.[26]

In the absence of detailed studies of Transvaal workers during the 1940s and 1950s, interviews with women who entered the factories during this time provide an impressionistic supplement to the more formal Cape Town surveys and to the studies of African urban family life. While possessing no statistical validity, the life histories of these women provide a rich sense of individual circumstances,[27] sometimes sustaining and sometimes contradicting the prevailing consensus about postwar urban women and families.

The overwhelming majority of women were born either in Johannesburg or in nearby areas of the Transvaal and were well educated for black women of their generation, most commonly attending school up to or through Standard 6 (8th grade).[28] Two of the women were educated at the Inanda Seminary in Natal, a pioneer in education for African girls.[29] Thus, they came primarily either from urban families or from families exposed to European contact through the labor-tenant and squatter relationships that prevailed in the rural Transvaal.[30] As relatively permanent urban residents, they formed the female counterpart of the men who were favored for skilled and semiskilled jobs during the period.[31]

The occupations of the women's parents reflected this social background, while illustrating pointedly the paucity of jobs open to African women: father, a clerk in the Roodeport mines, mother, a domestic worker in Johannesburg (although both were described as educated, and as former tutors at Inanda seminary); father, a milkman, mother, a domestic worker until the birth of her children and afterward, a housewife and dressmaker at home; father, laundry worker, mother, engaged in washing and charring for white families; father deceased, mother domestic worker; father, policeman, mother stayed home and did part-time washing; father worked in Crown Mines, mother did washing; father, milk delivery man, no information on mother. Only in one case, where both parents taught in a primary school, did they have equal positions.

Only a few women deviated from this pattern. A woman from Herschel, a rural area of the Eastern Cape, was the only African among them. Her father farmed his small plot of land, while her mother worked as a school cook. Of the coloured women, one father worked a small farm, helped by a wife who also cared for eleven children; the father of another was a farm laborer and the mother a housewife. That some daughters of domestic workers became machinists, trimmers, and pressers in garment factories indicates a pattern of mobility for women in working-class urban families, although many of the women began their working lives in 'domestic employment.

After finishing school, few of the women found jobs in the clothing industry immediately. Two patterns seemed to prevail, although clearly not everyone's lives fit into them. More common for African women than for coloured women, many sought their first job as a domestic, the most readily available form of work. Compelled to leave school after Standard 5, Harriet Phiri came to Johannesburg from Rustenburg to find a job at the urging of a friend. Unhappy about ending her studies, she recalled, "I was under twenty, 'twas just for the sake of suffering I had to go and work. Through the sake of suffering. I didn't want to go and work. So I went to work in the kitchens as a domestic." Reflecting the kinds of housing pressures that women faced, she and her intended husband married quickly because a house became available in Diepkloof. After they had moved there from Alexandra township, adjacent to the affluent northern suburbs of Johannesburg, she decided to find a job in a factory because the factories were closer to town.

Many of the other women also worked in white households for varying periods of time. Betty Matlaba soon turned to dressmaking at Indian shops in Fredadorp, the area of Johannesburg where she was born, leaving when she found a better-paying job in a garment factory in 1938. Others ceased domestic work when they married, either to drop out of the formal labor force temporarily or to take a more appropriate factory job. As Frances Baard explained, after marriage she left her domestic job in order to "look after the house for my husband." Following the birth of their children, she returned to work, "but now I went to work in the factories because I was a housewife."[32] Significantly, not a single woman in the group remained in household work after she had married, a choice that did indeed put them among the more fortunate urban women.

Only a few of the women escaped periods of domestic labor altogether. Like Betty Matlaba, Elizabeth Nkadimeng began working as a dressmaker in an African-owned private shop that employed six or seven people, including her future husband, a tailor. Having learned dressmaking at school, she was also among the earliest African women to find work in a garment factory. The only two women who moved directly into industrial jobs after finishing school were coloured: Ethel McCallum began working in a Cape Town shirt factory at the age of fourteen (a year below the legal minimum), while Rosaline Barnes found a job in a factory through a cousin shortly after she arrived in Johannesburg at the age of fifteen. Only Queenie Elizabeth Lenton, following a pattern common among coloured women at the Cape, stayed home for a period to help with domestic work.[33]

The age structure of black workers in the Transvaal clothing industry during the 1950s confirms the representative life-cycle patterns of this small group of women. Nearly half of the coloured and Asian women were 15–25, and roughly a third 25–34, reflecting the tendency to enter factory work directly as a first job, and then to drop out, if economically possible, at marriage. Fewer African women began so young: less than a third in the 15–24 age group (the overwhelming majority of whom were 20–24), and nearly half, 25–34. Again, the figures validate the personal testimony suggesting that, while most African women sought their initial jobs in domestic service, they also found factory work more compatible with marriage and family. Compared with their coloured coworkers, they managed less often to conform to the domestic ideal of the period by withdrawing from the labor force altogether to raise their families.[34]

Only Constance Belle and Nthana Mokale remained in the countryside for long periods while their husbands, both policemen, worked in Johannesburg. Married to a man who joined the police force in 1949, Belle remained in the Herschel District, farming their small mountainous plot of land with help from her father-in-law and neighbors. Combining her husband's wages and the food they grew, she was able to support her family. In 1965, however, after a forced move to the flatlands, sufficient food production became impossible. With her family on the verge of starvation, Belle joined her husband in Johannesburg. Eight months of washing and cleaning jobs convinced her to enter a six-month course in dressmaking at the Mupedi Tribal Club, which led to her present job.[35] Mokale married at the age of thirty, after working in Johannesburg as a domestic for eleven years. Returning to live with her in-laws in Phokeng, she only began working in a food factory after her husband's death in 1946. At the time of the interview (in 1982), she had returned to Phokeng and was caring for the children of a son, who lived in her house in a Johannesburg township.

Comparable to the husbands of white garment workers in the 1930s, the spouses of most of the women held both skilled and semiskilled positions, reflecting the entry of urban black men into new areas of the economy from the late 1930s onward. They included a salesman, tailor, presser in the clothing industry, manager of a dry cleaner, driver, clerk, driving school instructor, auto worker, tractor driver, engineering worker, transport worker, two policemen, and a teacher. All were apparently relatively stable jobs that allowed many of the women to become housewives for varying periods of time, either after marriage or after their children were born. Emma Mashinini was not atypical. Marrying in 1947 at the age of eighteen, she stayed home to care for her children and only began work as a machinist in 1956. Following tradition, she lived with her mother-in-law in rural Mafeking for a brief period after the birth of her first child.

Despite the prevalence of a strong ideology of female domesticity, economic necessity was inescapable; hence only two women, both coloured, spoke of incurring male disapproval for doing factory work. One quit for awhile because her father disliked her doing this work. The other, married to an African man, began to work secretly after her first child was born because her husband preferred that she remain at home. "He was a bit on the jealous side," she explained; but with many of her friends in the factories, the temptation to earn an independent income was too great to resist. Although, like most of these women, she handled the money in the family, her husband once found her pay slip and demanded, "Is this what you're working for every week? Neglecting the house for this money?"[36]

The high social status that Mia Brandel ascribed to garment workers did not free them of economic anxiety. Although a few of the women suffered from occasional ill health, a striking number of husbands were disabled or died when their wives were relatively young, thus confirming Pauw's finding that households tended to lose the father at an early stage. Their deaths added severe new strains to the lives of women already working in factories and prompted wives not formally employed to seek factory work. Among those already working were Lucy Mvubelo, whose husband was attacked in 1956 and left incapacitated until his death twenty-two years later; Elizabeth Nkadimeng, whose husband suffered a crippling illness in the 1950s; Harriet Phiri, in her early 50s at the time of the interview with a husband too ill to work; Sinah Jacobs, not yet thirty in 1950 when her husband died; Frances Baard, whose husband died in 1952; and Olga Williams, whose husband was killed in a car accident in 1966 when she was 40.

Among those who began factory work only as widows were Eliza Lebagoa, who came to Johannesburg with her husband in 1946 but only took a factory job in 1958, several years after his death, and Nthana Mokale, whose husband died in 1946, only eight years after their marriage, while she was living in Phokeng with their children and her in-laws. Betty Matlaba, born in 1916, only lost her husband later in life, in 1975, while Caroline Motsoaledi's situation was more singular: she was a former housewife who found work in a garment factory after her politically active husband was sentenced to life imprisonment on Robben Island along with Nelson Mandela and other leaders of the African National Congress. Yet her position as a young woman forced by circumstances to support a family on her own was not unique.

The number of women factory workers compelled to assume sole responsibility for their families, often at an early age, is in accord with the statistical data on single parent households in urban townships. The high incidence of death or illness rather than divorce or desertion, suggests that the pattern of marrying older men may have intensified women's economic problems.[37] It is striking, however, that most of these women breadwinners held their jobs before their forced financial independence, rather than taking them as a response to a personal economic crisis. Thus, for a surprisingly large number of women, the often-debated issue of whether independent economic resources contributed to enhanced authority in domestic relations was relevant only to a portion of their lives. The self-reliance foisted on them by circumstances was simply accepted as one more obstacle in the struggle for survival, not as an abstract measure of independence.

Though some of the women had managed to stay home as housewives while their children were young, virtually all faced the strain at some time of combining childcare with full-time work in the factories, a not inconsiderable burden with the five to seven children their families averaged. Yet, indicative of their urban roots and low level of rural ties, only one of the women sent her children to live with rural relatives (in this case, a grandmother in Rustenburg who also had raised the woman while her own mother worked as a domestic). This absence of rural kin networks contrasts sharply with household workers of the same period, whose conditions of work usually necessitated separation from their children; it also confirms the impression that female industrial workers were a highly proletarianized group.

By contrast with the easy generalizations about the breakdown of family ties in the cities, most women who worked while their children were young relied on close relatives for childcare, usually mothers, sisters, or mothers-in-law (one of whom kept the children at her house in Sophiatown during the week). Much more rarely, children were cared for by an unrelated woman. Similarly, many of the women with adult children provided child care for their grandchildren. Elizabeth Nkadimeng, who had retired, stayed home and looked after her grandchildren. Sinah Jacobs had a nine-year-old granddaughter who lived with her during the week, returning to her mother, a single parent, on weekends. Nthana Mokale, retired from her job, looked after her son's children in Phokeng. Only Betty Matlaba, who had recently adopted her sister's grandchildren after their mother and her sister died, mentioned the use of a crèche.

Family members also provided other forms of assistance, helping unmarried women newly arrived in Johannesburg, caring for aged parents, and continuing to house adult children and often their families. Rosaline Barnes, who came to the city from Somerset East (Cape) at the age of fifteen, lived with an aunt for fifteen years until she married; Sinah Jacobs found her first job in a garment factory through her mother's younger sister; when Constance Belle first arrived in Johannesburg, cousins "working in the kitchens," as domestic labor was described, found jobs for her. And Ethel McCallum continued to have her unmarried daughter of twenty-three and her granddaughter living with her. Caroline Motsoaledi, at the time of the interview, was living with her married daughter, while Queenie Elizabeth Lenton housed and cared for her 72-year-old mother, explaining, "She's very old and she doesn't want to go in a home now. I think it's better for you to mind your own mother than to have her in a home, than to have heartbreaks and all that, you know . . . and it's more safe because when the children come from school, there's always somebody with them."[38]

Only one of the women, a more recent urban arrival, spoke of more intense extended family obligations. As her husband was the only surviving member of a family of four brothers, he was often called upon to provide housing and other assistance to members of his brothers' families. On the receiving end of such assistance when her children were young, Elizabeth Nkadimeng and her family moved from Sophiatown, where they had been tenants, to Orlando East, where her father's brother had a two-room house. With his family in Natal, he was anxious to have their company.

Not only did most of these women provide much of the economic sustenance for their families, but they also sustained the social and emotional bonds of kinship, forming especially strong links among mothers and daughters, in contrast to the patrilineal ties of most rural South African communities. Though the range of kin who might be called upon for assistance was significantly narrower than in ethnically based peasant areas, immediate family members continued to represent an important resource for most of the women interviewed. Significant relationships centered less on the husband and his family than on support networks among grandmothers, mothers, and daughters which provided childcare, care for aged and sick family members, and housing for adult children, particularly single mothers and unemployed women and men.

In the most impoverished situations, and at the most desperate of times, relatively young children also represented an economic resource. One woman, unable to withhold tears, explained that a son in Standard 8 had left school to sell ice cream after her husband's death. Still visibly upset at the hardship they had suffered, she recalled, "I survived, I survived. Through the help of God." Another, who joined her husband in Soweto after the government had confiscated their land in the Transkei, relied partly on the children's selling newspapers during the two years before she found a job as a machinist. Olga Williams, a coloured woman married to an African man, also mentioned her children's assistance after her husband died. Using the skills she had acquired at work, she bought a knitting machine so that they could make caps to sell.

Not unexpectedly, adult children also represented another possible source of support. One woman, mentioning that her daughter was unable to help her financially, added, "Now I can't expect anything from somebody who's married because she's not yet working even." Though another daughter employed as a teacher was anxious to assist her mother, her meager wages under the terms of "Bantu education" made it difficult. Elizabeth Nkadimeng, whose husband has been ill since the 1950s, received some money from a daughter who continued to live with her and her husband. Another daughter, recently divorced, "gives me whenever she can, but I don't want to force her."

Although it is not unlikely that others, particularly those who were widowed, received assistance from their children, women tended to emphasize the ways in which they intensified their own labor to earn extra money (by working at home in the evening) rather than the external help they received. Nonetheless, several women felt strongly that children no longer worked as hard as their parents had done. Betty Matlaba, who housed an unemployed twenty-year-old uncle of her recently adopted children, was quite direct: "You know that children now are very lazy, they're not like we were."[39]

Overall, it might be argued, that, while striving to sustain their families economically was a central preoccupation for most women, they did not, in their later years, see a struggle for social independence (whether from the constraints of fathers or husbands) as an important preoccupation in their lives. Whether interviews thirty years earlier would have yielded different results is difficult to predict. But throughout their life histories, immediate family connections, particularly with other women, represented an essential resource and a critical source of personal support.

If their wages were necessary for survival, most women also seemed to enjoy their work, which gave them a sense of accomplishment and provided a satisfying social environment. Whether this would necessarily apply to all garment workers is questionable, however. Clearly, those factory owners willing to allow interviews were not necessarily typical and some women, perhaps uneasy about my intentions, might have felt constrained to sound positive about their jobs. Furthermore, women who disliked the work would have been more likely to leave after a short period of time, whereas I deliberately sought out older women, some of whom had worked in clothing factories for twenty-five to thirty years. Nonetheless, in the factory whose employees provided the most detailed interviews, the favorable attitude toward their jobs seemed genuine. Several women pointed out the positive features of factory work as compared with domestic labor, adding that it gave them skills they could use at home and offered a sociable setting in which they could meet other people and share ideas. Many of the workers expressed great appreciation for an owner who lent women money to buy their own sewing machines. Noting the absence of problems in the factory, Betty Matlaba observed, "We are at home here." At sixty-six, she saw continuing to work as an antidote to old age. When asked if she liked her job, she replied, "Well, to stay at home, what will I do? . . . Staying at home, I'm going to get old, get, you know, sickly. I've got arthritis, you know. I think it's best exercise to work."[40] Harriet Phiri, thanking God for her good health, reflected, "I come to work, I've got a headache. When I talk to my friends here, working, working the headache is over now." Constance Belle, pleased with pay rates superior to those for cleaning, was equally positive. "By my own feelings, I like my job. Perhaps I wanted to do sewing from the word go. It's a pleasure to work on the machine. I feel very satisfied." Caroline Motsoaledi expressed a real sense of pride in her progress from finisher to machinist to button-hole machine operator, noting "I'm a perfect machinist today." In order to gain each promotion, she had successfully persuaded her boss that she could do the new job. Most coworkers shared her affirmative feelings. "In fact, it's better than a domestic job because they get their wages weekly, while in a domestic job they get them monthly. I really like the factory job, with all my heart."

Many of these responses point to a distinct association of "work" with health, friendship, pride, and achievement, suggesting that for some women the collective atmosphere of the factory provided their lives with a stability and well-being that were absent both at home and in previous domestic jobs. In the context of forced removals, the illness, death, and imprisonment of their husbands, and anxieties about feeding, clothing, and educating their children, the women quoted above seem to have found their "haven in a heartless world" at work rather than at home. This portrayal of the personal satisfaction of industrial labor contrasts markedly with the usual associations attached to "work" and "home" in a way that calls into question the content of both categories.

The relatively small size of the two factories in which most of the women worked may have influenced their attitudes, which also reflect present conditions, not those when they first entered the industry. Olga Williams was adamant about the contrast. At the beginning, working under very strict conditions, she switched jobs every six to twelve months in order to escape the shouting and abuse of set leaders and supervisors, often Afrikaner women. Having entered the industry during a period of relatively routinized negotiations, some women recalled few strikes where they had worked. Elizabeth Nkadimeng, expressing bitterness, saw this quiescence as a result of pressure: although wages were consistently low, the white leadership successfully prevented women from striking in protest.

Yet Emma Mashinini, who worked from 1956 onward in one of the largest Transvaal factories (with over one thousand workers), recalled a history of racial friction, wildcat strikes, and intensive conflict over low wages and the arrogance and violence of management. Racial friction was intense. "So if we are told to do some work, we would be told move your hat, move your ass, hey you kaf . . . you know all the mud-slinging slurs were going on." She also felt that white women, who had only recently managed to gain their positions, could be the worst supervisors. Wildcat strikes were extremely important in forming the consciousness of ordinary workers. "So those strikes really brought out something very good that we could fight the problem of why must there be police involved in workers' problems. And why must people [representatives from the Labour Department] claim to represent *us* when we don't know who they are and who had elected them to represent us. And who gave them the mandate to speak on our behalf." Like Frances Baard, Mashinini had to challenge her job classification as she rose through the hierarchy from machinist to assistant manager, the designation she was given despite the absence of anyone above her. After she had waged a bitter struggle, the Industrial Council finally granted her the correct classification of "manageress." She also recalled the impersonal and demoralizing process by which black women were selected at random from a crowd gathered in the streets. "We used to stand as a mob of people and the employer would come and just pick out and say you, you, you, you, you."

Reacting to recent conditions, several women, particularly those who were older or in ill health, criticized pressure to rationalize the work process and enhance productivity by timing women at their jobs. Such an emphasis created an unpleasant situation for slower workers. In one of the factories, organized around production teams that worked together on each garment, a worker was asked what happened if the production quota was not met. She responded: "Hmm, you just do your job. They come and warn you and you try to do better."[41] In another the reaction was less subtle. "We have to give more production now. They are very strict that you are giving the production." Those unable to keep up with the pace lost their jobs.

Yet many women also felt that certain common practices in the industry had helped to protect their jobs, and a few, recognized by employers as exceptional workers, had received preferential treatment at various times in their working lives. For many of the women, the tendency to retain the workers when a factory was sold had guaranteed stable jobs over a long period of time, including several changes of ownership. One woman explained, "We didn't actually change jobs. The boss who buys our company, he never used to put us off. We are fortunate that we're here. Otherwise perhaps we would have been in the street."[42] There also were examples of small groups of experienced workers switching to a preferred employer. When Caroline Motsoaledi's former boss, who had sold his factory four years earlier, opened another factory and invited some of his old employees to work for him, she organized a group of eight women to return, despite the formal condemnation of such moves as "enticement." This employer consistently supported her during periodic police harassment; when pressured to fire her, he responded by praising her responsible and effective performance. Betty Matlaba and another woman worked closely with a designer, who brought them along each time she changed jobs.

In addition to social relationships, the work culture of the 1950s also exposed black women to a new political discourse, leading many, as Brandel noted, to identify themselves as part of a self-conscious working class. This sentiment emerges most forcefully in women's discussion of events during the 1940s and early 1950s. The exuberant references to May Day picnics and, most often, to the demonstration following Sachs's banning, suggest a high level of personal loyalty to him and a generalized attachment to the union reminiscent of white women in the 1930s. The feelings women discussed were not simply political, but referred to a political culture that involved them emotionally and socially as well. As the 1950s progressed, and the combined pressure of the state and the white GWU forced a separation between politics and trade unionism, the union lost the ability to define its own social and symbolic occasions and seems to have become more remote from its black members. By the early 1980s, some continued to find union participation personally satisfying, but others were extremely critical of the union's subordinate status and its bureaucratic indifference—a trend that had intensified under the repressive conditions of the 1960s. The force of this repression, felt by all the political movements and by the unions affiliated with SACTU, the South African Congress of Trade Unions, may account partially for the skepticism and cynicism some women expressed toward political involvement. Knowing of the risks many ordinary people had taken, they were uncertain that the resulting benefits compensated for the dangers people had incurred.

In keeping with these personal and political differences, attitudes toward the trade union and toward politics varied enormously, from full-time leadership and political commitment, to participation in the union as shop stewards and committee members, to total lack of interest in unions or in politics. To the active women, the union clearly imparted a sense of self-respect. Sinah Jacobs observed, "For the years I've worked in the clothing industry, I've always enjoyed it, because I've been active." Olga Williams, no longer a shop steward because of illness, related with pride, "They all wanted me to come back to be a shop steward." Explaining the responsibilities of shop stewards, she emphasized particularly their role in mediating disputes among the women.

> The shop stewards are there to see that everything goes right in the factory, that the girls not fight. They must try and help the boss to see that they don't steal, they must try and get the girls to live like friends, not enemies, and things like that because some girls can be very nasty, like fighting over the work.[43]

The union also gave some women a sense of personal and political solidarity, perhaps best expressed in an enthusiastic description of the annual May Day celebrations of all union women, black and white, during the 1940s and early 1950s. "We used to get together, sometimes we had meetings, tea, all the nice things. And some of us used to get home very late. Even if you were sick, even if you were far from home, but when that day draws nearer, you would be together with the other workers."[44] Many of the women recalled Solly Sachs with fondness and vividly remembered the turmoil after he was banned. With great animation, Sinah Jacobs spoke of a lively march in 1952. After the bosses had closed the factories in response to a strike, women paraded through the streets chanting, "We want work, we want work; open up the factories, we want work!" The demonstration to protest Sachs's banning came shortly thereafter. Crowding on the steps of the Johannesburg City Hall, women removed their shoes and turned spiked heels into weapons against the charging mounted police.

Yet, later in the decade, as the registered union placed greater political restraints on the African union, a former activist recalled that women involved in the ANC and the Women's League had to conceal their politics because of the white union's disapproval; its concurrence with the bosses on this issue made political organizing in the factories impossible. Alleging also that election returns were manipulated to keep the black union under control, she charged that she had been elected president of the union several times, but because of her politics, "they would steamroll it," making her vice president instead. Voicing a rank-and-file view of the break between the African women's union and SACTU (the South African Congress of Trade Unions), she expressed clearly what Shula Marks has termed the "ambiguities of dependence." "The garment workers had decided not to work with these people because we saw that the garment workers, the white workers, the white union, would neglect us and where would we be? We needed them. We would have been nowhere. That is when we decided that half a loaf is better than nothing."[45]

Understandably, in view of past repression and of the frequent attacks on political activists in the late 1970s and early 1980s, virtually everyone perceived any discussion of politics as extremely risky. Nonetheless, one of the women who professed a lack of interest in such issues managed to convey profoundly political sentiments. During the course of the interview, she criticized Bantu education, forced removals, and low wages, ending with a casual reference to Nelson Mandela as "my home boy."

Other women revealed anger at forced removals, which had affected the lives of many of the women and could become a powerful source of political consciousness. Yet this awareness did not always lead to political involvement. Emma Mashinini experienced such dislocation twice, first as a child whose family was forced out of Prospect Township in the late 1930s, and then as an adult driven from Sophiatown. The state pressure and police raids that uprooted families from this lively, culturally vibrant freehold community of Africans, coloureds, Indians, and Chinese, was a formative political experience for many young people during the 1950s. Nthana Mokale voiced these sentiments most eloquently. "Life in Sophiatown was very enjoyable. Then a white man intervened and pierced our hearts with a spear," by demolishing the area and "removing us from that rich land, . . . like a chief's kraal" and resettling people in places "where poverty was the order of the day."[46] Although she supported the protests against removal, the long hours in the canning factory where she worked made it difficult to take part fully. The results of the move were quite tangible to her, however: having to leave the house an hour earlier, at 4 a.m., in order to reach work on time. Olga Williams, a coloured woman married to an African man, also was forced to move from Sophiatown to Soweto. Although upset at the brutal way in which people were driven from their houses and at the distance from town, she explained that, as home owners able to buy another house in Dube, they were not as involved in the protests as tenants had been. The grievance of Edith McCallum, a coloured woman who had lived with her husband on land outside Johannesburg, was slightly different. When the area was declared European, they were compelled to move to the highly urbanized township of Alexandra where they were unable to grow their own food.

Few women admitted to active involvement in the protests of the 1950s. One, not yet in the industry, was a full-time housewife at the time she took part in the ANC Women's League and the Women's Federation, suffering arrest and detention during the early 1960s when her husband was on trial for treason. Another, already a garment worker and on the executive committee of the ANC Women's League, was jailed for several days for opposing passes. Articulate about the perils of political involvement, she noted, "I used to belong to the ANC until it was banned and then . . . I stopped my actions because I could see my background was very poor. If I the breadwinner goes to jail, then the whole family would go down. So I stopped, I shut my mouth."[47] Sinah Jacobs, a black woman married to a coloured man, and very active in the union, explained her lack of political involvement in much the same way: there was no chance of change and the risk was simply too great. As the sole supporters of their families during the 1950s, these women were understandably cautious. Betty Matlaba's similar sentiments, relating more to the present than to the past, certainly reflected her new status as a single adoptive mother in her late 60s. "I don't want to be involved. Who will look after those children if I die or if I get crippled? It's too dangerous. I think to stay where you are, it's always the best. And not to be involved in such groups. You see?"[48]

Material on Johannesburg factory workers tends to support the two major generalizations on black women's involvement during the 1950s. As noted earlier, many active garment workers, particularly Lilian Ngoyi and, for a brief period, Lucy Mvubelo, were indeed in the vanguard of political organizing as officials of the Women's Federation and SACTU respectively. For a number of reasons, however, this commitment on the part of union leaders did not necessarily draw in ordinary workers; many of them, as some of these interviews suggest, found the risks of political activity greater than the incentives. Julia Wells proposes that the women's anti-pass movement in Johannesburg found its strength among nonworking wives threatened by the prospect of proletarianization and, more specifically, by the prospect of limited options for wage labor outside of domestic employment. This raises the question of why factory workers tended to be less involved than unemployed wives. Did their structural position lead them to experience the threat of passes in a different way? Or did union opposition to politics combine with the absence of a coherent factory-centered working-class community able to bridge the gap between home and work? Certainly the political obstacles were enormous and cannot be underestimated. But it is also clear that, with wages relatively high for black women of the period, women clothing workers contributed significantly more to family support than did the housewives who filled the ranks of anti-pass campaigns. In this position, they may have shared some of the characteristics of black men, whom politically involved women sometimes accused of timidity in taking risks. For those who were the sole source of family income, the dangers were immediately obvious.

With hindsight, several of the women (among them two who were politically active), expressed strong disillusionment with unnamed political leaders during the 1950s, sentiments that must have influenced their attitudes. In the words of one woman, "Some of the leaders were not sincere; they misled us." Nthana Mokale felt a similar disenchantment, charging, "They burnt them [passes], fools burnt them only to discover that some people . . . our leaders, never burnt theirs. They deceived many people." Based on the failure to prevent the destruction of Sophiatown, she also feared that all protest was doomed to fail. "There is no black man who can defeat a white man. I repeat, a white man is god of the earth."

Reflecting some of the same skepticism toward leadership, but from a more class-oriented perspective, Harriet Phiri argued that politics was only for educated people.

> I've never involved myself in that. Especially people who are not educated are never involved in such things because we live there and there. We are not interested. People who can be involved in such things is people who say they are from school. The rest of those people who are at prison they are educated people. The rest which give police troubles here, it's for people who are educated. Now if you are not educated, so long as you've got bread for your children, you've got meat for your children . . . I'm satisfied for my life.[49]

Not surprisingly, the two most politically conscious women both had sons who had fled the country during the 1970s, suggesting the intergenerational power of political tradition within some families.

If many of these factory workers expressed profound ambivalence about politics, they were intimately involved in the numerous community organizations that Ellen Kuzwayo connects with the energy of the new, independent urban women she celebrates. For young, unmarried women in the most independent phase of their life-cycle, dancing at the Bantu Men's Social Club and the Jubilee Center on Eloff Street ranked high among their favored leisure activities. Betty Matlaba recalled with enthusiasm and intensity, "Before I got married, I used to be a dancer. Yes, it's where I used to enjoy life. . . . Now I've got no time for all that jazz, you know."[50]

After they married and bore children, however, church involvement assumed priority. Describing the importance of religion for African women, Lucy Mvubelo observed, "We pray and cry and think that all of our problems will be solved. In church you find two hundred women and ten men."[51] Betty Matlaba has turned her early enthusiasm for dancing to the benefit of the Methodist church and the local school board. As an Anglican, Sinah Jacobs has taken an active part in the church Mother's Union and in group trips to places like Sun City. "That is what I really enjoy," she explained. Rosaline Barnes has been involved in the Catholic Women's League (which supports the church and runs tea parties) and also in the Pioneer Association, a group for nondrinkers. Queenie Elizabeth Lenton, although identifying herself as an Anglican, professed a lack of time to be active (she had an elderly mother living with her). Emphasizing a sense of peace and closeness to her children, Mashinini recalled:

> I think that was the only loving time I had with my children. Just holding their hands and walking with them to church.
> That was the happiest time. They would be sitting there, and going off to Sunday school, or whatever, and you could sit down and relax, and listen to someone. Even today I love to go to church, only now my company is my grandchildren instead of my children.[52]

Despite the concerns of some theorists writing about the consciousness of working women in South Africa, religion and politics were perceived neither as conflicting loyalties nor as opposed forms of awareness. One of the most politically active clothing workers also was very involved in church clubs and in a burial society of the United Congregational Church (formerly the American Board Mission). Frances Baard, the AFCWU leader in Port Elizabeth, attended church every Sunday. Her autobiography recalls a revealing encounter with Ray Alexander, who summoned her from services one day, arguing that she was wasting her time and should be out organizing the women.[53] For Baard, however, who related the incident with amusement, the conflict was nonexistent.

Only one woman, also skeptical about politics for those without education, expressed any doubts about religion. A former Lutheran, she explained:

> I used to be a church member. . . . But it just happened that I stopped going to church. I'm collecting things from people's minds that my mind tells me I'm wasting my time at church. That man is talking there, I don't believe to him and I start leaving church. . . . I don't know what to tell you. I found that now I don't like this church business. I'm not interested. I mean, why should I go take my book and sit in a church while I'm not interested.[54]

Perhaps most striking about the religious lives of these women is their universal commitment to established denominations rather than to the thousands of independent churches so characteristic of South African urban women. Notwithstanding the economic hardships that most of them experienced at various points in their lives, their religious affiliation confirms Brandel's analysis, placing the garment workers of the townships among the more privileged members of their communities. Domestic workers, by contrast, were more likely to belong to charismatic, independent churches.

In addition to the burden of housework (only one of the workers, a coloured woman, had domestic help for a brief period), all of those interviewed made economic use of their sewing skills, easing the family budget by making clothes at home for their children and grandchildren and augmenting their incomes by selling items to neighbors and friends. While their skills gave them the ability to move easily between factory work and self-employment according to the needs of their families, the life histories of most women suggest that they did both simultaneously. The sole support of her family, Elizabeth Nkadimeng often awoke at midnight to sew items for sale. More than their formal work, their independent sewing gave them a distinct identity in the townships, with a stable and legal means of adding to family income. In addition to sewing, one woman also had another business. With a loan from her boss, she had purchased a table and furniture, which she rented out for weddings and funerals. This pattern suggests that a rigid division between wage workers and those in casual employment misrepresents the reality of most women's lives.

Although the division of domestic responsibility was never perceived as a political issue in the 1940s and 1950s, most women were adamant that they alone bore prime responsibility for children and the family. A few expressed resentment at the unequal division of labor and would have agreed with Kuzwayo that men's more limited sense of obligation to their families was a potential source of domestic conflict. Harriet Phiri was angry that husbands were free to come and go as they pleased, often without letting their wives know when they would return. "Sometimes my husband just vanished. . . . Now it's for the wife to stay in."[55] She went on to describe women's primary responsibility for children: "I must work for my children to eat. I don't care whether your husband is good or not good. But the children come first." She continued: "I think the life is too hard for a woman. Women here in South Africa is working more than the men. The men don't care. Three years not working, but it's for you the woman to struggle for food in the house. . . . She must take any jobs around, so the children get food. I think our husbands take everything very easy."[56]

Examining individual lives in detail dissolves some of the generalizations found in the literature on urban women during the 1950s and 1960s. Rather than simply breaking down, family relationships were being reconstructed in new ways that stressed the connection among women, children, and other female kin. This reorganization of family life occurred because so many women became actual or de facto household heads at an early stage of their lives. Thus, many acquired an independence not chosen, but forced on them by the death, illness, or arrest of their husbands, and most bore a major responsibility for managing household finances (particulary for food, clothing, and child-related expenses).[57] This was not the "independence" from family control of young, working women, but a tougher, more mature form of self-reliance that rested on a wide range of family and community ties. To women in this position, factory work afforded many advantages. In the 1940s and 1950s, female clothing workers in particular, highly paid by comparison with other women, also had a skill on which they could rely to supplement formal family income. Well-placed socially, and relatively established as urban residents, they became staunch members and leaders of religious, community, and sometimes political organizations.

Yet to celebrate these women for their "independence" without considering the impact of forced removals, political repression, and racially exploitative legislation would negate their own perception of their position. For virtually without exception, they saw their lives as difficult and whatever stability they achieved as fragile. Constance Belle, although content with her work and able to support her family on her wages and her husband's pay as a policeman, noted nonetheless, "I have never seen money written non-white. We go to the same shops for the whites, but the money's not the same." Never politically involved, she felt unable to change things, "but I don't like it."[58]

Thus, evidence from the lives of black industrial workers suggests that the assumptions about "modernization" that dominated contemporary social science in the 1950s and 1960s rested on some fundamental misunderstandings. By defining "family" too narrowly along Western, middle-class lines, many observers failed to see the new kinship networks that were allowing women to cope with their difficulties. Equally important, by not perceiving the patriarchy embedded in the Western societies held up as models, they overestimated the degree to which economic independence alone conferred more power on women. Finally, by focusing so heavily on concepts related to personal behavior like individualism and independence, they sometimes failed to take full account of the racial and class structures that constrained, and sometimes controlled, women's lives.

IV
Decentralization and the Rise of Independent Unions

-13-

CITY AND PERIPHERY, 1960–1980

The tragic shooting of anti-pass demonstrators at Sharpeville on March 21, 1960, made the year a dramatic turning point. Shortly afterward both the ANC and the breakaway Pan-Africanist Congress were banned. Forced underground, they carried out separate campaigns of sabotage until the leaders who remained in the country were arrested and, in 1964, sentenced to life imprisonment. Several years were to pass before political life rekindled in the Black Consciousness Movement of the late 1960s. With its emphasis on psychological liberation and its strength in the schools and universities, this new movement fueled the massive uprising of Soweto students in 1976, which was sparked by a new requirement of instruction in Afrikaans. In combination with renewed labor unrest during the 1970s, the school-based protests initiated an era of intense political organizing that the apartheid state has been unable to quell.

Inevitably, as repression crushed the broader political movement, women's struggle against passes effectively ended. With pass laws for women firmly in place, all Africans faced comparable restrictions on their movement and their labor. No longer were women simply incidental victims of policy decisions made for other reasons; controlling them had become a fundamental aspect of apartheid. Indeed, with many more men than women deemed necessary to the urban labor market, it is arguable that the Group Areas Act, which carved South Africa into carefully designated racial and ethnic enclaves, was primarily an effort at the massive resettlement and control of women and children.

The period from 1940 to 1960 had a certain organic unity as the wartime boom led into a new era of economic development under a state representing the joint interests of Afrikaner capitalists, farmers, and workers. The internal conflicts that opened the next two decades, between the apartheid state and its opponents, had equally significant economic consequences in their effects on the ebb and flow of overseas investment, which since World War II had underpinned the country's prosperity in secondary industry as well as in mining. Despite the sometimes contradictory needs of industry and the state, the two worked closely together to their mutual benefit during the 1960s. Only in the following decade did severe crises (massive strikes in 1973–74, the Soweto uprising of 1976, anti-apartheid pressures on foreign capital, and by late 1977, acute recession) punctuate the calm working relationship that had fostered the growth of Afrikaner capitalism and had encouraged a decentralization of industry affecting women in particular.[1] Indeed, as the political and economic crisis in South Africa has intensified since the late 1970s, one response has been a restructuring of the sexual division of labor, involving not only decentralization, but also a dramatic increase in the number of black female wage workers, the use of white women in formerly male jobs, and an urban labor preference policy, giving legally urbanized black women priority over migrant men.[2] These policies were a response both to a shortage of skilled labor, which threatened continued economic development, and to growing black resistance. By creating a more stable black middle class, the state hoped not only to fill essential job openings, but to create a group with enough stake in the economic system to support its measures of limited reform.

Economic growth and change also prompted a series of new laws governing the movement of women. The 1952 legislation extending passes to women meant that women, like men, required the permission of rural labor bureaus to seek work in the cities; but those who were dependents of men resident in towns still were eligible to join their fathers or husbands. In 1964, however, this right was rescinded. Women already working in towns and those with rights of residence might remain, but henceforth all other women could come to towns only as contract workers. Lacking approved jobs, they might remain in urban areas for no more than seventy-two hours. Reinforcing this restrictive policy, the government stopped building family accommodation in cities after 1968.[3]

Attempting to roll back the demographic trends of the previous three decades, these new regulations meant that women probably would be refused entry to cities unless they consented to fill the only job routinely assigned to black women, domestic service. Industrial jobs would go to permanently urbanized women, already too plentiful for official opinion, not to migrants hired on contracts. Thus, for women in established urban industries, there was little possibility of divisions emerging between contract workers and permanent residents.[4]

But "influx control" regulating entry into cities was only one side of an integrated policy. The obverse side meant that those unable to meet the stringent requirements of legal residence were expelled from the cities and that rural dwellers who lived outside of the ethnic or racial boundaries the apartheid state had assigned to them were forcibly resettled. Labor tenants and squatters expelled from white farms also were prime targets for resettlement.[5]

These involuntary removals, uprooting over three-and-a-half million people between 1960 and 1983, had disproportionate and disastrous effects on women. Removed most often to crowded, barren areas ill-equipped to support their inhabitants, women have to cope with high infant mortality rates from malnutrition and illness, inadequate medical and educational services, and insufficient access either to independent income or to productive land.[6] Often landless, many in these rural areas would be more aptly termed a rural proletariat than a peasantry.[7] The more fortunate among them have received remittances from husbands working in the cities; but many rural women, often the primary breadwinners in their households, lack even this source of income. These conditions have compelled them to accept the most arduous and ill-paid jobs: doing casual farm labor or heavy manual work in the reserves, such as digging roads and irrigation trenches, building dams and fences, and working in quarries.[8]

Beginning on a small scale in the 1950s as part of the move to disperse blacks to isolated, economically underdeveloped "bantustans," the movement of industrial production to these ethnic enclaves and to the nearby "border" areas has become a primary facet of economic policy. Voicing the state's position on industrial development in 1970, the Prime Minister argued that certain industries were "bound to the metropolitan areas." But others, which were labor intensive, "should never have developed there, and could move. If enough of them did so, the natural increase of Africans already in the cities would provide labour for the rest."[9] Often drawing on contract workers rather than on permanent local inhabitants, these new factories have extended the migrant labor system to women industrial workers, thus making female organizers and strikers as vulnerable as men to the combined threat of deportation and job loss.

Not surprisingly, clothing and textiles, both labor intensive low-wage industries, are among the most prominent in these rural centers. In some areas women also produce electrical parts, motor components, furniture, and chemical products.[10] Under the restrictions on black trade union organizing that prevailed until 1979, these workers had limited means of improving their situation. Since then some "homelands" have applied their own restrictions in order to gain the favor of investors.

Although not originally intending to draw a predominantly female labor force, the combination of meager wages and an overabundance of women in the rural periphery has created a distinct gender imbalance in the decentralized industries. Figures for factory employment in the "homelands" show women holding from half to two thirds of such jobs.[11] Of the 16,404 positions created during the first ten years of the Xhosa Development Corporation, for example, a high percentage were for women.[12] In one resettlement township of the Ciskei, the two factories hired mainly women because, having limited options, only they would accept such low wages.[13] For those who worked in rural industries the burdens of daily life were compounded. Often living without electricity or plumbing, women had to gather their own water and firewood after a day's work.[14]

Unfortunately, labor statistics on African women do not fully reflect their economic and political situation, particularly in the rural areas. Not only have the criteria for defining women as peasants or as agricultural workers been shifted or left unclear from one census to the next, but many women counted as farm laborers are, in fact, household employees. Those who do farm work on a casual or seasonal basis may escape the notice of census takers completely, although they have grown more numerous since the 1960s as agriculture has become more mechanized and capital intensive.[15] Finally, the population of the ostensibly independent "homelands," disproportionately female, was excluded from official manpower surveys after 1979. These difficulties notwithstanding, statistical data do provide insights into labor force trends for black women in other categories of employment during this period.[16]

For white women, the move out of industry and into white-collar jobs continued. By 1970, only 3.6 percent of employed women worked in manufacturing. The decline continued in the next decade not only among production workers, but also among supervisors and other skilled workers. At the same time, the number of white women in the clerical, sales, and professional/technical occupations rose gradually, but with the only notable increase in the numbers in administrative and managerial positions. This willingness to move women upward in the job hierarchy undoubtedly reflected the acute shortage of skilled labor to fill positions usually designated for whites.

The situation of coloured women, still heavily involved in wage labor, also showed strong continuity with the past.[17] A drop in the percentage of women in service occupations between 1960 and 1970 formed part of a pattern of continuing decline over the course of the twentieth century, as did the rise in the proportion of production workers, from 20.3 percent to 29.2 percent of the coloured female labor force. (The annual rate of increase in production, however, has been falling since 1936.) The numbers in clerical, sales, and professional/technical work remained small, although significant increases were beginning to occur, especially in the first two categories.

The percentages of African women in each occupational category cannot be compared between 1960 and 1970 because of the discrepancies in defining "peasants"; but the most numerically significant increase came in the number of women in production, followed by an important expansion of professional/technical workers.[18] In 1969, the number of African women industrial workers was only 54.3 percent of that of coloured/Asian women; by 1981 the proportion had risen to 85.9 percent. Although both African and coloured professional women became more numerous during these two decades, the overwhelming majority still worked either as teachers or as nurse/midwives, a fact that accounts for the discrepancy in the numbers of female and male black professionals.[19] Another important trend of the 1970s was black women's encroachment at a rapid rate into sales and clerical jobs.

Despite a sharper increase of black women in office work, the number involved in sales was more significant. Whereas, in 1969, 86 percent of female sales workers were white, by 1981, they held only 62.9 percent of these positions. During the same period the coloured/Asian percentage doubled, while the percentage of black women almost quadrupled.[20] For female clerical employees, however, the trend favored coloured rather than African women, although whites continued to hold the overwhelming majority of jobs.[21]

Most striking in industrial labor was the rising proportion of African women, who went from 30 to 42.7 percent of all female workers between 1969 and 1981. Coloured/Asian women fell from 55.3 percent to 49.7 percent of the female industrial labor force during this period and white women from 14.5 percent to 7.4 percent.[22] The pairing of coloured and Indian women in the manpower surveys, however, obscures another significant trend: a rising number of Indian women in industry during the 1970s.[23] The vast majority of them have assumed jobs in clothing manufacturing.[24]

While the number of African women in service jobs (primarily domestic) rose much more slowly between 1960 and 1970 than in other categories, these numbers remained overwhelming. Even Trudi Prekel's overly optimistic assessment of black women's increasing place in the South African economy concludes by cautioning:

> But to these numbers have to be added the 48 percent of economically active black women in domestic and agricultural employment, and even more in subsistence level agriculture, who were not included in the manpower surveys. It appears that in many cases black women have moved upwards into positions formally recognised in the economy and listed in the manpower surveys from unlisted positions, as black men and white men and women moved on into other, often higher level positions.[25]

Still, changes were occurring in the nature of domestic labor and in the service sector more generally as domestic servants began to comprise a slowly declining proportion of all service workers during the 1970s. Some of the shift came from women who broke with established South African routine during the recession of the 1970s and began to do their own housework. More significant, however, were the numerous capitalist enterprises operating outside the household such as launderettes, dry cleaners, and fast food shops, which have taken over many reproductive tasks hitherto performed in the home. These establishments have provided black women with jobs in new locations. But the tasks they perform remain identical to those of their mothers and grandmothers who were servants or washerwomen. Indeed, many jobs classified as "sales" and "commerce" in fact involve laboring, cleaning, cooking, and serving tea. Coloured and Indian women now occupy many of the better-paid middle-level female positions that these job categories would suggest.[26]

By 1981, despite the increase of black women in factory production, African, coloured, and Asian women still held less than 15 percent of all industrial positions and they remained heavily concentrated in traditional female manufacturing sectors. Clothing, textiles, and cleaning, grouped together in the manpower surveys, employed two thirds of both black and coloured/Asian women in industry. Large numbers also processed food and tobacco. Only jobs in the metal industry represented a new trend in women's industrial employment. Among white women, the demise of their traditional place in industry is evident in the fall from 18.6 percent to 8.4 percent of the number in clothing and textiles; instead, by 1981 nearly two thirds worked in transportation, delivery, and communication, jobs more closely akin to semiskilled service work than to traditional factory production.[27]

Industrial pay rates represent another index of women's position as wage laborers. In 1973, those earning less than R10 per week included 61.9 percent of black women, 28.3 percent of coloured women, 24.8 percent of Asian men, 12.5 percent of black men, and 7.1 percent of coloured men. Despite these wage differences, there were actually fewer African women in the lowest-skilled group than African men, and slightly fewer women than men in the lowest three groups. This discrepancy between wages and skill level indicates that the pay difference lay not in the relative difficulty of jobs held by women and men, but in gender-based wage differentials. Among coloured workers, however, the wage discrepancy between women and men was matched by a skill differential, with 82.7 percent of women and 76.7 percent of men in the lowest three categories. The difference between black and coloured women also is striking: 44.6 percent of the former, but only 29.8 percent of the latter held jobs classified in the lowest group.[28]

While the number of black women in wage labor was increasing, and influx controls kept down the number of wives in urban areas, high levels of unemployment, large numbers of illegal urban residents, and the preference of some women for home-based and independent economic activities kept women's place alive in the informal economy. One study of Durban begins with "socially acceptable" ways of supplementing income, which had changed little over the years: knitting, dressmaking, cake-making, and peddling meat, vegetables, and other goods.[29] Child care, particularly for older women, should be added to this list. Also socially acceptable to the women concerned, if not to outside researchers, was brewing, which remained the most lucrative independent source of income "almost exclusively in the hands of housewives."[30] A recent Soweto study shows a similar range of activities, with women involved primarily in selling, usually food and vegetables, but also clothes, beer, other hand-made articles and, in one case, detergents on a door-to-door basis. If the low incomes provided continuity with the past, by comparison with earlier periods, the context of informal labor in the cities had changed. Most of the Soweto women saw themselves as unemployed and in search of work, conceiving of casual labor as a means of survival in-between jobs.[31] Although many had lacked jobs for some time, their attitude suggests that wage labor had replaced informal work as the desired norm.

Although difficult to document statistically, the number of women in rural areas and smaller towns engaged in petty trade probably rose as the productivity of rural land continued to erode and, more important, as increasing numbers of people were dumped into regions lacking any economic potential. A sample of street traders in Transkei towns found that 88 percent were women. Working on a very small scale, often operating outside of official rules and regulations, all were unskilled except for the 22 percent of women who were dressmakers. Not surprising in view of the greater demand for male labor, the women were better educated than the men in similar occupations. They also occupied a different position from earlier generations of peasant women who routinely marketed their surplus crops; no longer able to grow their own food, these women and others in similarly destitute rural areas, depended solely on their income from trade. For the 86 percent of them who were the sole source of support for their households, as for their counterparts elsewhere, casual labor was not a supplement to household income, but a "last desperate attempt" at self-sufficiency (or, perhaps more accurately, at survival), one that redistributed scant income within the working class, while providing little return in terms of labor time invested.[32]

The ability to subsist on casual labor did not compensate for the high levels of female unemployment by the late 1970s. Official figures put the level of joblessness among black women at double or triple the rate among black men.[33] Even this stark appraisal almost certainly understates the problem, since housewives are generally regarded as "not economically active" rather than as unemployed, and in rural areas they may be forced to survive on pensions or remittances, both periodic and unreliable sources of income.[34]

As in earlier periods, economic insecurity and deprivation strongly influenced women's communal activities, both secular and religious. Rotating credit and mutual aid associations continued to flourish, offering members in turn the opportunity to collect the month's pooled contributions and to give a party, profiting from the sale of food and beer. A primary source of income for single women, particularly divorcees and widows,[35] these groups promoted a spirit of female self-sufficiency and mutual aid found also in the thousands of separatist churches characteristic of black urban communities.[36]

In the Durban township of Kwa Mashu, according to anthropologist

J. B. Kiernan, Zionist churches directly reflected women's economic insecurity and dependence. Forced to rely on men for economic support and for their legal and residential status in the community, women often accepted their accountability to men for their purported failures as wives and mothers, further reinforcing their lack of autonomy. Particularly attractive to widows and poorer women, Zionism offered an alternative system of beliefs and social ties. By making women and men jointly responsible for family behavior and by banning men from participation in drinking sets that diverted scarce household income from children's health and welfare, township women (like poor nineteenth-century women in Europe and America who supported the temperance movement) received religious sanction for their efforts to redirect male resources and responsibility.[37]

Despite the structural changes that opened new jobs for African women, then, they remained in the lowest paid, least secure positions, most frequently performing reproductive tasks in new settings. White and, to a lesser extent, coloured and Indian women who moved up in the job hierarchy followed well-established gender divisions in the economy rather than transcending such distinctions. Furthermore, significant numbers of black women, particularly in the textile industry, were joining the ranks of migrant industrial workers for the first time. Yet, if racial divisions always had made "women" problematic as a unified category in South Africa, new distinctions between black women also were growing increasingly significant. Particularly in clothing manufacturing, conflicting interests were intensifying between established, relatively well-paid urban employees and "homeland" and border area workers earning a fraction of their wages. Although urban women were spatially removed from their competitors, the potential conflict of interest between them was comparable to that two and three decades earlier between black and white women in the Transvaal and between clothing workers on the Witwatersrand and on the coast.

As the number of black women in industrial labor increased dramatically during the 1960s, many entered industries in which state repression had left unions severely depleted. Although the South African Congress of Trade Unions (SACTU) never was outlawed, its leaders were banned and imprisoned, silencing a generation of formidable female trade unionists. Some of those banned earlier went into exile during the 1960s, Ray Alexander in Zambia, Bettie du Toit in Ghana, then Great Britain. Others, like Mary Mafeking, Frances Baard, Mary Moodley, and Liz Abrahams were arrested, banned, or banished for the first time. Only black women such as those in the Transvaal clothing industry, willing or forced to settle for second-class status in nonpolitical parallel unions, escaped the repression of the early 1960s.

Baard, for example, already charged and then released during the Treason Trial, was rearrested in 1963 and held in solitary confinement for a year. When finally taken to court and shown the lengthy list of charges against her she responded, "I contravened all this? Rubbish!" Ignoring her rebuttal, authorities returned her to prison for five more years. Rather than allow her to return to Port Elizabeth at the end of the sentence, authorities banished her to a tiny, filthy house in Mabopane, a township an hour from Pretoria where her neighbors initially feared that she was a police informant. In keeping with the jobs available in the "homeland" of Bophuthatswana, Baard worked for a time in a newly established textile factory at Rosslyn.[38]

Receiving similarly harsh treatment, Rita Ndzanga and her husband, both organizers in SACTU unions, were banned and prohibited from attending public gatherings. Like other couples in similar circumstances, they required special permission to communicate with each other. As the banning period came to an end, the two suffered successive periods of detention and banning that ended with her husband's death in prison in 1976. Authorities refused to release her to attend the funeral.[39]

The relative inactivity of the 1960s meant limited organized interest in working-class women. When the registered Garment Workers' Union turned its attention to women's issues in the latter part of the decade, its concern was informed less by gender than by increasing awareness of a growing shortage of white labor. Seeking solutions to the problem, some experts in government and industry hoped to entice educated white women into joining the work force.[40] Urging the government to take the lead in this effort, Anna Scheepers stressed the importance of crèches "to encourage women to work and take domestic worries off their minds."[41] As part of the campaign to transform the attitudes of women reared on an ethos of domesticity, the Garment Workers' Union, in conjunction with the National Council of Women and the Federation of Business and Professional Women, planned a conference for March 8, 1969, to coincide with International Women's Day. Speakers highlighted two issues in particular: legal inequalities in a marriage system based on community of property, and workplace discrimination in wages and promotions, both particularly damaging "at a time when the economy is needing the help of women."

The meeting focused on issues of theoretical relevance to all women; but it represented in fact an elite group of white women, working in cooperation with the state and capital to solve the problem of "the utilisation of womanpower in the country." Opened by the Minister of Labour, the agenda included discussion of "the manpower shortage, the utilisation of the employment potential of housewives, the psychological and social aspects of the working mother and practical aspects of the dual role of the working mother."[42] While contributing to an awareness of women's concerns, the class and racial composition of those attending and the close alliance with representatives of government agencies made the dialogue meaningless to the vast majority of South African working women.

Expressing somewhat different interests, the South African Electrical Workers' Union had mounted a similar campaign two years earlier. With two thousand white women then employed in the industry, the general secretary hoped at once to decrease their use as cheap labor undercutting white men and to dampen the influx of black workers. Explaining the union's new charter for women he observed: "The association sees in White women the last hope of stopping a complete racial fragmentation of the engineering industry."[43] To encourage white women to fill the labor shortage, he urged equal pay for equal work, the provision of crèches "so that mothers need never be more than a few yards from their babies," apprenticeship and training schemes, equal opportunities for advancement, and retraining programs for older women. The plea to white women was urgent, for employers were pressing for the downgrading of white women's work and their replacement with black men.[44]

Once again, whether for racial reasons or because their wage rates were somewhat higher, white women seemed less threatening than black men to skilled white male workers. By the early 1970s, even some government officials were beginning to admit that only the admission of black workers into skilled jobs formerly designated as white would overcome the labor shortage.[45] Nonetheless, by the 1980s, white women driving buses in Johannesburg or operating trucks and cranes at ISCOR, the state-run iron and steel corporation, indicate that in some sectors of society transcending gender boundaries proved less repugnant than transcending those of race.[46]

If an awakening of white female awareness and militancy characterized labor organizing during the 1930s, black women developed a comparable consciousness in the 1970s and 1980s. As the repressive sixties shaded into the following decade, a new labor movement was gradually coming to life, prompted by continued low wages and steep price increases, especially in the cost of such essential items as food, clothing, and transport.[47] Expressed first in the massive strikes of 1973 and 1974 that nearly brought Durban to a standstill, the pressure of this period led to a burgeoning of "works committees" and "liaison committees." With black unions still not recognized, these groups provided the only forms of legal organization open to workers who wished to voice their grievances. Limited to single factories, the committees had little power and left leaders highly vulnerable to victimization.

Under these repressive conditions, the period following the 1973–74 strikes was difficult for trade unions. But they continued to grow slowly, aided by student support groups and, on occasion, by registered unions. Prompted by this growth and by the political and economic crisis after the Soweto student uprising of 1976, the government appointed a commission to explore possible changes in labor legislation.[48] Its report, discussed later in this chapter, provided a framework in which the burgeoning independent unions would thrive and expand during the 1980s.

Rarely on the sidelines of labor activity, women as well as men took an active part in the organizing efforts of the 1970s. Their grievances centered around wages, working conditions, industrial control, and trade union recognition. In many actions of the period, minor disputes led rapidly, and seemingly spontaneously, to an expression of long-standing, fundamental injustices. At the Turnwright Sweet Factory in Johannesburg, for example, three hundred employees, mainly women, walked out during a conflict over working conditions on August 21, 1974. Upset at first over a unilateral management decision to change the time at which the factory gates opened in the morning, the workers soon began to shout for wage increases, to complain about long working hours and about the need to clock in and out when they went to the bathroom, and to voice their wish to be represented by the Black Allied Workers' Union.[49]

In the heady atmosphere of unrest, historic centers of organizing like Port Elizabeth became active once again, although the results could be risky. In October 1978, 230 coloured women, all members of the National Union of Motor Assembly and Rubber Workers of South Africa, went on strike at the Eveready plant, a subsidiary of a London-based corporation. The strike, following a long struggle for formal recognition, led company officials to fire all the women, whom they classified as unskilled, and thus easily replaceable. Backed by an international boycott of Eveready products, the women held out to win back their jobs. Their efforts to prevent others from taking their places faltered, however. Within two days, hundreds of women braved pouring rain to claim the vacant positions, and those who remained unhired grew angry, throwing stones and raising their fists in black power salutes after learning that all openings had been filled.[50]

Like the women at Eveready, others involved in protests also worked in the newer areas of female employment, where women had a dual struggle—not only against employers, but also against the attitudes of their male coworkers. At the Heinemann Electric Plant in Elandsfontein, east of Johannesburg, the Metal and Allied Workers' Union (MAWU) quickly organized the 606 workers, mainly women, in 1974. "Mama" Lydia Ngwenya (Kompe) was chosen as a shop steward and executive committee member of the union. Dismissed after a strike in 1976, she became the only female MAWU organizer in the Transvaal. In an interview in 1983, Ngwenya, then working for the Transport and General Workers' Union, discussed the role of women in the Heinemann strike. Although half of the twelve shop stewards were women, she recalled:

During meetings we tried to fight the undermining of women's suggestions. They thought we were not saying strategic things. But we managed to fight that. If a woman stands up and puts a motion or a suggestion it should be taken into consideration. We succeeded in Heinemann because . . . women outnumbered men. The women were taking the lead when we were on strike.

They weren't scared even when the police were trying to thrash us and scare us with dogs. I think that's when the women realised that women can be determined.[51]

But life at home did not go smoothly during these events. Ngwenya's husband resented her frequent meetings, sometimes lasting so late that she spent the night with friends instead of returning home, and often consuming entire days on weekends. She continued:

That made him very unhappy and it made our life very miserable. He couldn't see why I was involved in this. He was scared that I'd be in politics and land in jail.

He'd get very unhappy and think I was making excuses about meetings when I was going out jorling [having an affair].

When we got dismissed it was worse because he felt I deserved it. . . .

You know what husbands are like. He'd complain that I don't do anything—cook, make tea or do washing for him.[52]

Similar complaints about household responsibilities increased during the 1980s. As trade union women began to vocalize new ideas on gender, a growing body of scholarly and political writing on working-class women provided a forum for their expression.

The year 1979 marked a dramatic shift in state policy. In an effort to bring the burgeoning black labor movement under the control of the existing system of industrial relations, a White Paper accepted the recommendation of the government-appointed Wiehahn Commission that African trade unions be granted official recognition. Although the new independent unions differed on how to respond to this legislative shift, the space now granted to working-class organization led to a wave of concentrated strike activity in 1980–81.

In addition to reevaluating the place of black unions, the Wiehahn Commission sought to redefine the legal position of working women. In doing so, it relied primarily (though not exclusively) on the testimony of the Study Group on Women in Employment, a body established by the commission, but proceeding with complete independence. In a worldwide intellectual and political climate in which gender had assumed a place alongside class and race as a legitimate political issue, and in which some female labor leaders were becoming increasingly vocal in their advocacy of women's rights, the study group produced a cogent statement of the new attitudes.

Representing the opinion of established women trade unionists,[53] its memorandum to the Wiehahn Commission broke from earlier left-wing analyses and ascribed the disabilities of working women to household relationships as well as to capitalism, the state, and the legal system. The memo highlighted three causes of discrimination against women: tradition and prejudice (such as sex stereotyping of jobs) by employers and by society in general; marriage, maternity, and homemaking which deny mobility to women; and the historically subservient attitude of women originating in the family and reinforced through their education and training. The women involved recommended legislation that would outlaw wage differentials based on sex, age, or marital status. They also advocated that domestic and agricultural workers (still the overwhelming majority of women) be included in the benefits of social and labor legislation.[54]

In its most novel recommendation, the Study Group memorandum compared pregnancy leave to military service, arguing that the Defence Act provided a precedent for not depriving temporarily absent workers of seniority, wage increments, or long-term benefits. Most important, they could return to their jobs at the end of their leave.[55] Although the Wiehahn Commission accepted this recommendation, it was not surprising that subsequent government legislation did not.[56]

Responding positively to such testimony, the Wiehahn Commission report on women shed the blatant sexism of the 1935 Industrial Legislation Commission and made a number of recommendations of undoubted benefit to women. Its members recognized that "the time has come for a fundamental revision of the existing approach toward the employment of women," particularly appropriate at a time when the country needed "to optimise the utilisation of its human resources." Included in this reevaluation was the recognition "that communal provision will have to be made to accommodate working women who have family responsibilities."[57] Accordingly, the commission concluded that all laws contrary to the principle of equal treatment for women and men should be abolished, including discrimination in any area of employment based on sex or marital status; that maternity benefits should be improved and extended and that women should be guaranteed their jobs after leave; that domestic and agricultural employees should be included in maternity benefits; that part-time employees should receive benefits on a prorata basis; and that the state should provide increased levels of support for day care and should allow working parents tax deductions for child-care expenses.[58]

Although, on the surface, these conclusions appear potentially beneficial to all working women, there were nonetheless some problems with the commission report. Addressing the position of "women" as an undifferentiated group, the report explicitly eschewed consideration of the special restrictions on black women under the Group Areas Act, explaining that this issue fell under the terms of reference of the Riekert Commission, which was working simultaneously on the question of influx control.[59] Furthermore, the recommendation to remove restrictions on night and overtime work in the interests of equity was controversial.

In its response to the Wiehahn Report, the government acted to prohibit wage discrimination on the basis of sex, a provision applied first to

Industrial Council agreements in 1981 and then to all wage rates three years later.[60] But legislators rejected some of the recommendations of greatest benefit to women, particularly those advocating improved maternity benefits; they also made changes in existing law detrimental to seasonal workers, who no longer are eligible for benefits. Although wage equality was a step forward in theory, the high level of gender segregation in the labor force and the ease of maintaining inequities by reclassifying jobs meant that few women have received increased pay as a result of the new law.

The most controversial outcome of this reevaluation of gender-based laws came in the area of protective legislation. Using guidelines more solicitous of the needs of employers than of workers, the state accepted the Wiehahn recommendation that restrictions on overtime work for women should be abolished. While praised by some as a step forward, others (including officials of the Garment Workers' Union) were wary of such a change without a reduction in women's domestic and child-care responsibilities and measures to insure their safety while returning from work at night.[61] Joining in the criticism, J. Cock interpreted the government's response as fully congruent with other dubious "reforms" of the late 1970s and early 1980s.

> In relation to all aspects of reproduction, health, housing, child care, etc., we hear murmurings of 'reform'. But in every case, such reform is in fact part of a directed policy of the state and capital towards improving conditions for a small part of the working class, as an attempt to incorporate them on an ideological level, whilst continuing or increasing the levels of control and oppression of the majority, who are left to carry the burden of reproduction on their own.[62]

Outside the industrial sector, labor unrest spread during the 1970s to the growing ranks of black shop employees and to domestic workers. The Commercial, Catering and Allied Workers' Union, created in 1975 by the registered distributive workers' union, quickly took on its own identity and independence under the capable and energetic leadership of Emma Mashinini. A former Executive Committee member of the National Union of Clothing Workers, Mashinini has created a highly successful union in which gender issues have assumed unusual importance.[63]

As in previous periods of working-class militancy (such as late 1930s), even domestic workers have once again come together in an effort to overcome the structural obstacles that persistently plague their efforts to organize. Under the leadership of former household employees Maggie Oewies and Florence de Villiers, the South African Domestic Workers' Association has drawn up demands for higher wages and improved working conditions, organized literacy classes, taken up cases of sexual harassment, and encouraged workers "to see themselves as women not as slaves."[64]

Speaking of the spirit in the newer unions, Mashinini highlighted the high level of demand for workers' education.

There are endless seminars. People don't spend weekends at their homes. They spend weekends educating the workers. And trade unions today are working *excessively* long hours. You know you'll find we work around the clock and every weekend because the workers *demand* to know, they *demand* to be educated.[65]

While Mashinini speaks as a woman primarily organizing other women, some male trade unionists of the period recognized the central role of women in the events of the 1970s and early 1980s: one former textile union official noted the "advanced political consciousness" of African women, and a shop steward, speaking of the 1980 textile strike, praised women for having "fought like men."[66] No doubt a double-edged compliment in lauding women for their male attributes, the two comments nonetheless suggest that during the 1970s, black women working in factories were fully involved in a decade of reemerging labor protest, part of an ongoing struggle that has intensified in the 1980s. In each of the main industrial sectors employing women, however, the nature of women's involvement reflected not only the immediate context of the decade, but also historical patterns of organization and change.

$-14-$

REPRESSION AND RESISTANCE

The economic and political environment of the 1960s and 1970s profoundly affected the working lives of women in food, textile, and clothing factories. As in earlier periods, the distinctive history of each industry depended on both financial and technological developments and on the gender and racial composition of the work force. But the new peripheral industries and expanding "homeland" labor reserves reshaped the economic climate for low-wage, nonunionized labor-intensive enterprises. Whereas in the past, employers seeking cheaper, presumably more pliable workers had sought female or black employees and had chosen to locate along the coast rather than in the more expensive Transvaal, they now had an added option: the border and "homeland areas," where women migrants were being drawn into industrial jobs.

Although produced locally by a set of policies unique to South Africa in their form and in their cynical disregard for human well-being, the movement of low-wage, predominantly female industries to peripheral areas was a global tendency. Textile, clothing, and electronics plants scattered to cheap, unorganized labor markets like Taiwan, Singapore, Korea, Hong Kong, and Mexico and, within single countries like the United States, moved from the high-wage, well-organized North to southern states willing to encourage nonunion shops. In the core industrial countries, sections of the clothing industry, still able to operate without costly technological input, also have relocated from unionized factories into homes and small sweatshops. They rely on the labor of poor, immigrant women from Third World countries, in some cases unable to protest because of their illegal residency status, in others constrained by the isolation of working at home or by the organization of production through male-run family networks.[1]

The food and canning industry in South Africa did not have to move to take advantage of the trend toward decentralized production. The Western Cape, the early center of the industry, was a low-paying rural

area in which abysmal farm wages offered the only competition to industry. The Eastern Cape had the advantage of proximity to the impoverished Transkei and Ciskei, which provided a reserve of migrant workers
for East London and Port Elizabeth, as well as for factories to the west.
The expulsion of thousands of black families from the Western Cape in
the late 1950s and early 1960s did not, in fact, reduce the number of black
workers (despite the official policy of making the Cape a "coloured labor
preference area"), but merely increased the proportion of migrant men
recruited on a contract basis. After the early 1960s most African workers
in the food and canning industry were no longer permanent residents of
the areas in which they worked.[2] As early as 1963, 250 of the 400 members of the African Food and Canning Workers' Union in Paarl were single men.[3]

The implementation of the coloured labor preference policy had two
facets: expelling Africans from the Western Cape and giving priority to
coloured workers. Employers could receive certificates to recruit black
workers from the Xhosa-speaking areas only if suitable coloured labor
was unavailable. As of 1966, the black labor complement in all industrial
and commercial enterprises was frozen and a 5 percent annual reduction
was imposed in the future. And under the Physical Planning Act, effective a year later, employers in the major centers of food production who
wished to establish or to expand factories could do so only with coloured
or white workers. Where labor shortages existed, Africans might be hired
only with government permission.

Although some of the regulations that reshaped labor conditions in the
Western Cape were gender specific, others also had consequences for
women. Between January 1954 and March 1962, the measures to make
the Western Cape a coloured area had led to the "endorsement out" of
over eighteen thousand men and 5,975 women. Reflecting the view of
many officials that women and children were simply the "superfluous
appendages" of male workers, the Minister of Bantu Administration announced in February 1964 that additional "Bantu women" would not be
permitted to enter the Western Province to assume employment or to
remain in the area permanently. This regulation, combined with the exclusion of domestic service from occupations for which exemptions would
be granted, meant that only a negligible proportion of contract workers
were women. Indeed, by the 1980s, legally employed women made up
less than 14 percent of the registered African work force in the Cape.[4]

Such stringent controls covering the Western Cape inevitably decreased
the number of black female food and canning workers in these centers.
By 1979, African women comprised only 3 percent of food processing
employees in the Western Cape.[5] The immediate consequences of restrictive regulations could be devastating. In November 1966, for example, a
group of black factory and farm workers in rural Grabouw were given an
ultimatum: the men must move immediately to the single sex compound,

while their wives and families must leave the area. Bantu Administration Department officials removed four African women from their factories, and on November 9, eight more were ordered to leave the area at once. Found holding his baby, one man was fined R5.[6]

If labor policies toward the Cape significantly shaped the racial and gender composition of the work force in the food and canning industry, rapid changes in the labor process as a result of automation reinforced the tendency to find the cheapest possible workers and to employ them in new ways. Unemployment attributed to mechanization caused great distress in the early 1960s, as new machines were introduced to pit peaches, core and peel pears, grade apricots, and to close cans and pack them into cartons. High-speed conveyer lines replaced slower means of moving from one production process to another, and new technology soon prevailed in labeling, warehousing, and packing. Discussing the large number of people out of work in 1961, Liz Abrahams urged each branch, factory, and department to describe the new machinery in use and to tabulate the number of workers dismissed.[7]

Union efforts notwithstanding, by 1968 much of the manual labor formerly employed to wash, sort, clean, peel, stone, and grade fruit and to fill containers had been mechanized, ousting workers at all levels and demanding new skills from those who remained.[8] Yet, by international standards, manual labor remained important. A United States Department of Agriculture report observed in 1969: "The striking feature of canneries in South Africa is the labor intensiveness of the operations. Large numbers of seasonal workers, especially women, are employed, on a much more extensive scale than in California canneries. This vast use of labor reflects the very low wages paid."[9] Statistics suggest, however, that the full impact of mechanization was not felt until the 1970s. Whereas up until 1970, the value of output and the size of the labor force both increased steadily, between 1970 and 1976, despite a slight drop in the number of employees, the value of output rose dramatically.[10]

This context of increasing automation and deskilling favored the lowest paid, least stable workers. Employers in the Western Cape increased the numbers of migrant African men; elsewhere in the country, the number of African women rose dramatically. During 1960–61, while the percentages of black men and coloured women remained at roughly the same level, the proportion of coloured men dropped from 13.5 percent to 8.5 percent and that of black women nearly doubled, going from 15.9 percent to 30.9 percent of the work force.[11]

The reorganization of work as a result of automation diversified women's work in the industry, while also leading to changes in the wage structure that probably encouraged employers to hire women instead of men in lower grade occupations. Whereas in 1960 different male and female wages were laid down only for Grade 4 and Grade 5 workers and supervisors, by the time of the 1975 agreement, women were also working as can packers, chargehands, fruit checkers, feeders of peach-pitting or repitting machines, feeders of pear-peeling and coring machines, and protective clothing attendants. Over time, for the women in supervisory positions, the degree of pay inequity decreased slightly. For the lowest-grade employees, however, the gap widened, perhaps because the weakened union was unable to protect men on the lowest levels of employment from replacement by women, previously a deliberate reason for not allowing too great a gender gap to develop. Between 1960 and 1975, the pay of Grade 5 adult women dropped from 89.3 to 80 percent of comparable male pay.[12]

Political repression during the 1960s worked in concert with changing production techniques to weaken the union. In 1963 and 1964, the Minister of Labour enlisted employers in the effort to destroy the working unity of the African and coloured unions. Several companies complied, including L.K.B. in Ashton and Worcester, which henceforth prohibited joint gatherings of the black and coloured branches on factory premises and refused to meet jointly with officials of the two unions. Such policies, accompanying the shift to migrants among the black workers, promoted greater distance between the two groups of workers.

During these same years, the police and Special Branch engaged in harassment campaigns, searching the head office, repeatedly questioning and sometimes arresting officials, and sending police officers to meetings. The effects of this intimidation were particularly devastating in rural areas where, according to union charges, "the union is isolated and in any event exposed to much hostile pressure by some employers, and where there is no other organisation to defend and advance the people."[13] Frances Baard, then secretary of the Port Elizabeth branch of the AFCWU, was served with three banning orders that excluded her from factories and prevented her from addressing union gatherings or from meeting with individual members who lived outside her own location of New Brighton. Arrested in 1963 and imprisoned for five years, she also suffered a year in solitary confinement. Lydia Kazi, the general secretary of the African Food and Canning Workers' Union, who was then expecting a baby, was detained and held in solitary confinement in the Paarl jail. In 1963, Mabel Balfour of the AFCWU in Johannesburg was banned, Mary Moodlay, FCWU secretary in Benoni, was detained, and Lily Diedrichs, organizing secretary of the union's Sick Fund, was issued a five-year banning order, making her the first coloured woman to receive this punishment. But perhaps the gravest blow to the union since Ray Alexander's forced departure was the banning of Liz Abrahams on August 28, 1964. She was prohibited from holding the post of general secretary, forbidden to do any union work, and confined to the Paarl area for five years. The union condemned this final action as part of the government's policy of "degrading the African and Coloured majority to the level of serfs."[14]

Under the dual threat of increased mechanization and loss of established leadership, the difficulties of organizing a seasonal and increasingly migrant work force were intensified, making it harder to sustain branch organization[15] and easier for employers to intimidate union activists. In some cases workers elected to union committees were dismissed at once. Noreen van Dyke, a worker at Gants Food, Somerset West, was let go at the height of the peach season. After other workers walked out of the factory for three days, she and another union leader were reinstated. But as soon as the slack season came, van Dyke was fired again and ninety-eight of her supporters were charged with illegal striking and fined.[16] If workers were able to take advantage of the seasonal demand for labor by timing their actions accordingly, employers could use similar tactics.

In other cases as well, charges against workers for striking illegally reflect the diminished power of the union. On March 10, 1963, for example, a dispute broke out at L.K.B. Daljosaphat in protest against the dismissal of two workers and the manager's use of abusive language. After four hours of negotiation, during which workers successfully blocked a Labour Department effort to speak to the African workers alone, one of the dismissed men was reinstated. After this apparent success, however, 320 people, mainly coloured women, were charged with striking illegally. Found guilty after two days of hearings, they were cautioned and discharged.[17]

Despite these difficulties, in the early years of the 1960s the union continued to espouse a nonracist political policy, to support SACTU and the Women's Federation, and to speak out on local issues. On occasion, members who opposed arbitrary state power were successful. In 1961, twenty-two interracial families employed at Lamberts Bay Canning Company were ordered out of their houses. The men, all black, were assigned to the African compound, and the women, all coloured, were evicted with their children, but given no alternative residence. When they refused to leave, the adults, all of whom had lived in the area for anywhere from fifteen to thirty-six years, were arrested and fined. Although their affront to apartheid left them little ultimate chance of success, union intervention gained temporary respite for these families.[18]

The early 1970s also brought new sets of problems in the fishing industry, as the "ocean of gold" that had sustained it dried up. The industry had been prosperous enough in 1963 to establish a fund that paid women 15 percent of their normal earnings during the slack period, but the fund was now depleted. The factory at Port Nolloth virtually closed down, leaving workers without alternative employment. One told union officials:

> My feet are sore of going about looking for work. I am a sickly woman and cannot go on my knees doing house work. I have a baby of six month's old and a child at school at Steinkopf, and I have to pay R12 p.m. board. I am willing to do any work—but there is no work.[19]

Her story was not atypical. The signs of distress showed up most acutely not among women, however, but among their children. During the first four months of 1970, of the twenty-one deaths registered, eighteen were children under the age of two. Half of them had died of gastroenteritis, a disease not usually fatal to healthy infants.

The combined effect of repression, mechanization, and a changing labor force was severe. Between 1965 and 1975, only the core union groups in the Western Cape remained active, and political participation ceased almost entirely. Outside of Paarl, there was little branch-level organization among fruit and vegetable workers, while the closure of many fish canneries completed the union's decline on the west coast. Because migrants were vulnerable to expulsion and many employers refused to negotiate jointly with the FCWU and the AFCWU, African branches also collapsed. A 1976 review of trade unions in the Western Cape depicted the level of organization in the food and beverages industry as "extremely weak."[20] In this discouraging context, while the union never altered its policy of nonracialism, leaders tended to adopt a more conservative outlook.[21]

During this bleak period, union records dwell at great length on issues of working conditions and benefits, many affecting women: complaints about nonpayment of confinement allowances and workers' compensation, about unjust dismissals, the use of abusive language by foremen, and general conditions such as inadequate cloakrooms, excessive overtime, and lack of protective clothing. Richard Goode argues that as the union lost the power to win substantial wage concessions, these issues, over which it retained some leverage, assumed greater relative importance.[22]

The impediments to renewed organization appeared overwhelming in 1970. But just a few years later the revival of militant working-class organization was creating a new political environment. Black food and canning workers in East London, exempt from the stringent controls on African labor, were particularly drawn to the large-scale, often spontaneous, actions typical of the late 1970s. Although Western Cape workers were poorly represented in the 1973 strikes, the development that year of the Western Province Advice Bureau (later the Western Province General Workers' Union), aimed at organizing unskilled laborers, began to create a new climate for labor in the region. At the same time, the AFCWU and the FCWU launched a reorganization campaign, relying on older leaders whose banning orders had expired (like Oscar Mpetha of the AFCWU) and on newly recruited staff. Their earliest successes occurred in the rural areas of the Western Cape, where many workers remembered the union and were eager to rejoin.[23] Chastened by the lessons of the 1960s, organizers decided against the overt political involvement of the past. This decision did not spare them from repression, however. Among those banned at the end of 1976, in the wake of the Soweto uprising, was Wilma van Blerk, a union office worker who was one of the few to survive from the organization's stronger days.[24]

Although hesitant to become politically involved, the new organizers apparently retained a concern for gender equity. A list of delegates and alternates submitted to the Department of Labour for a Conciliation Board in 1974 listed women as five of the eleven delegates, and six of eleven alternates.[25] Pay equity for women was one of the union's demands to the Wage Board during the reorganization period of the 1970s.[26]

If the union structure was reforming only slowly, many workers in the industry were quite willing to join in the spontaneous activity of the 1970s. In 1973 and 1974, African food workers in Natal were among those who took part in strikes for higher wages.[27] Later in the decade, the issue of overtime pay triggered a stoppage among 850 African women at L.K.B. in East London. Like many other workers of the period, these women also were dissatisfied over grievance procedures. One woman criticized the liaison committee for collaboration with management: "They are now 'ja baas' [yes boss] instead of putting things right."[28] No doubt encouraged by such militancy, Oscar Mpetha, the former general secretary of the AFCWU, and Lizzie Phike, then a union activist in Paarl, initiated an organizing campaign in East London.[29] As labor unrest increased in late 1979, seven hundred coloured women went on strike at the Sea Harvest fish factory in Saldanha Bay, north of Cape Town on the west coast. Protesting over unsuccessful wage negotiations, their stoppage was the culmination of a series of conflicts over pay, long working hours (often twelve hours a day in season), unhealthy working conditions, and the union's right to operate freely in the plant.[30]

The most significant action of the food and canning workers in the 1970s, however, preceded the Sea Harvest stoppage, the strike at the Fattis and Monis factory in Bellville, South Cape, which was supported by a nation-wide consumer boycott. In a remarkable victory, African contract workers eventually won back the right to their jobs. The action, which Steven Friedman credits as "the first indication of a resurgence of the union movement,"[31] attained prominence and publicity for a number of reasons: the solidarity between coloured workers, primarily women, and black migrants; the extraordinary risks that the latter group took; and the extensive community and political ties necessary to sustain a nationwide consumer boycott for seven months.

The dispute ignited in the context of efforts, beginning in 1978, to revive a union at the plant. The company failed to respond to union letters regarding workers' complaints and refused to negotiate jointly with the three sections of the factory or to recognize the African Food and Canning Workers' Union. A year later, in March 1979, coloured and African workers together drew up a petition authorizing the union to demand higher wages and to bargain on their behalf. Receiving no response, the union asked the Minister of Labour to appoint a Conciliation Board and sent a copy of the application to Fattis and Monis.

From the time this letter arrived, the disagreements flared into an open confrontation. Calling together the workers in the milling section of the factory on April 19, the manager informed them they would have to choose between the union and the liaison committee he had recently established, which the milling workers had refused to join. The choice was not entirely open, however, for he threatened "difficult times" ahead if they chose the union. When officials contacted the manager to inquire about the threat, he refused to speak to them, forcing the secretary to inform the company's director in Johannesburg. Peter Moni's assurances that employees would not be threatened proved valueless, and four days later events came to a head.

On April 23, five coloured women active in the union were given their pay and then dismissed without explanation. The following day, as the news spread, five more coloured workers who demanded to know the reason for this action also were fired. According to the general secretary, "When the Union pointed out that the workers were breadwinners, he replied that that was something the Union should have thought of." [32]

A high degree of solidarity between black and coloured workers prevailed throughout the conflict. On April 24, both groups came together; they demanded to speak to the manager and refused Department of Labour efforts to deal with them separately. In response to their determination, the manager instead fired all of the workers present, making a total of eighty-eight dismissed. Among them were forty African contract workers whose support of their coworkers put them in immediate danger of being deported to the Ciskei or arrested for pass offenses. The manager promptly engaged scab labor and refused to discuss the dismissals with the union.

For the next seven months, until the dispute was settled in November, negotiations between the FCWU and the company centered on efforts to have all the workers reemployed in their former jobs or in comparable, equally paid positions and to insure that the contracts of the African workers would be renewed. The cost to the union and to individual strikers was enormous. Payment of over R30,000 was necessary to support the strikers, and one worker lost a child because he refused to collect money from the company to cover her medical treatment. The union was correct to judge the action as a victory, however. A consumer boycott, organized and sustained by an impressive number of community organizations (and, most critically, by Cape Town's African traders), put sufficient pressure on Fattis and Monis to force them to agree to the union's demands,[33] the workers showed "unheard of endurance and determination," and the union played an active and effective role in keeping the strikers together.[34]

With the strength of this victory to sustain its position, the Food and

Canning Workers' Union regained its place as an active and viable organization. During the controversy in the early 1980s over whether independent unions should register with the Department of Labour, the AFCWU held out for several years in protest against the controls implicit in registration. The momentum from the Fattis and Monis strike also gave both sections the necessary energy to reactivate old branches, to revive those at a low ebb, and to establish new ones. During 1980 and 1981, strikes broke out in rural areas of the Cape, part of a wave of unrest throughout the area during these years. All occurring during the season to take advantage of the greater leverage at this time, significant wage increases were won. Once again, however, the risk was greatest to black contract workers, who sometimes were victimized at the season's end.[35]

As worker militancy began to revive in the late 1970s, the union added to its long-standing opposition to regional wage differentials a concern with gender inequity. In support of a request to the Wage Board for the elimination of sex and age differentials, the union reasoned that women's low wages depress pay throughout the food industry and that there can be "no substantial increase in the minimum wage until sex differentials are eliminated or reduced." Furthermore, "The argument that the women [sic] worker is supported by a male breadwinner is often not the case. A significant proportion are sole breadwinners with dependants."[36] At the time of these discussions, female wages were set at 25 percent less than those of men. But in fact male wages in the main centers were considerably higher than the minimum, while those of women, especially in Durban, were rarely above this level. Agreeing to close this gap only slightly, the board recommended a shift to a 20 percent differential.[37]

By the mid-1980s, the union's decline had been reversed. With twenty-two branches, membership stood at over twenty-five thousand. Having officially amalgamated with the AFCWU in 1985, the union more recently joined with the Sweet, Food and Allied Workers' Union. Successfully addressing the perennial problem of regional wage variation, it was one of the few emerging unions to develop an effective national organization.[38] And despite employers' deliberately divisive tactics, good relationships between African and coloured members prevailed.

This remarkable resurgence of activity notwithstanding, many problems remained. One study of country areas of the Western Cape (Ceres and Grabouw, two of the strongest rural branches) depicted conditions of seasonal labor, low wages, arduous and unhealthful working conditions, and racial and sexual harassment little changed from the 1950s. Furthermore, with coloured men continuing to predominate among permanent workers, they also made up the majority of branch committee members.[39] This apparent difference from the 1940s and 1950s may be a result of a deliberate policy change in recent years. With the union less involved than before in community and political activities,[40] the vehicles for organizing women and for encouraging their continuous participation in union-related affairs during the off-season may have been reduced. If officials continue to be wary of ambiguous political connections, they may need to seek other ways to insure that women again become active members.

For clothing workers in the Transvaal, the most significant political development of the early 1960s involved the merger in June 1962 between the Garment Workers' Union of African Women and the smaller, but more left-wing black male union to form the National Union of Clothing Workers (NUCW). While continuing as a female-dominated organization under the leadership of Lucy Mvubelo, the group voted to join the moderate Federation of Free African Trade Unions of South Africa (FOFATUSA), affiliated with the Trade Union Council of South Africa (TUCSA), thus bringing the radicalism of the male workers more firmly under the control of the registered Garment Workers' Union. In a recent interview Mvubelo alluded to some opposition to the merger on feminist grounds, explaining that when she tried to encourage unity between the two unions, women responded: "Lucy, you want to bring in the men? Men are dominating us enough at home. We don't want to be dominated by men." [41]

Although the GWU had joined the ranks of moderate unions by the beginning of the 1960s, even its white members did not escape the deleterious influence of apartheid. Most serious was legislation designed to intensify "homeland" and border industry development by limiting the growth of clothing production in the Transvaal, presumably to undermine employment possibilities for black women there. The Physical Planning and Utilisation of Resources Act of 1967 imposed further limits on the number of African garment workers employed in the region. Amended in 1974 as the Environmental Planning Act, this legislation gained added credence with the appointment of an inspectorate to police its implementation. J. H. Thomas, Secretary of the Industrial Council for the Transvaal Clothing Industry, felt that his industry had been targeted because of its high concentration of black labor and its potential for geographical mobility. [42] These measures accomplished their goals, causing a decline of clothing manufacturing in the Transvaal and a corresponding rise in two areas: the Cape, where coloured women had long predominated in the workforce, and Natal, which as a declared "border area" was exempt from controls on the ratio of black to white employees. [43]

In an effort to enable the Transvaal clothing industry to exist under the strictures of the 1967 act, a training college was established to encourage people already employed in the industry to remain and to retrain others for better positions. [44] Several years after its establishment, however, Thomas acknowledged the experiment's failure to attract suitable white or coloured students, even to training programs for supervisors. Only a course to train production managers and designers achieved any success in attracting whites. But the total numbers were "hopelessly inadequate" to meet the industry's projected needs. [45]

Employment statistics graphically display the absurdity of the industry's position. While job reservation legislation had fixed the percentage of whites for the Transvaal at 25 percent, by 1967 the number employed had dwindled to 9 percent of clothing workers. If the primary trend of the years 1940–60 had been the massive influx of coloured women into the industry, during the next two decades, black women became dominant. Whereas in 1959, of 11,604 Transvaal garment workers, 45.05 percent were coloured, 28.50 percent white, and 26.45 percent black, by 1979 the figures were drastically different: with 16,076 workers, 82.11 percent were black, 15.60 percent coloured, and a meager 2.29 percent white.[46]

The climate in the Transvaal was grave in the 1960s and 1970s, a result of factory displacement and an acute shortage of skilled labor. During the last four months of 1968, unable to increase the number of their black employees, four Transvaal clothing factories closed because of insufficient labor, leaving one thousand workers without jobs. Other firms quickly hired most of the skilled and semiskilled white, coloured, and Asian employees; but the majority of blacks did not readily find work.[47] Thus, although the shortage of skilled and semiskilled labor remained acute, the law prevented employers from drawing on African women to fill vacant positions. Many potential coloured employees were unwilling to move to the Transvaal, citing housing problems and the lack of crèches.[48]

In an effort to address these difficulties, the union urged the Deputy Secretary for Bantu Administration and Development to remove restrictions that prohibited coloureds and Indians from employing African domestic workers.[49] A memorandum argued that this ban "forced [these women] to stay at home to do their own domestic chores and look after their children. . . . Just as Whites cannot afford to employ White servants, even if they should find them available, so the Coloureds and Indians cannot afford or obtain people from their own race groups to work as domestic servants."[50] Ironically, laws forbidding the hiring of new black women as skilled workers were forcing the union to argue for their expanded employment in a more menial capacity, as domestic employees.

Amidst these fears in the Transvaal, new factories continued to expand in the border areas. In 1968, the South African Clothing Factory began operating at Mobeni, Durban. Three years later, Arbeter Fashions of Johannesburg announced plans to employ eight hundred people to manufacture dresses in East London.[51] The factory that opened at Hammarsdale in Natal hired one thousand women who lived in the reserves. With little more than Standard 2 schooling, most were significantly less educated than their urban counterparts.[52]

Although manufacturers who invested in border factories had hoped to escape the union pressure of the Transvaal, they were not exempt from the wave of protests that swept the country in 1973 and 1974. During March and April 1973, immediately following the Durban strikes, clothing workers staged a number of stoppages. The first two occurred in a border area, where the employees were unorganized and earned substantially lower wages than their counterparts in the major urban centers. On March 26, 1973, undoubtedly spurred by events in nearby Durban, a thousand workers at the Veka Clothing Company in Charlestown went on strike for increased wages, leading police to impose a curfew on the nearby township and to prohibit meetings of more than five people. Four days later, seven hundred workers at Rump Clothing, also in Charlestown, struck for higher pay in support of the Veka strike. Although both groups returned to work without promise of an increase,[53] these actions represented a significant political awakening in areas where clothing manufacturers had hoped to maintain a quiescent labor force. Nonetheless, strikers' failure to win concessions underlines the obstacles to organization under these conditions.

Even before the events of 1973, the intense pressures on the Transvaal industry produced unrest. In August 1970, the twenty-six thousand workers in the Transvaal decided to work-to-rule, banning overtime and suspending bonus schemes in protest against a deadlock in wage negotiations.[54] In 1972, Anna Scheepers, with a prescience growing out of her long years of trade union experience, and perhaps sensing the tensions building up in her own industry, warned of further Sharpevilles and Ovambo-type strikes if the government refused to allow the development of African trade unions. Speaking of the potential "danger" of politically aware labor organizations, she warned, "No police force would be large enough to control a general strike situation."[55]

As if in response to Scheepers's predictions, the stoppages of garment workers in and around Johannesburg in March and April of 1973 achieved greater success than those in the border areas. Fueled by an expected cost-of-living increase, 4,608 black garment workers took part in some twenty-one stoppages during a three-week period. With quick intervention by the registered Garment Workers' Union and/or the parallel African body, the National Union of Clothing Workers, employers usually announced concessions and workers returned to their jobs. Only two of the incidents lasted more than five hours.[56] In 1980–82 another series of clothing industry strikes on the Witwatersrand culminated in February and March of 1982 in a strike of eighteen hundred workers in at least twenty factories, all demanding an immediate wage increase of R3.[57]

Garment workers in the largest cities also were involved in other forms of protest that were more anarchistic and more purely political than the 1973 stoppages. During a strike in the early 1970s at a clothing factory in Johannesburg, large numbers of finished garments were slashed, while in another Johannesburg factory an experienced worker emptied a fire extinguisher onto imported materials worth thousands of rands.[58] Garment workers also numbered among the most active supporters of the stay-at-homes that followed the Soweto uprising in 1976. The clothing industry came to a complete halt during the August protest in the Transvaal, despite the fact that trade union leaders appealed to their members not to withdraw their labor. The three hundred African shop stewards, mainly women, probably were responsible for organizing the workers.[59]

Clothing workers at the Cape, overwhelmingly coloured women, also showed signs of revolt, in this case against a corrupt, unrepresentative, male-dominated trade union. The large labor force in the Cape clothing industry made this effort extremely important to the climate of labor relations in the area.[60] Indirect forms of resistance probably had gone on for some time in the form of absenteeism, go-slows, demonstration strikes, and sabotage, geared primarily against production targets coupled with incentive bonus schemes. Indeed, in 1961, despite appeals from the leadership, the garment industry was severely disrupted by the stay-away commemorating the Sharpeville demonstration.[61] But the late 1970s also saw more organized resistance in the formation of the Action Committee, aimed at democratizing the union, and in massive support for politically oriented stay-aways in 1976 and 1980. In 1976, women reportedly led the September stay-at-home in the Cape during which the clothing industry, whose workforce of fifty thousand was 90 percent female, lost two days of production. And on June 16 and 17, 1980, during actions to commemorate the Soweto uprising, production "came to a standstill" in Cape garment factories.[62] By 1987, the impetus for reform gained a firmer structural footing. The garment unions in the Western Cape and Natal merged to form the Garment and Allied Workers' Union, based on the principles of nonracialism and workers' control.

Garment industry work stoppages usually were extremely brief. Those in border areas were rapidly repressed, while in the Transvaal, well-established procedures for handling disputes were tacitly accepted by employers, the unregistered National Union of Clothing Workers, and the registered Garment Workers' Union. During the 1973 actions, officials of one or both unions intervened immediately. In the opinion of one authority, more generous toward the union than many of its members, "The existence of an established union such as the NUCW enjoying the confidence of the workers was undoubtedly one reason for the speed in which the disputes were settled."[63] At the same time, the activities of the NUCW in helping members to find work, in administering a burial fund, and in assisting them in such tasks as applying for unemployment and maternity benefits theoretically should have helped to create a sense of collective identity.

Nonetheless, the suppressed anger, evident in the instances of industrial sabotage and the widespread support for the 1976 stay-at-home, against the expressed wishes of union officials, suggest only minimal loyalty to a union that many workers perceived as weak and ineffective. One of the more political Johannesburg workers interviewed in 1983 found the black union leadership unresponsive to issues in the factories:

The union, in fact, they don't work. They don't do their job properly because they don't visit the factories, they don't educate the shop stewards. You don't know [as a shop steward] whether you are right or wrong, because you are not educated about it. They just sit in their office there; they don't educate people, "When things are like this, you must do this."[64]

There are many other reasons for this dissatisfaction as well. Extremely low wages continue in the industry, and a tendency to demand a stepped-up work pace, enforced with production goals and bonus payments, has put more pressure on workers, particularly on older women, who find it difficult to keep up. Despite the union's nominal acceptance, the inferior position of the NUCW gave African garment workers less than full representation. In several instances after the 1973 strikes Department of Labour officials deliberately excluded the NUCW spokesperson from negotiations.

On a structural level, the need to negotiate through the registered GWU created a dependent relationship the details of which were revealed in a series of allegations and denials published in the *Financial Mail* in 1976.[65] The article, drawn from sources within the union, alleged that Anna Scheepers, president of the registered union, dominated the "sister" African body and influenced the actions of its leaders, vetoing decisions of which she did not approve. It reported, "She calls the executive in and lectures them like grade school children and then tells them to go back and reconsider. Usually they do." Furthermore, although employers in the 1970s were willing to negotiate directly with the NUCW, Scheepers insisted that the African unionists were "not ready." The numerical situation in the union alone underlined the insulting nature of this inequality. As of the early 1970s, the registered GWU represented 1,377 white and 6,901 coloured workers, while black employees numbered 17,191.[66]

This "mother-daughter" relationship between the two unions resulted both from what Douwes Dekker terms the "understandable caution" of the GWU leaders and from the continuing dependence of the NUCW.[67] Yet the independent action of the shop stewards in 1976 suggests a growing resentment of "maternalism," particularly on the part of younger workers who have entered the industry since the late 1960s. As second or third generation urban dwellers, these women are politically sophisticated and skeptical about supporting a moderate trade union that puts them in a subordinate position.[68] Some of the more politically aware older women, who felt the union was inadequately active on behalf of its members, shared this critical attitude. An incident in 1983, when twenty-two retrenched garment workers fought successfully for reinstatement, brought out some of these feelings. Workers interviewed explained that members had been dissatisfied for a long time. "The union does not really consult and represent us." During negotiations, the workers insisted on the union's following conditions that they had set out. A spokesperson explained:

"Not only were we taking a stand against recession and the bosses, but also against the union. This made the victory all the more difficult, but sweeter."[69] One of the few workers interviewed in 1983 who defended the union directly was an older woman, who had been a shop steward for ten years. She appreciated its protective value, arguing, "Without the union we are nothing. The boss can do what he likes." Expressing gratitude rather than anger toward the registered union, she observed, "Blacks are here because of the efforts of the whites and coloureds."

The economic pressures on garment workers, combined with a racially and sexually biased division of labor, have created yet another source of discontent. In urban factories the labor process has operated to the detriment of black women, who still occupy the least-skilled jobs in disproportionate numbers, despite their long history of organization and the shortage of white garment workers. In the Transvaal as of 1973 European men continued to hold the vast majority of the highest paid supervisory positions. Although a surprisingly high 62 percent of the 120 European female employees earned only R10–20 a week, 98 percent of the coloured women and 99 percent of the African women fell into this category. Furthermore, black women (78 percent African and 20 percent coloured) held virtually all of the unskilled positions.[70]

On one level, then, the collective activity of garment workers has drawn on the organizational strength generated by membership in an informally recognized trade union that operates through hundreds of shop stewards and provides a variety of material benefits to its members. Yet, the protests of the 1970s came from rank-and-file workers, not from union officials, and the spirit that animated them emerged not as much through the unions as from opposition to existing union leadership. In the eyes of many women, this leadership accommodated too readily to an industrial system that hampered the emergence of strong, independent black unions and that continues to rely on the exploitation of cheap black labor power. Although explicitly women's issues did not figure in the collective action of the garment workers, a high degree of female solidarity was undoubtedly present in an industry with few male employees and a union organized and led by women.

The 1980s brought a new series of changes to the Transvaal garment unions. The report of the Wiehahn Commission and the government White Paper that followed incited a rare spark of militancy. Explaining the NUCW's refusal to register until the ban on migrant workers belonging to recognized unions had been lifted, Lucy Mvubelo snapped, "This is not the pass office."[71] Within a short time after the black union was officially recognized, however, dwindling white membership and new laws permitting multiracial unions led to pressure for another structural shift. During the early 1980s the registered GWU repeatedly urged the NUCW to merge with it. Although Mvubelo agreed, her executive committee did not. By 1985, when the two finally joined, GWU membership was so small that it was forced to disband and become a branch of the formerly African union.[72]

The textile industry, concentrated around Durban, though scattered throughout the low-paying border areas and "homelands," was among the economic sectors hardest hit during the protests of the 1970s. This geographical concentration was not accidental. Durban's proximity to the KwaZulu "homeland," resulting in its classification as a border area, made it exempt from controls on industrial growth and made its industries eligible for varied economic incentives. Operating on a capital-intensive basis that brought together thousands of workers in each mill, the textile factories only began to employ significant numbers of women again during this period. The turn to African women in the 1960s was partly a product of the changing labor process that accompanied intensified mechanization, and partly an effort to break the unity of organized labor in the industry.[73] Roughly half the textile workers in Durban were migrants, whose housing in company dormitories enhanced the possibility of mass action, as did the heavy concentration of ownership by the Frame company, a vast industrial empire spread over South Africa, Zimbabwe, Zambia, and Malawi.[74]

Despite many signs of discontent, the 1973 strikes took many trade unionists by surprise. According to Harriet Bolton, who had taken over the Natal Garment and Furniture Workers' Union from her husband after his death in 1964 and who worked closely with those seeking to form an independent textile union:

It was just like it came out of the air. I mean, we knew about the dissatisfaction, obviously we had a part in it because we had been organizing for two or three years. We had been talking to them [the textile workers], had been addressing groups of workers, having plays, songs, informal meetings, home meetings, and so on. But we had not advocated that particular direction. That seemed to be a spontaneous thing.[75]

Women formed only a small percentage of the work force in 1970. But their numbers began to increase dramatically shortly thereafter, under circumstances that undoubtedly contributed to their willingness to protest. Until the mid-1960s, in the heavy or woollen section of the industry, which was covered by an Industrial Council agreement, no separate wage rates for women were set. (Workers in the light or cotton section were largely unorganized.) At this time, however, under continual threat from lower-priced imports, the National Textile Manufacturers' Association (NTMA) began an offensive to force employees to accept a gender-based wage differential. In 1965 and 1966, the union resisted their effort to grant women only 75 percent of the wages to be paid after a proposed increase, and the NTMA position won only partial and conditional acceptance by an arbitrator. He agreed to lower wages in certain restricted classes of work,

provided that the categories in question be "suitably diluted" and that
the work assigned to women be clearly specified. By the early 1970s, only
452 of the 3,747 women in the industry were receiving the lower wage,
fixed at 80 percent of male pay. But in June 1972, after several break-
downs in both negotiation and arbitration, the union finally accepted the
NTMA's conditions. This ruling undoubtedly accounts for the increased
number of women textile workers during the 1970s. In a pattern typical
for the industry as a whole, the proportion of women employed in the
Frame factories rose from 40 percent to 70 percent of the total workforce
between 1972 and 1980.[76]

These women came both from local urban townships and from sur-
rounding rural areas; indeed, in the early 1970s, many Pinetown factories
recruited country women directly, bringing them to town on cattle trucks.
Paid extremely low wages, these recent rural migrants saved money on
shoes by binding their feet with cloth. Generally, Durban workers were
relatively young; in one survey of nearly one thousand female factory
employees, half were under thirty. Nonetheless, this youth was not a
uniform pattern, for a quarter of the women exceeded forty. According to
Fatima Meer's study, about half had been married, but many were divorced or widowed and therefore economically independent. And, whether
single or married, many had children. Relatively well-educated, 55 percent had been to primary school and slightly over a quarter (27.5 percent)
through Standards 8 and 9. Significantly, nearly half had left school because their families needed their earnings, although slightly over one
quarter of the African women had quit because of pregnancy. Continuing
a pattern of family wages, an unmarried young woman usually turned
over her entire pay check to her mother, who then granted her a personal
allowance.[77]

Thus, some of these women were as young as their white counterparts
a generation earlier. But they were more varied in terms of age and marital status, and many more had dependents to support on their meager
wages. Furthermore, many were migrants, a new category of working-
class women, who occupied the lowest-paid, most insecure positions.

In addition to receiving less pay than men, women held the lowest-
paid, least skilled jobs. Although the sexual division of labor differed in
each branch of the textile industry, most supervisors were men, and women
had little chance for advancement. More men than women were employed as weavers, a position that offers both a higher wage and a greater
degree of control over one's working conditions than is possible for spinners, the other main category of semiskilled workers.[78]

Despite the large number of female textile workers, the detailed study
of the 1973 strikes published by the Institute for Industrial Education leaves
many gaps in its information about women.[79] A list of the percentages of
workers in each grade of employment contains no breakdown by sex, and
more important, the sample of workers interviewed gives information on

Indian women but not on their African counterparts. This discussion concerns Indian women's fears of African men, thereby conveying the impression that women workers posed a threat to interracial solidarity. The gap in the available information on women is partly remedied by a series of interviews conducted with women textile workers in Durban following the strike. But, although it provides insights into women's concerns, the study's statistical imprecision leaves important question unanswered.

On January 19, ten days after the Durban strikes began, the first stoppages occurred in the textile industry. Wages throughout the industry were roughly 20 percent lower than those in manufacturing as a whole. At the Frame Cotton Mills in New Germany, male pay apparently had risen by only R1 per week, from R6 to R7, between 1964 and 1972 (excluding a R1 attendance bonus). Women at the later date earned R5 with a R1 bonus. But a survey conducted at the Nortex and Seltex mills in July 1972 revealed that some women were earning only R3.50 in basic salary.[80] Textile workers stopped work first in East London, at Consolidated Fine Spinners and Weavers. By January 25 and 26, the "isolated brush fires became a conflagration" as strikes spread to the Frame Group factories and over seven thousand cotton workers at the New Germany mill left their jobs. The other adjacent cotton mills followed in quick succession. In at least one of the textile industry stoppages, it was African women, working for D. Pegler and Company in New Germany, who were first to down their tools.[81] On January 29, the workers at Consolidated Woolwashing and Processing Mills in Pinetown, mainly women rag sorters, came out on strike after the management had ignored a written statement of their grievances presented through a union representative. By that day, not a single Frame factory in Natal remained in operation.[82] Lasting from one to seven days, the strikes in the industry ended with concessions of R1–R2.50 per week from employers.

These settlements did not curtail the unrest in the industry, however. In April 1973, three hundred Indian and African women working as sorters in a woolwashing and processing firm in the Durban suburb of Pinetown were locked out after striking and then refusing an unspecified pay offer. In July, the stoppages spread to women weavers in Umtata, the capital of the Transkei in the Eastern Cape.[83] Again, on August 8, some one thousand workers struck at the Frame Group's Wentex Factory in Durban after six hundred workers had lost their jobs in the wake of wage demands.[84] By January 1974, ten thousand Durban textile workers in eleven mills were again on strike, demanding that government-ordered increases for new workers in the cotton mills also be extended to employees with seniority.[85] These actions led to the rapid development of a new unregistered union, the National Union of Textile Workers (NUTW), which signed its first agreement in 1974 with Smith and Nephew. Only after a heated struggle in 1982 did the Frame group recognize the union.[86]

Despite the intensity of these outbursts, the issue of gender inequity seems to have been submerged in the wake of other grievances. As recently as July 1972 the textile union had demanded the removal of wage discrimination against women; but this provision rarely was brought up in the negotiations during the strikes. In the IIE report, the issue of a gender-based wage differential comes out only once, in the description of negotiations at the relatively progressive firm of Smith and Nephew, a British-based multinational where the workers demanded a basic wage of R18 "even if it meant that all workers irrespective of sex and skill be paid that amount."[87] Indeed, the factory was initially unionized through the actions of a militant group of Indian women who demanded that the National Union of Textile Workers come there to organize.[88] That they settled eventually for a male minimum of R18 and a female minimum of R12 probably was related to the intimidating presence of carloads of plainclothes police at the meeting during which the offer was accepted. More generally, the issue of the recently instituted wage differential may have been ignored because of the nature of the only union operating before the NUTW was formed; closed to blacks, it had few women members and little power on the shop floor.[89]

Subsequent actions by textile workers reveal patterns of racial and gender relationships that varied from factory to factory. In the August 1973 strike at Consolidated Textile Mills, male weavers concerned with piece rates demanded that women join them. But the women at the mill, who had not been included in the decision to strike, hesitated to lend support until they had been assured that their demands as spinners also would be voiced. In the Braitex Factory in the Transvaal, however, organizers Evelyn Selora and David Hemson found a very different situation. With greater job security, the men were more skeptical about their ability to effect change and were slower to support the union until they could see how it would work out. The women, by contrast, were immediately enthusiastic, and with their support the factory was organized rapidly.[90]

In 1980 another massive strike broke out in the Frame factories around Durban. Beginning among weavers in the Frametex plant and lasting for twelve days, the stoppage was triggered by continuing anger at low wages, the manipulation of the bonus system, and the manager's unwillingness to consult with the liaison committee. Women, by then 70 percent of the work force, were involved from the beginning and took an active part in meetings, demonstrations at the bus terminal, and organization at Kranzkloof, the hostel where most of the workers, as migrants, were forced to live. The only grouping of strikers from which they were excluded was the *impi* or "regiment," which acted as the main strikers' defense force. The following description by the Natal Labour Research Committee, based on interviews with participants, summarizes women's activities succinctly:

Within twenty-four hours of its beginning the women workers at Kranzkloof had organized themselves into two groups, one of which was stationed at the main gate, the other at the opposite end of section D. Here they waited for those women workers who were defying the strike, to return from the factories. The latter were then prevented from entering the premises, and only later that night (Friday) after the police dispersed the women strikers with tear gas, were they able to steal back into the hostel. Thereafter the women decided to visit each room occupied by one or more strike-breakers. This resulted in violent confrontation, with some of the strike-breakers leaving the hostel for fear of being attacked. Throughout the strike, the women continued to meet regularly in the hostel corridors, as well as in the grounds near the bus rank where most of the action took place. Their gatherings were coloured by much discussion, militant chanting and singing.[91]

The militancy of women in these protests undoubtedly arose from some of the same factors that fueled and shaped the resistance of their male coworkers: extraordinarily low wages in a time of rapid inflation, rigidly controlled working conditions, and a lack of adequate procedures for communicating their grievances. The vast scale of production, with several thousand workers in a single factory, the densely packed hostels in which they resided, and the "packed and gregarious" buses on which they rode to and from work fostered communication and collective consiousness among textile workers, male and female alike. The homogeneity of the largely Zulu workforce also figures in discussions of unrest in the Durban area.

Numerous aspects of women's working situation and living conditions probably helped to generate a sense of female solidarity among the strikers. Adding to the frustrations of women's generally disadvantageous position in the labor process, management relied on male dominance as a means of enforcing industrial discipline. Male supervisors might grant permission to go to the bathroom or the "privilege" of resting during a bout of menstrual cramps in exchange for sexual favors. Women interviewed after the 1973 strike also complained of sexual harassment.

The women reported that the men workers in their factories have no respect for them. On the factory floor, men ill-treat the women, make fools of them and become vulgar by 'touching the women in embarrassing parts'. Others mentioned male assaults on the women they worked with, one noting that if this is reported to the authorities, the latter take the part of the men.[92]

Coercive intrusion into workers' personal lives also was common, particularly with respect to women's fertility. In one engineering factory, black women were forced to take the pill daily under a nurse's supervision.[93] In the Frame factories, prospective female employees who survived a mandatory pregnancy test were then subjected to the probing eye of factory doctors instructed to watch for signs of impending motherhood. Until early 1980, Frame managers routinely dismissed pregnant women; but a later policy change provided for reemployment eight weeks after confinement. Women alleged, however, that supervisors retained the arbitrary power to determine whether a woman would be reinstated. Those allowed to return were required to undergo a "retraining" period (of six weeks according to the industry, three months according to women), during which they were excluded from bonuses and overtime work.[94] Accounts differ on women's attitudes toward compulsory birth control in the factories. Whereas David Hemson, a former textile workers' organizer, recalls great controversy over the Frame factories' insistence on women taking pills or injections of Depo Provera, Meer reports as a collective sentiment: "We are glad to have this control otherwise we would be in great trouble."[95]

Other arbitrary and sometimes humiliating regulations dominated the lives of women textile workers, both in the factories and at the hostel where a majority of them lived. Company policy, for example, forbade them from using any company toilet paper or cotton scraps to supplement the single sanitary napkin they were issued. And, while men were frisked for company property at the end of each day, women had to leave through a special "searching room," where they were scrutinized more thoroughly. Trade union material found during these searches might provide grounds for dismissal.[96]

In Kranzkloof hostel a high degree of paternalism regulated women's daily lives. Whereas men had greater mobility within the hostel grounds, women were largely confined to a fenced-in area that was permanently under guard. The rules were applied more strictly to them than to men. They were prohibited from smoking or drinking in their rooms and forbidden from having babies or young children as visitors. But the threat of arbitrary expulsion by the superintendent generated the most extreme bitterness. Women complained of facing removal for questioning unreasonable demands, such as being selected at random to collect litter in the corridors. Individuals also could be victimized arbitrarily for misusing communal facilities, with neither investigation nor recourse to a hearing. The study of the 1980 strike concluded: "Because women live in constant fear of arbitrary expulsion, they have tended to unite in mutual self-defence against the capricious actions of the authorities. The solidarity and steadfastness of these women were certainly evident during the strike."[97]

Women living in dormitories experienced conditions very different from those in black townships. Run like mining compounds, with efforts to exert total control over their inhabitants, these hostels must have strongly shaped women's attitudes toward their work. Whereas most women have favored industrial jobs because they allowed a more stable family life and a less-regulated existence than domestic work, these women lived under strictures harsher than those of most household servants, and with equally dismal opportunities for seeing their children or husbands. That so many women have sought such jobs during the past two decades attests to the desperate conditions in the "homelands."

In the disorder connected with the 1980 strike, women's sexual vulnerability became politicized. Female strikers were the target of police violence and of youth gangs or *tsotsi*, whose motivation may have been unrelated to the labor dispute. Since the security and regulation system at the hostel broke down, nonresidents had freer access to women's rooms; numerous incidents of theft and rape were reported. Other women were sexually assaulted by nonstrikers, who then instructed them to return to work. In one area, women successfully organized themselves to prevent such attacks, but in another part of the hostel they were less successful. Women were often forced to flee the hostel to seek accommodation in the nearby African township of Clermont, frequently in the safest place available: other men's beds. "Once again," according to the 1980 study, "women found themselves having to choose between the lesser of two abuses—rape by, or involuntary submission to male coworkers."[98]

The prevalence of migrant workers among the women is also a significant issue. By the early 1980s, they comprised 90 percent of the female cotton workers in Frame factories around Pinetown. Like other migrants, those who supported the 1980 strike risked losing their jobs and accommodation and being forced to return to their "homelands." They were ethnically divided between Zulu, who generally were strikers, and Xhosa from the Transkei, whose insecure employment situation in Durban made them less likely to strike.[99] Although violent confrontation between striking and nonstriking women in the hostel did occur, the study of the 1980 strikes seems to imply that the high degree of solidarity generated by fear of expulsion may have mitigated these tensions somewhat among women. Thus, the impact of migrancy is complex. Lacking daily obligations to their families, women migrants had more time to devote to labor activities than did many other women, and the crowded hostels generated both solidarity and personal and ethnic tensions. Yet the degree of risk women were willing to take may have varied with their sense of job security. Whether such fears affected women and men in different ways remains to be investigated.

Few South African documents spell out the ideological justification of women's exploitation more fully than the report from the National Association of Textile Manufacturers to the industrial arbitrator in 1966, when the organization sought to justify its request for a 25 percent wage differential between women and men.[100] The authors relied on stereotyped arguments, apparently so widely accepted that they felt little need to substantiate them: women's alleged physical weakness, their lower educational attainments, and their minimal financial needs.

Yet a later study of women textile workers belies these facile conclusions. Conducted by the National Institute of Personnel Research, this survey found a high degree of financial responsibility among respondents, who were not migrants but settled residents of a border area in the Eastern Cape. Shattering the myth of the dependent working woman, it exposed the economic self-sufficiency that pushed women into their jobs. Nearly half (47 percent) were single, 32 percent formerly married (widowed, divorced, and deserted) and only 21 percent were married—a very low percentage considering that 64 percent of the women were between twenty-one and thirty-five years old. The figures are important in correcting the notion of wives left behind when men migrate to larger urban centers; for the ravages of apartheid have left many women unmarried at relatively late ages. Although often lacking "male breadwinners," these women did not lack dependents. On the contrary, many "occupied a key role in the households to which they belonged, for one-quarter of them were household heads and over one half (52 percent) were the main breadwinners of their families." Not only were most of the women self-supporting, but they were, as a group, much better educated than the men employed in the factory. Furthermore, although the women's absenteeism and turnover rates were slightly higher than those of men (another contention of the textile manufacturers), the report judged both figures to be low. According to the author, women's high degree of family responsibility as household heads and as main breadwinners "apparently caused them to be stable."[101]

Although in recent years a significant number of female workers have withdrawn their labor in support of political and economic goals, how to interpret their participation in collective action remains unclear. Many historians and social theorists caution against automatically interpreting strikes as a reflection of class consciousness. Furthermore, recent sociological studies of women industrial workers in South Africa suggest the difficulty of generalizing accurately about their attitudes toward politics or trade unions.

Two surveys in the early 1980s, for example, uncovered a lukewarm or even negative attitude toward unions. Women in the Johannesburg knitting factory studied by Jane Barrett were more inclined to express their resentment of working conditions through chatting with each other (forbidden during working time), quarreling, petty theft, and lingering during toilet breaks than by organizing collective resistance, either independently or through the union (the National Union of Clothing Workers). Their perception of the union as weak and ineffective undoubtedly shaped such responses. Indeed, many were reluctant to act as shop stewards for fear of being unprotected in case of victimization.[102] Studying women factory workers in Natal, Fatima Meer found a similar lack of interest in unions. Only half of those interviewed were members.[103] Yet, based on a smaller, earlier study she did conclude that African women, then without trade union rights, appeared more union-conscious than their Indian and coloured coworkers. It was they who initiated most complaints against management.[104]

The comments of veteran Natal unionist Harriet Bolton are more optimistic, however. Speaking primarily about the Natal garment industry, she observed in particular the relevance of age differences among Indian women:

> The women have always been very active and, as shop stewardesses, mainly coloured women and young Indian girls. . . . The coloured women were the most marvelous trade unionists, quite fearless, and quick to understand the principles of it, as were the African women when they came in. The older Indian women were more diplomatic and tactful and a bit more placid. They would stand by you, but they would be afraid.[105]

Informed by Bolton's perspective, further analysis suggests that the contradiction between Barrett's and Meer's conclusions and women's participation in collective action during the 1970s and 1980s may be more apparent than real. Indeed, the conflict may be a product of the common but unspoken assumptions that often inform political and scholarly discussion: either women are conscious of themselves as members of a working class or they are not. And, if they perceive themselves as class-conscious, they will express their awareness through a trade union. The contradictory data suggest that the question is much more complex. Apart from the difficulties of defining consciousness in an ostensibly "universal" fashion, it seems necessary to formulate the issues differently: to ask in what situations women have been mobilized successfully or have organized themselves spontaneously, how they have formulated their grievances and concerns in those instances, what form their resistance has taken, and how the gender-related aspects of their lives have shaped their actions and their attitudes. Finally, it is important to understand women's lives from their own perspective and not to impose outside frameworks and expectations on their behavior and then to find them lacking with reference to those theories or by comparison with men.

The conflicting information does not end with studies of work, but also permeates interpretations of women's attitudes toward their home lives and toward the division of labor and authority at home. All the women Barrett and Meer interviewed felt the burden of cooking, cleaning, and washing clothes after working a full day outside the home, and many resented the men in their families for expecting to be waited on. But the degree of resentment varied, and none of the women perceived the household division of labor as amenable to change. Certainly the strongest statement in support of male authority came from Meer's summary of the collective feelings of the women interviewed in her study:

The men in our lives are our fathers, brother, husbands and boyfriends. These are the people who control us and whom we must obey.

We live in a man's world and men are superior to women. As daughters and as wives we must respect and listen to our brothers and husbands and it is only right that we should seek their permission before we do anything or go anywhere. Men are the breadwinners. They need jobs more than women do. It is worse for a man to be out of a job than it is for the woman.

About a third of us do all the housework ourselves single-handed and most of us feel that it is not right that men should do housework.[106]

The women Barrett interviewed also accepted their double burden as unalterable. But their varied individual comments convey an edge of bitterness that is curiously absent in Meer's composite opinion:

It would be nice if the men would cook, but they won't do it . . . they like to drink all the time. He tells you he is tired, that he needs to relax. When I get home I don't relax, I have to cook. There is no rest.

My father just sits down. He says he wants his tea. And he wants this and that. Its not fair—he must try it.

My husband he just look! He is reading the paper while I cook. He says he is tired. I am also tired but I must cook. I am used to it because it is our custom.

Ooh, that one [her husband on the weekends] is drinking. He is not at home but in the shebeens.[107]

Outside of work and home, the strongest influences on the "Knitmore" women whom Barrett studied came from their participation in religious and voluntary associations, which involved most of the women despite their limited leisure time. Like the older Johannesburg women discussed earlier, most belonged to established churches rather than to smaller, more independent charismatic groups. They found in church women's associations and in collective credit groups scope for shared activities (like Bible-reading, sewing, trips, or choir singing); support in dealing with illness and personal or family problems; and economic cooperation. Fundamental to these leisure activities was their gender-segregated character. (Many of the men in the factory were involved in sports, and most women mentioned their husbands' drinking, either at home or in shebeens). Significantly also, although only one woman (a shop steward) regularly attended political gatherings, the others were not altogether lacking in political consciousness. Virtually all identified Nelson Mandela as their "true leader."[108]

Thus, the material from the 1970s, combined with interview data from the early 1980s, may not be at odds with women's behavior. In this decade of renewed labor activity, women clearly were very involved in strikes and in often-spontaneous labor activities, although most women were not particularly committed trade unionists. The situational and historical reasons for their attitudes vary from one industry to the next. Garment workers in the Transvaal perceived their union as weak and ineffective, in the Cape, as corrupt. The Food and Canning Workers' Union was just in the process of reorganizing by the latter part of the 1970s, although the Fattis and Monis strike and boycott provided a stunning example of its potential. Yet the concerns of women as a distinct group were not articulated as clearly during this reorganization period as they had been in the 1940s and 1950s. Similarly, though many women took part in the textile strikes in 1973–74 and in 1980, gender-specific issues of pay equity, sexual harassment, reproductive control, and the sexist assumptions of male organizers rarely were raised. Thus, most working women had little reason to perceive trade unions as a primary means of addressing their concerns. By 1980, none of the unions in which they were involved was as active in responding to their needs as women or in linking their concerns and their lives at home, at work, and in the community as either the GWU or the AFCWU and FCWU had been in earlier years. The nascent consciousness of gender issues among a few female leaders had not been articulated in ways that reached a significant number of working women.

Yet to conclude that women accepted their oppression and exploitation with docility would be an error, involving a narrow and restrictive understanding of consciousness. Helen Safa, who has analyzed the lives of Latin American women workers, found that those who were economically independent showed a higher level of class consciousness than others.[109] Significantly, most studies of women factory workers in South Africa during the 1970s and early 1980s suggested that a large proportion of them provided the sole income or a major part of the income for their families. With this high level of responsibility, these women felt acutely the results of low wages and the all-pervasive political and economic restraints of apartheid, and did not hesitate to voice their anger and frustration in strikes and stay-at-homes commemorating political events. Expressing a kind of populist consciousness informed by class and racial grievances, they had no doubt that they required higher wages and vastly transformed political conditions to be able to support themselves and their children without anxiety. Yet their domestic responsibilities created strains in going to meetings and in becoming involved in activities that require sustained after-work commitments. They also, understandably, created fears about what would happen to their families if they were arrested. In some respects, then, some of the events of the 1970s might be understood as "rituals of rebellion." They allowed women occasional collective opportunities to act out their rage and anxiety, but rarely drew them into ongoing organizations with the power to effect significant change. Like the strikes of the late 1920s, they provided a kind of rehearsal for the more systematic organizing of the coming decade.

Thus, throughout the twentieth century, the social, economic, and political factors that shaped the consciousness of working-class women have been complex. Clearly, racial and ethnic identity have mediated their perception of class. But women of different racial groups also have shared common concerns, which have influenced the agendas of the more responsive trade unions in similar ways. Under the divisive conditions prevailing in South Africa, however, gender could only rarely provide a basis for unity. Yet the country has undergone an enormous transformation since 1900. The "working class" is now black, female and male, rather than white and male, and dependency no longer governs the lives of most working women.

By 1980, after nearly a decade of renewed unrest, many of the black women involved in industrial labor were willing once again to act spontaneously or to be mobilized on occasion to voice grievances articulated in terms of class and race. Few as yet perceived gender as an equally political issue. But that situation would begin to change in the coming decade as a small number of trade unionists articulated a new understanding of women's issues.

EPILOGUE

Common Threads, Past and Present

As I waited to conduct an interview in the office of a progressive Johannesburg lawyer, I struck up a conversation with the man seated next to me. Noting the journal he was reading—a special issue on women's health—I inquired about the source of his interest in the subject. He explained that, as an official of a trade union with a large female membership, he had to be well informed on such issues.

This experience aptly illustrates a new awareness of gender within the independent trade union movement. In part a result of the growing number of women in industrial and commercial jobs, the attitude also has external sources. As a global dialogue on women's issues intensified during the 1970s and 1980s, international labor organizations became a vehicle for diffusing these concerns among constituent unions. Similarly, stimulated by the feminist scholarship proliferating in Britain and North America, some students and faculty at South African universities translated their interest into studies of women's work. Others became organizers or researchers for the new unions.

Although working-class women in South Africa hardly require outsiders to verify the difficulty of their daily lives, the broad recognition of gender as a political issue has helped to legitimize an interest in new questions and to provide the concepts and the language to discuss them. In this sense, it might be argued, feminism provided working-class women in the 1980s with a "language of gender" that supplements Marxism's long-established "language of class." This politicized conception of gender has emerged despite a deep suspicion of "feminism," which some progressive women in South Africa have considered an essentially bourgeois ideology with divisive implications for the liberation struggle.[1]

South Africa provides rich material for a feminist critique. Although the relationship between racism and sexism is complex, social and intellectual change during the twentieth century has reinforced a tendency to classify people according to strictly drawn categories based on race, ethnicity, and gender. Such classifications are thought to "describe one's essential being."[2] Thus, the country remains in many respects a bastion of attitudes and practices demeaning to women. Even respected newspapers display a

blatant sexism unmatched in most western countries. The separate, gen-
der-biased legal systems that applied to black and white women in the
early 1900s persisted relatively unchanged until the 1980s. Only recently
have marriage laws been amended to allow most women equal rights
with their husbands.[3] And, for black women, legal treatment as minors
has compounded the ravages to personal and family life caused by the
migrant labor system and racial restrictions.

In assessing the place of women's industrial labor as a product of economic and social transformation and as an agent of change in itself, many
questions remain to be answered from the vantage point of the entire
period under discussion. How has industrial labor influenced women's
perception of themselves, as workers and as women? What are the implications of the South African case for the general issue of how and when
women are likely to organize? How does the inclusion of women and of
gender alter established views of South African labor history and of class
relationships? And what does this case study add to a more general understanding of the relationship among race, gender, and class?

The far-ranging effects of industrial transformation, both direct and indirect, create a unique lens through which to view and to assess women's
experience. During the first quarter of the twentieth century, most women,
black and white, were firmly integrated into families and households organized around some form of patriarchal power, and women of all ages
were treated officially as dependents. In areas of the country where black
female domestic labor was not long-established, many families only reluctantly allowed their daughters to enter this unprotected occupation. The
voices against the paternalism and dependency of the status quo were
few and isolated.

By the late 1920s and early 1930s, the inexorable push of proletarianization was forcing larger numbers of women into wage labor, most blacks
as domestics and many white Afrikaans-speaking and coloured women
as factory workers. At first, most white women in these positions were
single, quite young, and economically tied to the households of their birth.
Some, however, had made a psychological break, moving to morally
"questionable" urban communities against the wishes of their parents.
Many, in becoming primary wage-earners for their families, were driven
by necessity to overstep accepted patterns of gender and age relationships, even if they had no intention of openly challenging them. As these
women were swept into the waves of union organizing during the 1930s,
however, their actions definitively established a new fact of labor history:
that working women were perfectly capable of asserting their own interests and of demanding change on their own behalf. The garment workers' defiant posture toward Afrikaner nationalist efforts to take over their
union, which continued into the 1940s, presented an equally blatant challenge to notions of women as necessarily weak, passive, and dependent.
Similarly undermining traditional assumptions, women's wartime labor

in the engineering industry affirmed their ability to do work hitherto reserved for men.

By the 1940s and 1950s, labor migration and the flood of black families moving to the cities had severely eroded rural patriarchal controls over black women in many areas. Furthermore, many of those who took the newly available factory jobs were widowed or became the primary breadwinners in large families at a relatively young age. Whatever "independence" they gained from earning steady wages at respected jobs was illusory because of their heavy domestic responsibilities and because of the increasing intervention of a repressive, racist regime into every aspect of their lives. Some black women who worked in industries with active, progressive trade union organization did develop a new consciousness of themselves as workers, which, depending on local circumstances, sometimes led them to take part in their unions and in the women's protests of the 1950s. But because of women's strong position in the most active unions and because the discourse of the 1950s defined race and class as the salient "political" issues, the question of male power was rarely discussed.

As many industries moved to the periphery or to urban areas adjacent to populous rural "homelands" in the 1960s and 1970s, the new black women drawn into industrial production were likely to be less well educated and more destitute than their predecessors a decade or two earlier: no longer the township "elite" described by Brandel. Many, in addition, were migrants rather than settled urban residents. Like an earlier generation, however, they tended to bear responsibility for large families and to be independent breadwinners at some stage of their working lives. Given their appallingly low wages and the relentless pressures of apartheid, many women were drawn to the spontaneous mass protests of the 1970s, signs of a union movement struggling for rebirth after a decade of fierce repression. But the nascent state of most of the new unions by the end of the 1970s meant that few of the new entrants to factories and mills had, as yet, become part of ongoing organizations. Defining their attitudes in both class and nationalist terms, many women rightly connected their work-related grievances to their general anger at the conditions of life under a white-dominated government.

Throughout the twentieth century, changing conceptions of factory work and the relative viability of informal income-generating options also has influenced women's views of themselves. The young Afrikaner women of the 1920s and 1930s, who had been relatively successful in refusing domestic jobs, often judged factory work with disdain by comparison with openings in shops and cafes. But economic crisis temporarily made industrial work more palatable, although domestic jobs remained the last resort of the most desperate and ill-educated. For black women in the 1940s and 1950s, by contrast, factory employment had more positive attractions. In the absence of industrial jobs, those who required steady wages had no other option but household labor or, in the rural Cape, arduous work on farms.

In the 1980s, domestic work remained a "choice" born of desperation. But as low-wage, peripheral industries became more prevalent, the contrast between domestic and factory labor diminished in some areas. In many of the new factories, female workers were migrants, forced to live apart from their children and families in overcrowded, closely regulated hostels. Meanwhile, increasing state pressure and greater spatial distances between black and white residential areas progressively narrowed the possibilities for informal economic activities to a point where some women who pursue them today consider themselves "unemployed."

Turning to the question of organization, the South African material supports the idea that women are drawn to trade unions that allow them the space to express personal and community concerns that extend beyond their lives in the factories. Thus, in groups responsive to women's needs and to their leadership potential, women have been able to reshape the notion of "class" in terms that reflect their own experience. In the process their actions have challenged the boundaries of categories like work, family, and community common to both scholarly and political discourse, implying instead a series of interconnected relationships that provide a context for defining political and personal issues. Even under supportive circumstances, however, women have been more likely to engage in collective action when their behavior does not threaten male power and when structural features of a particular industry are conducive to organizing.

The chapters on the Transvaal garment industry and on food and canning workers at the Cape emphasize in particular the broad appeal of successful unions, whose activities transcended the divisions among work, community, and politics. The GWU came to occupy an important part in the lives of young Afrikaner women by filling a variety of social needs and by developing an ideological position that integrated class and ethnicity. Operating under different conditions with black members, the AFCWU and the FCWU in the 1940s and 1950s provided women with a means of incorporating into union activities their concerns with daily community life and their struggles against new forms of racial domination. In both instances, the importance of "nonclass" elements came to form an important aspect of women's working-class identity, as did the bonds that women were able to build among themselves and between their lives inside and outside the workplace.

But in both cases, also, structural aspects of the union or the industry helped to create conditions that supported successful organizing. GWU officials in the early 1930s were able to circumvent the politically explosive issue of uniting black men and white women in the same group because the former already were organized into a viable union. (Textile organizers who faced this problem, like Bettie du Toit, had a rockier path to trod.)

Among food workers, women's precarious place as seasonal employees gave them less to lose than men who became union leaders or activists. In this respect, they were comparable to female anti-pass resisters in South Africa and to women nationalist organizers in Tanzania: able to take greater risks than men because they were less bound by the controls of authoritarian colonial states.[4]

The second observation, concerning the relationship between women's organizing and threats to male power, encompasses a wide range of circumstances. In situations as diverse as that of the young, white factory workers of the late 1920s and early 1930s and the food and canning workers at the Cape several decades later, living in a supportive working-class community meant that women inclined to strike or to become involved in unions did not have to surmount barriers of political antagonism within their own communities in addition to those of gender. For other young Afrikaner women, living apart from their families gave them space to carve out their own paths of personal involvement and identity. In this regard, it is not surprising that many of the white women who became the most engaged union leaders during the 1930s had come to Johannesburg on their own.

The assumption about independence also applies to the large number of female family-heads who, while overloaded with responsibility, also have had the personal autonomy to make their own political decisions. In the trade union and community struggles of the 1980s, as in the Industrial and Commercial Workers' Union of the 1920s, observers have noted that women living on their own have shown a greater propensity to become politically involved. According to Helen Bradford's description of exuberant and militant ICU beer boycotts in Natal in 1929–30, for example, women "accustomed to fighting their own battles in a patriarchal world" were disproportionately represented in leadership positions.[5]

Nonetheless, this generalization invites numerous exceptions. In times of severe repression, such women may be reluctant to incur the risks associated with political or union activity. Personal life histories also suggest that women with the strength to pursue organizing careers have had equal determination to resist the constraints of husbands anxious to have them spend more time at home.

In addition to illuminating working-class life in South Africa from a new perspective, the addition of women's experience and of gender as a category of analysis also transforms received ideas about labor history and class relationships. Perhaps most critically, it challenges the standard narrative of "the white working class" as a highly paid, skilled group that, from the late 1930s onward, climbed the social ladder into supervisory places in the labor process. From their newly won, lofty position, they related to black workers strictly from a position of superiority. Based on mining, engineering, and other protected trades, this portrayal, widely accepted as it is, applies only to men.

By contrast with their male counterparts, the white women working in industry in the 1930s were designated as semiskilled employees and were paid little more than black men. They gained a more privileged position than black women only gradually during the forties and fifties. Thus, in certain respects, their experience of "class" and of interracial relationships was very different from white men's. Particularly in the Transvaal garment industry, a small group of women of all races worked at similar or identical jobs, sometimes in the same factories, and belonged to the same trade union, even if to different branches. In a society in which most working relationships between black and white women were wrought in the crucible of domestic labor, this situation of relative equality was virtually unique. To some, prodded by the admonishments of Afrikaner nationalist organizations, it was also threatening. But others sought, under increasingly difficult circumstances, to structure connections between the two groups of women that retained some vestiges of fairness and comradeship, some thread of solidarity.

The integration of gender into working-class history also suggests the need to reshape accepted ideas about "proletarianization." The notion of a linear process from dependence on the land to reliance on the sale of labor power is not easily applicable to women. Seldom in control of the fields they farmed in the countryside, women moved more slowly into formal wage labor in the cities. Furthermore, marriage often mediated their economic choices, sometimes providing them with the option of wholly or partially relying on male incomes for support. In this respect, the dependent situation of married women in urban settings scarcely differed from that in rural areas, where African women gained access to land through their husbands and where white women relied heavily on their husbands' agricultural labor. Even when low male incomes, marital instability, and widowhood forced poor urban women to earn a livelihood, many avoided wage labor, turning instead to the income they could generate from independent, home-based economic activity. This was particularly true where domestic work was the only wage-earning alternative and became less so as female jobs diversified. Moreover, women tended to fluctuate among different income-producing strategies according to the phases of their life cycle. Even when employed in factories, many continued to supplement family resources in varied ways.

This complexity in women's economic position underscores the strong ties they maintained between wage labor and home-based work. Furthermore, regardless of their income-generating activities, women's unpaid household labor (rarely considered "work") profoundly shaped their lives.

Thus, the study of women in industrial labor and trade unions illuminates a number of aspects of the relationship among race, class, and gender. It verifies that in South Africa, as in other segmented labor markets, employers continually have sought new groups of workers who, because they were black or female or both could be used to undercut established and usually better-organized employees. In understanding these patterns of change, however, it is very clear that gender has been as important as race in defining individual employment paths. Apart from domestic service, which has borne both a gendered and a racial stamp, most work has been defined as female or male, and new arrivals to the wage-labor track have entered through doors clearly designated "women" or "men." Yet the racially defined rifts of South African society have grown so deep that only in rare circumstances, particularly striking among Cape food and canning workers, have the common problems of gender and class fostered truly egalitarian joint organization among women of different groups. Nonetheless, for a small group of white women in the 1940s and 1950s, the experience of working alongside women of other races, both in the factories and in the unions, did provide a challenge to accepted notions of racial superiority and separation.

Although black women's subordinate position in the labor force has improved little since 1980, the articulation of gender-based grievances has intensified. Not surprisingly, one of the newest predominantly female unions has been the most aggressive in raising issues central to women's ability to juggle the twin demands of home and family. Headed until recently by Emma Mashinini, the Commercial, Catering and Allied Workers' Union (CCAWUSA), which has worked since the mid-1970s to organize the legions of new black shopworkers, has insistently emphasized the issue of maternity benefits. In the course of several militant strikes, the union won contracts with some of South Africa's largest commercial employers that provided new mothers with a one-year leave and guaranteed reemployment in a comparable position without loss of pay or status. In 1988, in a Parental Rights Agreement covering over eighteen thousand workers, the right of both women and men to childcare leave was recognized.[6]

As women like Mashinini aggressively confronted women's issues in their contract demands, they also began to speak more openly of their concerns at larger trade union gatherings. One of the most dramatic public moments in the discussion of gender occurred at a 1983 education workshop sponsored by the Federation of South African Trade Unions (FOSATU), then one of the largest and most influential groupings of independent unions. The four speakers were Refiloe Nzuta (general secretary of the Paper, Wood and Allied Workers' Union), Maggie Magubane (general secretary of the Sweet, Food and Allied Workers' Union), Lydia Kompe (branch secretary of the General Workers' Union), and Tembi Nabe (an organizer and former vice president of the Metal and Allied Workers' Union). While they surprised no one with their descriptions of women's disabilities and problems at work, their frank discussion of household labor and sexuality in the context of male domination induced a shocked and nervous response among the audience. As reported in the *South African Labour Bulletin*, Tembi Nabe described the home life of the average female worker.

> Endless rounds of providing tea and food for her husband; making the bed; cleaning the house; carting the baby around; making the fire; ironing, etc. . . . In contrast to her husband who feels free to read the newspaper and watch t.v. ("always with his 'little darling' bottle of whiskey beside him") on returning home from work. . . . "When he gets to bed he then starts to demand another overtime from you" (the third overtime), . . . "if you refuse that's when the divorce starts and then his 'little darling' makes him think to batter you".[7]

In the unenviable position of having to follow up these explosive remarks, Lydia Kompe, among the most outspoken advocates of women's rights during the 1980s, suggested that this heavy burden of domestic labor was part of the reason for women's relative invisibility among the upper ranks of union officials.

Based on the discussion at the meeting, some FOSATU leaders found these remarks extremely controversial and provocative; but there also were men in the audience who acknowledged the truth of the accusations. Although it would be difficult indeed to find simple organizational means to address such questions, this meeting dramatically highlights the new ferment and the new awareness that has been developing among the leaders of working-class women since the late 1970s. For the first time since the era of Mary Fitzgerald, a group of women trade unionists is raising feminist issues that transcend class, although working women are at the heart of their concerns and some would reject the label of "feminist."

Reflecting a growing willingness to acknowledge the political nature of gender relationships, the platform of COSATU (Congress of South African Trade Unions), the new federation that united most of the independent unions in 1985, included a broad-ranging statement on women's issues. Promising to fight against "all unequal and discriminatory treatment of women at work, in society and in the federation," the platform went on to advocate a number of specific means to achieve this objective: equal pay for work of equal value, restructuring employment to allow women equality of opportunity, improved childcare and family facilities, maternity and paternity leave, and support for the struggle against all forms of sexual harassment.[8]

This integration of gender into the concerns of a federation with over a million members is a significant achievment. But such resolutions, as statements of intent, by no means erase women's problems overnight. Some have argued that little progress was made on gender issues during COSATU's early years. Indeed, the drawings submitted as logos for the organization provided a graphic reminder of common conceptions of "the working class"; not one included a female image.[9] Recently, however, women have begun to address internal issues within the organization more explicitly. During the COSATU National Women's Seminar, held in early 1989, they demanded greater representation within the federation and formal procedures to handle complaints of sexual harassment. Raised again at the Third Congress in July, 1989, a resolution to promote greater women's leadership won the approval of the assembled delegates. This success notwithstanding, more controversial resolutions condemning the effects of unwanted sexual attention on women activists were voted down.[10]

A 1986 article by June Nala, a former textile worker, eloquently reflects the new level of consciousness among female leaders, while at the same time detailing the monumental problems that remain to be addressed. She speaks from her experience as a full-time official of the National Union of Textile Workers and then of the Metal and Allied Workers' Union. Particularly illuminating is her account, derived from first-hand experience, of women's participation at different stages of the organizing process. In the early phase of shop-floor and lunchtime meetings and informal contacts, women's union activities become "part and parcel" of their work. But when it comes to electing shop stewards, the balance shifts in the direction of men because they tend to be more articulate in the official foreign language, better able to attend meetings and seminars, and perceived as strong and brave. She continues, "Women themselves also often have a low self-image which they are socialized into and they see men as superior to them. They therefore elect male workers as their leaders. The social relations at the workplace whereby male workers are always overseers over women workers reinforce this form of socialization."[11] Furthermore, as others have pointed out, women's family responsibilities, coupled with pressures from husbands or male partners, interfere with their ability to attend meetings after work. Agreeing with other observers, Nala describes single women as most likely to be able to break through this barrier.

After noting these impediments to women's leadership, Nala then tackles some of the more subtle aspects of male domination in the unions, asserting that men rarely question the absence of women in leadership positions, since they assume it is "how things should be naturally." Furthermore, when male leaders argue that addressing women's issues and their role in the union is divisive, "Most women fall into the trap of accepting this argument since their commitment to union unity is strong and they do not wish to be seen as aiding a divisive process." Consequently, most women continue with their work unaware that "they are misdirected from issues that affect them in particular, to issues that they have in common with men," a trend that leaves men as the main beneficiaries of union action while women's particular concerns "go to the bottom of the list."[12] Having begun with household inequality as a primary cause of women's exclusion from leadership roles, Nala perceptively concludes this section by observing that unquestioned acceptance of male union leadership, particularly in industries like textiles with a majority of women workers, filters down to the shop floor and back into the home, thus reinforcing stereotyped attitudes toward gender.

She ends her article with a strong warning concerning the future direction of change:

> When women today consider the argument that "when capitalist apartheid is removed there will be freedom," they realise that this is an empty promise. It is not only capitalist apartheid that must go, but also patriarchy which is prevalent throughout South African society. Women must fight for a society where they will regain their dignity and respect.[13]

Thus, during the 1980s, as a record number of black women have taken jobs spinning and weaving, making clothing, and working in shops, and as women have entered formerly all-male industries, a few female labor leaders have articulated their problems from a feminist perspective more widely and forcefully than ever before. This awareness also has generated a new understanding of the deeply rooted and complex nature of working women's position. Consequently, although no one doubts that the destruction of apartheid is an essential component of meaningful change, it has become more difficult to assert with confidence that socialism, or even freedom from white capitalist domination, will automatically bring equality for women.

Efforts to read the future are hazardous at best. But if the labor movement maintains its strong position among opponents of the Nationalist regime, and if the number of black working-class women continues to rise, this new women's voice may have a profound influence on a postapartheid society. Just as female trade unionists in the 1950s took the lead in contesting efforts to force women to carry passes, their descendants of the 1980s and 1990s (perhaps a new generation of "rebels' daughters") may be pioneers in another collective struggle: to demonstrate the integral connections among women's oppression at work, at home, and in the wider community and to persuade men "to question [and reject] their role in the patriarchal system." It is only then, in June Nala's words, "that the seeds of freedom can flourish and people's real strength be mobilized against injustice and exploitation."[14]

Notes

Preface

1. Albie Sachs, "Judges and Gender: The Constitutional Rights of Women in a Post-Apartheid South Africa," *Agenda* 7 (1990), 1.

1. Gender, Community, and Working-Class History

1. Tembi Nabe was then an organizer and ex-vice president of the Metal and Allied Workers' Union.

2. The relative lack of transformation in women's work with industrialization is a central argument of the most influential study of European working women, Louise A. Tilly and Joan W. Scott, *Women, Work and Family* (New York: Holt, Rinehart, and Winston, 1978).

3. Ester Boserup, *Woman's Role in Economic Development* (New York: St. Martin's Press, 1970), pp. 114–17.

4. Lourdes Benería and Martha Roldan, *The Crossroads of Class and Gender: Industrial Homework, Subcontracting, and Household Dynamics in Mexico City* (Chicago: University of Chicago Press, 1987), pp. 102–103.

5. These stages are outlined in Helen I. Safa, "Runaway Shops and Female Employment: The Search for Cheap Labor," *Signs* 7, no. 2 (Winter 1981), 418–33. Her model applies particularly to the northeastern United States. This pattern of development would not apply to the Cape Province of South Africa, where the labor force in the clothing industry did not shift as significantly.

6. Ivy Pinchbeck, *Women Workers and the Industrial Revolution* (London: Routledge and Kegan Paul, 1930; repr., London: Virago, 1981), p. 316. The difference between writers stressing the independent behavior of young, female factory workers and those emphasizing the continued influence of family and household on their actions continues to pervade the literature. See, for example, the references of Tom Dublin and Alice Kessler-Harris to Tilly and Scott, in Dublin, *Women at Work: The Transformation of Work and Community in Lowell, Massachusetts, 1826–1860* (New York: Columbia University Press, 1979), p. 40; and Kessler-Harris, "Problems of Coalition-Building: Women and Trade Unions in the 1920s," in *Women, Work and Protest: A Century of U.S. Women's Labor History*, ed. Ruth Milkman (Boston: Routledge and Kegan Paul, 1985), p. 135 n. 18.

7. David Montgomery, *The Fall of the House of Labor: The Workplace, the State, and American Labor Activism, 1865–1925* (Cambridge: Cambridge University Press, 1987), p. 144.

8. Montgomery, *House of Labor*, p. 145. Leslie Woodcock Tentler, by contrast, suggests in *Wage-Earning Women: Industrial Work and Family Life in the United States, 1900–1930* (Oxford: Oxford University Press, 1982), pp. 4, 9–10, that industrial work, in which women had little power, reinforced circumscribed female roles and women's attachment to the home.

9. See Joan Kelly, "The Doubled Vision of Feminist Theory," in *Sex and Class in Women's History*, ed. Judith L. Newton, Mary P. Ryan and Judith R. Walkowitz (London: Routledge and Kegan Paul, 1983).

10. See Belinda Bozzoli, "Marxism, Feminism and South African Studies," *Journal of Southern African Studies* 9, no. 2 (April 1983), 139–71.

11. Though writing about the United States, this analysis by Evelyn Nakano Glenn, "Racial Ethnic Women's Labor: The Intersection of Race, Gender, and Class Oppression," may also be applicable to South Africa. It appears in *Hidden Aspects of Women's Work*, ed. Christine Bose, Roslyn Feldberg and Natalie Sokoloff (New York: Praeger, 1987), pp. 70–71. Focusing on resistance, Mina Davis Caulfield makes a similar argument in "Imperialism, the Family, and Cultures of Resistance," in *Feminist Frameworks: Alternative Theoretical Accounts of the Relations between Women and Men*, ed. Alison M. Jaggar and Paula S. Rothenberg (New York: McGraw-Hill, 1984), pp. 374–79.

12. Benería and Roldan, *Crossroads*, pp. 9–10.

13. These accounts include Richard Goode, "For a Better Life: The Food and Canning Workers Union 1941–1975," B.A. Hons. thesis (University of Cape Town, 1983); Leslie Witz, "Solly Sachs: Servant of the Workers," M.A. dissertation (University of the Witwatersrand, 1984); D. Y. Soudien, "The Food and Canning Workers Union," B.A. Hons. dissertation (University of the Witwatersrand, 1981), and B. M. Touyz, "White Politics and the Garment Workers Union 1930–1953," M.S. dissertation (University of Cape Town, 1979). An exception to this pattern is Elsabé Brink, "The Afrikaner Women of the Garment Workers Union, 1918–1939," M.A. dissertation (University of the Witwatersrand, 1986). Since I make use of a number of B.A. Hons. and M.A. theses, it is important to note their frequent high quality in English-speaking South African universities. See also Jon Lewis, "South African Labor History: A Historiographical Assessment," *Radical History Review* 46, no. 7 (1990), 213–35.

14. Among works taking this perspective are Amelia Marie Mariotti, "The Incorporation of African Women into Wage Employment in South Africa, 1920–1970," Ph.D. thesis (University of Connecticut, 1979); V. M. Martin and C. M. Rogerson, "Women and Industrial Change: The South African Experience," *The South African Geographical Journal* 66, no. 1 (April 1984), 32–46; Joanne Yawitch, "The Incorporation of African Women into Wage Labor, 1950–1980," *South African Labour Bulletin* 9, no. 3 (December 1983); and Georgina Jaffee and Collette Caine, "The Incorporation of African Women into the Industrial Work-Force: Its Implications for the Women's Question in South Africa," in *After Apartheid: Renewal of the South African Economy*, ed. John Suckling and Landeg White (London: James Currey; Trenton, N.J.: Africa World Press, 1988). These works do not ignore human agency totally, but they rarely see it operating to shape the places women fill in the economy.

15. The use of this concept is explored in Louise A. Tilly, "Women and Family Strategies in French Proletarian Families," *Michigan Occasional Paper* no. 4, Fall 1978.

16. Richard Goode, "Struggle and Strikes in the Cannery: The Great Wolseley Strike," unpublished paper presented to the Conference on the History of the Western Cape, University of Cape Town, July 1987, p. 47. Translated from Afrikaans by Goode.

17. Rose L. Glickman, *Russian Factory Women: Workplace and Society, 1880–1914* (Berkeley: University of California Press, 1984), p. 204. She discusses the impact of the legacy of female subordination and submissiveness on women's labor activism on pp. 215–16. Ruth Milkman also discusses the attitudes of male trade unionists in "Organizing the Sexual Division of Labor: Historical Perspectives on 'Women's Work' and the American Labor Movement," *Socialist Review* 49, no. 1 (January–February 1980), 95–150.

18. See, for example, Sheila Rowbotham, *Women, Resistance and Revolution: A History of the Modern World* (New York: Pantheon, 1972), p. 113.

19. Temma Kaplan, "Female Consciousness and Collective Action: The Case of Barcelona, 1910–1918," *Signs* 7, no. 3 (Spring 1982), 548. Her apparent argument,

that women were concerned only with issues of community preservation and survival and not with economic issues, cannot necessarily be generalized to other cases.

20. Dolores E. Janiewski, *Sisterhood Denied: Race, Gender, and Class in a New South Community* (Philadelphia: Temple University Press, 1985), p. 177. The view of trade unions as inadequate from women's perspective is also strongly expressed in Diane Elson and Ruth Pearson, "Third World Manufacturing," in *Waged Work: A Reader,* ed. Feminist Review [journal's editorial board](London: Virago, 1986), pp. 89–90, and in Roslyn L. Feldberg, "Women and Trade Unions: Are We Asking the Right Questions?" Bose et al., *Hidden Aspects.*

21. Joan W. Scott makes this argument in "On Language, Gender, and Working-Class History," *International Labor and Working Class History* 31 (Spring 1987), 1–13.

22. Several of the articles in Milkman, *Women, Work and Protest,* take this approach. See especially Colette A. Hyman, "Labor Organizing and Female Institution-Building: The Chicago Women's Trade Union League, 1904–24"; Ardis Cameron, "Bread and Roses Revisited: Women's Culture and Working-Class Activism in the Lawrence Strike of 1912"; and Alice Kessler-Harris, "Problems of Coalition-Building: Women and Trade Unions in the 1920s." For writing with a focus on work cultures, see the articles in *Feminist Studies* 11, no. 3 (Fall 1985).

23. See Louise A. Tilly, "Paths of Proletarianization: Organization of Production, Sexual Division of Labor, and Women's Collective Action," *Signs* 7, no. 2 (Winter 1981), 400–417.

24. Carole Turbin, "Reconceptualizing Family, Work, and Labor Organizing: Working Women in Troy, 1860–1890," Bose et al., *Hidden Aspects,* p. 192; Helen Safa, "Class Consciousness among Working Class Women in Latin America: A Case Study in Puerto Rico," in *Peasants and Proletarians,* ed. Robin Cohen, Peter Gutkind, and Phyllis Brazier (New York: Monthly Review Press, 1979), pp. 447–48; Iris Berger, "Sources of Class Consciousness: South African Women in Recent Labor Struggles," in *Women and Class in Africa,* ed. Claire Robertson and Iris Berger (New York: Holmes and Meier, 1986), p. 232.

25. This approach is similar in this respect to those of Evelyn Glenn and Mina Davis Caulfield cited above.

26. Among the works of these authors that establish this perspective are Herbert G. Gutman, "Work, Culture, and Society in Industrializing America, 1815–1919," in *Work, Culture and Society in Industrializing America: Essays in American Working-Class and Social History* (New York: Alfred A. Knopf, 1976); Virginia Yans-McLaughlin, *Family and Community: Italian Immigrants in Buffalo, 1880–1930* (Ithaca: Cornell University Press, 1977); and Tamara Hareven, "Family Time and Industrial Time: Family and Work in a Planned Corporation Town, 1900–1924," in *Family and Kin in Urban Communities, 1700–1930,* ed. Tamara K. Hareven (New York: New Viewpoints, 1977). In contrast to these approaches, John T. Cumbler emphasizes the formal and informal institutions comprising the new industrial community in *Working-Class Community in Industrial America: Work, Leisure, and Struggle in Two Industrial Cities, 1880–1930* (Westport, Conn.: Greenwood Press, 1979).

27. For two books dealing specifically with work, see Jacqueline Jones, *Labor of Love, Labor of Sorrow: Black Women, Work, and the Family from Slavery to the Present* (New York: Basic Books, 1985) and Joe William Trotter, Jr., *Black Milwaukee: The Making of an Industrial Proletariat, 1915–45* (Urbana: University of Illinois Press, 1985).

28. This rich and insightful essay, "Class, Community and Ideology in the Evolution of South African Society," appears in *Class, Community and Conflict: South African Perspectives,* ed. Belinda Bozzoli (Johannesburg: Ravan Press, 1987), p. 26.

29. Bozzoli, "Class, Community and Ideology," p. 6.

30. In this part of her discussion (on pp. 9, 13, and 18), Bozzoli relies on George Rude's distinction between "inherent" traditional attitudes based on direct experience, oral tradition, or folk memory and more structured "derived" ideologies as discussed in *Ideology and Popular Protest* (London: Lawrence and Wishart, 1980), pp. 27–29.

31. Benedict Anderson, *Imagined Communities: Reflections on the Origin and Spread of Nationalism* (London: Verso, 1983). This definition comes from pp. 15–16.

32. The African percentage has risen in recent years.

33. Gutman, *Work, Culture and Society*. A. P. Cheater argues for a more complex, situational conception of "worker consciousness" among men as well, one that does not resort to labels like "false consciousness" to explain behavior that fails to conform to narrowly defined Marxist norms. See "Contradictions in Modelling 'Consciousness': Zimbabwean Proletarians in the Making?" *Journal of Southern African Studies* 14, no. 2 (January 1988), 293, 303.

34. This is a central theme in many of the essays in Robertson and Berger, *Women and Class*.

35. Montgomery, *House of Labor*, p. 139.

36. Bill Freund suggests this distinction between African and western family patterns in *The African Worker* (Cambridge: Cambridge University Press, 1988), p. 87. Freund draws his examples from West African cases in which women asserted an extraordinary degree of independence from men.

37. At times, women's perceptions and actions raise questions about the accepted meanings of these distinctions, although the important differences between work-based and community-based struggles suggest that the question of categories and their validity requires further and more systematic exploration.

38. Emma Mashinini, *Strikes Have Followed Me All My Life: A South African Autobiography* (London: The Women's Press, 1989), p. 119.

39. See the examination of this process in Ian Goldin, "The Reconstitution of Coloured Identity in the Western Cape," in *The Politics of Race, Class and Nationalism in Twentieth-Century South Africa*, ed. Shula Marks and Stanley Trapido (London: Longman, 1987).

2. Dependency and Domesticity: Women's Wage Labor, 1900–1925

1. Elaine N. Katz, *A Trade Union Aristocracy: A History of the White Workers in the Transvaal and the General Strike of 1913* (Johannesburg: University of the Witwatersrand, 1976), pp. 298–99, 307, 312; see also Ivan Walker and Ben Weinbren, *2000 Casualties: A History of the Trade Unions and the Labour Movement in the Union of South Africa* (Johannesburg: South African Trade Union Council, 1961); E. Gitsham and J. F. Trembath, *A First Account of Labour Organisation in South Africa* (Durban: E. P. and Commercial Printing Co., 1926); Louise Haysom, "Mary Fitzgerald," unpublished manuscript, pp. 46–49. Neither Fitzgerald nor other trade union leaders of the period questioned the racially exclusive character of the labor movement. I am grateful to Louise Haysom for permission to use this manuscript and to Baruch Hirson for bringing it to my attention.

2. White women only gained the right to vote in 1930.

3. Bill Freund, *The Making of Contemporary Africa* (Bloomington: Indiana University Press, 1984), p. 178.

4. Julia Wells, "Why Women Rebel: A Comparative Study of South African Women's Resistance in Bloemfontein (1913) and Johannesburg (1958)," *Journal of Southern African Studies* 10, no. 1 (October 1983), 69.

5. Cherryl Walker, "The Woman's Suffrage Movement in South Africa," Communications No. 2, Centre for African Studies, University of Cape Town, 1979, p. 57; Belinda Bozzoli, "Marxism, Feminism and South African Studies," *Journal*

of Southern African Studies 9, no. 2 (April 1983), 151–52. The best general survey of women's legal position is H. J. Simons, *African Women: Their Legal Status in South Africa* (Evanston: Northwestern University Press, 1968).

6. Deborah Lyndall Gaitskell, "Female Mission Initiatives: Black and White Women in Three Witwatersrand Churches, 1903–1939," Ph.D. thesis (University of London, 1981), p. 109.

7. Deborah Gaitskell, " 'Wailing for Purity': Prayer Unions, African Women and Adolescent Daughters, 1912–1940," in *Industrialisation and Social Change in South Africa*, ed. Shula Marks and Richard Rathbone (London: Longman, 1982); and "Building a Nation from Words: Afrikaans Language, Literature and Ethnic Identity, 1902–1924," in *Race, Class and Nationalism in Twentieth Century South Africa*, ed. Shula Marks and Stanley Trapido (London: Longman, 1987), pp. 113–14. For a theoretical overview of the issue of women and proletarianization in South Africa, see Bozzoli, "Marxism, Feminism and South African Studies." See also Cherryl Walker, ed., *Women and Gender in Southern Africa* (London: James Currey, 1990).

8. Sheila van der Horst, *Native Labour in South Africa* (London: Frank Cass, 1971), p. 105.

9. From p. 226, par. 5403, cited in Stanley Trapido, "Landlord and Tenant in a Colonial Economy," *Journal of Southern African Studies* 5, no. 1 (October 1978), 55.

10. Trapido, "Landlord and Tenant," p. 31; see also Report of the Carnegie Commission, *The Poor White Problem in South Africa*, vol. 5 (Stellenbosch: Pro Ecclesia-Drukkery, 1932), 173.

11. These events are discussed in Wells, "Why Women Rebel."

12. See Alys Lowth, *Women Workers and South Africa* (London: Kegan Paul, 1903) and Alicia M. Cecil, "The Needs of South Africa, II: Female Emigration," *The Nineteenth Century* (April 1902), 683–92. Jean Jacques Van-Helten and Keith Williams explore more fully the campaign to encourage British women to immigrate to South Africa in " 'The Crying Need of South Africa': The Emigration of Single British Women to the Transvaal, 1901–10," *Journal of Southern African Studies* 10, no.1 (October 1983), 17–38.

13. Lowth, "Women Workers," p. 41.

14. Cecil, "Needs of South Africa," p. 685.

15. Lowth, "Women Workers," pp. 92–93.

16. Cecil, "Needs of South Africa," p. 688. Van-Helten and Williams in "Crying Need" also emphasize the role of "imperial motherhood" in producing a British "race" majority in South Africa.

17. Cecil, "Needs of South Africa," p. 689.

18. *Rand Daily Mail* (hereafter *RDM*), April 15, 1919.

19. Union of South Africa, *Report of the Commission Appointed to Enquire into Assaults on Women* (Cape Town, 1913), U.G. 39–'13, p. 26.

20. The following section comes mainly from Charles van Onselen's splendid essay, "The Witches of Suburbia: Domestic Service on the Witwatersrand, 1890–1914," in van Onselen, *Studies in the Social and Economic History of the Witwatersrand, 1886–1914*, vol. 2. *New Ninevah*, (London: Longman, 1982).

21. J. H. Balfour Browne, *South Africa: A Glance at Current Conditions and Politics* (London: Longman, Green, 1905; repr., New York: Negro Universities Press, 1969), p. 200.

22. South Africa, *Assaults on Women*, p. 26.

23. Union of South Africa, Union Education Department, *Report of the Committee on Industrial Education* (Cape Town, 1916), U.G. 9–1917, p. 8.

24. Agnes Cooke, "Report on the Industrial Conditions of European Women and Girls in Cape Town and District," Cape Town, May 9, 1917, MNW 1881/17, p. 12.

25. South Africa, *Assaults on Women*, p. 27; see also Union of South Africa, Department of Mines and Industries, *Annual Report, 1913* (Cape Town, 1914), U.G. 21–'14, p. 69.

26. van Onselen, *History of the Witwatersrand*, vol. 2, 15–16.

27. The figures come from Deborah Gaitskell, Judy Kimble, Moira Maconachie and Elaine Unterhalter, "Class, Race and Gender: Domestic Workers in South Africa," *Review of African Political Economy* 27/28 (1983), 96. They discuss the complex reasons for these different regional patterns on pp. 98–100.

28. Deborah Gaitskell, "Laundry, Liquor and 'Playing Ladish': African Women in Johannesburg 1903–1939," Unpublished paper presented to the South African Social History Workshop, Centre of International and Area Studies, University of London, 1978, pp. 7–8.

29. Gaitskell, "Laundry," p. 17.

30. *RDM*, March 28, 1917.

31. "Women's Work in Johannesburg in the Native Yards," *The Mission Field* (October 1913), 308.

32. Gaitskell, "Laundry," p. 19, citing an article by Selby Msimang in *Umteteli wa Bantu*, March 17, 1923.

33. *RDM*, February 8, 1922.

34. Union of South Africa, *Report of the Select Committee on Subject Matter of the Regulation of Wages (Specified Trades) Bill* (Cape Town, 1917), S.C. 4–'17, p. 108.

35. *RDM*, March 14, 1917.

36. *RDM*, January 5, 1917.

37. *RDM*, January 19, 1915; January 5, 1917; March 22, 1917. Other writings that refer to illegal liquor sales include "Women's Work in Johannesburg," p. 309, and Carnegie Commission, *Poor White Problem*, vol. 5, 43.

38. David Welsh, "The Growth of Towns," in *The Oxford History of South Africa*, vol. 2, *South Africa 1870–1966* (New York and Oxford: Oxford University Press, 1971), 186.

39. van Onselen, *History of the Witwatersrand*, vol. 1, *New Babylon*, 146; and *RDM*, February 21, 1921.

40. *RDM*, January 17, 1921.

41. South Africa, South African Native Affairs Commission 1903–05, vol. 1, *Report of the Commission* (Cape Town, 1905), 83.

42. Ibid.

43. South Africa, *Assaults on Women*, p. 26.

44. Union of South Africa, Union Education Department, *Report of the Committee on Industrial Education* (Cape Town, 1916), U.G. 39–'13, p. 8. Several witnesses testified to the Transvaal Indigency Commission in 1906–08 on the desirability of raising the standards of domestic workers through industrial education. See, for example, p. 73.

45. South Africa, *Industrial Education*, p. 8.

46. Cooke, "Industrial Conditions," p. 12.

47. South Africa, *Industrial Education*, p. 4.

48. Between 1911 and 1921 the percentage of economically active white women formally employed as domestic workers dropped from 18.3 percent to 13.8 percent of the labor force, an absolute decline from 14,932 to 12,255. Figures for 1921 come from tables in Union of South Africa, Bureau of Census and Statistics, *Union Statistics for Fifty Years, 1900–1960* (Pretoria, 1960), pp. A30–A33, for 1911 from Union of South Africa, Office of Census and Statistics, *Census*, Pretoria, 1911. Figures from the two surveys can be compared only after adjusting the 1911 data in two ways: eliminating those counted as "dependents," primarily children under 15 and those counted in Category I of domestic labor, applying to "wives,

widows, daughters and other relatives engaged in domestic duties." See pp. 448–49, 472–73.

49. In 1921, white men performed most clerical work in South Africa; there were 48,248 white male clerical workers and only 18,372 white women.

50. South Africa, *Industrial Education,* p. 10.

51. Compiled from tables in *Union Statistics,* pp. A30–A33. These trends were not dramatically different from those found in the 1911 census, although for white women the "clerical" category was new, and there was a dramatic drop in the number of women counted as agricultural workers (from 24,172 to 4,218). Interestingly, the number of industrial workers also declined, from 11,962 to 8,831. For African women, the most significant trend was a rise of 97.7 percent in the number of women engaged in domestic work, although the percentage of women so employed remained small.

52. South Africa, *Assaults on Women,* p. 22.

53. Transvaal Indigency Commission, *Minutes of Evidence, 1906–08,* Pretoria, 1908, p. 59. W. H. Macmillan's discussion of poverty in Grahamstown mentions the particular plight of widows. See *Economic Conditions in a Non-Industrial South African Town* (Grahamstown: Grocott and Sherry, 1915), p. 13.

54. Indigency Commission, *Evidence,* p. 61.

55. C. W. de Kiewiet, *A History of South Africa: Social and Economic* (London: Oxford University Press, 1957), p. 221.

56. Indigency Commission, *Evidence,* p. 266.

57. Ibid., p. 76.

58. Mines and Industries, *Annual Report,* p. 58.

59. *RDM,* February 21, 1921.

60. The first figure comes from Harry Beynon, the Labour Registration Officer for the Cape; it is cited in *Regulation of Wages,* p. 15. The second appears in Cooke, "Industrial Conditions," p. 1.

61. From statistics in South Africa, *Statistics,* pp. G-4 to G-7. The number of African and Asian women was negligible.

62. South Africa, *Regulation of Wages,* p. 1.

63. Ibid., p. 16.

64. Ibid., p. 58.

65. Ibid., p. 96. Despite the difference in spelling, this is clearly the same person who wrote the document "Industrial Conditions."

66. Cooke, "Industrial Conditions," p. 9.

67. South Africa, *Regulation of Wages,* p. 30.

68. Ibid., pp. 21, 24, 51, 78.

69. Ibid., p. 20.

70. Ibid., p. 52.

71. Ibid., pp. 100–102, 128.

72. Ibid., p. 70.

73. Ibid., pp. 108–109.

74. Ibid., see pp. 42, 87, 94, 103.

75. Letter from R. Stuart to W. Freestone, Labour Department, December 15, 1920, Correspondence, TUCSA, AC 1.2. The setting of minimum wages for different age groups would have encouraged employers to hire more younger workers.

76. *RDM,* February 22, 1922.

77. See *RDM,* January 7, 1915.

78. South Africa, *Regulation of Wages,* p. 19.

79. Ibid., pp. 50–51, 57.

80. Ibid., p. 97.

81. Ibid., p. 125.

82. Ibid., p. 31.

83. Ibid., p. 22.

84. Calculations were made from figures in Union of South Africa, *Report of the Economic and Wage Commission (1925)* (Cape Town, 1926), U.G. 14–'26, Table I (d), p. 9. Women in the trades earned an average of 95 percent of the earnings of waitresses and saleswomen.

85. Cited in Cooke, "Industrial Conditions," p. 8.

86. This figure is very close to the nonindustrial average of 41.8 percent for the year. The statistical data come from *Economic and Wage Commission*, Table "I," p. 272, and Table I (a) and (d), pp. 8–9. Women boot machinists earned 50.3 percent of the wages of male boot and shoe operators, while tailoresses and dressmakers earned 46.5 percent and 48.1 percent respectively of what their male counterparts did.

87. The comparison is between "European adult female workers in manufacturing" and "non-European unskilled workers in general manufacturing industry."

88. South Africa, *Economic and Wage Commission*, Tables J and K, pp. 272–73.

89. Ibid., Table I, p. 90.

90. S. C. Cronwright Schreiner, ed., *The Letters of Olive Schreiner* (London: Unwin, 1924), p. 387.

91. Ibid., p. 386.

92. *Voice of Labour*, July 31, 1909.

93. Haysom, "Mary Fitzgerald," p. 16; *Voice of Labour*, August 21, 1907, and December 4, 1909.

94. Haysom, "Mary Fitzgerald," pp. 16–36, 139, 142. The prosuffrage journal she edited, along with Margaret Bruce and British journalist Nina Boyle, was called *Modern Woman in South Africa*.

95. Walker and Weinbren, *2000 Casualties*, p. 59; see also *RDM*, February 6–14, 1917. Among the five trades cited in South Africa, *Economic and Wage Commission*, Table I (d), printers' assistants on the Rand received the lowest wages.

96. Walker and Weinbren, *2000 Casualties*, p. 77; *RDM*, January 27, 1921.

97. Haysom, "Mary Fitzgerald," pp. 145–50. The South African Industrial Federation was headed by her new husband, Archie Crawford. See pp. 151–53 for an account of an incident in which white waitresses protested against the hiring of waiters from St. Helena. Little is heard of the League after the early 1920s.

98. *RDM*, April 15, 1919.

99. *RDM*, April 14, 1919.

100. Letter to H. Levine from H. Joseph, n.d., n.p., GWU, Asb 1.157.

101. Letter from the Secretary, WTA to Fellow Workers, Johannesburg, January 24, 1920, GWU Aab 1.157.

102. D. du Toit, *Capital and Labour in South Africa: Class Struggle in the 1970s* (London: Kegan Paul, 1981), p. 102. Wells, "Why Women Rebel," p. 65, explains this militancy by the threat of passes to force women into full-time domestic service.

103. Sheridan Johns III, "The Birth of Non-White Trade Unionism," *Race* 9, no. 2 (1967), 180; Helen Bradford, "Organic Intellectuals or Petty Bourgeois Opportunists: The Social Nature of I.C.U. Leadership in the Countryside," unpublished paper, Johannesburg, 1983, p. 5; Helen Bradford, *A Taste of Freedom: The ICU in Rural South Africa 1924–1930* (New Haven: Yale University Press, 1987), pp. 3–4. Maxeke, best known as the leader of the 1913 campaign against passes for women, was at the meeting representing the South African Native National Congress.

104. Louise A. Tilly, "Paths of Proletarianization: Organization of Production, Sexual Division of Labor, and Women's Collective Action," *Signs* 7, no. 2 (Winter

1981), 416. See also Jane L. Parpart, "Class and Gender on the Copperbelt: Women in Northern Rhodesian Copper Mining Communities, 1926–1964," in *Women and Class in Africa*, ed. Claire Robertson and Iris Berger (New York: Holmes and Meier, 1986). Other examples include the Senegalese railway workers' strike as depicted in Ousmane Sembene's classic *God's Bits of Wood* and the miners' strikes in Great Britain in 1984–85, discussed in Vicky Seddon, ed., *The Cutting Edge: Women and the Pit Strike* (London: Lawrence and Wishart, 1986).

105. Katz, *Trade Union Aristocracy*, p. 19.
106. Haysom, "Mary Fitzgerald," pp. 69, 95–96.
107. *RDM*, January 27, 1922.
108. *RDM*, February 25, 1922.
109. *RDM*, February 15, 1922.
110. *RDM*, February 13, 1922.
111. *RDM*, February 8–9, 1922.
112. *RDM*, March 7, 1922; see also February 8–9, 13–16, 18, 20, 25 and March 3, 7.
113. Katz, *Trade Union Aristocracy*, pp. 150–51.
114. *RDM*, February 5, 1915.
115. *RDM*, January 8, 1917.
116. *RDM*, January 8, 1917.
117. *RDM*, February 4, 1915; February 3, 1917.
118. *RDM*, February 21, 1921.
119. *RDM*, February 26, 1915.
120. van Onselen, *History of the Witwatersrand*, vol. 2, 26–27.
121. Ibid., 54–60. See also *RDM*, September 11, 1908.
122. *RDM*, January 12, 1922.

3. Patterns of Women's Labor, 1925–1940

1. P. L. Bonner, " 'Desirable or Undesirable Basotho Women?' Liquor, Prostitution and the Migration of Basotho Women to the Rand, 1920–1945," in *Women and Gender in Southern Africa*, ed. Cherryl Walker (London: James Currey, 1990), pp. 247–49.
2. C. W. de Kiewiet, *A History of South Africa: Social and Economic* (London: Oxford University Press, 1957), p. 224.
3. Economic and Wage Commission, "Evidence of the South African Women Workers' Union," part 2, September 3, 1925, p. 2, SATLC, Cd 9.2–5. This fall is documented in Union of South Africa, *Report of the Economic and Wage Commission (1925)* (Cape Town, 1926), pp. 268–70, U.G. 14–'26.
4. Report of the Carnegie Commission, *The Poor White Problem in South Africa*, vol. 1 (Stellenbosch: Pro Ecclesia-Drukkery, 1932), 215.
5. In the 1926 census, in the ten largest urban centers, there were 58,153 men and 64,057 women of Afrikaner origin, 476 men and 524 women per thousand. For the total European population, the ratio was 496 men to 504 women. In 1931 the urban areas had a ratio of 505 white women to 495 white men, the rural areas 531 men to 459 women.
6. Carnegie Commission, *Poor White Problem*, vol. 1, 214.
7. *Economic and Wage Commission*, pp. 312–13.
8. Louis Franklin Freed, *The Problem of European Prostitution in Johannesburg* (Cape Town: Juta and Co., 1949), p. 32.
9. *The Social and Industrial Review* 2, no. 2 (February 1926), 125–27.
10. *The South African Labour Gazette* 1, no. 5 (August 1925), 130; 2, no. 2 (February 1926), 93–94; 2, no. 3 (March 1926), 195–96; 2, no. 9 (September 1926), 741;

4, no. 18 (July 1927), 585–86; 4, no. 19 (July 1927), 59–61; 7, no. 42 (June 1929), 516–17.

11. *The Social and Industrial Review* 4, no. 20 (September 1927), 239.

12. *The Social and Industrial Review* 4, no. 19 (July 1927), 59.

13. Carnegie Commission, *Poor White Problem*, vol. 1, xvi; vol. 5, 202–212.

14. See, for example, *The Star*, June 20, 1935, reporting on the discussion at a meeting of the East Rand Juvenile Affairs Board in 1935.

15. *Report of the Department of Labour for the Year Ended 31st December 1939* (Pretoria, 1940), U.G. no. 36, 1940, p. 23 and *Report of the Department of Labour for the Year Ended 31st December 1938* (Pretoria, 1939), U.G. no. 51, 1939, p. 27. See also *Report of the Department of Labour and Social Welfare for the Year Ended December 1936* (Pretoria, 1937), U.G. no. 44, 1937; and "Report of the Athlone Club for Girls, 1934," SATLC, AH 646,1 Dc 5.16.

16. See *Cape Times* articles from June 24, 1936; July 8 and 14, 1937; October 9, 1937.

17. Ibid., July 14, 1937.

18. Ibid., July 8, 1937.

19. Ibid., June 24, 1936.

20. *Rand Daily Mail* (hereafter *RDM*), October 5, 1929.

21. *RDM*, October 5, 1929.

22. *The Social and Industrial Review* 3, no. 16 (April 1927), 351.

23. *Cape Times*, October 21, 1927.

24. Ibid.

25. "Some Occupations for Girls," *The Social and Industrial Review* 8, no. 45 (September 5, 1929), 819–22.

26. *Cape Times*, October 21, 1927.

27. Union of South Africa, Department of Labour, *Annual Report of the Chief Inspector of Factories for the Year 1927* (Pretoria, 1928), U.G. no. 38, 1928, p. 7.

28. This is the judgment of Bill Freund in "The Social Character of Secondary Industry in South Africa, 1915–1945 (with Special Reference to the Witwatersrand)," African Studies Seminar Paper, African Studies Institute, University of the Witwatersrand, April 22, 1985, p. 24. He also cites Ian Phillips's opinion that the board was determined from the outset not to tamper with the gender definition of jobs. See Phillips, "The 'Civilised Labour Policy' and the Private Sector: The Operation of the South African Wage Act 1925–37," Ph.D. dissertation (Rhodes University, 1984). Jon Lewis suggests a contrary view: that the Wage Board was of some benefit to African workers and their trade unions. See *Industrialisation and Trade Union Organisation in South Africa, 1924–55: The Rise and Fall of the South African Trades and Labour Council* (Cambridge: Cambridge University Press, 1984), pp. 57–58.

29. Union of South Africa, *The Work of the Wage Board, Report to the Honourable Minister of Labour by the Wage Board upon the Work of the Board for the Three Years Ended 28th February, 1929* (Pretoria, 1929), p. 7.

30. South Africa, *Work of the Wage Board*, p. 8.

31. F.A.W. Lucas, "The Determination of Wages in South Africa," *South African Journal of Economics* 1, no. 1 (March 1933), 55.

32. *The South African Worker*, November 12, 1926.

33. Anne Phillips and Barbara Taylor make this argument for women in "Sex and Skill," in *Waged Work: A Reader*, ed. Feminist Review [journal's editorial board] (London: Virago, 1986).

34. Lucas, "Determination of Wages," pp. 55–56.

35. See "Evidence of South African Women Workers' Union," part 1, pp. 1–4 for figures. As is customary with state-collected statistical data, the assessment of

laundry work ignored the input of women who performed this laborious task in their homes.

36. "Evidence of South African Women Workers' Union," part 3, p. 3.

37. South Africa, *Work of the Wage Board*, p. 16.

38. *RDM*, May 16, 1928, citing the opinion of a government sericulture expert in testimony to the Witwatersrand Juvenile Affairs Board at Benoni.

39. "Memo from the Department of Labour and Social Welfare to the Secretary for Labour and Social Welfare, Pietermaritzburg," March 1, 1937, ARB 1546, File no. C1146.

40. "Evidence of South African Women Workers' Union," part 1, p. 6.

41. Unless otherwise noted, the material in this section is based on calculations from the statistics in Union of South Africa, Bureau of Census and Statistics, *Union Statistics for Fifty Years, 1910–1960* (Pretoria, 1960), pp. A-30 to A-33 and pp. 38–41.

42. The number of white women in industrial jobs rose from 8,831 to 24,115 and the number of shop assistants from 6,620 to 15,532. Union of South Africa, *Report of the Industrial Legislation Commission* (Pretoria, 1935), U.G. 37, 1935, p. 26, observes that retail trade had changed considerably in recent times with the growth of "bazaar" type chain stores in which selling had come to be "almost a mechanical process." The duties of assistants were more like "policemen and wrapping robots than of salesmen." Women were allegedly so suitable for this work that they were employed in preference to men. (Their substantially lower wages were perhaps a more salient explanation.)

43. In 1928 newspapers referred to a growing problem of unemployment among young women teachers as a result of their reluctance to take jobs in country schools; at the same time the large number of lucrative positions for urban nurses was pointed out. These trends are noted in *RDM*, May 23 and 24, 1928. The Natal Native Teachers' Conference, in 1935, passed a resolution stating that no married women should be employed as teachers while there were unmarried teachers who lacked jobs. Cited in *The Star*, July 8, 1935. See Shula Marks's unpublished paper, "Class, Race and Gender in the South African Nursing Profession," [London, 1987], for a historical overview of the profession.

44. The figures for Cape Town are cited in Ian Goldin, *Making Race: The Politics and Economics of Coloured Identity in South Africa* (London: Longman, 1987), p. 45.

45. Hansi Pollak, "Women Workers in Witwatersrand Industries," *South African Journal of Economics* 1, no. 1 (March 1933), 64.

46. Letter of Divisional Inspector, Natal, to the Secretary for Labour, Durban, February 9, 1938, ARB 1546, file no. C1146.

47. C. W. Pearsall, "Some Aspects of the Development of Secondary Industry in the Union of South Africa," *South African Journal of Economics* 5, no. 4 (December 1937), 421; "Report to the Honourable the Minister of Labour by the Wage Board. Garment Making Trades," April 12, 1935, p. 27.

48. Pearsall, "Secondary Industry," p. 421.

49. Freund, "Secondary Industry," p. 14, observes that white male workers included an increasing proportion of juveniles who, like white women, could be paid lower wages than adult men.

50. And in the Cape clothing industry, for example, the largest beneficiaries of expansion were female juveniles, white and coloured. Although the number of white juveniles increased by a greater percentage, 439 coloured employees were hired as compared to 250 whites. See Martin Nicol, " 'Joh'burg Hotheads' and the 'Gullible Children of Cape Town,' " Cape Town, n.d., Table 1. [The table is not included in the published version of the article.]

51. Calculated from figures in South Africa, *Union Statistics*, pp. G-6–G-7. Ame-

lia Mariotti, "Women in the South African Labor Force: 'Poor White' Women in Industry," paper prepared for the Fourth Annual Meeting of the Social Science History Association, November 1–4, Cambridge, Mass., 1979, pp. 4–5, examines shifts during this period and argues that women were responsible for most of the gains made by whites in industrial work between 1924–25 and 1934–35.

52. Carnegie Commission, *Poor White Problem*, vol. 5, 43.

53. In another case, a woman who pleaded guilty to the offense was sentenced to six months hard labor, suspended for two years. From *RDM*, May 23, 1928. According to *The Star* of June 26, 1935, Syrians, relying on African "runners," had been targeted as the main suppliers of illicit liquor.

54. Freed, *European Prostitution*.

55. This material comes from V. P. Steyn, "Prostitution and Houses of Ill-Fame in Johannesburg," n.p, n.d., ARB 2017, file no. C.F. 13 unless otherwise specified.

56. Freed, *European Prostitution*, p. 182.

57. Bertha Solomon, *Time Remembered* (Cape Town: Howard Timmins, 1968), pp. 190–91.

58. Hansi P. Pollak, "Women in Witwatersrand Industries," M.A. thesis (University of the Witwatersrand, 1932), p. 72.

59. David Welsh, "The Growth of Towns," in *The Oxford History of South Africa*, vol 2, *South Africa 1870–1966*, ed. Leonard Thompson and Monica Wilson (New York and Oxford: Oxford University Press, 1971), 198. Bonner argues on p. 243 that this legislation had little effect because it was so easy to evade.

60. Sheila van der Horst, *Native Labour in South Africa* (London: Frank Cass), 1971, p. 268.

61. Union of South Africa, *Report of Native Economic Commission, 1930–1932* (Pretoria, 1932), U.G. 22, 1932, p. 141; Ray E. Phillips, *The Bantu in the City: A Study of Cultural Adjustment on the Witwatersrand* (Lovedale: The Lovedale Press, 1938), p. 13.

62. J. D. Rheinallt Jones, "Social and Economic Condition of the Urban Native," in *Western Civilization and the Natives of South Africa*, ed. I. Schapera (London: G. Routledge and Sons, 1934; repr., London: Routledge and Kegan Paul, 1967), p. 189. Rheinallt Jones also notes that access to wage jobs was making young women less subject to parental control. Shula Marks documents this movement in Natal in "Patriotism, Patriarchy and Purity: Natal and the Politics of Zulu Ethnic Consciousness," in *The Creation of Tribalism in Southern Africa*, ed. Leroy Vail (Berkeley: University of California Press; London: James Currey, 1989). See also Bonner, "Basotho Women," pp. 228–29.

63. *The Social and Industrial Review*, January 5, 1930.

64. *The Star*, July 4, 1935.

65. Van der Horst, *Native Labour*, p. 268. This source notes the possible undercounting of the population because of fears that the Urban Native Census of 1938 would be used to limit African movement to towns.

66. "The Employment of Native Girls Trained in Domestic Service at Native Training Institutions," *The South African Outlook* (January 2, 1932).

67. W. G. A. Mears, "The Educated Native," in Schapera, *Western Civilization*, p. 96.

68. Deborah Gaitskell makes the first point in "Housewives, Maids or Mothers: Some Contradictions of Domesticity for Christian Women in Johannesburg, 1903–39," *Journal of African History* 24, no. 2 (1983), 241–56.

69. *Guardian*, May 20, 1938.

70. Ibid., April 23, 1937.

71. Mears, "Educated Native," p. 96. In 1936 there were only 669 African nurses in the entire country.

72. City of Johannesburg, Non-European and Native Affairs Department, "Survey of the African in Industry," Johannesburg, 1939, p. vii.

73. *The South African Worker*, September 30, 1929.

74. Eileen Jensen Krige, "Some Social and Economic Facts Revealed in Native Family Budgets," *Race Relations Journal* 1 (1934), 99.

75. Mears, "Educated Native," p. 94.

76. Johannesburg, "Survey of the African," pp. xii–xiv.

77. Ellen Hellmann, *Rooiyard: A Sociological Survey of an Urban Native Slum Yard,*(Cape Town: Oxford University Press, 1948), p. 39.

78. Phillips, *Bantu in the City*, p. 18.

79. This new climate is referred to in Helen Bradford, *A Taste of Freedom: The ICU in Rural South Africa 1924–1930* (New Haven: Yale University Press, 1987), p. 248; in Eddie Koch, " 'Without Visible Means of Subsistence': Slumyard Culture in Johannesburg 1918–1940," in *Town and Countryside in the Transvaal: Capitalist Penetration and Popular Response*, ed. Belinda Bozzoli (Johannesburg: Ravan Press, 1983), p. 166; and in Bonner, "Basotho Women," pp. 222–26. Ellen Hellmann found that women who did not participate in brewing were characterized as "bad" wives. See "The Importance of Beer-Brewing in an Urban Native Yard," *Bantu Studies* 8 (1934), 41, 44.

80. Hellmann, *Rooiyard*, p. 6.

81. Slightly over half of the 239 children in families she surveyed lived with relatives in the country.

82. See Deborah Gaitskell, "Laundry, Liquor and 'Playing Ladish': African Women in Johannesburg 1903–1939," unpublished paper presented to the South African Social History Workshop, Centre of International and Area Studies, University of London, 1978, p. 24.

83. Gaitskell, "Female Mission Initiatives," pp. 112, 138.

84. Phillips, *Bantu in the City*, p. 48. Taking in lodgers is widely documented as an income-earning activity in African urban areas; but most accounts do not make it clear whether this income accrued to women or to men. In those areas where municipalities rented houses only to men, it is not unlikely that they controlled this resource. Discussing East London in the late 1920s, however, William Beinart and Colin Bundy mention renting rooms as a primarily female activity. See *Hidden Struggles in Rural South Africa: Politics and Popular Movements in the Transkei and Eastern Cape, 1890–1930* (London: James Currey, 1987) pp. 275, 302.

85. Bonner, "Basotho Women," p. 227, discussing the Pretoria-Witwatersrand-Vereeniging area.

86. Hellmann, *Rooiyard*, p. 38.

87. Gaitskell, "Laundry," p. 5. See Hellmann, *Rooiyard*, pp. 11–17, for a fuller discussion of the lives of black female domestic workers in the 1930s.

88. Gaitskell, "Laundry," pp. 22–23.

89. Krige, "Native Family Budgets," pp. 96–97.

90. See Luise White, *The Comforts of Home: Prostitution in Colonial Nairobi* (Chicago: University of Chicago Press, 1990).

91. Hellmann, *Rooiyard*, p. 50.

92. Krige, "Native Family Budgets," p. 97.

93. Hellmann, *Rooiyard*, pp. 40–41.

94. Krige, "Native Family Budgets," p. 96.

95. Hellmann, "Beer-Brewing," p. 60.

96. Hellmann, *Rooiyard*, p. 38.

97. Ibid., p. 18; also Krige, "Native Family Budgets," p. 96. In general, on women, work, and family, see pp. 18, 21, 37–39 and 89–91. Gaitskell, "Laundry," p. 6 notes that as "slumyards" like Rooiyard were closed down, Africans could live either in municipal locations where only men had direct access to housing, in

suburbs like Sophiatown where living with a man was not necessary, or on the premises of white employers.

98. Hellmann, *Rooiyard,* pp. 43–44.

99. Ibid., p. 46.

100. Krige, "Native Family Budgets," p. 102.

101. Ibid., pp. 94, 97.

102. Ibid., p. 95.

103. Bonner, "Basotho Women," p. 227.

104. *Umsebenzi,* August 18, 1934. Baruch Hirson documents another important struggle against police attacks on brewing in "The Bloemfontein Riots, 1925: A Study in Community Culture and Class Consciousness," Collected Seminar Papers on the Societies of Southern African in the 19th and 20th Centuries, University of London, Institute of Commonwealth Studies, May 13, 1983. The role of women in the riots has not been determined.

105. Baruch Hirson, *Yours For the Union: Class and Community Struggles in South Africa, 1930–1947* (London: Zed Press, 1989), pp. 69–70.

106. Bradford, *Taste of Freedom,* pp. 247–50.

107. Bonner, "Basotho Women," p. 224.

108. Ezekiel (Es'kia) Mphahlele, *Down Second Avenue* (Berlin: Seven Seas Publishers), pp. 39, 41.

109. Hellmann, *Rooiyard,* p. 46.

110. Bradford, *Taste of Freedom,* pp. 69, 90, 260; and Beinart and Bundy, *Hidden Struggles,* pp. 286, 302–305.

4. Daughters of the Depression

1. Union of South Africa, *The Work of the Wage Board, Report to the Honourable Minister of Labour by the Wage Board upon the Work of the Wage Board for the Three Years Ended 28th February, 1929* (Pretoria, 1929), p. 13.

2. Ibid.

3. Ibid.

4. E. S. (Solly) Sachs, *Rebels Daughters* (London: MacGibbon and Kee, 1957), p. 55.

5. Ibid. pp. 23, 27–28.

6. Hansi P. Pollak, "Women in Witwatersrand Industries," M.A. thesis (University of the Witwatersrand, 1932), p. 101.

7. Leslie Witz, "Support or Control: The Children of the Garment Workers' Union," seminar paper, University of the Witwatersrand, June 24, 1983, p. 14.

8. Letter to Mr. Sacks [sic] from Jean Ghent, Parktown, December 2, 1929, GWU, Aab 1.16.

9. Letter from Annie Stodes to the Secretary, Tailors' Association, Doornfontein, March 9, 1929, GWU, Aab 1.16.

10. Letter to the Secretary, Witwatersrand Tailors' Union, from Mrs. C. Le Grange, March 12, 1929, GWU, Aab 1.16.

11. Letter from the General Secretary to Miss D. Emmerson, Mrs. C. Le Grange, and Mrs. A. Hodes, March 22, 1929, GWU, Aab 1.16.

12. H. A. F. Barker, *The Economics of the Wholesale Clothing Industry of South Africa* (Johannesburg: Pallas Publications, 1962), p. 20.

13. Letter of the General Secretary to the Honourable the Minister of Labour, April 3, 1930, GWU, Bbc 1.50.

14. *Cape Times,* August 8 and August 11, 1931.

15. Pollak, "Women in Witwatersrand Industries," pp. 118–19, 178, 224; Wage Board, "Report to the Honourable the Minister of Labour by the Wage Board.

Garment Making Trades," April 12, 1935, pp. 18, 26, came to some of the same conclusions.

16. See ARB 2017, file no. C.F. 13/2.

17. Report of the Carnegie Commission, *The Poor White Problem in South Africa*, vol. 5 (Stellenbosch: Pro Ecclesia-Drukkery, 1932), 208.

18. Customs Tariff Commission, "Record of Evidence," testimony of the Transvaal Clothing Manufacturers' Association, October 9, 1934, p. 706.

19. *The Star*, September 2, 1932, cited in Elsabé Brink, " 'The Whole Lot Were Cross,': A Narrative of the Strikes in the Clothing Industry 1931 and 1932," unpublished seminar paper, University of the Witwatersrand, n.d., p. 26.

20. The Apprenticeship Act was specifically designed to protect young men from such job loss, but no comparable protection was accorded to women. Under the "task work" system workers had to meet daily production targets that were raised periodically.

21. "Facts About the Present Strike in the Clothing Industry, Witwatersrand," September 1, 1932, GWU, Bch 7.2; "Dispute at Clothing and Shirt Manufacturers, Johannesburg," 1931, GWU, Bch 1.50. Arguing that the high level of sexual harassment facilitated the "short step" to prostitution, Louis Franklin Freed, *The Problem of European Prostitution in Johannesburg* (Cape Town: Juta, 1949), pp. 193–94, provides graphic examples of the coercive uses of sexuality in factories and restaurants.

22. Pollak, "Women in Witwatersrand Industries," p. 193.

23. See Sachs, *Rebels Daughters*, pp. 40–57.

24. See "Membership Lists of Garment Workers' Union (Cape)," [probably 1935], ARB 896, file no. 1058/27, and Interview, Anna Scheepers, Johannesburg, July 1, 1983.

25. Pollak, "Women in Witwatersrand Industries," p. 143.

26. *The Star*, June 28, 1935.

27. Pollak, "Women in Witwatersrand Industries," p. 251.

28. Ibid., p. 255, citing a woman she interviewed; see also pp. 252–53.

29. Ibid., p. 255.

30. Wage Board, "Garment Making Trades," p. 22.

31. Calculated from "Membership Lists of Garment Workers' Union." Of 496 members reported in 1935, 288 were married.

32. Pollak, "Women in Witwatersrand Industries," p. 251.

33. Union of South Africa, *Report of the Industrial Legislation Commission* (Pretoria, 1935), U.G. 37, 1935, p. 23; Customs Tariff Commission, "Testimony of Transvaal Textiles Ltd.," September 26, 1934, pp. 219, 223; "Testimony of Clothing Industry, Johannesburg," October 5, 1934, pp. 599–600; Union of South Africa, *Report of the Customs Tariff Commission, 1934–35* (Pretoria, 1936), U.G. No. 5, '36, p. 18. Although clothing manufacturers were anxious to stress the high turnover in the industry to emphasize the high costs of production and therefore the need for tariff protection, other evidence supports these observations.

34. Wage Board, "Garment Making Trades," p. 23.

35. South Africa, *Industrial Legislation Commission*, p. 23.

36. Confinement Allowance, Factory Act Section 18, "Applications Refused During 1932." Apart from one man who was in jail, job information on the others was unavailable.

37. Pollak, "Women in Witwatersrand Industries," pp. 258–59. In sweets and food, 37.5 percent of women were under eighteen and only 5.7 percent over twenty-five, whereas in the clothing industry, the median age was twenty, but 29 percent were over twenty-five.

38. From Martin Nicol, " 'Joh'burg Hotheads' and the 'Gullible Children of Cape Town,' " Cape Town, n.d., Tables 1 and 2.

39. Carnegie Commission, *Poor White Problem*, vol. 1, 214, 216–17.

40. Hansi Pollak, "Women Workers in Witwatersrand Industries," *South African Journal of Economics* 1, no. 1 (March 1933), 65.

41. Carnegie Commission, *Poor White Problem*, vol. 1, 217.

42. Customs Tariff Commission, "Testimony of the Transvaal Clothing Manufacturers' Association (TCMA)," October 9, 1934, pp. 683–84.

43. Data come from the figures in Wage Board, "Garment Making Trades," Tables 2 and 3. Writing of the 1920s, Bill Freund, "The Social Character of Secondary Industry in South Africa, 1915–1945 (with Special Reference to the Witwatersrand)," African Studies Seminar Paper, African Studies Institute, University of the Witwatersrand, April 22, 1985, reports a classic urban wage rate for blacks of one pound a week, compared with an ideal skilled white man's wage of one pound per day.

44. Letter from A. D. Allen, Divisional Inspector to the Secretary of Labour, East London, October 11, 1939, ARB 1546, file no. C1146.

45. Pollak, "Women in Witwatersrand Industries," p. 77.

46. Customs Tariff Commission, "Testimony of the TCMA," October 9, 1934.

47. *Cape Times*, January 8, 1936.

48. Wage Board, "Garment Making Trades," p. 24.

49. Calculated from Wage Board, "Report to the Honourable the Minister of Labour and Social Welfare by the Wage Board," August 19, 1936, ARB, file no. 1009/36, Table I.

50. Memo of S. Liebenberg to the Divisional Inspector, Cape Town, August 3, 1939.

51. Customs Tariff Commission, "Testimony of Transvaal Textiles Ltd.," Johannesburg, September 28, 1934, pp. 220, 226.

52. Pollak, "Women in Witwatersrand Industries," p. 214.

53. Wage Board, "Garment Making Trades," pp. 8–9, 12.

54. Press Clippings, 1938, SATLC, Dg.

55. Customs Tariff Commission, Johannesburg, September 25, 1934, pp. 157, 168–69.

56. "Report by Factory Inspectors Mr. Orkin and Miss E. Winter to the Divisional Inspector," Johannesburg, December 30, 1938.

57. Press clippings, 1938, SATLC, Dg.

58. Pollak, "Women in Witwatersrand Industries," p. 230.

59. Ibid. pp. 64, 76, 291, and Allister Macmillan, *Environs of the Golden City and Pretoria* (Cape Town: Cape Times, 1934), pp. 61–71.

60. Carnegie Commission, *Poor White Problem*, vol. 5, p. 215.

61. From figures in Nicol, "Joh'burg Hotheads," Table 1.

62. *Cape Times*, August 14, 1934.

63. Ibid., July 30, 1935.

64. Ibid., February 6–7, 1935.

65. Memo from the Divisional Inspector, J. Martens, to the Secretary for Labour, Cape Town, September 14, 1939, ARB 1546, file no. C1146.

66. Nicol, "Joh'burg Hotheads," Table 1.

67. South Africa, *Customs Tariff Commission*, p. 18.

68. Union of South Africa, *Report of the Industrial Legislation Commission* (Pretoria, 1935), U.G. 37, 1935, pp. 23–27.

69. The white women included 938 adults and 606 juveniles and the African men, 468 adults and 71 juveniles. The white men numbered 150. Calculated from "Recommendation to the Honourable Minister of Labour by the Wage Board. Clothing Manufacturing Industry, Witwatersrand and Pretoria, 1929," Table "A". For a broad survey of the "shape of wages" on the Rand, see Freund, "Secondary Industry," pp. 6–13.

70. Calculated from figures in Sheila T. van der Horst, "Labour," Ellen Hellman [sic], ed., *Handbook on Race Relations in South Africa* (Cape Town: Oxford University Press, 1949), Table XV, p. 131. Whereas female garment workers earned 28 percent of the average European wage, black wages were 67 percent of those of these women.

71. See Customs Tariff Commission, "Testimony of the TCMA, Johannesburg," pp. 632–33. These representatives assured the commission that the association would try for a 100 percent European female labor force in the Transvaal clothing industry if granted the necessary tariff protection.

72. Witz, "Support or Control," p. 18, and Pollak, "Women in Witwatersrand Industries," p. 78, both refer to complaints about Africans (presumably men) sitting next to white women.

73. *Rand Daily Mail* (hereafter *RDM*), September 22, 1934. Unless otherwise indicated, the material on this issue all comes from ARB 1546, file no. C1146, Parts I and II.

74. See *RDM*, September 29, October 4, and October 6, 1934, and Letter from the Honourable Secretary, South African League of Women Voters to the Secretary for Labour, Pretoria, October 24, 1934.

75. *The Star*, October 10, 1934.

76. Memo from Ivan Walker, Secretary for Labour and Social Welfare, June 14, 1935, to the Secretary for the Interior. A report of the situation printed in *The Star* on April 14, 1937, counted 128 European female employees of Asians in the Transvaal, almost all in sales or office work, and six in Durban.

77. Memo from S. Liebenberg, Industrial Inspector, Cape Town, 3rd August, 1939.

78. The similarity of this proposed legislation to the Nuremburg laws in Nazi Germany is unmistakable; under the German regulations of 1935, Jewish men were prohibited from supervising "Aryan" women under the age of forty.

79. Jeffrey Butler, "Afrikaner Women and the Creation of Ethnicity in a Small South African Town, 1902–1950," in *The Creation of Tribalism in Southern Africa*, ed. Leroy Vail (Berkeley: University of California Press; and London: James Currey, 1989), p. 76.

80. Deborah Gaitskell, " 'Christian Compounds for Girls': Church Hostels for African Women in Johannesburg, 1907–1970," *Journal of Southern African Studies* 6, no. 1 (October 1979), 55. Unless otherwise noted, information on hostels for African women comes from this source.

81. Louise A. Tilly and Joan W. Scott, *Women, Work and Family* (New York: Holt, Rinehart, and Winston, 1978), p. 109. They suggest that factory owners attempted to recruit young girls by providing the "conditions of protected migration" found in domestic service.

82. Gaitskell, "Christian Compounds," p. 58, quoting from Leeds, AT/c43, Clara Bridgman to E. Little, 17/9/1930.

83. *The Social and Industrial Review* 2, no. 6 (June 1926), 415.

84. Ibid., 416.

85. Remarks reported in *Umsebenzi*, December 12, 1936.

86. *The Social and Industrial Review* 2, no. 6 (June 1926), 414.

87. Ibid., 417.

88. Ibid., 3, no. 16 (April 1927), 350.

89. ARB 2039, file no. F 10/1.

90. Frida Hartley, "The Urban Girl Worker," *The Star*, December 17, 1938.

91. ARB 2039, file no. F 10/3. In June 1940 the Transvaal Clothing Manufacturers' Association agreed to donate twenty-five pounds a year to the club, according to the minutes of a meeting of the Executive Committee held on June 6, 1940.

92. *Garment Worker* (February 1939), p. 11. Earlier discussions of the possibility

of a hostel in Germiston are found in *RDM*, February 2, 1935 and *Umsebenzi*, December 12, 1936. The government had set aside £25,000 for the hostel, and Germiston manufacturers were prepared to donate £800 annually.

93. *Garment Worker* (April 1939), p. 14, and (March 1940), p. 10.

94. *Guardian*, November 3, 1939 notes that the Trades and Labour Council had appointed Anna Scheepers, an official of the Garment Workers' Union, to the Committee of Control of the residential club at Brixton.

95. Carnegie Commission, *Poor White Problem*, vol. 5, 211. The hostel at Paarl is mentioned in the file on Asian supervision of white women.

96. Butler, "Afrikaner Women."

97. Interview, Anna Scheepers, Johannesburg, July 1, 1983.

98. "Report to the Witwatersrand Central Juvenile Affairs Board on the Activities of the Girls' Lunch Hour Club for August and September, 1930," GWU, AH 1092, Asb 1.84.

99. Union of South Africa, *Report to the Department of Labour* (Pretoria, 1934), U.G. No. 37, 1933, p. 26.

100. Anna Scheepers made this point in the interview cited above.

101. Elsabé Brink, " 'Maar'n Klomp "Factory" Meide': Afrikaner Family and Community on the Witwatersrand during the 1920s," in *Class, Community and Conflict: South African Perspectives*, ed. Belinda Bozzoli (Johannesburg: Ravan Press, 1987), p. 190.

102. Bertha Solomon, *Time Remembered: The Story of a Fight* (Cape Town: Howard Timmins, 1968), p. 102.

103. *Umsebenzi*, December 12, 1936.

104. Brink, " 'Factory' Meide," p. 184. Although the total sample was very small (167 in Johannesburg and 40 in Germiston) these conclusions support Pollak's observation on the association of factory workers with men who were in the building trades or in public service.

105. Interview.

5. Commandos of Working Women

1. Union of South Africa, *The Work of the Wage Board. Report to the Honourable Minister of Labour by the Wage Board Upon the Work of the Board for the Three Years Ended 28th February, 1929* (Pretoria, 1929), p. 13.

2. Ibid., p. 27.

3. Economic and Wage Commission, "Evidence of South African Women Workers' Union," September 3, 1925, part 2, p. 1, SATLC, Cd 9.2–5.

4. *Rand Daily Mail* (hereafter *RDM*), October 4, 1929.

5. For a summary of South African reactions to the strike, see Baruch Hirson, "The Homeboat Strike of 1925: British Seamen and South African Community Reactions," Collected Seminar Papers, The Societies of Southern Africa in the 19th and 20th Centuries, University of London, Institute of Commonwealth Studies, vol. 14, October 1984–June 1986.

6. This statement and other personal material on Klenerman come from a personal interview, Johannesburg, November 26, 1979.

7. Her party membership was brief, however; in September 1931 she was among a group of trade unionists expelled for "reformist tendencies."

8. Klenerman, Interview. There is no evidence to confirm this allegation.

9. The South African Women's Union, "Constitution," ARB 729, file no. 1054/171. I am grateful to Baruch Hirson for the information on Eva Green. Klenerman called publicly for a democratic defense force on several occasions in 1924 and 1925 and, later, ran literacy classes for the ICU. See Baruch Hirson, "Death of a

Revolutionary: Frank Glass/Li Fu-jen/John Liang: 1901–1988," *Searchlight South Africa* 1, no. 1 (September 1988), 33–35.

10. Letter to C. F. Glass from Fanny Klenerman, Johannesburg, April 24, 1925. In this letter to the Bespoke Tailors' Association, she noted that the Builders' and Engine Drivers' Unions, the Communist party, and the South African party already had contributed.

11. Jon Lewis, *Industrialisation and Trade Union Organisation in South Africa, 1924–55: The Rise and Fall of the South African Trades and Labour Council* (Cambridge: Cambridge University Press, 1984) p. 61.

12. Letter to the Secretary, South African Association of Employees' Organizations from the Registrar of Trade Unions and Employees' Associations, Johannesburg, July 11, 1925. The South African Women's Union, ARB 729, file no. 1054/171.

13. E. Gitsham and J. F. Trembath, *A First Account of Labour Organisation in South Africa* (Durban: E. P. and Commercial Printing Co., 1926), pp. 112–13; Letter to A. C. v.d. Horst from Fm.C.G., March 7, 1927, The South African Women's Union, ARB 729, file no. 1054/171.

14. *The South African Worker*, July 8, 1927; at this time Klenerman was the secretary of the Sweet Workers' Union.

15. "Evidence of South African Women Workers' Union," part 1, pp. 1–2.

16. Ibid. The final quote is from part 1, p. 7.

17. Ibid., part 1, p. 6.

18. Ibid., part 4, pp. 3–4.

19. *RDM*, May 24, 1928.

20. *RDM*, May 22, 1928.

21. *Cape Times*, May 22–23 and May 25, 1928; *The South African Worker*, May 15, 1928.

22. May 22, 1928.

23. *RDM*, May 22, 1928.

24. Robin Cohen, "Introduction," in A. T. Nzula, I. I. Potekhin, and A. Z. Zusmanovich, *Forced Labour in Colonial Africa*, ed. Robin Cohen (London: Zed Press, 1979), p. 9. In 1928, the various Communist-led unions combined to form the FNETU. The group was affiliated with the Red International of Labor Unions.

25. Lewis, *Industrialisation*, pp. 64–66.

26. "Memorandum in Respect of the Employment of Persons in the Clothing Industry (Transvaal) Who Are Not Covered by the Industrial Agreement for that Industry," submitted by the Witwatersrand Tailors' Association to the Honourable the Minister of Labour, February, 1929.

27. *Cape Times*, June 8, 1928; *The South African Worker*, June 22, 1928.

28. *RDM*, October 5, 1929.

29. *Cape Times*, October 5, 7, 8, 12, 1929.

30. Hansi Pollak, "Women in Witwatersrand Industries," M.A. thesis (University of the Witwatersrand, 1932), p. 48.

31. Wage Board, "Report to the Honourable Minister of Labour by the Wage Board, Garment Making Trades," April 12, 1935, p. 19.

32. E. S.(Solly) Sachs, *Rebels Daughters* (London: Mac Gibbon and Kee, 1957), p. 85.

33. "Biography of Johanna Catherina Jacoba Cornelius," p. 4, GWU, Bcc 1.45.

34. *The Hammer*, November 1931, p. 4. Sachs's expulsion from the Communist party in September 1931 was clearly an important factor in these attacks. One of the reasons given at the time was his failure to lead action against the "white chauvinism" of union members. According to Cohen, "Introduction," p. 9, the African Federation of Trade Unions was formed when a black party member, A. T. Nzula, broke off from the Federation of Non-European Trade Unions to

organize a group more firmly under his own control. Jack Simons and Ray Simons in *Class and Colour in South Africa, 1850–1950* (Harmondsworth: Penguin, 1969, repr., London: International Defence and Aid Fund for Southern Africa, 1983), pp. 443–44, imply that Douglas Wolton was instrumental in the AFTU's formation, under the impetus of the 5th Congress of the Red International of Labor Unions in Moscow.

35. Sachs, *Rebels Daughters*, p. 88.

36. *The Hammer*, November 1931, pp. 2–3. In August 1931, according to Elsabé Brink, the GWU and the black male South African Clothing Workers' Union had agreed to assist each other in case of a dispute. Instead, the strike was conducted unilaterally and the locked-out African workers received no pay. See " 'The Whole Lot Were Cross': A Narrative of the Strikes in the Clothing Industry 1931 and 1932," Seminar paper, University of the Witwatersrand, n.d., p. 19.

37. Martin Nicol, " 'Joh'burg Hotheads' and the 'Gullible Children of Cape Town': The Transvaal Garment Workers' Union's Assault on Low Wages in the Cape Town Clothing Industry, 1930–1931," in *Class, Community and Conflict: South African Perspectives*, ed. Belinda Bozzoli (Johannesburg: Ravan Press, 1987), pp. 209–17. For a fuller discussion of unions in the Cape garment industry, see Martin Nicol, "Riches from Rags: Bosses and Unions in the Cape Clothing Industry 1926–1937," *Journal of Southern African Studies* 9, no. 2 (April 1983), 239–55; and Martin Nicol, "A History of Tailoring and Garment Workers in Cape Town, 1900–1939," Ph.D. thesis (University of Cape Town, 1984), which analyzes this history in the context of conditions of class struggle in Cape Town.

38. *Cape Times*, August 20 and 25, 1931.

39. Nicol, "Joh'burg Hotheads," pp. 217, 221. The judgment of the strike as "suicidal" comes from the unpublished version of the paper.

40. *Cape Times*, August 26, 1931.

41. Nicol, "Joh'burg Hotheads," p. 221.

42. "Facts About the Present Strike in the Clothing Industry, Witwatersrand," September 1, 1932, p. 8.

43. Unless otherwise indicated, the recollections of Cornelius in this section come from Johanna Cornelius, "My Experience of the Germiston Gaol in 1932," ICS, Trade Unions, South Africa, File on GWU, and from "Biography of Johanna Jacoba Cornelius," GWU, Bcc 1.45.

44. Cornelius, "Germiston Gaol," p. 2.

45. "Biography of Johanna Cornelius," p. 8. Practically, however, according to Brink, "Narrative of Strikes," p. 29, support from other unions was extremely limited in 1932. Most were unable to contribute because of the severe economic conditions, and all of the gold mines on the Rand refused to allow the women to collect money on their premises.

46. Belinda Bozzoli, "Class, Community and Ideology in the Evolution of South African Society," in Bozzoli, *Class, Community and Conflict*, p. 7.

47. Sachs used this reference in Cornelius's speech as the title of his book.

48. Sachs, *Rebels Daughters*, p. 92.

49. *Cape Times*, August 24, 1932.

50. Jon Lewis, "The Germiston By-Election of 1932: The State and the White Working Class During the Depression," in *Working Papers in Southern African Studies*, ed. P. Bonner, vol. 2 (Johannesburg: Ravan Press, 1981), 103.

51. *Cape Times*, September 2, 1932.

52. Ibid., September 3, 1932.

53. Ibid., September 6, 1932.

54. Ibid., September 12, 1932.

55. Sachs, *Rebels Daughters*, p. 95.

56. "Minutes of Proceedings of Mass Trial (Adjourned) Held in the Trades Hall,

Johannesburg, on Thursday the 6th April, 1933," Testimony of Malan, p. 1, GWU, Bch 7.3. The trial also highlights the ambiguous position of the skilled male workers. Although some were Communist party members and considered themselves revolutionaries, their supervisory role in the factories and their high wages gave them substantial arbitrary power over the women under them. See "Proceedings of Mass Trial," p. 12 for one acknowledgement of this contradiction.

57. "Proceedings of Mass Trial," Testimony of Sachs, p. 3.

58. B. A. Touyz, "White Politics and the Garment Workers' Union 1930–1953," M.A. dissertation (University of Cape Town, 1979), p. 25, n. 53.

59. *The Star*, November 6, 1931.

60. Ibid., November 3, 5, 6, 1931.

61. Ibid., September 2, 1932.

62. Lewis, "Germiston By-Election," pp. 100–101, 104.

63. Even up to the period just preceding the split, one member of the Central Executive Committee alleged, "The girls never said a word at the meetings." From "Proceedings of Mass Trial," Testimony of Groer, p. 9.

64. Leslie Witz, "Servant of the Workers: Solly Sachs and the Garment Workers' Union, 1928–1952," M.A. thesis (University of the Witwatersrand, 1984), p. 101.

6. A Lengthening Thread

1. This strategy of cooperation with the industrial conciliation system left Sachs open to charges of reformism and class collaboration. See *The Spark* 1, no. 9 (December 1935), 13–14.

2. Letter from E. S. Sachs to the Secretary, South African Trades and Labour Council, Johannesburg, November 5, 1935, GWU, Bbc 1.50. Their effort was not misplaced. According to Martin Nicol, " 'Joh'burg Hotheads' and the 'Gullible Children of Cape Town,' " unpublished paper, Cape Town, n.d., Table 2, in 1929 average weekly wages on the Rand and at the Cape were not far apart: £1 14s. 10d. and £1 12s. 8d. respectively. By 1934, Cape wages had dropped to £1 10s. 6d. per week and by 1937–38 had risen only to £1 12s. 6d. (less than in 1929), whereas by the latter year the average Rand garment worker earned £2 2s. 6d.

3. "Biography of Johanna Jacoba Cornelius," GWU, Bcc 1.45, p. 13. According to Martin Nicol, "Riches from Rags: Bosses and Unions in the Cape Clothing Industry 1926–1937," *Journal of Southern African Studies* 9, no. 2 (April 1983), 252, one of the few active women among the Cape garment workers, Rose Crawford, sided with the Transvaal organizers at this time.

4. Press clipping, June 22, 1935, SATLC, Dg. A list of representatives sent to a Wage Board sitting in the late 1930s indicates the differing character of the Cape and the Transvaal unions with respect to women: whereas six of the eight Transvaal representatives were women, four of the five Cape delegates were men.

5. Press clipping, June 15, 1935, SATLC, Dg.

6. "Membership Lists of GWU (Cape)." In response to Transvaal intervention, management instituted a compulsory stop order in favor of the compliant Cape union, which laid the foundations for its growth from then on.

7. "Memorandum of Proceedings At Protest Meeting Held on Steps of Johannesburg City Hall on 16/11/35," ARB 1464, file no. C1069/98.

8. *Cape Times*, March 5, 1936.

9. Ibid., March 11, 1936.

10. "Biography of Johanna Cornelius," pp. 13–14.

11. *The Spark* 2, no. 6 (May 1936), 13.

12. *Guardian*, August 19, 1938.

13. *Umsebenzi*, February 19, 1938. The perception of favoritism toward whites remained at this time, although in fact the great drop in coloured workers came

between 1934 and 1936; between 1936 and 1937–38 their numbers rose again. See Nicol, "Joh'burg Hotheads," Table 1. Ian Goldin, *Making Race: The Politics and Economics of Coloured Identity in South Africa* (London and New York: Longman, 1987), p. 47, suggests that by accepting wage settlements unacceptable to white workers, the union insured that they would not compete with coloureds. In 1941 a closed-shop agreement formally excluded Africans from the industry.

14. *Umsebenzi*, May 4, 1935.

15. Ibid., January 23, 1937.

16. Ibid., August 28, 1937.

17. Ibid., August 13 and 21, 1937.

18. *Guardian*, October 29, 1937.

19. *Umsebenzi*, November 20, 1937.

20. *Guardian*, October 21, 1938; February 10, June 30, July 7, July 21 and August 11, 1939. *Garment Worker*, June 1939, discusses the difficulties of organizing in Port Elizabeth.

21. Letter of I. Wolfson to the Secretary, South African Trades and Labour Council, Johannesburg, May 13, 1935, SATLC, Dc 8.19. Discussion concerning wages and working conditions at Consolidated Textile Mills had been ongoing for several months. See *The Star*, June 27, 1935.

22. "Textile Workers Strike." SATLC, Dc 8.19.

23. *Cape Times*, June 10, 1935. At the time, fifty-nine women and eight men were employed as spinners, as compared with 170 women and thirty-five men as weavers. Figures come from *The Star*, June 27, 1935. By contrast with the spinning section, the weaving section of the industry was protected from foreign competition by tariffs.

24. *Cape Times*, May 15, 1935.

25. Ibid., June 18, 1935.

26. Ibid., June 18, 1935.

27. Ibid., June 26, 1935.

28. Bettie du Toit, *Ukubamba Amadolo: Workers' Struggles in the South African Textile Industry* (London: Onyx Press, 1978), p. 22. Other women arrested during the course of the strike included Ellen Claasen (28), Susannah Coetzee (20), E. Wadge (24), Gwendoline Gray (23), Violet Rudman (33), Martha Venter (19), Bettie Swanepoel (26), and Maria van der Walt (40). The various charges against them included disturbing the peace, obstructing members of the police in executing their duties, and malicious assault.

29. Du Toit, *Ukubamba Amadolo*, pp. 23–24.

30. "Biography of Johanna Cornelius," p. 10.

31. Interview, Bettie du Toit, London, October 26, 1979.

32. "Biography of Johanna Cornelius," pp. 11–12.

33. Du Toit, Interview.

34. *Cape Times*, June 29, 1935. It is interesting to note that accounts of the strike in *Umsebenzi* never refer to the replacement issue.

35. Du Toit, *Ukubamba Amadolo*, p. 124.

36. *Umsebenzi*, July 6, 1935.

37. *Cape Times*, June 29, 1935.

38. *Umsebenzi*, June 29, 1935.

39. Ibid., July 13, 1935.

40. Ibid. According to the *The Star*, July 20, 1935, the agreement gazetted the previous day ruled that everyone should be reemployed; but the lack of specific reference to the fate of women spinners suggests that the union may have lost on the issue of their retention in these jobs.

41. *Umsebenzi*, July 27, 1935.

42. *Guardian*, June 24, September 2, October 28, 1938; February 24, 1939.

43. Ibid., December 9, 1938 and September 1, 1939.

44. Ibid., June 23, 1939.

45. Ibid., February 24, 1939.

46. Alex la Guma, *Twenty Five Proud Years: the Story of the Textile Workers' Union* (Johannesburg, n.d.), p. 3.

47. Du Toit, *Ukubamba Amadolo*, p. 60.

48. Letter from Secretary Organiser to The General Secretary, South African Trades and Labour Council, July 2, 1935, SATLC, Dc 8.19.

49. September 30, 1935, SATLC, Dc 2.26, TWIU, 1935.

50. Letter to the Secretary-Organiser, Salt River, from I. Wolfson, October 3, 1935, SATLC Dc 2.26, TWIU, 1935.

51. *Umsebenzi*, August 3, 1935.

52. Ibid., August 3, 1935.

53. Ibid., June 1 and August 3, 1935.

54. Ibid., June 16, 1939.

55. Interview.

56. Du Toit, *Ukubamba Amadolo*, p. 39.

57. Interview.

58. Du Toit, *Ukubamba Amadolo*, pp. 40–41.

59. Interview.

60. Edward Roux, *Time Longer Than Rope* (Madison: University of Wisconsin Press, 1966), p. 330.

61. *Guardian*, July 2, 23, 30, September 24, and November 12, 1937; see also *Cape Times*, July 19–22, 1937.

62. *Guardian*, May 21 and July 30, 1937.

63. *Cape Times*, July 22, 1937.

64. *Guardian*, July 23, 1937; see also *Cape Times*, July 20, 1937.

65. *Cape Times*, July 20, 1937.

66. Ibid., July 22, 1937, and *Guardian*, July 30, 1937; see also *Guardian*, April 23, May 21, June 18, and July 30, 1937; and *Umsebenzi*, May 22, 1937.

67. *Umsebenzi*, May 22, 1937.

68. *Guardian*, February 19, July 2, July 9, July 16, 1937; January 7, March 11, 1938; and *Umsebenzi*, July 10, September 3, 1937.

69. *Guardian*, March 3, July 14, July 21, August 18, October 6, October 13, and November 24, 1939; February 23, 1940.

70. Interview with Ray Simons [Alexander], Popular History Trust, p. 22.

71. *Guardian*, March 18, August 5, and September 16, 1938.

72. Norman Herd, *Counter Attack: The Story of South African Shopworkers* (Cape Town: National Union of Distributive Workers, 1974), pp. 24–25, 60–66.

73. *Garment Worker*, October, 1938.

74. Anna Scheepers, Interview, Johannesburg, July 1, 1983.

75. *Guardian*, November 10, 1939.

76. Deborah Gaitskell, "Laundry, Liquor and 'Playing Ladish,': African Women in Johannesburg 1903–1939," Unpublished paper presented to the South African Social History Workshop, Centre of International and Area Studies, University of London, 1978, p. 17. The League, though formed in 1935 by coloured activists at the Cape, sought to represent the interests of all "non-Europeans."

77. *Cape Times*, April 29, 1937.

78. *Guardian*, February 24 and November 10, 1939.

79. *Cape Times*, July 14, 1937.

80. July 8, 1937.

81. Gaitskell, "Laundry," pp. 16–17.

82. *Guardian*, September 22, 1939. He died in August 1938.

83. Letter from G. J. Coka, Johannesburg, n.d., SAIRR, File G 193.

84. *Guardian,* September 22, 1939.

85. Baruch Hirson, *Yours For the Union: Class and Community Struggles in South Africa, 1930–1947* (London: Zed Books, 1989), p. 60. See also all of chapter 5. The presence of D. R. Twala in a leading role suggests a possible connection between this group and that of Lucy Twala, although the relationship between them is unknown.

86. *Guardian,* April 24, 1937.

87. Ibid., June 4, 1937; March 11, September 16, December 9, 1938; March 24, 1939.

88. Ibid., April 30, 1937.

89. *Umsebenzi,* March 16, 1935.

90. *Umsebenzi,* July 11, 1936.

91. "Report of the General Secretary E. S. Sachs on his visit to Durban and Cape Town," May 1935, GWU, Reel 5.

92. *Umsebenzi,* May 11, 1935. The regular publication of the bimonthly newspaper, *Garment Worker/Klerewerker,* was itself part of the campaign against right-wing ideas.

93. See Jon Lewis, "Solly Sachs and the Garment Workers' Union," *South African Labour Bulletin* 3, no. 3 (October 1976), 72. The fullest accounts of Christian nationalism and its onslaught against the Garment Workers' Union are found in Jon Lewis, *Industrialisation and Trade Union Organization in South Africa, 1924–55: The Rise and Fall of the South African Trades and Labour Council* (Cambridge: Cambridge University Press, 1984), pp. 69–75; and in Dan O'Meara, *Volkskapitalisme: Class, Capital and Ideology in the Development of Afrikaner Nationalism, 1934–1948* (Cambridge: Cambridge University Press, 1983), pp. 86, 94.

94. Elsabé Brink, "Plays, Poetry and Production: The Literature of the Garment Workers," *South African Labour Bulletin* 9, no. 8 (1983–84), 52, n. 34.

95. See Brink, "Plays, Poetry and Production," pp. 39–41, for further detail.

96. "Biography of Johanna Cornelius," p. 15.

97. Basil Davidson, *Report From Southern Africa* (London: Jonathon Cape, 1952), p. 197.

98. O'Meara, *Volkskapitalisme,* p. 86.

99. Du Toit, *Ukubamba Amadolo,* p. 44; Interview.

100. *Umsebenzi,* March 30, 1935.

101. From a flyer by A. Scheepers and Maria Beggs, Johannesburg, n.d., but probably 1952.

102. "Why I Left My Home on the Land to Come and Work in a Factory," typescript, 1938, p. 3, GWU, Bch. Based on her birth in Lichtenburg, the statement may come from either Johanna or Hester Cornelius.

103. O'Meara, *Volkskapitalisme,* p. 149.

104. See Cherryl Walker, "The Woman's Suffrage Movement in South Africa," Communications No. 2, Centre for African Studies, University of Cape Town, 1979. Only a small, relatively privileged group of black men at the Cape was allowed to vote. Africans lost this right in 1936, coloured men in the early 1950s.

105. *Garment Worker,* November 1936.

106. Hansi P. Pollak, "Women in Witwatersrand Industries," M.A. thesis (University of the Witwatersrand, 1932), p. 49.

107. See, for example, *Garment Worker,* August 1939.

7. Nimble Fingers and Keen Eyesight

1. Subsequent chapters will discuss the labor movement in the early 1940s and the impact of rising production on women's work.

2. Eddie Webster, *Cast in a Racial Mould: Labour Process and Trade Unionism in the Foundries* (Johannesburg: Ravan Press, 1985), p. 57.

3. R. J. Randall, "Full Employment in War-Time," *South African Journal of Economics* 10, no. 2 (June 1942), 123.

4. Randall, "Full Employment," p. 124.

5. The figures come from D. Hobart Houghton, *The South African Economy* (Cape Town: Oxford University Press, 1973), p. 123 and D. Hobart Houghton, "Economic Development, 1865–1965," in Monica Wilson and Leonard Thompson, eds., *The Oxford History of South Africa*, vol. 2 (New York and Oxford: Oxford University Press, 1971), 36.

6. H. M. Robertson, "The War and the South African Economy," *South African Journal of Economics* 20, no. 1 (March 1954), 102, makes this point with regard to automation. Jon Lewis, *Industrialisation and Trade Union Organisation in South Africa, 1924–55: The Rise and Fall of the South African Trades and Labour Council* (Cambridge: Cambridge University Press, 1984), p. 88, discusses these changes more broadly.

7. Jack Simons and Ray Simons, *Class and Colour in South Africa, 1850–1950* (Harmondsworth: Penguin, 1969, repr., London: International Defense and Aid Fund for Southern Africa, 1983), p. 535.

8. Dan O'Meara, *Volkskapitalisme: Class, Capital and Ideology in the Development of Afrikaner Nationalism, 1934–1948* (Cambridge: Cambridge University Press, 1983), p. 147.

9. *The Star*, n.d., Dg SATLC, Press clippings, 1941.

10. *Guardian*, February 27 and July 17, 1941.

11. Letter to the Secretary, Mechanic Unions' Joint Committee, from A. J. Limebeer, Secretary, Transvaal Chamber of Mines Gold Producers' Committee, Johannesburg, March 25, 1941, ARB 1558, file no. 1183/9.

12. Letter to the Director of Technical Production, War Supplies Board, from G. H. Beatty, Johannesburg Consolidated Investment Co., Johannesburg, November 19, 1940, ARB 1558, file no. 1183/9. The wages agreed upon in March 1941 were considerably lower, beginning at 1s. 4d. per hour and rising to 1s. 9d.

13. See correspondence in ARB 1558 file no. 1183/9.

14. Letter from R. Glastonbury, Secretary, Amalgamated Engineering Union, to Mr. D. B. Reay, Johannesburg, September 20, 1941, ARB 1959, file no. C.O.M. 1/37 Sc. IV, Part I (hereafter ARB 1959).

15. Letter from E. A. Clements, Secretary, Amalgamated Engineering Union, to the Controller of Industrial Man-Power, Johannesburg, March 30, 1942, ARB 1959.

16. Letter from R. Glastonbury, Secretary, Amalgamated Engineering Union to the Secretary, Transvaal Chamber of Mines, Johannesburg, October 20, 1942, ARB 1959.

17. "Memorandum on Moulders-Dilution," from A. C. Payne, November 9, 1942, ARB 1959.

18. The specific occupations included the following: fitters, turners, electricians, moulders, boilermakers, patternmakers, and blacksmiths.

19. "Memorandum on Employing Female Emergency Workers without Controller's Permission," October 30, 1942, ARB 1959.

20. "Memorandum on Female Emergency Workers Returns," March 11, 1943, ARB 1959.

21. "Memorandum on Women Operators," February 15, 1942, ARB 1959. The two firms under discussion here were the Group Workshop and Grootvlei.

22. Letter from J. M. Torrance, Manager, Leon Robert, Limited to the Controller of Industrial Man Power, Johannesburg, June 5, 1942, ARB 1959; Letter from

West Rand Engineering Works Limited to the Controller of Industrial Manpower, June 5, 1942, ARB 1959.

23. Letter from the Chief Engineer to the Controller of Industrial Man Power, Pretoria, September 14, 1942, ARB 1959.

24. "Memorandum on Cofac—Women's Training Scheme," Johannesburg, March 22, 1943, ARB 1959.

25. Letter from Gregor MacGregor, Office of the Director General of War Supplies, to the Secretary of Labour, Johannesburg, February 21, 1942, ARB 1157, file no. 1183.

26. Letter from E. Penrose to the Controller of Industrial Man-Power, Durban, February 15, 1943, ARB 1959.

27. Female Workers in the Engineering Industry. Return for the Month Ended April 30, 1943, ARB 1960, file no. C.O.M. 1/37 Sc. IV B.

28. The figures were 2,754 on the Witwatersrand, 1,471 in Pretoria, and 335 in Cape Town. Letter from J. A. Wagner to the Secretary, Safema, January 28, 1944, ARB 1960, file no. C.O.M. 1/37 Sc. IV B.

29. Monthly Return of Female Emergency Workers Employed in the Engineering Industry for the Months of June, July, August, and September, 1944, October 12, 1944, ARB 1960, file no. C.O.M. 1/37 Sc. IV B. Monthly totals for June, July, August, and September respectively were 3,333, 3,389, 3,480, and 3,449—a rise of 4.4 percent between June and August and then a slight drop in September.

30. Letter from the Controller of Industrial Man Power to the Secretary, Chief Mechanicians Workshops, Johannesburg, August 24, 1942, ARB 1959.

31. Letter from the Chief Engineer to the Controller of Industrial Man-Power, Pretoria, September 14, 1942, ARB 1959.

32. *Guardian*, February 27, 1941.

33. Simons and Simons, *Class and Colour*, p. 554.

34. This quote and other information on the case come from Letter of F. Reeves Barratt, Managing Director, Barratt and Pillans, Ltd., to the Secretary, Industrial Council for the Iron and Steel Manufacturing and Engineering Industry, Tvl., Luipaardsvlei, June 23, 1942. A handwritten note on the letter observes that the two women dismissed for refusing to follow instructions were interviewed and denied the allegations against them.

35. *Guardian*, April 16, 1942.

36. *Guardian*, April 24, 1941.

37. *Guardian*, September 8, 1939.

38. AH 646/Dd. 17.117, SATLC.

39. *Guardian*, March 13, 1941. Johanna Cornelius cited these figures during a speech at an International Women's Day celebration.

40. Ibid., March 20, 1941.

41. Letter from E. A. Clements, Secretary, Amalgamated Engineering Union, to D. A. Mackintosh, Acting Secretary, South African Trades and Labour Council, Johannesburg, January 7, 1942, AH 646/Dc 5.37, SATLC.

42. Letter from L. Bezuidenhout, Secretary, Pretoria and District Trades and Labour Committee, to the Secretary, South African Trades and Labour Council, Pretoria, January 20, 1942, AH 646/Dc 5.37, SATLC.

43. Letter from the Secretary to the Secretary, Amalgamated Engineering Union, February 2, 1942, AH 646/Dc 5.37, SATLC. According to H. M. Robertson, the Pretoria mint already had converted to the production of small arms ammunition between 1934 and 1938, following the devaluation of the South African pound in 1932. During the early years of the war, it became the "main nerve-centre" of armament production. See *South African Journal of Economics* 20, no.1 (March 1954), 101–102.

44. Letter from E. A. Clements, Secretary, Amalgamated Engineering Union, to W. J. de Vries, Secretary, SATLC, February 16, 1942, AH 646/Dc 5.37, SATLC.

45. Letter from the Secretary to Mrs. F. J. Engela, March 2, 1942, AH 646/Dc 5.37, SATLC.

46. *Forward*, October 27, 1944, Dg, SATLC, Press Clippings, 1942–44.

47. Letter from the Director to the Secretary, SATLC, Pretoria, April 18, 1942, AH 646/Dc 5.37, SATLC.

48. Letter from W. J. de Vries to the Director, South African Mint, April 21, 1942, AH 646/Dc 5.37, SATLC.

49. Letter from the Secretary to the Secretary, Transvaal District Committee, Amalgamated Engineering Union, May 15, 1942, AH 646/Dc 5.37, SATLC.

50. Letter from the Director, South African Mint, to the Secretary, Trades and Labour Council, Pretoria, June 25, 1942, AH 646/Dc 5.37, SATLC.

51. Letter from the Secretary to Mr. A. C. Heiberg, July 8, 1942, AH 646/Dc 5.37, SATLC.

52. F. J. Engela, "Report on Visit to Kimberley for the Purpose of Organising the Mint Workers (Women Engineering Workers' Union)," p. 1, GWU, Bba 2.3.26.

53. Ibid., "Report," p. 2.

54. Ibid.

55. Letter from Frances Engela to Mr. de Vries, Kimberley, July 23, 1942, AH 646/Dc 5.37, SATLC.

56. Letter to Mr. de Vries, Kimberley, July 23, 1942, AH 646/Dc 5.37, SATLC.

57. The Kimberley statistics come from "List of Kimberley Emergency Workers [1942]," ARB 1959. The median age of single women in Pollak's study was twenty. The 1930s figures come from "Women in Witwatersrand Industries," M.A. thesis (University of the Witwatersrand, 1932), p. 259. The racial composition of the Kimberley sample is unclear; but the proportion of white women must have been higher than it would have been later, since a large number of coloured female workers were hired during a brief period in 1943.

58. Engela, "Report," p. 2.

59. "Hostel accommodation—S. A. Mint," handwritten report, August 29, 1942, ARB 1959.

60. Engela,, "Report," p. 2.

61. Unless otherwise indicated, material in this paragraph and the following section comes from Women Engineering Workers' Union, "Memorandum on Conditions at the Mint in Pretoria," AH 646/Dd 9.18, SATLC.

62. South African Mint Employees Union, "Memorandum for the Controller of Man Power on the Second Agreement," November 26, 1943, AH 646/Dd 9.18, SATLC. Despite the use of another name in this memorandum, there is no evidence to suggest that the Mint Employees' Union was a separate organization.

63. WEWU, "Memorandum," p. 3.

64. SAMEU, "Memorandum," p. 2.

65. *Guardian*, June 24, 1943.

66. Ibid.

67. *Report of the Department of Labour for the Year Ended 31st December, 1945* (Pretoria, 1947), U.G. No. 9, 1947.

8. A New Working Class, 1940–1960

1. See Union of South Africa, *Report of the Industrial Legislation Commission of Enquiry* (Cape Town, 1951), U.G. 62–1951, p. 14, for the dramatic shifts in the "masculinity rate" in major urban areas between 1921, 1936, and 1946.

2. "Industrial Legislation Commission Report," Pretoria, July 22, 1935, pp. 127–

28, 130–31; *Cape Times,* June 30, 1936; *Umsebenzi,* March 27, 1937; *Report of the Department of Labour for the Year Ended December 31, 1939* (Pretoria, 1940), U.G. No. 36, 1940.

3. "Minutes of Monthly Meeting of the Executive Committee of the Transvaal Clothing Manufacturers' Association (TCMA)," June 29, 1942, p. 5.

4. TCMA, "Minutes," Special Meeting, June 12, 1943, p. 3.

5. TCMA, "Minutes," October 13, 1942, p. 7.

6. S. G. Hutton, "An Investigation into European Labour Supply in Port Elizabeth," *Personnel Research Bulletin No. 3* (1945), p. 140.

7. TCMA, "Minutes," June 6, 1940, p. 5.

8. Ibid., March 17, 1941.

9. TCMA, "Minutes of Special Meeting of the Executive Committee," February 10, 1942.

10. "Minutes of Special Meeting of Germiston Members of the TCMA," April 17, 1943, pp. 1–2, 4–5. According to War Measure 6 of 1941, the Secretary of Labour was authorized to fix wages and settle disputes in controlled industries.

11. TCMA, "Minutes," April 29, 1943, p. 1.

12. TCMA, "Minutes of Special General Meeting," May 17, 1943, pp. 3, 6.

13. "Minutes of Meeting of C.M.T. Section of the TCMA," February 21, 1942, p. 4.

14. TCMA, "Minutes," June 6, 1940, p. 5.

15. Ibid., September 10, 1940, p. 125.

16. *Report of the Department of Labour for the Year Ended 31st December 1945* (Pretoria, 1947), U.G. No. 9, 1947; "Problems of the Clothing Industry of South Africa," Memorandum submitted by E. S. Sachs to the Arbitration Tribunal, Clothing Industry, Transvaal, August 1948, SATLC, Dc 8.73.

17. *South African Industry and Trade,* 42, no. 1 (January 1946), 115.

18. Ibid. On the labor shortage in Port Elizabeth, see also Hutton, "Investigation," pp. 45–47.

19. See Hutton, "Investigation," and I. H. R. White, "Investigation on Need for Increased Crèche Facilities for Married Workers in Boot and Shoe Factories in Port Elizabeth," *Personnel Research Bulletin No. 3,* pp. 268–69.

20. *Forward,* August 24, 1951.

21. These incidents are documented in GWU, Bbe 1.1.2.

22. *Guardian,* May 29 and June 5, 1941. The relationship between this group and the Federation of Women Workers, formed in 1938 under the auspices of the GWU, is unclear.

23. Ibid., April 10, 1941. The issues of July 17 and 24, 1941 describe organizing efforts in Cape Town. The overwhelming majority of white women in the industry were classified as Grade 2 workers (out of 3 grades), whereas black men were more numerous among laborers.

24. See accounts in the *Cape Times,* September 24, October 1, 2, 5, 9, 17, and December 3, 1940. At the start of the action, company officials told the newspaper that only about 25 percent of the workers were out, mainly the younger ones.

25. *Garment Worker,* August/September, 1940, p. 11, and October/November, 1940, pp. 2–4, discuss the strikes in the tobacco industry. The issue of November 1940 describes the celebration on p. 5.

26. *Garment Worker,* May/June, 1941, p. 6.

27. Unidentified press clipping, February 18, 1943.

28. The following information comes from Interview of E. J. Burford by Baruch Hirson, London, 1976 [Edited and typed from a transcript by E. J. Burford]. I am grateful to Baruch Hirson for sharing a copy of this interview with me. On sweetworkers in the early 1940s, see also *Garment Worker,* May/June 1941 and Press Clippings, SATLC, Dg. 1942.

29. Burford, Interview.

30. Ibid.

31. Jon Lewis, *Industrialisation and Trade Union Organisation in South Africa, 1924–55: The Rise and Fall of the South African Trades and Labour Council* (Cambridge: Cambridge University Press, 1984), p. 67.

32. *Guardian*, August 21 and 28, 1941.

33. Ibid., July 16, August 6 and 13, 1942. Wages for women rose from the appalling low level of five shillings per week to eight shillings, plus a two shilling cost-of-living allowance. Roussouw thanked E. S. Sachs, Bettie du Toit, and Johanna Cornelius for their assistance.

34. Union of South Africa, "Report No. 303 of the Board of Trade and Industries on the Clothing Industry," Pretoria, December 9, 1947.

35. Quoted in "Report of the Industrial Tribunal to the Honourable Minister of Labour on the Reservation of Work in the Clothing Industry," Pretoria, October 2, 1957, p. 12. In the Cape Province in 1925, 52 percent of pupils went on to Standard 7, whereas by 1943, the number had risen to 77 percent. Those who had not gone beyond Standard 6 tended to supply the majority of white factory workers.

36. Dan O'Meara, *Volkskapitalisme: Class, Capital and Ideology in the Development of Afrikaner Nationalism, 1934–1948* (Cambridge: Cambridge University Press, 1983), discusses some of the evidence for this transformation on p. 220.

37. Union of South Africa, Board of Trade and Industries, "The Textile Manufacturing Industry," Report No. 323, April 23, 1951, pp. 32–37. In 1945 and 1946 Transvaal Textiles, Ltd., experimented with female labor available from munitions plants, according to *South African Industry and Trade* 42, no. 1 (January 1946), 150.

38. Bettie du Toit, *Ukubamba Amadolo: Workers' Struggles in the South African Textile Industry* (London: Onyx Press, 1978), p. 58; "Schedule. National Industrial Council for the Textile Industry of the Union of South Africa. Agreement," p. 4, Dc 8.77, SATLC, TWIU, 1948.

39. See, for example, "Report to the Honourable Minister of Labour by the Wage Board, Textile Industry: King William's Town," August 29, 1952, SATLC, Dc 2.26.

40. *Umsebenzi*, March 12, 1938.

41. *Guardian*, February 27, 1941.

42. Alexandra Women's League, "Features of the Grievances Regarding the Transport Operating Between Alexandra Township and the City of Johannesburg," July 11, 1943, A. B. Xuma Papers, 430711b. I am indebted to Alf Stadler for referring me to this source. Women's part in these protests is discussed later in this chapter.

43. TCMA, "Minutes of Special Meeting of the Executive Committee, Transvaal Clothing Manufacturers' Association," February 15, 1945, p. 4.

44. South Africa, "Report No. 303."

45. Bantu Welfare Trust, "Survey of Resident Bantu Domestic Servants in One Suburb of Johannesburg conducted in September and October 1946," Johannesburg, July 12, 1947, p. 1, SAIRR, File on Domestic Workers 1925–50.

46. Ibid., pp. 5–6. It is important to note women's underrepresentation in the survey.

47. Ibid., pp. 3–6, 10–14.

48. S. P. Viljoen, "Report of the Interdepartmental Committee on Native Juvenile Unemployment on the Witswatersrand and in Pretoria," Pretoria, 1951, p. 11. The Bantu Welfare Trust Survey bears out this observation; only three of the fifty-seven women were born in Johannesburg.

49. Ellen Kuzwayo, "The Role of the African Woman in Towns," South African Institute of Race Relations, Johannesburg, November 22, 1960, RR.207/60.

50. South African Institute of Race Relations, "The Cato Manor Framework," p. 4, RR.66/59.

51. Olive Gibson, *The Cost of Living for Africans: The Results of an Enquiry into the Cost of Living for Africans in the Locations and African Townships in Johannesburg and Alexandra* (Johannesburg: South African Institute of Race Relations, 1954), p. 5.

52. Kuzwayo, "African Woman," p. 2.

53. Ibid.

54. Mia Brandel, "The Needs of African Women," Research Report, February 1955, pp. 128–29.

55. Ethel Wix, *The Cost of Living* (Johannesburg: South African Institute of Race Relations, 1950), pp. 6–7.

56. Ibid., p. 8, based on figures for Johannesburg, Pretoria, and the Reef towns.

57. A. Lynn Saffery and Julian Rollnick, "Social and Economic Position of Unskilled Workers at Kimberley," n.p., n.d., p. 11.

58. C. Kros, "Urban African Women's Organisations, 1935–1956," Africa Perspective, Dissertation Number 3, Johannesburg, n.d.

59. Ibid., pp. 45–50. In interviews in *Drum*, February 1959, several shebeen owners also complained of the need to pay monthly protection money to gangsters and of the sexual pressure from those who saw shebeen queens as "easy."

60. See Joanne Yawitch, "Natal 1959—The Women's Protests," Conference on the History of Opposition in South Africa, (Students) Development Studies Group, January 1978, on the 1959 disturbances in the Durban African area of Cato Manor.

61. A report of a meeting to settle the dispute over bus fares between the bus owners and the people of Alexandra Township in Johannesburg had delegates from five groups, one of them the Alexandra washerwomen. See *Guardian*, November 5, 1942.

62. Tom Lodge, *Black Politics in South Africa since 1945* (London: Longman, 1983), pp. 147–50, and Ken Luckhardt and Brenda Wall, *Organize . . . or Starve!: The History of the South African Congress of Trade Unions* (London: Lawrence and Wishart, 1980), pp. 303–304.

63. Ibid., pp. 277, 280.

64. Baruch Hirson, *Yours for the Union: Class and Community Struggles in South Africa, 1930–1947* (London: Zed Press, 1989), Chapter 11; Alf Stadler, "A Long Way to Walk: Bus Boycotts in Alexandra, 1940–1945," in *Working Papers in Southern African Studies*, vol. 2, ed. P. Bonner (Johannesburg: Ravan Press, 1981), 237; Tom Lodge, " 'We Are Being Punished Because We Are Poor': The Bus Boycotts of Evaton and Alexandra, 1955–1957," in Bonner, *Working Papers*, p. 277; and Baruch Hirson, personal communication, June 26, 1989.

65. H. E. Reitz, "Occupations in Cape Town," M.A. thesis (University of Cape Town, 1962), pp. 49, 51, 52, 55, on flower sellers and pp. 138–41, 144–46, on washerwomen.

66. These statistics come from Amelia Marie Mariotti, "The Incorporation of African Women into Wage Employment in South Africa, 1920–1970," Ph.D. dissertation (University of Connecticut, 1979), pp. 278–87. Mariotti has adjusted the census classifications to make the categories more consistent over time. Figures in the following section come from this source unless otherwise indicated. Most of the increase in the "service" category occurred between 1936 and 1946.

67. Women went from 35.1 percent of clerical workers in 1936 to 48.5 percent in 1951, although only a minute number of men ever became stenographers (207 in 1951, as opposed to 39,429 women).

68. The number of female teachers did not change drastically during this period; in fact, only in 1951 did the figure rise (slightly) above the number in 1921. The number of nurses showed a steady rise, especially between 1936 and 1946 (from 8,497 to 13,957), and then a slight increase to 15,963 in 1951.

69. A rise in the number of coloured household workers, from 68,310 in 1946 to 100,920 in 1960 was the sharpest since 1921. One study of employment patterns in Cape Town found that 40 percent of the coloured women surveyed in one factory had started work in domestic service; but the majority had moved into the factory after a single domestic job. See Sheila van der Horst, *African Workers in Town: A Study of Labour in Cape Town* (Cape Town: Oxford University Press, 1964), p. 54.

70. Union of South Africa, Bureau of Census and Statistics, *Union Statistics for Fifty Years, 1900–1960* (Pretoria, 1960), pp. G-6, 9, 10. Clothing and footwear, 68 percent white in 1933–34, declined to 24 percent white in 1955–56, while textiles, 47 percent white in 1933–34, had dropped to 24 percent white in 1955–56.

71. Mariotti, "Incorporation of African Women," citing Trevor Bell, *Industrial Decentralization in South Africa* (Cape Town: Oxford University Press, 1973), pp. 128–29. The ranking from wage figures was reflected in life expectancy patterns from 1945–47: 66 years for Europeans, 42.5 for coloureds, and 30 for Africans. (The Asian figures give too wide an age range to be meaningful.)

72. Baruch Hirson, *Yours for the Union*, pp. 199–201.

73. Luckhardt and Wall, *Organize . . . or Starve!*, pp. 311–30, describe women's role in SACTU in greater detail. Phyllis Altman, originally an office worker for SACTU, became heavily involved in all aspects of the organization's operation.

74. du Toit, *Ukubamba Amadolo*, pp. 93–94. See *New Age*, December 3, 1959, which attributes the women's dismissal to their union membership.

75. Goldin, *Making Race: The Politics and Economics of Coloured Identity in South Africa* (London: Longman, 1987), pp. 121–22.

76. Lewis, *Industrialisation*, p. 151. Hirson, *Yours for the Union*, discusses a strike in 1942 on p. 97. The name change, from SATUC to TUCSA, occurred in 1962.

9. Solidarity Fragmented

1. These figures come from the Industrial Council for the Clothing Industry, Transvaal, GWU, Bch. 1.

2. See "President's Address" and "Minutes of the Annual General Meeting," Transvaal Clothing Manufacturers' Association, December 1, 1947 and "Minutes of Monthly Meeting of the Executive Committee of the Transvaal Clothing Manufacturers' Association," May 18, 1948. Jon Lewis, *Industrialisation and Trade Union Organisation in South Africa, 1924–55: The Rise and Fall of the South African Trades and Labour Council* (Cambridge: Cambridge University Press, 1984), p. 118, does note the widespread use of incentive bonus schemes, which were popular because they enabled some machinists to increase their earnings substantially.

3. Anna Scheepers, "Trade Unions Face Challenge," address delivered at the 3rd Research Workshop of the Abe Bailey Institute of Interracial Studies, University of Cape Town, January, 1973, pp. 11–12. The successful case was filed on behalf of Christine Okolo; a simultaneous case on behalf of an African man exempt from carrying a pass failed.

4. This is discussed more broadly in Stanley Greenberg, *Race and State in Capitalist Development* (New Haven: Yale University Press, 1980), pp. 284–85.

5. E. S. (Solly) Sachs, *Rebels Daughters* (London: MacGibbon and Kee, 1957), p. 36.

6. Interview by Stanley Greenberg. I am indebted to him for providing me with a transcript.

7. Union of South Africa, Board of Trade and Industries, "Investigation into Manufacturing in the Union of South Africa," Report No. 282, Cape Town, 1945, p. 45.

8. "Memorandum Submitted by the Garment Workers' Union to the Wage

Board Investigating into the Clothing Industry of South Africa," August 1946, pp. 7–8.

9. Ibid., p. 15.

10. See Dan O'Meara, *Volkskapitalisme: Class, Capital and Ideology in the Development of Afrikaner Nationalism, 1934–1948* (Cambridge: Cambridge University Press, 1983), pp. 161–62, 220, for a discussion of these changes in the context of rising Afrikaner nationalism.

11. Ibid., p. 149.

12. This view of Sachs's concerns is central to Leslie Witz's University of the Witwatersrand M.A. thesis, "Solly Sachs: Servant of the Workers," completed in 1984. See the attack on Sachs in *The Spark* 2, no. 6 (June 1936), 14. It is also important to note that professions against "racism" from the late 1930s and early 1940s might be referring to antisemitism or to relations between whites of British and Afrikaner backgrounds rather than to antiblack sentiment. B. M. Touyz makes this point about antisemitism on p. 18 of "White Politics and the Garment Workers' Union 1930–1953," M.A. dissertation (University of Cape Town, 1979).

13. Jack Simons and Ray Simons, *Class and Colour in South Africa 1850–1950* (Harmondsworth: Penguin 1969; repr., London: International Defense and Aid Fund for Southern Africa, 1983), p. 535. Gana Makabeni, head of the black men's Clothing Workers' Union, felt that separate unions gave blacks increased opportunity to assume responsible positions. Albie Sachs, in a recent interview, also argued that, in his father's view, only black workers powerful in their own unions could "destroy the racism in the minds of the white workers." Popular History Trust, p. 384.

14. *Guardian*, September 26, 1940.

15. Sachs, *Rebels Daughters*, pp. 118–19.

16. "Minutes of the First National Conference, Garment Making Trade Unions," Johannesburg, August 23, 1942, reprinted in *Garment Worker*, September/October 1942, pp. 10–14.

17. O'Meara, *Volkskapitalisme*, pp. 161–62, 220.

18. Reports of Hetty du Preez, the No. 2 branch organizer, contain some instances of such conflict. See GWU, Bba 2.3.26.

19. Commission of Inquiry into the Garment Workers' Union, "Statement of Anna Elizabeth Scheepers (Venter)," pp. 10–11, and "Statement of Dulcie M. Hartwell," p. 20, GWU, Bca 3.

20. Evidence presented in the Supreme Court of South Africa (Witwatersrand Local Division), in the matter of Emil Solomon Sachs versus Dr. A. B. du Preez, Johannesburg, October 24, 1945, and Witz, "Solly Sachs," p. 276.

21. "Minutes of the Executive Committee of the No.2 Branch of the Garment Workers' Union," Johannesburg, February 28, 1942, p. 1, GWU, Bbb 1.2.

22. "Minutes," February 28, 1942, p. 2. Sachs also argued in these discussions that once a national union was formed race would no longer be an issue, since the majority of garment workers would be coloured. The conflict over representation eventually led to the temporary suspension of the No. 2 branch in 1944.

23. The issue was discussed in joint executive committee meetings on August 8 and August 14, 1957. During the course of these discussions, officials of the No.1 branch were able to persuade their No.2 branch counterparts that unity was of overwhelming importance. See GWU, Bbb 1.2.

24. "Minutes of the Executive Committee of the No.2 Branch," Johannesburg, January 29 and February 28, 1942, GWU, Bbb 1.2.

25. These issues were discussed respectively in minutes of February 10, 1949, January 29, 1952, and January 21, 1953 and in "Minutes of No. 2 Branch Executive Committee Meeting," Johannesburg, January 29, 1953 and "Minutes of a Special

Executive Committee meeting of the No.2 Branch," Johannesburg, February 12, 1953, GWU, Bbb 1.2.

26. E. S. Sachs, "Report of C.E.C. Re State of Office of No. 2 Branch," January 13, 1951, and Letter from J. Cornelius to Miss H. du Preez, January 26, 1951, GWU, Bba 2.3.26.

27. Industrial Council for the Clothing Industry (Tvl.), "Number of Employees All Factories-Transvaal," GWU, Bch 1.

28. Calculated from statistics in "Report of the Industrial Tribunal to the Honourable Minister of Labour on Reservation of Work in the Clothing Industry," Pretoria, October 2, 1957, p. 22.

29. Most single women now were widows.

30. Garment Workers' Union of South Africa, "Why Is Your Daughter Not a Garment Worker?" Johannesburg, March 1957.

31. Letter to the General Secretary, GWU, from E. Reyneke, TCMA, February 28, 1950, SATLC, Dc 8.87. In 1955, manufacturers discussed at length, but then rejected, a proposal to divide the industry into women's and men's clothing sections, paying lower wages in the latter and employing black workers.

32. Letter from [J. Cornelius] to E. S. Sachs, December 10, 1953, GWU, Bce 2.1.

33. *Garment Worker*, March 12 and 19, April 30, 1954.

34. Letter from [J.Cornelius] to Solly Sachs, March 18, 1954, GWU, Bce 2.1.

35. Letter from [J. Cornelius] to Solly Sachs, April 3, 1954, GWU, Bce 2.1.

36. *Garment Worker*, June 4 and 11, 1954; Scheepers, "Trade Unions," p. 15.

37. Correspondence between the GWU and the Department of Labour, August 30, 1955–March 13, 1956, TUCSA, Memoranda.

38. H. A. F. Barker, *The Economics of the Wholesale Clothing Industry of South Africa* (Johannesburg: Pallas Publications, 1962), p. 387.

39. It is interesting to note that, despite the employers' claim that wages had become too high from a competitive standpoint, workers no longer were as uniformly well off as they had been in 1946. In that year the hourly wage rates of all workers were well above the retail price index, whereas by 1958 the wages of many fell substantially below it.

40. Considerably more African women than coloured women worked as pressers, 29.5 percent and 13 percent respectively, whereas the percentages as general workers were more even, 24 percent and 21 percent. Of the general workers, 3.5 percent were white women. See Clothing Industry, Transvaal, "Analysis of Employees by Occupation, Race and Sex on Reserved Jobs as at August 1957," and "Analysis of Employees by Occupation, Race and Sex on Unreserved Jobs as at August 1957," GWU, Bba 2.3.15.

41. Barker, *Wholesale Clothing Industry*, pp. 150–52. The rates for the main classes of work were about 56 percent lower for men and 49 percent lower for women than those in Natal District No. 2 (Pietermaritzburg and Lower Tugela), the lowest paying areas covered by an Industrial Council agreement.

42. Between 1952 and 1956 at least 182 clothing establishments withdrew from the Transvaal.

43. Letter to the Honourable Senator J. de Klerk, Minister of Labour, from E. F. Else and H. Cornelius, October 11, 1956, GWU, Bba, 5.1.3.4.

44. *Garment Worker*, April 20, 1956.

45. Ibid., June 22, 1956.

46. Barker, *Wholesale Clothing Industry*, p. 387.

47. "Report on the Reservation of Work," p. 15.

48. "Second Annual Conference of the South African Congress of Trade Unions Held at No. 3 Trades Hall," Johannesburg, April 12–14, 1957, Carter-Karis Collection, 2:LS2:30/7.

49. Ray Adler, "The Garment Workers," *Liberation* 27 (September 26, 1957), 26.

50. "Extracts from 105th Meeting of the Central Executive Committee," April 16, 1956, GWU, Bba.1.

51. Ray Alexander and H. J. Simons, *Job Reservation and the Trade Unions* (Cape: Enterprise, 1959), p. 32.

52. "Report and Recommendation by the Industrial Tribunal to the Honourable Minister of Labour on Reservation of Work in the Clothing Industry," February 11, 1960, p. 7.

53. *New Statesman and Nation*, August 4, 1951.

54. Letter from [J. Cornelius] to Solly Sachs, December 10, 1953, GWU, Bce 2.1.

55. Letter from [J. Cornelius] to Solly Sachs, March 18, 1954, GWU, Bce 2.1.

56. Touyz, "White Politics," p. 173 observes that nearly one third of the opposition votes came from Germiston/East Rand. Because of multiracial voting, it is difficult to isolate the white vote on the rest of the Rand.

57. The "Minutes of a Meeting of the C.E.C. and the No. 2 Branch Executive Committee," February 17, 1953, GWU, Baa 2.2 suggest the pressure from the number one branch to avoid participating collectively in organizations "outside the trade union movement."

58. Industrial Legislation Commission of Enquiry, Pretoria, July 28, 1950, "Minutes of Proceedings," pp. 13462–63.

59. "Minutes of an Executive Committee Meeting of the No. 2 Branch," Johannesburg, April 6 and May 19, 1949, GWU, Bbb 1.2. The branch joined the ANC on behalf of its African members.

60. Cherryl Walker, *Women and Resistance in South Africa* (London: Onyx Press, 1982), pp. 139, 155; "Conference to Promote Women's Rights," Trades Hall, Johannesburg, Saturday April 17, 1954, Carter-Karis Collection, 2:WF1:47/3.

61. Helen Joseph, *If This Be Treason* (London: Andre Deutsch, 1963), p. 165. The Garment Workers' Union of African Women was created in 1953 when a new law prohibited African membership in racially mixed trade unions.

62. South African Congress of Trade Unions, "Annual Report and Balance Sheet for the Year Ended March, 1957," presented to the 2nd Annual National Conference, Johannesburg, April 12–14, 1957, Carter-Karis Collection, 2:LS2:30/8.

63. *Golden City Post*, November 23, 1958, Leo Kuper Papers, Ser. 4, Box 20, "Status of Women." See also "Interview with Lucy Mvubelo by G.M.G.," November 1973, Carter-Karis Collection, 2:XM1:70, and "The National Union of Clothing Workers: Interview with Mrs. Lucy Mvubelo General Secretary," *South African Labour Bulletin* 5, no. 3 (October 1979), 97–100. Both interviews note that she disapproved of the close relationship that developed between FOFATUSA and the Pan-Africanist Congress. Yet, two days before the fateful demonstration at Sharpeville on March 21, 1960, Mvubelo presided over a FOFATUSA-sponsored meeting supporting the planned PAC action.

10. Food and Canning Workers at the Cape

1. Since the two branches, forcibly separated by the state under conditions described in chapter 11, continued to consider themselves a single union, references to "the union" should be taken as indicating both branches.

2. Richard Goode, "For a Better Life: The Food and Canning Workers Union 1941 to 1975," B.A. Hons. thesis (University of Cape Town, 1983), pp. 3–5. Other work on the Food and Canning Workers' Union includes: D. Y. Soudien, "The Food and Canning Workers Union: The Organisation of the Food and Canning Workers Union during the South African Congress of Trade Union Years," B.A. Hons. dissertation (University of the Witwatersrand, 1981); Mark Stein, "The Food

and Canning Workers' Union, 1950–1960," University of York, Centre for Southern African Studies, March 26–28, 1979; and Di Cooper, Untitled paper, 1977; Dennis Rubel, Untitled manuscript, 1989. Three other works refer more specifically to women's experience: J. Schreiner, "Thina singoomama asinakubulawa," [We Are the Women and We Shall Not Be Killed], B.A. Hons. dissertation (University of Cape Town, 1982); Nomatamsanqua Nomvete, "The Participation of the Female Working Class in Trade Union Struggles in South Africa from 1950," Occasional Papers No. 6, Centre of African Studies, Edinburgh University, 1984; and J. Schreiner, "Women Working For Their Freedom: FCWU and AFCWU and the Woman Question," M.A. thesis (University of Cape Town, 1986). My thanks to Ray Simons for access to the Rubel manuscript.

3. Goode, "Better Life," Table 2, and *Guardian*, September 4, 1941, citing a *Star* article of July 6. In addition, during the five years of the war, the number of factories in the industry nearly doubled.

4. Union of South Africa, Board of Trade and Industries, "The Fruit and Vegetable Canning Industry," Report No. 296, Pretoria, 1947, p. 7.

5. Goode, "Better Life," pp. 7, 12, 16, 19, 20. Similar concentration took place in the fish industry at this time. For a self-congratulatory piece on the L.K.B, see *The South African Food Trades Journal* (November 1949), pp. 23–34. Hermann Gilomee discusses the active support of Paarl and Stellenbosch farmers for Afrikaner nationalist projects in the 1920s and 1930s in "The Beginnings of Afrikaner Ethnic Consciousness, 1850–1915," in *The Creation of Tribalism in Southern Africa*, ed. Leroy Vail (Berkeley: University of California Press; London: James Currey, 1989), pp. 44–45.

6. Union of South Africa, *Report of Commission of Inquiry Regarding the Cape Coloured Population of the Union* (Pretoria, 1937), U.G. 54–1937, pp. 69–70.

7. Ibid., p. 69.

8. Ibid., p. 123.

9. Food and Canning Workers Union, "Search for a Workable Relationship," *South African Labour Bulletin* 7, no. 8 (July 1982), 56.

10. Native Laws Commission of Enquiry, "Minutes of Evidence," vol. 5, Evidence of H. J. Simons, Cape Town, September 19, 1946, p. 293. My thanks to Deborah Posel for this reference.

11. Ibid., p. 15.

12. Tom Lodge, *Black Politics in South Africa since 1945* (London: Longman, 1983), pp. 45–60.

13. Ibid., p. 55, and Tom Lodge, "Political Mobilisation During the 1950s: An East London Case Study," in *Race, Class and Nationalism in Twentieth-Century South Africa*, ed. Shula Marks and Stanley Trapido (London: Longman, 1987), pp. 330–31.

14. *Guardian*, December 15, 1939.

15. *Food and Canning Workers' Union* 1 (January 15, 1942), 3, and Union of South Africa, Department of Social Welfare, "Report of a Committee of Enquiry Appointed to Enquire into Conditions Existing on the Cape Flats and Similarly Affected Areas in the Cape Division," 1942, p. 45. The minimum effective wage was £3 19s. 11d. for women and £4 6s. 8d. for men.

16. *Guardian*, June 18, 1942.

17. Ibid., December 15, 1939. See also August 21, 1941 and "Elizabeth Mafekeng," FSAW, F (1).

18. *Cape Times*, November 29, 1941.

19. "Report on Organization of African Workers in Port Elizabeth by A. Lynn Saffery for the South African Committee on Industrial Relations," Johannesburg, April 17, 1942, RR 63/42, A. L. Saffery Papers.

20. *Guardian*, January 8, 1942.

21. FCWU, "Minutes of Second Quarterly Branch Delegates Conference," Cape Town, July 6, 1952, p. 9.

22. Rubel, manuscript, chapter 4, p. 3.

23. "Quarterly Branch Minutes," p. 8.

24. FCWU, "Circular Letter no. 15/48," October 18, 1948. By the late 1950s, only food workers in large urban centers could collect unemployment benefits. From 1946 to 1951, however, those in the country areas had contributed to the fund; they were excluded from benefits under the Unemployment Insurance Act of 1949. The Minister of Labour revealed the political pressures to which he was responding when he ruled in 1959 that unemployed seasonal workers in canning "must seek work on the farms." Quoted in *New Age*, October 22, 1959.

25. This alternative work is mentioned in several different sources: Richard Goode, "Struggle and Strikes in the Cannery: The Great Wolseley Strike," unpublished paper, Cape Town, p. 6; Frances Baard, personal communication, January 27, 1984; and "Elizabeth Mafekeng."

26. According to BTI, "Fruit and Vegetable Canning," p. 7, during the war, whereas the number of Europeans increased by 139 percent, the number of "non-Europeans" rose by 521 percent, shifting the ratio from 3.2 to 1 in 1938/38 to 8.3 to 1 in 1944/45.

27. The statistics are from "Langeberg Kooperasie Beperk, List of employees present and absent on 27/1/48," ARB 1052/679.

28. Percentages in this section of the paper are calculated from data in Goode, "Better Life," Table 2.

29. The proportion of coloured workers would have remained higher in the Cape than elsewhere.

30. By the late 1950s a Grade 5 category had been added; during negotiations, according to the *Cape Times*, employees argued for an absence of sex or age differentiation for this category because employers were hiring lower-paid females and juveniles "for work that should be done by men."

31. These differentials are calculated from FCWU lists for the districts of the Cape, Wynberg, and Simonstown, 1947, SATLC, Dd 9.39.

32. R. Lan, "Objections of the Food & Canning Workers' Union to the Wage Board's Recommendations for the Metal Containers and Allied Products Industry and the Preserved Food Industry in the Union of South Africa," November 25, 1955, p. 1.

33. FCWU, Lists, 1947. The other group of women in the industry, probably predominantly white, worked as clerical employees. Although beginning at the same wage as male clerks (interestingly, £1 16s. 11d., less than that of women moulders and packers), by their sixth year, as qualified employees, their wages of £3 9s. 6d. were only 60 percent of those of qualified men.

34. Between 1945 and 1960, the ratio of lower paid to higher paid workers increased, according to Board of Trade and Industries, "Investigation into the Fruit and Vegetable Canning Industry," Report No. 676, August 1960, p. 45.

35. *Food and Canning Workers' Union* 4, no. 2 (August 1945), 2–3.

36. Frances Baard as told to Barbie Schreiner, *My Spirit Is Not Banned* (Harare: Zimbabwe Publishing House, 1986), p. 23.

37. Goode, "Struggle and Strikes," pp. 7–8.

38. Rex Close, *New Life* (Cape Town: Food and Canning Workers' Union, 1950), pp. 27–32, and FCWU, "Proud Record of Ray Alexander."

39. "Proud Record."

40. "Minutes of Special General Meeting," October 3, 1953.

41. See Goode, "Better Life," for a detailed chronology of these developments.

42. FCWU, "Annual Report," submitted to the 13th Annual National Conference, Cape Town, August 28–29, 1954.

43. Baard, *My Spirit,* p. 23.

44. *Guardian,* September 4, 1941.

45. Ibid., August 20, 1942.

46. *Cape Times,* November 29, 1941.

47. *Guardian,* December 23, 1941, and February 12, 1942.

48. Muriel Horrell, *South Africa's Non-White Workers* (Johannesburg: South African Institute of Race Relations, 1956), p. 82.

49. Goode, "Better Life," p. 112.

50. *Guardian,* July 22, 1943. The next determination for the industry, in 1958, recommended wage rates lower than those most employers were paying.

51. *Guardian,* January 13, 1944.

52. Ibid., January 27, 1944.

53. Letters from R. Lan to the Divisional Inspector, Labour Department, January 11, 1954, January 18, 1954, January 20, 1958, SATLC, Dc 8.108. McKenzie's life illuminates the ambiguities of efforts at racial classification. Born a Damara (a group classified as coloured), she spoke Xhosa and lived as an African. From Rubel, manuscript, chapter 4, p. 3.

54. Letter from Oscar Mpetha, General Secretary, to Mrs. Francis Baart [*sic*], July 12, 1951, RA/VY, REF. AFCWU/127/51, and Letter from O. Mpetha to the Branch Secretary, AFCWU, Port Elizabeth, September 25, 1951, OM/VY, REF. AFCWU/51.

55. See "Statement by Food & Canning Workers Union Relating to the Contraventions of the Industrial Conciliation Act by Messrs. Wolseley Fruit Canning Company of Wolseley," p. 1; *Cape Times,* December 15 and 17, 1953; Goode, "Struggle and Strikes," p. 46; Goode, "Better Life," p. 88; *Morning Star/Ikwezi Lomso* 2, no. 2 (February/March 1954), 2; and FCWU, "Annual Report," August 28–29, 1954, p. 6. Six of eight members of the strike committee were women.

56. Ray Simons (Alexander), Interview, Lusaka, Zambia, July 20, 1989.

57. Letter from Ray Alexander, Cape Town, September 8, 1953.

58. Baard, *My Spirit,* p. 25.

59. Union of South Africa, *Report of the Commission of Enquiry into Policy Relating to the Protection of Industries* (Pretoria, 1958–59), U.G. 36/1958, p. 58.

60. L. Abrahams, "Memorandum Submitted to the Industrial Tribunal: Labour Position in the Western Province in Terms of Section 17 (8)(g) of the Industrial Conciliation Act, 1956," November 14, 1958, p. 1.

61. FCWU "Annual Report," September 12–13, 1959, p. 2.

62. Goode, "Better Life," p. 105.

63. "Annual Report," 1959, p. 10 and "Minutes of Branch Executive Committee and Shop Stewards Meeting of FCWU, Paarl Branch," April 22, 1959.

64. "Minutes of Management Committee Meeting, FCWU, Zuider Paarl," November 29, 1959, p. 4.

65. See "Minutes of Special Management Committee Meeting, FCWU," April 28, 1959, p. 1, for an account of the attack.

11. Standing United

1. FCWU, "Circular Letter No. 38/45," December 3, 1945.

2. FCWU, "Annual Report," January 1948.

3. Cited in letter from Ray Alexander to Oscar Mpetha, Cape Town, August 20, 1951, RA/VY, REF, FCWU/906/BL. Apparently, the Department of Labour in Cape Town had been unwilling to make such a ruling; the judgment regarding African women came from the Port Elizabeth office, according to "Minutes of Meeting of the Central Executive Committee," September 9, 1951.

4. Letter, Alexander to Mpetha.

5. Frances Baard as told to Barbie Schreiner, *My Spirit is Not Banned* (Harare: Zimbabwe Publishing House, 1986), p. 24.

6. Ibid., p. 29.

7. Ray Alexander, "Trade Unionism in South Africa," *Discussion* 1, no. 6 (December 1952), 35–38. The FCWU in Johannesburg, which was a separate union until 1951, did belong to the CNETU and comprised 40 percent of its membership in 1950.

8. "Annual Report by the Acting General Secretary, L. Abrahams," submitted to the 16th Annual Conference of the FCWU, Langvlei, Paarl, September 14–15, 1957, p. 10.

9. "How to Organise for the £1 a Day Campaign," attached to "FCWU Circular Letter No. 23/57."

10. Jenny Schreiner, "Women Working for their Freedom: FCWU and AFCWU and the Woman Question," M.A. thesis (University of Cape Town, 1986), p. 68.

11. FCWU, "Circular Letter No. 2/57," p. 5.

12. Willie Hofmeyr, "Rural Popular Organisation and its Problems: Struggles in the Western Cape, 1929–1930," *Africa Perspective* 22 (1983), 28–30, 32, 47, and Ian Goldin, "The Reconstitution of Coloured Identity in the Western Cape," in *The Politics of Race, Class and Nationalism in Twentieth-Century South Africa*, ed. Shula Marks and Stanley Trapido (London: Longman, 1987), pp. 164–65.

13. FCWU, "Minutes of Adjourned Branch Executive Committee Meeting, Zuider Paarl," June 17, 1954.

14. Jenny Schreiner, "Thina Singoomama asinakubulawa [We Are the Women and We Shall Not Be Killed]," B.A. Hons. dissertation (University of Cape Town, 1982), p. 87.

15. FCWU, "Annual Report," submitted to the Annual Conference, August 27–28, 1955, p. 11.

16. Schreiner, "Thina Singoomama," pp. 116, 129.

17. M. Horrell, comp., *A Survey of Race Relations in South Africa* (Johannesburg: South African Institute of Race Relations, 1956/57), p. 71.

18. Schreiner, "Thina Singoomama," p. 39.

19. Tom Lodge, *Black Politics in South Africa since 1945* (London: Longman, 1983), pp. 43–45.

20. Tom Lodge, "Political Mobilisation During the 1950s: An East London Case Study," in Marks and Trapido, *Race, Class and Nationalism*, pp. 315, 318.

21. Schreiner, "Thina Singoomama," pp. 88–89.

22. Ibid, pp. 129–39.

23. D. Y. Soudien, "The Food and Canning Workers Union: The Organisation of the Food and Canning Workers Union during the South African Congress of Trade Union Years," B.A. Hons. dissertation (University of the Witwatersrand, 1981), pp. 84–86. The description of the incident at L.K.B., Port Elizabeth comes from *New Age*, November 29, 1956.

24. Baard, *My Spirit*, p. 49.

25. Soudien, "Food and Canning Workers Union," pp. 84–86.

26. Ibid., pp. 85.

27. Schreiner, "Thina Singoomama," p. 105.

28. See Julia Wells, "Why Women Rebel: A Comparative Study of South African Women's Resistance in Bloemfontein (1913) and Johannesburg (1958)," *Journal of Southern African Studies* 10, no. 1 (October 1983), 55–70.

29. Based on a survey of twenty-five households entitled "How Do the People Live," November 1953.

30. "Peasant Women in the Union of South Africa," report presented on behalf of the FSAW, n.p., n.d., p. 11, quoting from a letter by the FCWU to the Secretary for Public Health, FSAW, AD 1137, Aj 3.1.

31. Letter from C. Vink to the FCWU, Kraaifontein, October 9, 1954.

32. Ray Alexander, "Our Case for Increased Wages," handwritten notes, November 16, 1953.

33. Beata Lipman, *We Make Freedom: Women in South Africa* (London: Pandora Press, 1984), pp. 89–90.

34. "Minutes of the Food & Canning Workers' Union Special Conference," Paarl, November 25, 1955, p. 3.

35. FCWU, "Circular Letter no.19/57," p. 4.

36. Letter from R. Lan to the Divisional Inspector, Labour Department, March 8, 1954. One of the girls was twelve and the other, a fifteen year old, also had been at work the previous year.

37. FCWU, "Annual Report," submitted on September 8–9, 1956, p. 11.

38. "Report of Conciliation Board Meeting between Our Union and Jax Canning Co.," September 1, 1954.

39. Alexander, "Increased Wages."

40. Letter from Liz Abrahams, Acting General Secretary, to J. Fillies, October 15, 1956.

41. Quoted in FCWU, "Circular Letter No. 2/57," p. 3.

42. Ian Goldin, *Making Race: The Politics and Economics of Coloured Identity in South Africa* (London: Longman, 1987), p. 119.

43. *Guardian*, January 21, 1943.

44. *Morning Star/Ikwezi Lomso* 2, no. 3 (July 1954), 3.

45. *Guardian*, June 29, 1943.

46. Ibid., April 15, 1943.

47. Ibid., July 23, 1942.

48. Letter to the Chairman, Divisional Council, from the General Secretary, June 6, 1952. See *Cape Times*, June 2, 1952, for a description of the incident.

49. Interview, Ray Simons (Alexander), Lusaka, Zambia, July 20–21, 1989.

50. Letter from the Branch Secretary to the Mayor, Port Elizabeth, October 16, 1951.

51. Letter from Ray Alexander to the Secretary of Education, Cape Town, August 12, 1952.

52. Letter from Ray Alexander to the Postmaster General, Cape Town, October 11, 1952.

53. Letter from Ray Alexander to the Secretary, Paarl Transport and Services, Ltd., August 3, 1951.

54. "Minutes of Central Executive Committee Meeting," August 31, 1952. The Minister concerned with the matter referred to the minimum standards for "non-European" housing, which did not require the provision of ceilings.

55. Letter from Ray Alexander to the Branch Secretary, Zuider Paarl, March 3, 1953. Another crèche was being established in Noorder Paarl for employees of Associated Canners, Ltd. Schreiner, "Women Working," p. 130, notes, however, that the minutes of a General Meeting at Paarl on June 17, 1954, suggest that the Zuider Paarl crèche never went into operation.

56. Ordinarily, two circular letters per month were issued to branch secretaries, but on occasion there were as many as five.

57. *The Food and Canning Worker* 3, no. 11 (July 1944).

58. Letter from Ray Alexander to the Branch Secretary, Zuider Paarl, March 3, 1953.

59. "Minutes of the 8th Annual Conference," Cape Town, January 7–8, 1950, p. 11.

60. Schreiner, "Thina singoomama."

61. "Union's Memorandum and Evidence to the Women's Legal Disabilities Commission," *Food and Canning Worker's Union* 6 (May 1947), 4–6. Representatives

were Janie Lenton, Eva Carollisson, Betty Kearns, Joyce Ehrenreich, Rahima Ally, and Ray Alexander.

62. Ibid., p. 5.

63. Ibid., p. 6.

64. Interview by C. Sideris and D. Cachalia, Johannesburg, July 15, 1982, SAIRR Oral Archive No. 16, p. 23. I am indebted to F. Baard and the South African Institute of Race Relations for permission to use the transcript of this interview.

65. See, for example, Letter to Mr. W. Gant, Director, H. Jones & Co., from L. Abrahams, Acting General Secretary, April 30, 1956.

66. Letter to the Divisional Inspector, Department of Labour, from the Secretary, January 28, 1948.

67. "Proposed Agreement, 1949," p. 3, SATLC, AH 646/Dd 9.56.

68. FCWU, "Circular Letter No. 18/48," Cape Town, December 22, 1948, p. 1.

69. For one of the early discussions of the issue, see FCWU, "Minutes of Meeting of 1st Quarterly Branch Delegates Conference," Cape Town, April 6, 1952, p. 7.

70. FCWU, "Minutes of Management Committee Meeting," June 14, 1959, p. 3. In 1956, workers at several different factories argued unsuccessfully for double pay for night shift work.

71. FCWU, "Circular Letter No. 25/52," p. 4.

72. FCWU, "Minutes of Meeting of the 1st Quarterly Branch Delegates Conference," Cape Town, April 6, 1952, p. 7.

73. "Minutes of the Food and Canning Workers' Union, Paarl Branch," September 17, 1956.

74. Letter to the Divisional Inspector, Department of Labour, from L. Abrahams, June 6, 1956.

75. Letter to Ivan L. Walker, Secretary for Labour, from the Secretary, August 27, 1942. The Factories Act of 1941 denied benefits to seasonal workers; benefits were extended to them in October, 1942, only after an intense letter-writing campaign organized by the FCWU.

76. See, for example, FCWU, "Annual Report by the Executive Secretary," Cape Town, January 7–8, 1950, and FCWU, "Minutes of Meeting of the Central Executive Committee," Cape Town, March 9, 1952, p. 5.

77. FCWU, "Minutes of the Central Executive Committee Meeting," Cape Town, September 18, 1949.

78. FCWU, "Replies Submitted to Questionnaire Received from the Industrial Legislation Commission," Cape Town, n.d., p. 2.

79. FCWU, "Minutes of the 8th Annual Conference," Cape Town, January 7–8, 1950, pp. 8, 11.

80. FCWU, "Minutes of the Paarl Branch Executive Committee Meeting," January, 1955 and October 16, 1955.

81. Richard Goode, "Struggle and Strikes in the Cannery: The Great Wolseley Strike," paper presented at the Conference on the History of the Western Cape, University of Cape Town, 1987, p. 47.

82. Simons, Interview.

83. Letter from L. Abrahams to the Divisional Inspector, Department of Labour, November 16, 1960.

84. FCWU, "List of Committee Members and Addresses," [1952]. The three officers all were married women.

85. AFCWU, "List of Committee Members and Addresses," [1952]. Four of five of the women were married and all lived in New Brighton. Frances Baard was at that time the treasurer.

86. *Rand Daily Mail* (hereafter *RDM*), November 10, 1959. De Wet Nel, Minister of Bantu Administration and Development, had signed the banishment order.

87. FSAW F(1). See also *The Star* and the *Cape Times* of November 10.

88. Interview with Frances Baard, Mabopane, June 24, 1983 and Interview by C. Sideris and D. Cachalia.

89. *Guardian*, September 30, 1943.

90. Letter from L. Abrahams, General Secretary, to the Divisional Inspector, Department of Labour, March 31, 1959.

91. Both Liz Abrahams and Frances Baard have mentioned this problem in interviews.

92. Simons, Interview.

93. Goode, "Struggle and Strikes," p. 47, suggests this as one of the reasons for men's relative lack of involvement.

94. As the African men working in the Western Cape increasingly became migrants during the 1950s, it is likely that their level of union participation declined. Those who lost their jobs faced deportation from the area.

95. Letter to the Joint Secretary, South African Trades & Labour Council, from R. Alexander, Cape Town, November 24, 1952.

12. Never Far from Home

1. Anna Gertrude Weiss, "The Cape Coloured Woman: Within an Industrial Community and at Home," B.Soc.Sci. thesis (University of Cape Town, 1950), p. 5. At the time she wrote this thesis, Weiss had worked for three and a half years as the personnel welfare officer in a Cape Town clothing factory.

2. Pierre L. van den Berghe, *Caneville: The Social Structure of a South African Town* (Middletown, Conn.: Wesleyan University Press, 1964), p. 193.

3. B. A. Pauw, *The Second Generation: A Study of the Family among Urbanized Bantu in East London* (Cape Town: Oxford University Press, 1964), pp. 15–16.

4. E. M. Preston-Whyte, "The Making of a Townswoman? The Process and Dilemma of Rural-Urban Migration amongst African Women in Southern Natal," Papers from the First Congress of the Association for Sociologists in South Africa, University of Natal, Durban [1973], p. 283.

5. Ellen Hellmann, "The African Family Today," Conference on African Family Life, Johannesburg, November 18 and 25, 1967, Jean Sinclair Papers, AD 1457, C3.

6. See, for example, Monica Wilson and Archie Mafeje, *Langa: A Study of Social Groups in an African Township* (Cape Town: Oxford University Press, 1963), p. 81, and Laura Longmore, *The Dispossessed: A Study of the Sex Life of Bantu Women in Urban Areas in and around Johannesburg* (London: Jonathon Cape), p. 119.

7. Longmore, *The Dispossessed*, p. 119.

8. Wilson and Mafeje, *Langa*, p. 82.

9. Ellen Kuzwayo, "The Role of the African Woman in Towns," Johannesburg, South African Institute of Race Relations, Johannesburg, November 22, 1960, p. 2, RR.207/60.

10. Ibid., p. 4.

11. See Claire Robertson and Iris Berger, "Introduction," in *Women and Class in Africa*, ed. Claire Robertson and Iris Berger (New York: Holmes and Meier, 1986), p. 17.

12. Pauw, *Second Generation*, p. 33.

13. H. J. Simons, *African Women: Their Legal Status in South Africa* (Evanston: Northwestern University Press, 1968), p. 74.

14. Pauw, *Second Generation*, p. 149.

15. Hellmann, "African Family," p. 8, probably citing figures from a 1966 survey. This difference certainly relates to the policy of granting houses only to men.

16. Wilson and Mafeje, *Langa*, p. 82.

17. In the mid-1960s, for example, only fifty-two crèches were in operation in Soweto, with a population of 600,000, and only four in Alexandra Township, with 55,000 people. Not surprisingly, all had lengthy waiting lists. The figures come from Deborah Mabiletsa, "The Working Mother," presented to the Conference on African Family Life, Johannesburg, 1967, p. 2, Jean Sinclair Papers, C3.

18. Mabiletsa, "Working Mother," p. 4.

19. Simons, *African Women*, p. 282. Only those women born in or lawfully residing in a city continuously for at least fifteen years had the right to remain, although wives and daughters of qualified men were likely to be able to stay provided they had entered lawfully and continued to live with the qualified man. See Julia Wells, "Passes and Bypasses: Freedom of Movement for African Women under the Urban Areas Act of South Africa," in *African Women and the Law: Historical Perspectives*, ed. Margaret Jean Hay and Marcia Wright, Boston University Papers on Africa, no. 7 (Boston, 1982) on the earlier history of controls on women's movement.

20. Simons, *African Women*, p. 74.

21. Mia Brandel, "The Needs of African Women," Research Report, February 1955, p. 129. The social prestige of factory work at the Cape during the 1940s and 1950s is similarly described by Rosemary Ridd in "Where Women Must Dominate: Response to Oppression in a South African Urban Community," in *Women and Space: Ground Rules and Social Maps*, ed. Shirley Ardener (London: Croom Helm, 1981), p. 92. She observes that women recall the factory work of their teenage years "as though it were a finishing school."

22. Weiss, "Cape Coloured Woman," page numbers are illegible throughout much of the thesis. Unless otherwise indicated, the material in the following section comes from this source.

23. This section comes from the budget data rather than from the discussion of the poorest families, a section impossible to decipher in the microfiche copy available to me.

24. June Stevenson, "An Investigation of Absenteeism and Its Causes among Coloured Women Workers in a Section of the Cape Clothing Industry," Ph.D. thesis (University of Cape Town, 1969). Unlike Weiss's study, which was limited to a single factory, Stevenson surveyed women operatives in seven factories during the year 1964.

25. Ibid., pp. 23, 226–27.

26. Ibid., pp. 251, 321.

27. This section is based on sixteen interviews conducted primarily with women who began working in Johannesburg factories during the 1940s and 1950s. Most were African garment workers (one of whom began work somewhat later under more unique circumstances), but four were coloured; two worked in food and canning factories, one in Port Elizabeth, the other in Johannesburg. Although three of the women became national union leaders, their earlier life histories are quite typical. These women were interviewed in their offices; most others in two factories whose owners very kindly allowed me the time and space to interview. Three interviews were conducted in private homes. One was conducted not by me, but by researchers working with the Oral History Project of the African Studies Institute, University of the Witwatersrand. I am grateful to the project director, Charles van Onselen, for allowing me to cite this material. All but two of the women had no objection to their names being used. (One requested anonymity during the initial interview, another in response to a recent follow-up letter from me.) The women who did not wish to be identified are referred to by pseudonyms.

28. One woman only completed Standard 5 (7th grade), while another com-

pleted two years of the secondary school or Junior Certificate program. Only one of the women had little schooling, having completed only Standard 1 (3rd grade). Whether this small sample is representative remains to be investigated. Lucy Mvubelo, in an interview on June 17, 1983, observed that she was atypical of women in the industry, and that many of them were completely uneducated.

29. On the history of this institution, see Heather Hughes, " 'A Lighthouse for African Womanhood': Inanda Seminary, 1869–1945," in *Women and Gender in Southern Africa*, ed. Cherryl Walker (London: James Currey, 1989).

30. Only one of the African women came from a more predominantly peasant area, the Herschel District of the Transkei, and two of the coloured women came from rural areas of the Cape.

31. See Deborah Posel, "Doing Business With the Pass Laws: Influx Control Policy and the Interests of Manufacturing and Commerce in South Africa in the 1950s," Seminar on the Societies of Southern Africa in the 19th and 20th Centuries, University of London, February 27, 1987, for further discussion of these hiring patterns.

32. Frances Baard as told to Barbie Schreiner, *My Spirit Is Not Banned* (Harare: Zimbabwe Publishing House, 1986), pp. 17, 20.

33. This is an important theme in Valdo Pons's study of commercial workers, "A Social Investigation of Female Workers and A Related Study of their Absenteeism," M.S.S. thesis (University of Cape Town, 1949).

34. Statistics come from Transvaal Clothing Industry, Medical Aid Society, Secretary's Report, 1957, Table 4.

35. Interview, Johannesburg, July 1, 1983.

36. Interview, Johannesburg, June 28, 1983.

37. On age differentials in marriage and the disproportionate number of widows, see Simons, *African Women*, p. 70, and Monica Wilson, "Xhosa Marriages in Historical Perspective," in *Essays on African Marriage in Southern Africa*, ed. Eileen Jensen Krige and John L. Comaroff (Cape Town and Johannesburg: Juta and Co., 1981), pp. 142–43. Simons also observes on p. 71 that the death rate for men probably is higher than for women because men are more exposed to industrial accidents and disease and to violence.

38. Interview, Johannesburg, June 28, 1983.

39. Interview, Johannesburg, June 28, 1983.

40. Interview, Johannesburg, June 28, 1983.

41. Ethel McCallum, Johannesburg, June 28, 1983.

42. Interview, Sinah Jacobs, Johannesburg, June 28, 1983.

43. Interview, Olga Williams, Johannesburg, June 28, 1983.

44. Interview, June 30, 1983.

45. Interview, Elizabeth Nkadimeng, Johannesburg, June 30, 1983. The phrase comes from the title of Marks's book, *The Ambiguities of Dependence in South Africa: Class, Nationalism, and the State in Twentieth-Century Natal* (Baltimore: The Johns Hopkins University Press, 1986).

46. Interview, August 20, 1982.

47. Interview, June 30, 1983.

48. Interview, Johannesburg, June 28, 1983. Had these interviews been conducted more recently, different attitudes toward politics might have been expressed.

49. Interview, Johannesburg, June 28, 1983.

50. Interview, Johannesburg, June 28, 1983.

51. Interview.

52. Emma Mashinini, *Strikes Have Followed Me All My Life: A South African Autobiography* (London: The Women's Press, 1989), p. 16.

53. Baard, *My Spirit*, pp. 22–23. Ray Simons (Alexander) relates the incident slightly differently, recalling that she emphasized the work they had to do after church was over.

54. Interview, Johannesburg, June 28, 1983.

55. Interview, Johannesburg, June 28, 1983.

56. Interview, Harriet Phiri, Johannesburg, June 28, 1983.

57. Husbands often paid the rent since houses were usually in their names.

58. Interview, July 1, 1983.

13. City and Periphery, 1960–1980

1. Ian Goldin, *Making Race: The Politics and Economics of Coloured Identity in South Africa* (London: Longman, 1987) p. 128 sees the record rates of growth between 1962 and 1974 as a partial reflection of government success in overcoming the resistance of black workers.

2. Jacklyn Cock, "Introduction," *South African Labour Bulletin*, 9, no. 3 (December 1983), 3.

3. Hilda Bernstein, *For Their Triumphs & for Their Tears: Women in Apartheid South Africa* (London: International Defence and Aid Fund for Southern Africa, 1985), p. 18.

4. Douglas Hindson, in "Conditions of Labour Supply and Employment of African Workers in Urban Based Industries in South Africa, 1946–1975," prepared for the Workshop on Unemployment and Labour Reallocation, University of Natal, Pietermaritzburg, March 18–19, 1977, p. 21, discusses opposing views on the significance of this division.

5. The Bantu Laws Amendment Act of 1964 provided for a gradual end to the labor tenant system, under which African families were able to work for a farmer for part of the year in return for the right to live on the farm and, usually, to have a piece of land for pasture and cultivation. The system, prevailing particularly in the Transvaal and Natal, was abolished in 1979.

6. According to 1977 statistics, in Johannesburg, 47 percent of African women over the age of 16 were formally employed, whereas in the Kwazulu resettlement area of Limehill, only 13 percent were working. This statistic is cited in Cosmas Desmond, "Limehill Revisited: A Case Study of the Longer-Term Effects of African Resettlement," Development Studies Research Group Working Group, Working Paper No. 5, University of Natal, Pietermaritzburg, 1978, p. 13.

7. Hindson puts this somewhat differently on p. 11 of "Conditions of Labour Supply," arguing that they more closely fit the conditions of an urban proletariat than a peasantry. Citing a 1975 study of the Transkei and the Ciskei, he relates that 33 percent of households in the Ciskei and 14 percent in two districts of the Transkei had no arable land at all.

8. Joanne Yawitch, "African Women and Labour Force Participation," *Work in Progress* 10 (August 1979), 40–41. See the massive, multivolume study by the Surplus People's Project for the most comprehensive survey of the devastating effects of resettlement.

9. Muriel Horrell, comp., *Survey of Race Relations in South Africa, 1970* (Johannesburg: South African Institute of Race Relations, 1971), p. 100.

10. This is the case in Brits on the borders of Bophuthatswana, according to a study by Georgina Jaffee and Collette Caine. See "The Incorporation of African Women Into the Industrial Work-Force: Its Implications for the Women's Question in South Africa," in *After Apartheid: Renewal of the South African Economy* (London: James Currey and Trenton, N.J.: Africa World Press, 1988), p. 96.

11. See V. M. Martin and C. M. Rogerson, "Women and Industrial Change: The South African Experience," *The South African Geographical Journal* 66, no. 1

(April 1984), 44, Table 3. Based on figures from the late 1970s and early 1980s, the following percentages of manufacturing jobs were held by women: Venda, 63.5 percent; Ciskei, 64.2 percent; Bophuthatswana, 52.5 percent; Lebowa, 49.6 percent. Gazankulu, with a manufacturing workforce 5.3 percent female, was the only exception. This trend is also documented in Philippa Green and Alan Hirsch, "The Ciskei—The Political Economy of Control," *South African Labour Bulletin* 7, no. 4–5 (February 1982), 65–85.

12. *The Star*, October 9, 1974. The figure was 80 percent in the industries that the reporter visited.

13. *Inquiry* 2 (October 1979), 21. An important article on the area is Anne Mager, "Moving the Fence: Gender in the Ciskei and Border Textile Industry, 1945–1986," *Social Dynamics* 15, no. 2 (1989), 46–62.

14. Many women also had to travel long distances to and from work. Jaffee and Caine, "African Women," p. 96, observe that women from Brits, who live up to 80 kms. from their jobs, may spend up to three hours a day in transit.

15. Joanne Yawitch, "The Incorporation of African Women into Wage Labour 1950–1980," *South African Labour Bulletin* 9, no. 3 (December 1983), 85–86.

16. Because Amelia Mariotti's adjusted census figures only go up to 1970, it would be invalid to compare her 1970 figures with those of the 1980 census. For the decade of the 1970s, therefore, I have relied on the Department of Labour Manpower Surveys for 1969 and 1981 as reported in Truida Prekel, "Black Women at Work: Progress despite Problems," *South African Journal of Labour Relations* 6, no. 3 (September 1982), Tables 1, 2 and 3. The figures in this source group coloured and Asian women together.

17. According to the 1970 census, 46.4 percent of coloured women between 16 and 64 were "economically active" as compared to 38.4 percent of whites and 18.5 percent of Asians. Again, the African figure means little because of the undercounting of rural women involved in production.

18. Increases of over 400 percent in sales and clerical workers still involved very small numbers of women, each of whom represented less than 1 percent of employed African women.

19. This discrepancy increased sharply during the 1970s. Whereas in 1969 there were nearly 40 percent more women professionals than men, by 1981 the figure had risen to nearly 119 percent. The number of women teachers rose substantially more than that of men during this period. For nurse/midwives there is no comparable male category.

20. A clash was reported in 1967 in *Rand Daily Mail* (hereafter *RDM*), September 15, 1967, between employers and the National Union of Distributive Workers over a proposal to employ African shop attendants in white areas at reduced rates of pay. The annual turnover of white women was 62.4 percent.

21. Calculated from figures in Prekel, "Black Women," Table 2. In both years, black and white men each substantially outnumbered any single group of women in clerical work, whereas white women substantially outnumbered black men and were roughly equal to white men in sales occupations. According to an article in the *South African Gazette* on October 11, 1974, only "non-white" businesses and a few white businesses with substantial black clientele were hiring black female secretaries.

22. Calculated from figures in Prekel, "Black Women," Table 3. Between 1965 and 1973, the number of African women employed in Johannesburg industries rose by 100 percent, compared with an increase of 17.5 percent for men.

23. See Fatima Meer, ed., *Black Women: Durban 1975: Case Studies of 85 Women at Home and Work* (Durban, 1975), p. 49, on Indian women in industry. Despite a decline in the percentage of domestic workers, she observes on p. 38 that Indian society continued to consider young women safer in domestic service than in

factory work since they were confined to the house and under the supervision of elders.

24. Martin and Rogerson, "Women and Industrial Change," p. 41.

25. Prekel, "Black Women," p. 71. In 1970, 94 percent of African women in the service category were domestic workers as compared to 11 percent of African men. Whether the trend to substitute labor-saving appliances for domestic workers is a significant long-term development is as yet unclear. The tendency is documented and discussed in Jennifer Shindler, "The Effects of Influx Control and Labour-Saving Appliances on Domestic Service," *South African Labour Bulletin* 6, no.1 (July 1980), 22–34. According to Yawitch, "Incorporation," p. 83, in 1980, one third of African women in paid employment were engaged in domestic work.

26. Yawitch, "Incorporation," pp. 83–85, citing an unpublished paper by M. Favis, "Black Women in the South African Economy," January 1983.

27. Calculated from figures in Prekel, "Black Women," Table 3. The largest group of these women were telephonists and switchboard operators.

28. Report from a 1973 survey conducted by the National Development and Management Foundation, discussed in Muriel Horrell, comp., *A Survey of Race Relations in South Africa, 1973* (Johannesburg: South African Institute of Race Relations, 1974), pp. 203–204. Those who earned less than R10 per week were unable to qualify for unemployment insurance. These figures are not directly comparable to the wage ranking discussed in chapter 8 for the 1940s and 1950s. But it is interesting to note that at that time the lowest paid industrial workers were Africans, women and men, whereas by 1973 they were women, African and coloured. The new currency, the rand, was adopted after South Africa became a republic and withdrew from the British Commonwealth on May 31, 1961.

29. Gavin Maasdorp and A. S. B. Humphreys, eds., *From Shantytown to Township: An Economic Study of African Poverty and Rehousing in a South African City* (Cape Town: Juta & Co., 1975), p. 47.

30. Ibid., pp. 47–49.

31. Joanne Yawitch, "Tightening the Noose: African Women and Influx Control in South Africa 1950–1980," Carnegie Conference Paper No. 82, Cape Town, April 13–19, 1984, p. 26.

32. Nicoli Nattrass, "Street Trading in Transkei: A Struggle against Poverty, Persecution and Prosecution," Carnegie Conference Paper No. 237, Cape Town, April 13–19, 1984, pp. 11–17, and Yawitch, "Incorporation," p. 90. Eleanor Preston-Whyte and Sibongile Nene discuss the informal sector in a rural area of KwaZulu in "Where the Informal Sector is *Not* the Answer: Women and Poverty in Rural KwaZulu," Carnegie Conference Paper No. 235, Cape Town, April 13–19, 1984.

33. Pundy Pillay, "Women in Employment in South Africa: Some Important Trends and Issues," *Social Dynamics* 11, no. 2 (1985), 30–31. According to the 1980 census, three quarters of all African women were recorded as "not economically active."

34. Yawitch, "Incorporation," pp. 90–91.

35. David Webster, "The Reproduction of Labour Power and the Struggle for Survival in Soweto," Carnegie Conference Paper No. 20, Cape Town, April 13–19, 1984, pp. 6–7.

36. The discussion in Jane Barrett et al., *Vukani Makhosikazi: South African Women Speak* (London: Catholic Institute for International Relations, 1985), pp. 215–17, distinguishes between *stokvels*, now fund-raising parties; *mohodisano*, rotating credit associations; and *matshido* or *masibanbane*, groups that assist each other socially, morally, and sometimes financially in case of crises like unemployment or death.

37. J. B. Kiernan, "Preachers, Prophets and Women in Zion," Ph.D. thesis (Manchester University, 1972), pp. 106, 109–10.

38. Interview, Mabopane, June 24, 1983.

39. Interview, Johannesburg, June 30, 1983.

40. See Muriel Horrell, comp., *A Survey of Race Relations in South Africa, 1964* (Johannesburg: South African Institute of Race Relations, 1965), pp. 234–35, for a discussion of the range of groups concerned about a shortage of skilled workers.

41. *RDM*, December 5, 1968. See also *The Star*, January 13, 1969.

42. Clipping, March 1969, GWU, Bcf 2.1. In 1974, 20 percent of jobs available to white women remained vacant, but 32 percent of jobs for coloured women were unfilled according to *South African Financial Gazette*, September 13, 1974.

43. *RDM*, July 26, 1966.

44. Ibid., and South African Electrical Workers' Association, "A Charter for the Female Worker," Johannesburg, May 5, 1966.

45. *The Star*, February 2, 1973.

46. Cock, "Introduction," p. 3, mentions the employment of women in these positions.

47. David Hemson, "Trade Unionism and the Struggle for Liberation in South Africa," *Capital and Class* 6 (Autumn 1978), 19.

48. Steven Friedman, "Political Implications of Industrial Unrest in South Africa," in *Working Papers in Southern African Studies*, vol. 3, ed. D. C. Hindson (Johannesburg: Ravan Press, 1983), pp. 128–29. Friedman's book, *Building Tomorrow Today: African Workers in Trade Unions, 1970–1984* (Johannesburg: Ravan Press, 1987), gives an excellent, detailed account of the 1973 strikes and of the slow but deliberate pace of union development during the 1970s.

49. *RDM*, August 22, 1974.

50. "Eveready Strike," *South African Labour Bulletin* 5, no. 1 (May 1979), 25–28; see also Loraine Gordon et al., comp., *A Survey of Race Relations in South Africa, 1977* (Johannesburg: South African Institute of Race Relations, 1978), p. 261, and Gerhard Maree, "Eveready to Exploit," *Work in Progress* 7 (March 1979), 22–29.

51. "Women and Trade Unions," *South African Labour Bulletin* 8, no. 6 (June 1983), 66. Friedman, *Building Tomorrow Today*, discusses the Heinemann strike on pp. 114–16.

52. "Women and Trade Unions," p. 64. Lydia Ngwenya (Kompe) recounts her life and experiences more fully in Barrett, *Vukani Makhosikazi*, pp. 97–109.

53. Those involved included E. Mashinini, S. Chitja, J. Hlongwane, L. Mvubelo, F. Mandy, E. Seloro, and J. Siwani.

54. The Study Group on Women in Employment, "Memorandum on Women in Employment," submitted to the Commission of Inquiry into Labour Legislation, Johannesburg, February, 1978.

55. Ibid., pp. 42–43.

56. Barbara Klugman, "Maternity Rights and Benefits and Protective Legislation at Work," *South African Labour Bulletin* 9, no. 3 (December 1983), 44.

57. Republic of South Africa, Department of Manpower Utilisation, *Report of the Commission of Inquiry into Labour Legislation*, [Wiehahn Commission] Part 5 (Pretoria, 1981), RP 27/1981, p. 92.

58. Ibid., pp. 93–99.

59. Ibid., p. 93.

60. Under the Labour Regulations Amendment Act, Industrial Councils no longer have the power to discriminate on the basis of sex in setting wages and working conditions. The Basic Conditions of Emplyment Act of 1984 forbade the establishment of separate wage rates for women.

61. These issues are discussed in Shirley Millar, "The Basic Conditons of Employment Act: The Position of Women," *South African Labour Bulletin* 8, no. 6 (June 1983), 1–4. A common alternative argument, which the Wiehahn Commission did not consider, is to extend the protections for women to all workers.

62. J. Cock et al., "Child Care and the Working Mother: A Sociological Inves-

tigation of a Sample of Urban African Women," Carnegie Conference Paper No. 115, Cape Town, April 13–19, 1984, p. 14.

63. Between 1981 and 1984, membership rose from five thousand to thirty-three thousand. In August 1985, it became a nonracial union, after having included coloured and Indian workers a year earlier. Friedman, in *Building Tomorrow Today*, p. 504, cites members' reluctance to admit whites, fearing that their educational and other advantages would permit them to dominate the union. Mashinini's moving autobiography, *Strikes Have Followed Me All My Life* (London: The Women's Press, 1989), discusses these events in detail.

64. The quote comes from Diana E. H. Russell, *Lives of Courage: Women for a New South Africa* (New York: Basic Books, 1989), pp. 175–77. See also "Maggie Oewies Talks about the Domestic Workers Association," *South African Labour Bulletin* 6, no. 1 (1980), 35–36; Muriel Horrell, *A Survey of Race Relations in South Africa, 1976* (Johannesburg: South African Institute of Race Relations, 1977), pp. 312–13; *The Star*, November 25, 1974. In 1981 the South African Domestic Workers' Association was formed with branches in the Transvaal, Cape Town, Durban, and the Orange Free State. Friedman, *Building Tomorrow Today*, pp. 486–88, discusses the organization of domestic workers and the continuing difficulties they face.

65. Interview, June 23, 1983.

66. Hemson, "Trade Unionism," p. 32; Natal Labour Research Committee, "Control Over a Workforce—The Frame Case," *South African Labour Bulletin* 6, no. 5 (December 1980), 38.

14. Repression and Resistance

1. The literature on this topic is vast. The changes on an international scale are sketched by Folker Fröbel, Jurgen Heinrichs and Otto Kreye in "The New International Division of Labour," *South African Labour Bulletin* 5, no. 8 (May 1980), 3–15, which summarizes the main arguments of their book. Swasti Mitter's book, *Common Fate, Common Bond: Women in the Global Economy* (London: Pluto Press, 1987), is an important contribution to this discussion.

2. Richard Goode, "For a Better Life: The Food and Canning Workers Union 1941 to 1975," B.A. Hons. thesis (University of Cape Town, 1983), p. 133.

3. *Forward*, September 1963.

4. Information in the two preceding paragraphs comes from Ian Goldin, *The Poverty of Coloured Labour Preference: Economics and Ideology in the Western Cape*, Saldru Working Paper no. 59 (Cape Town: 1984), pp. 12–16. According to 1970 census figures for the Western Cape, 8,401 of 9,030 employed African women were in services, only 148 in industry. See Table 2 in Delia Hendrie and Dudley Horner, "The People and Workers of the Cape Peninsula: A Sketch," *South African Labour Bulletin* 3, no. 2 (September 1976), 9.

5. Goldin, *Coloured Labour Preference*, Table 15, p. 461. Coloured women were 43.5 percent, African men 24.1 percent, and coloured men 19.1 percent.

6. FCWU, Memorandum, "Re: Grabouw African Workers."

7. FCWU, "Circular letter No. 10/61," Cape Town, March 17, 1961.

8. FCWU, "Memorandum to all employers who are parties to the Conciliation Board Agreement," Cape Town, April 1968, p. 3.

9. United States Department of Agriculture, Foreign Agricultural Service, "The Canned Deciduous Fruit Industry of South Africa," Washington, D.C., 1969, p. 12.

10. Goode, "Better Life," Tables 1 and 2. The gross value of output rose by 120 percent, the net value by 148 percent. The regional shift in the industry was probably responsible in part for the loss of jobs at the Cape.

11. Calculated from figures in Goode, "Better Life," Table 2. The remaining

workers were primarily white men not in production jobs, with smaller numbers of white women and Indians, primarily men. The coloured percentage, for women and men, would have been higher in the Western Cape than in the industry as a whole. By the mid-1970s, approximately half of the industry's employees worked in the Western Cape, compared with over three quarters in 1945.

12. Based on FCWU, "Circular Letter No. 3/60," Cape Town, October 14, 1960, and FCWU, "Annual Report submitted to 35th Annual Conference," Huguenot, September 21–22, 1975, p. 10.

13. FCWU, "Minutes of Management Committee Meeting," Zuider Paarl, June 9, 1963, p. 1.

14. AFCWU, "Annual Report submitted to the 16th Annual Conference," Cape Town, September 14–15, 1963, pp. 5–9; FCWU, "Annual Report submitted to the 24th Annual Conference," Cape Town, September 19–20, 1964, p. 6; FCWU, "Circular Letter no. 17/64," September 3, 1964; *Forward*, September 1963, p. 3, and October 1963, p. 3.

15. See, for example, FCWU, "Annual Report submitted to the 21st Annual Conference," Zuider Paarl, September 9–10, 1961, p. 11; FCWU, "Annual Report submitted to the 20th Annual Conference," Zuider Paarl, September 24–25, 1960, pp. 6–9; AFCWU, "Annual Report," 1963, p. 1; "Minutes of National Executive Council Meeting," Zuider Paarl, January 22, 1961, p. 8.

16. FCWU, "Annual Report," 1964, p. 2.

17. FCWU, "Circular Letter No.8/63," Cape Town, March 12, 1963, and No. 16/63, June 18, 1963.

18. FCWU, "Minutes of Management Committee Meeting," Zuider Paarl, November 26, 1961, p. 3.

19. FCWU, "Annual Report," September 19–20, 1970, p. 6.

20. Dave Lewis, "Registered Trade Unions and Western Cape Workers," *South African Labour Bulletin* 3, no. 2 (September 1976), 53. Nationally, the proportion of unionized food workers was estimated at 30 percent. Jeremy Baskin, "Factoryworkers in the Countryside: The Food and Canning Workers' Union in Ceres and Grabouw," *South African Labour Bulletin* 8, no. 4 (February 1983), p. 51, estimates that at most twelve branches remained active. The annual report for 1963 had put the number then at twenty-five.

21. Goode, "Better Life," pp. 131, 134, 145–46.

22. Ibid., p. 145.

23. Steven Friedman, *Building Tomorrow Today: African Workers in Trade Unions, 1970–1984* (Johannesburg: Ravan Press, 1987) pp. 230–31 gives greater detail on the strategy of this rebuilding effort.

24. Goldin, *Coloured Labour Preference*, pp. 312, 314, and Friedman, *Building Tomorrow Today*, pp. 119, 139.

25. FCWU, "List of delegates and alternates for Conciliation Board," August 7, 1974.

26. Friedman, *Building Tomorrow Today*, p. 415.

27. FCWU, "Annual Report submitted to the 34th Annual Conference," Huguenot, September 21–22, 1974, p. 11.

28. *Daily Dispatch*, October 4, 1978. Accounts do not explain why men did not join in this strike; but it is likely that a higher proportion of them were migrants, who would have risked deportation from the cities if they lost their jobs.

29. An East London Worker, "Strike and Lockout at LKB, East London," *South African Labour Bulletin* 8, no. 4 (February 1983), 59. Phike also was instrumental in reuniting the Paarl union after a lengthy rift that followed the firing of a long-time branch secretary for misusing union funds.

30. "Strike at Sea Harvest," *Work in Progress*, No. 11 (1980), 26–27.

31. Steven Friedman, "Political Implications of Industrial Unrest in South Africa," in *Working Papers in Southern African Studies*, vol. 3, ed. D. C. Hindson, (Johannesburg: Ravan Press, 1983), p. 135.

32. This quote and account of the events comes from Jan Theron, "A Chronology of the Fattis & Monis Dispute," August 10, 1979. The number of African contract workers cited below comes from Ian Goldin, *Making Race: The Politics and Economics of Coloured Identity in South Africa* (London and New York: Longman, 1987), p. 222. It is interesting that gender is rarely brought into accounts of the strike. Only Pearl-Alice Marsh mentions that the first five to be fired were women. See "The Failures of Apartheid Industrial Decentralization Policies and the Rise of the Independent (African) Trade Union Movement in South Africa: 1968–1982," Ph.D. dissertation (University of California, Berkeley, 1984), p. 127.

33. Jan Theron, "Statement on the Settlement Reached between Fattis and Monis and the Food and Canning Workers Union and African Food and Canning Workers Union," November 12, 1979.

34. Friedman, *Building Tomorrow Today*, pp. 187–88.

35. Baskin, "Factoryworkers in the Countryside," p. 55. Friedman, "Industrial Unrest," p. 136, refers to the general strike-wave in the Western Cape.

36. Republic of South Africa, Department of Labour, "Report to the Honourable the Minister of Labour by Division B(III) of the Wage Board, Food Industry," 15/1978, Pretoria, 1977–78, pp. 16–17.

37. Ibid., pp. 17–20.

38. Friedman, *Building Tomorrow Today*, p. 34.

39. Baskin, "Factoryworkers in the Countryside," pp. 51–58. The "small, but significant" number of Africans were contract workers.

40. This policy was expressed in Food and Canning Workers Union, "Search for a Workable Relationship," *South African Labour Bulletin* 7, no. 8 (July 1982), 55, which stated: "A trade union is not a community organization. A union which tries to be a community or political organization at the same time cannot survive." Friedman, *Building Tomorrow Today*, chap. 14, discusses the difficult issue of unions and politics in the context of the 1980s.

41. Interview, June 17, 1983.

42. Erica Emdon, "The Planning Act and the Transvaal Clothing Industry," *South African Labour Bulletin* 3, no. 5 (March-April 1977), 60. According to the 1967 Act, written permission from the Minister was required in order to expand the number of "Bantu" employees in any factory in the Transvaal, Pretoria, Witwatersrand, and Vereeniging areas.

43. J. H. Thomas, "The Wage Structure in the Clothing Industry, South Africa," South African Institute of Personnel Management and South African Institute of Race Relations, Johannesburg, January 18–19, 1973, p. 2. Considerable incentives were given all along to manufacturers willing to locate in border areas. By 1982, they included a substantial cash subsidy for each worker and other generous financial assistance.

44. *Rand Daily Mail* (hereafter *RDM*), June 19, 1968.

45. Thomas, "Wage Structure," p. 2. His figures show the three dominant areas of clothing production to be the Cape with 40,888 workers, the Transvaal with 25,469, and Durban/Pietermaritzburg with 23,498. Most of the total "coloured" employees shown for Durban (19,717 of 21,705) were, in fact, Asian. See Annexure "E".

46. Figures are from "Address Delivered by Miss Sarah Chitja," Johannesburg, October 25, 1979, pp. 2–3.

47. One firm, taken over by British interests, was planning to move to a border area, the other two were moving to Cape Town and Durban, respectively, and the last was closing down.

48. *The Star*, January 29, 1969.

49. *RDM*, April 1, 1969.

50. *Evening Post*, April 7, 1969.

51. *The Star*, June 24, 1968; *Daily Dispatch*, July 15, 1971.

52. Fatima Meer, ed. and comp., *Factory and Family: The Divided Lives of South Africa's Women Workers* (Durban: The Institute for Black Research, 1984), p. 34.

53. *Sechaba*, June 1973, p. 9 and July 1973, p. 9.

54. Unidentified clipping, March 18, 1971, GWU, Bcf 2.1.

55. *RDM*, February 8, 1972. The latter reference is to a massive strike in Namibia that began in late 1971.

56. L. Douwes Dekker et al., "Case Studies in African Labour Action in South Africa and Namibia," in *The Development of an African Working Class: Studies in Class Formation and Action*, ed. R. Sandbrook and R. Cohen (Toronto: University of Toronto Press, 1975), p. 217.

57. "Wages in the Clothing Industry," *Work in Progress* 23 (1982), 45.

58. Institute for Industrial Education, *The Durban Strikes, 1973* (Durban: Institute for Industrial Education with Ravan Press, 1974), p. 160.

59. David Hemson, "Trade Unionism and the Struggle for Liberation in South Africa," *Capital and Class* 6 (1978), 32.

60. As of 1976, the Garment Workers' Union of the Western Province was the largest trade union in the country, with a total membership of 35,406; the vast majority were coloured women.

61. This is discussed in Goldin, *Coloured Labour Preference*, p. 315. He also notes that the union allegedly cooperated with management and the security police to identify the strike leaders and expel them from the union.

62. Dave Gool, "The Struggle for Trade Union Democracy," *South African Labour Bulletin* 10, No.4 (January–February 1985), 54, 56–58. On the 1976 protest, see also E. C. Webster, "Stay-aways and the Black Working Class since the Second World War—the Evaluation of a Strategy," unpublished paper, n.p., n.d., pp. 17, 23; Hemson, "Trade Unionism," pp. 31–32; Counter Information Service, *Black South Africa Explodes* (London: Counter Information Service, 1977), p. 40. This revolt against established leadership continued in the 1980s, marked by large strikes in 1980 and 1981 and by efforts, supported by the United Democratic Front, to organize a new and more progressive union. See also Joanne Bloch, "The Action Committee versus the Garment Workers' Union," in *Selected Research Papers on Aspects of Organisation in the Western Cape*, ed. Linda Cooper and Dave Kaplan (Department of Economic History, University of Cape Town, 1982), and Goldin, *Coloured Labour Preference*, pp. 416–19.

63. Douwes Dekker, "African Labour Action," p. 217.

64. Interview, Johannesburg, June 18, 1963.

65. *Financial Mail*, November 19, 1976. The article was written by Steven Friedman, who also discusses the situation in *Building Tomorrow Today*, pp. 78–79.

66. These figures come from J. H. Thomas, "The Wage Structure in the Clothing Industry, South Africa," Johannesburg, South African Institute of Personnel Management and South African Institute of Race Relations, January 18–19, 1973, Annexure "E".

67. Douwes Dekker, "African Labour Action," pp. 216–17.

68. Adam Klein, GWU general secretary 1973–76, Interview, Cambridge, Mass., June 8, 1981.

69. *Speak*, June 1983.

70. Thomas, "Wage Structure."

71. Friedman, *Building Tomorrow Today*, p. 160.

72. Friedman, *Building Tomorrow Today*, p. 422. In 1989, the two major unions in the garment and textile industries, the Amalgamated Clothing and Textile

Workers' Union and the Garment and Allied Workers' Union, merged, becoming one of the largest unions in the country.

73. According to Graeme Bloch, in "Room At the Top?—The Developing of South Africa's Manufacturing Industry 1939–1969," *Social Dynamics* 7, no. 2 (1981), 56, the proportion of women grew from 1 percent in 1951 to 7 percent in 1970. The development of industry in the Durban area is discussed in Ari Sitas et al., "Trade Unions, Monopoly Power and Poverty in Natal's Industries," Carnegie Conference Paper no. 108, Cape Town, April 13–19, 1984.

74. It is interesting to compare this degree of concentration with that in the clothing industry. In the latter, comparatively large firms with over one thousand workers employed less than 20 percent of the work force, while in the textile industry less than 10 percent of establishments employed nearly 60 percent of the work force. See Allan Hirsch, "An Introduction to Textile Worker Organization in Natal," *South African Labour Bulletin* 4, no. 8 (1979), 14. Bloch, "Room at the Top?" p. 50, discusses the development of this concentration with assistance from the state-funded Industrial Development Corporation and a number of large international companies. In addition to Frame, these firms include the Anglo-American Corporation and Barlow Rand.

75. Interview, Harriet Bolton, Harare, Zimbabwe, July 27, 1989.

76. See NTMA, "Submission to Dr. F. J. Viljoen," Durban, February 8, 1966; "Arbitrator's Report and Award," Pretoria, March 16, 1966; NTMA, "Wage Proposals," February, 1972; Bettie duToit, *Ukubamba Amadolo: Workers' Struggles in the South African Textile Industry* (London: Onyx Press, 1978), pp. 117–118, and IIE, *Durban Strikes*, p. 25. A "Gentleman's Agreement" of 1943 that accepted equal pay for women and men is mentioned in duToit, p. 54; but it is unclear whether this agreement (which was not legally binding) or the small number of women textile workers accounted for the wage equality of the mid-1960s. According to the *Financial Gazette*, February 9, 1983, the South African textile industry had suffered severely during the eighteen-month period preceding the 1973 strikes. A drastic drop in worldwide prices and a 70 percent increase in textile imports led the article to characterize the country as "the dumping ground of the world." Between 1960 and 1970, however, Hirsch reports that the average wage per employee increased by 140 percent, while profits grew by 365 percent. See "Textile Worker Organisation," p. 30.

77. This information comes from Fatima Meer, ed., *Black Women: Durban 1975: Case Studies of 85 Women at Home and Work* (Durban: 1975), pp. 60–64; Fatima Meer, ed. and comp., *Factory and Family: The Divided Lives of South Africa's Women Workers* (Durban: The Institute for Black Research, 1984), pp. 23–26; and David Hemson, Interview, London, June 1, 1987. It is important to note that Meer's studies include all Durban area industries, not just textiles.

78. This division varied with sections of the industry, however. In the cotton factories, for example, black women operated looms, whereas in heavier work such as blankets, weaving was dominated by men.

79. IIE, *Durban Strikes*.

80. Ibid., pp. 23–24.

81. *Natal Mercury*, January 30, 1973. The quote highlighting the importance of the Frame strikes comes from Friedman, *Building Tomorrow Today*, p. 38.

82. IIE, *Durban Strikes*, pp. 29–31.

83. *Sechaba*, April and July, 1973.

84. IIE, *Durban Strikes*, p. 16.

85. *Southern Africa*, March 3, 1974.

86. The agreement between the NUTW and Smith and Nephew was the first "recognition agreement" with a black union. Friedman, *Building Tomorrow Today*, pp. 94–96, describes the chance development of the concept of recognition agree-

ments, which gave the new union movement a critical new strategy. Junerose Nala, who worked as a weaver at the Afritex Mill in Durban, was among the new generation of women to become active in the NUTW. She was acting secretary from February 1974 until her banning in May 1976. Instrumental in starting the union and in making initial contacts with the university students who became its organizers was Harriet Bolton, an unusual TUCSA unionist who felt that the organization could not ignore the thousands of new black workers in Durban.

87. IIE, *Durban Strikes*, p. 35. Once again, the issue of wage equality could be double edged. Friedman, *Building Tomorrow Today*, p. 415, reports that in 1981, when workers at S.A. Fabrics struck to demand equal pay, the company retrenched almost all its women workers.

88. Interview with David Hemson, the NUTW organizer who negotiated on their behalf, London, June 1, 1987.

89. Interview, Halton Cheadle, former secretary of the National Union of Textile Workers, Johannesburg, June 21, 1983.

90. Both of these examples come from Hemson, Interview.

91. Natal Labour Research Committee, "Control over a Work Force: The Frame Case," *South African Labour Bulletin* 6, no. 5 (1980), 38.

92. Jean Westmore and Pat Townsend, "The African Women Workers in the Textile Industry in Durban," *South African Labour Bulletin* 2, no. 4 (1975), 26.

93. *The Star*, November 9, 1973.

94. Westmore and Townsend, "African Women," pp. 29–30.

95. Hemson, Interview and Meer, *Factory and Family*, p. 37.

96. Westmore and Townsend, "African Women," p. 30.

97. NLRC, "Control Over a Workforce," p. 39.

98. Westmore and Townsend, "African Women," p. 30.

99. This was a result both of the greater distance of the Transkei from Durban and of the fact that many companies had ceased to recruit workers from this now "independent" area.

100. NTMA, "Submission."

101. S. K. Hall, "An Exploratory Investigation into the Labour Stability and Attitudes of Bantu Women in a Textile Factory," Johannesburg, National Institute for Personnel Research, 1973. The study was based on data collected from 212 workers; 93 were interviewed to obtain more detailed demographic and attitudinal information. Most of the women were settled residents rather than temporary migrants; 63 percent of them had lived for over ten years in the same place.

102. Jane Barrett, "Knitmore: A Study in the Relationship Between Sex and Class," B.A. Hons. dissertation (University of the Witwatersrand, 1981), chapter 7.

103. Meer, *Family and Factory*, p. 47. The study surveyed 992 women in the Durban-Pinetown area, 454 African, 429 Indian, and 109 coloured. By reporting all the evidence collectively as representing the voice of black women workers, the study obscures differences among the three groups as well as among individuals.

104. Meer, *Black Women*, pp. 53, 65.

105. Bolton, Interview.

106. Meer, *Factory and Family*, p. 50. To place this statement in context, it should be noted that, among Africans, the Zulu (Natal's ethnic majority) have a stronger tradition of male domination than many other groups in South Africa, and that Indian women have been the most protected, and the last group to enter wage labor in any significant numbers.

107. Barrett, "Knitmore," chapter 8, pp. 2–4.

108. Barrett, "Knitmore," chapter 8, pp. 5–14.

109. Helen Icken Safa, "Class Consciousness among Working Class Women in

Latin America: A Case Study in Puerto Rico," in *Peasants and Proletarians: The Struggles of Third World Workers*, ed. Robin Cohen, Peter Gutkind, and Phyllis Brazier (New York: Monthly Review Press, 1979), pp. 442–43.

Epilogue

1. Such attitudes have begun to change, however. During 1990, the African National Congress resumed its position as a legal organization within the country. As its leaders have begun rebuilding the movement's structures inside South Africa and planning for a postapartheid future, they have also acknowledged the need to confront patriarchal attitudes and practices both within the ANC and in the larger society. See *Agenda* 8 (1990), 1–23.

2. Vincent Crapanzano, *Waiting: The Whites of South Africa* (London: Paladin, 1986), p. 18. Although Crapanzano does not include gender in his discussion of the tendency toward "exquisitely mechanical stereotyping," his discussion could apply equally to ideas about women.

3. For women married under Roman-Dutch law, these changes were made in the Matrimonial Property Act of 1984. The law regarding African civil marriage was similarly changed in 1988.

4. Tom Lodge makes this argument in *Black Politics in South Africa since 1945* (London: Longman, 1983), p. 141, as does Susan Geiger, discussing Tanzania, in "Women in Nationalist Struggle: TANU Activists in Dar es Salaam," *International Journal of African Historical Studies* 20, no. 1 (1987), 18.

5. Helen Bradford, *A Taste of Freedom: The ICU in Rural South Africa 1924–1930* (New Haven: Yale University Press, 1987), pp. 249–50. On the 1980s, see Elaine Unterhalter, "Class, Race & Gender," in *South Africa in Question*, ed. John Lonsdale (Cambridge: University of Cambridge African Studies Centre in association with James Currey, London and Heinemann, Portsmouth, N.H., 1988), pp. 162–63, and Debby Bonnin and Karen Hurt, "The O.K. Strike: A Battle on Many Fronts," *Agenda* 1 (1987), 38–42.

6. "CCAWUSA Maternity Agreement," *South African Labour Bulletin* 8, no. 7 (August 1983), 64–66; "Parental Rights Proposal," *Agenda* 1 (1987), 25–26; and "CCAWUSA Wins a New Deal for Working Parents," *Agenda* 3 (1988), 10. The union also has organized militant campaigns against humiliating strip searches of black women in some of the country's leading retail stores. See Emma Mashinini, *Strikes Have Followed Me All My Life: A South African Autobiography* (London: The Women's Press, 1989), pp. 116–17. CCAWUSA is now the South African Commercial, Catering, and Allied Workers' Union (SACCAWU).

7. Johannesburg Correspondent, "Workshop on Women," *South African Labour Bulletin* 9, no. 3 (December 1983), 10.

8. Martin Murray, *South Africa: Time of Agony, Time of Destiny* (London: Verso Press, 1987), p. 194. See also COSATU, "Women and the Living Wage Campaign," n.p., n.d. The National Council of Trade Unions (NACTU), a federation of exclusively black unions formed in 1986, also has adopted a strong policy statement on equal rights for women. The statement's cover boldly portrays a women's symbol encircling a clenched fist.

9. COSATU, "Cosatu Women's Education Conference," *Agenda* 2 (1988), 56–58 and Mashinini, *Strikes*, p. 118.

10. Debby Bonin, "COSATU Congress," *Agenda* 5 (1989), 19–20 and *Weekly Mail* 5, no. 28, July 21–27, 1989. Another important development has been the organization of separate women's forums within a number of unions. See Barbara Klugman, "Women Workers in the Unions," *South African Labor Bulletin* 14, no. 4 (1989), 13–36, and Tammy Shefer, "The Gender Agenda: Women's Struggles in the Trade Union Movement," paper presented to the Conference on Women and

Gender in Southern Africa, University of Natal-Durban, January 30–February 2, 1991.

11. June Nala, "Active, Loyal—But Banned From Leadership," *Third World Women's News* 1, no.1 (1986), 10.

12. Ibid., p. 11.

13. Ibid.

14. Ibid.

Documentary Sources and Interviews

Documentary Sources

Central Archives Depot, Pretoria
  Department of Justice
  Department of Labour (abbreviated: ARB)
  Department of Mines and Industries (abbreviated: MNW)
International Defence and Aid for Southern Africa, London
  Cuttings collection
Johannesburg Public Library
  Wage Board reports
Northwestern University
  Alex Hepple Papers
  Carter-Karis Collection
  Leo Kuper Papers
Popular History Trust, Harare, Zimbabwe [now South African History Archives, Johannesburg]
  Interview collection
Rand Daily Mail cuttings collection, Johannesburg
South African Institute of Race Relations (abbreviated: SAIRR)
  Dulcie Hartwell Labour Collection
  Oral History Archive
South African Library, Cape Town
  Cuttings collection
Transvaal Clothing Manufacturers' Association, Johannesburg
  Minutes (abbreviated: TCMA)
University of Cape Town
  Food and Canning Workers' Union and African Food and Canning Workers' Union Papers (abbreviated: FCWU and AFCWU)
University of London, Institute of Commonwealth Studies (abbreviated: ICS)
  Albie Sachs Papers
  A. L. Saffery Papers
University of the Witwatersrand
  A. B. Xuma Papers
  Federation of South African Women Papers (abbreviated: FSAW)
  Garment Workers' Union of South Africa Archive (abbreviated: GWU)
  Jean Sinclair Papers
  Rheinallt Jones Papers
  Trade Union Council of South Africa Collection, including the South African Trades and Labour Council (abbreviated: SATLC)

Interviews

Ray Alexander (Simons), Lusaka, Zambia, 1989
Frances Baard, Mabopane, 1983
Rosaline Barnes, Johannesburg, 1983

Constance Belle, Johannesburg, 1983
Harriet Bolton, Harare, Zimbabwe, 1989
Halton Cheadle, Johannesburg, 1983
Rose Crawford, Durban, 1979
Bettie du Toit, London, 1979
Dulcie Hartwell, Durban, 1979
David Hemson, London, 1987
Sinah Jacobs, Johannesburg, 1983
Morris Kagan, Johannesburg, 1983
Adam Klein, Cambridge, Massachusetts, 1981
Fanny Klenerman, Johannesburg, 1979
Rebecca Lan (Sacks), London, 1987
Elizabeth Lebagoa, Johannesburg, 1983
Queenie Elizabeth Lenton, Johannesburg, 1983
Emma Mashinini, Johannesburg, 1983
Betty Matlaba, Johannesburg, 1983
Ethel McCallum, Johannesburg, 1983
Caroline Motsoaledi, Johannesburg, 1983
Lucy Mvubelo, Johannesburg, 1983
Rita Ndzanga, Johannesburg, 1983
*Elizabeth Nkadimeng, Johannesburg, 1983
*Harriet Phiri, Johannesburg, 1983
Anna Scheepers, Johannesburg, 1983
Ray Simons (Alexander), Lusaka, Zambia, 1989
J. H. Thomas, Johannesburg, 1983
Olga Williams, Johannesburg, 1983

*Pseudonyms

Index

IRIS BERGER, Director of the Institute for Research on Women and Associate Professor of History, Africana Studies, and Women's Studies at the State University of New York at Albany, is the author of the award-winning book *Religion and Resistance: East African Kingdoms in the Precolonial Period* and coeditor (with Claire Robertson) of *Women and Class in Africa*.